SECOND EDITION

FINANCIAL STATEMENTS
Construction, Analysis, and Forecasts

MICHAEL L FETTERS

Babson College

ROBERT F HALSEY

Babson College

VIRGINIA E SOYBEL

Babson College

Cambridge
BUSINESS PUBLISHERS

Cambridge Business Publishers

FINANCIAL STATEMENTS, Construction, Analysis, and Forecasts, Second Edition, by Michael Fetters, Robert Halsey, and Virginia Soybel

ISBN: 978-1-61853-179-7

Bookstores & Faculty: To order this book, contact the company via email customerservice@cambridgepub.com or call 800-619-6473.

Students: To order this book, please visit the book's website and order directly online.

Printed in Canada

10 9 8 7 6 5 4 3 2 1

ACKNOWLEDGMENTS

We are enormously grateful to our colleague, Shay Blanchette Proulx, who has contributed her thoughtful analysis, professional experience, and meticulous editing to all aspects of this text. Her willingness to experiment with creative approaches to teaching first-year undergraduate students gave us additional insights, and her energy, clarity, and student-centered perspective have improved this book through numerous revisions.

We also wish to express our gratitude and thanks to our colleagues, Bill Lawler and Richard Bliss, who were so critical in the genesis of this book and to Tom Buttacavoli, Bill Coyle, and Aaron Shimoff who teach introductory financial accounting with us and who continue to provide suggestions that improve the text.

Finally, we want to express our sincere gratitude to George Werthman and his staff at Cambridge Business Publishers for their valuable suggestions and careful editing of our text.

Michael L Fetters   *Robert F Halsey*   *Virginia E Soybel*

BRIEF CONTENTS

CONTENTS

Chapter One

Business Models and Financial Statement Formats

LEARNING OBJECTIVES

When you complete this chapter you should be able to:

1. Identify and define the basic elements of financial statements.
2. Understand and describe the purpose and format of the balance sheet.
3. Understand and describe the purpose and format of the income statement.
4. Describe the connections between industry business models and financial statement characteristics.

INTRODUCTION

Before digging into the details, mechanics, and vocabulary of financial reporting, we need to understand the broader context in which financial statements are generated and used. All companies record their transactions and produce periodic reports to summarize their financial performance and condition. All companies adhere to the same concepts and principles of financial reporting, and all use the same statement templates. Yet no two companies produce the same financial results, as each company makes unique strategic and operating decisions. The focus of this text is on understanding corporate financial statements and using them in systematic, detailed ways to assess historical performance and to forecast future performance. Before we introduce specific tools of analysis, however, we should consider the big picture: how are industries structured, and where do corporate strategies fit within an industry?

The industry *value chain* is one conceptual framework that provides a specific context in which to consider and evaluate an industry's basic business model and a company's financial performance, given its strategy for competing in the industry.[1] The process of providing a good or service to a consumer involves multiple steps, links in a chain, in which each step adds measurable incremental value. For example, a person with a sinus headache might find value in medication to relieve the pain. The process of making such a product available involves the following broad steps: basic research and development (R&D), raw materials procurement, manufacturing, distribution, and sale to the consumer. Each step or link in the pharmaceutical products chain is complex, and companies in the industry choose how much of the chain their operations will span. A biotechnology firm would focus on a narrow link if it is devoted to basic R&D projects, and its product would be patents sold to manufacturers. A large diversified pharmaceutical firm might span the R&D, manufacturing, and distribution links, thus adding proportionately more value from the beginning to end of its operating process. While covering greater breadth of the chain allows the company to capture more of the value, it also requires a much larger investment in resources. The R&D biotechnology company needs laboratories, but the more diversified company needs not only laboratories, but also large complex manufacturing facilities, warehouses, and fleets of trucks to distribute products. At the other end of the value chain, a small convenience store that sells a pain reliever to a consumer plays a critical role in completing the process, but operates in a narrow sliver with very little investment in resources and an inevitably small fraction of the total value added.

---

[1] See Porter, *Competitive Strategy: Techniques for Analyzing Industries and Competitors,* 1980 and 1998.

A company's placement within its industry value chain also determines the nature of its customers. The small convenience store serves individuals in face-to-face transactions, while a large pharmaceutical company markets and sells to hospitals, clinics, health management organizations, and physicians. Consequently, the retailer will focus on its location, its product mix and product displays, and quick customer service. The large diversified pharmaceutical company will focus on the development of new patented products and serving the particular needs of physicians and their patients. So while both of these companies participate in the same value chain, their business models and the metrics used to evaluate them are different.

As another example, consider the steps in the process of providing a t-shirt to an individual. The first step in the value chain would be growing, harvesting, and processing cotton. Subsequent links would include dyeing and manufacturing the cotton into t-shirts, packaging them, and distributing them to retailers for sale to customers. Within the industry value chain, companies such as The Gap focus on the retail link in the chain as it subcontracts the manufacture of its products. American Apparel, however, has chosen to cover a broader span as it manufactures, distributes, and sells its products, a strategic decision called vertical integration. In contrast, a graphic designer might participate in a small slice of this value chain by creating graphics to add to existing t-shirts, an operation that would require little investment and, most likely, a proportionately lower fraction of the total value added.

The companies doing business along a value chain may all be affected by similar trends or events, but the consequences will vary. For example, if a new biotech company discovers a superior, cost-effective pain-relief process, the existing biotech company may experience a severe decline in demand for its patents and technologies, while the larger company may be able to purchase the new process and add a new product to its portfolio, and the small corner store will simply adjust its inventory to include the new product. Each of these companies would generate financial statements that reflect the effects of both management decisions and external events.

Throughout this text we will use and analyze financial statements to assess and understand the consequences of management choices and external forces, both for large corporations and for small companies. We introduce the specific financial statements first in the context of a small company and then consider the statements for large corporations.

FINANCIAL STATEMENTS: SMALL COMPANY

When John Palmer was an MBA student, he pursued his passion for cycling while learning all he could about the business of the industry. While he understood the issues of product development and manufacturing, he wanted interaction with end-use customers—his fellow cyclists—and focused on the last link in the industry's value chain. As he worked toward his goal of owning a bicycle retail store, he developed a business plan and considered multiple alternatives related to the primary activities of any business: *financing activities*, *investing activities*, and *operating activities*.

Financing the business is the necessary first step, as he would need a location, store equipment, and plenty of inventory before he made a single sale. How should the company be financed? As the owner, John would contribute a significant amount of the capital, but the company would need more than he could provide. He could find co-owners to contribute capital, but then he would have to share any profits with them. Alternatively, he could seek financing from lenders, such as a bank, but he would have to be confident that the company could cover interest and principal payments.

Once John decided on the sources of financing for the company, he needed to consider how to invest the cash. Should he buy a store? Could he lease a location instead? How much and what kind of display equipment would be needed? Would the company need substantial computer equipment?

His financing and investing decisions all laid the groundwork for the core operating activities of the company. How much inventory did he need to fulfill his strategy? How many employees should he hire and at what compensation? Which credit cards should he accept

EXHIBIT 1.3	KW Bookkeeping Services Statement of Cash Flows for the Year Ending December 31, 2015	
Received from customers		$112,000
Paid for salaries		(58,000)
Paid for rent		(30,000)
Paid for utilities		(5,400)
Paid for interest		(600)
Net operating cash flows		$ 18,000
Financing cash flows:		
Paid bank loan		(10,000)
Change in cash		$ 8,000

Through the first year, KW Bookkeeping Services operated entirely on a cash basis. That is, the company did not extend credit to customers, but collected as soon as it provided its services. Similarly, the company paid immediately for all the services that it used. Consequently, an income statement for the company for 2015 would be identical to the statement of operating cash flows in Exhibit 1.3, except that the terms are different (Exhibit 1.4).

EXHIBIT 1.4	KW Bookkeeping Services Income Statement for the Year Ending December 31, 2015	
Revenues		$112,000
Salaries expense		(58,000)
Rent expense		(30,000)
Utilities expense		(5,400)
Interest expense		(600)
Net income		$ 18,000

Generally accepted accounting principles (GAAP) require that **net income** be measured on an accrual basis, which, for most companies, does not equal cash flow during the same period because of differences in timing. Specifically, revenues are recognized when the company has provided goods or performed services, and expenses are subtracted when the company uses goods or services. In 2015, KW Bookkeeping earns revenue and collects from customers at the same time, but suppose KW Bookkeeping acquires new clients that are companies for which standard practice is to extend credit for 30 days. If KW Bookkeeping provides services and bills a client $4,000 in January, but does not collect from the client until February, we would still recognize revenue of $4,000 in January, when it is actually earned. For the first year, however, KW Bookkeeping did not extend credit to its customers. We see, however, that the total cash flow of $8,000 is less than KW Bookkeeping's net income for the year because of the repayment of the $10,000 bank loan—a financing activity. This payment required cash, but has no effect on net income, as it is a return of principal to the lender. The company's balance sheet at the end of the year would be as shown in Exhibit 1.5.

EXHIBIT 1.5	KW Bookkeeping Services Balance Sheet as of December 31, 2015		
Assets		**Liabilities & owners' equity**	
Current assets		Current liabilities	
Cash	$48,000	Bank loan payable	$ 0
Total current assets	$48,000	Total liabilities	$ 0
Long-term assets		Owners' equity	
		Contributed capital	$30,000
		Retained earnings	18,000
		Total owners' equity	$48,000
Total assets	$48,000	Total liabilities & owners' equity	$48,000

We can see that the cash balance has increased by $8,000 since the beginning of the year, as explained in the statement of cash flows, that the bank loan has been repaid, and that owners' equity has increased by the $18,000 of net income earned during the year. The new account, **retained earnings**, exists to indicate increases in the owner's claim that are the result of the company's profitability, as distinct from an owner's direct payment to the company to acquire shares. Every time KW Bookkeeping earns income, the value of the company and specifically of its owners' equity in the company increases. A company's profit, or net income, belongs to its owners, and is reflected by the increase in retained earnings. Because a company's owners have a claim on all profits the company earns, they have the right to require that the company distribute its profits to them as a dividend. If they do, the dividend will reduce the company's retained rarnings account because a dividend or distribution is essentially the opposite of retaining or reinvesting profits back into the company. So for any company, the following relationship holds:

> Retained earnings, beginning balance
> Plus: Net income for the period
> Less: Dividends to owners during the period
> ───────────────────────────
> Retained earnings, ending balance

For our simple KW example, we will assume that the company does not pay a dividend to the owner, as the owner chooses to increase her investment in the company.

In 2016, the second year of its operations, KW Bookkeeping Services decides to expand its client base to include small businesses and, in order to be competitive, offers them credit terms of 30 days after invoice before they must pay for their services. Also, KW Bookkeeping decides to purchase some of its own office and computer equipment and discontinues those leasing arrangements. On January 2, 2016, KW Bookkeeping paid $21,000 for equipment that it expects to use for the next three years. The company also borrowed $5,000 from the bank on a note requiring interest payments of $25 each month, and the repayment of the principal of $5,000 in three years (on January 2, 2019). The company's cash flows during its second year of operations are detailed below (Exhibit 1.6).

EXHIBIT 1.6	KW Bookkeeping Services Statement of Cash Flows for the Year Ending December 31, 2016
Received from customers	$123,000
Paid for salaries	(64,000)
Paid for rent	(24,000)
Paid for utilities	(5,900)
Paid for interest	(300)
Net operating cash flows	$ 28,800
Investing cash flows:	
Purchase of equipment	(21,000)
Financing cash flows:	
Proceeds from bank loan	5,000
Change in cash	$ 12,800

During 2016, KW Bookkeeping provided services to clients, billing a total of $133,500 for its work. The company's total revenue for the year, therefore, was $133,500, and the difference between the revenue earned and the $123,000 cash collected from customers is $10,500, the amount KW Bookkeeping is entitled to receive from its customers. In 2016, the company's income statement will therefore not be the same as its statement of operating cash flows (Exhibit 1.7).

EXHIBIT 1.7	KW Bookkeeping Services Income Statement for the Year Ending December 31, 2016	
Revenues		$133,500
Salaries expense		(64,000)
Rent expense		(24,000)
Depreciation expense.		(7,000)
Utilities expense		(5,900)
Interest expense		(300)
Net income		$ 32,300

In addition to the difference between revenues earned and cash collected, we see another difference between the measurement of KW Bookkeeping's net income and its cash flows. The company's office and computer equipment is an essential component of its earnings process for the year, and the equipment will support the company's operations for three years. To allocate the cost of $21,000 systematically over its useful life, we recognize ($21,000/3) = $7,000 per year in **depreciation** expense. This expense measures the cost of using the equipment for the year, but it does not involve any operating cash outflow, as the equipment was purchased (as an investing activity) and paid for at the beginning of the year.

The company's balance sheet at the end of its second year of operations is shown below (Exhibit 1.8).

EXHIBIT 1.8	KW Bookkeeping Services Balance Sheet as of December 31, 2016			
Assets			**Liabilities & owners' equity**	
Current assets			Long-term liabilities	
Cash	$60,800		Bank loan payable	$ 5,000
Accounts receivable	10,500			
Total current assets	$71,300		Total liabilities	$ 5,000
Long-term assets			Owner's equity	
Equipment (net)	$14,000		Contributed capital	$30,000
			Retained earnings	50,300
			Total owners' equity	$80,300
Total assets	$85,300		Total liabilities & owners' equity	$85,300

Cash has increased by $12,800, as disclosed in the statement of cash flows, and retained rarnings has increased due to net income of $32,300 earned during the year.

Retained earnings, beginning balance	$18,000
Plus: Net income for the period	+ 32,300
Less: Dividends to owners during the period	(0)
Retained earnings, ending balance	$50,300

The net value, or book value, of the equipment is $14,000—the $21,000 original cost less the $7,000 that was depreciated during the year. With one-third of its life used, the equipment's remaining balance sheet value is two-thirds of its original cost. As the company grows, KW Bookkeeping will undertake other transactions that will add complexity to its financial statements, but the fundamental structure and formats will remain unchanged.

FINANCIAL STATEMENTS: LARGE CORPORATIONS

The same structure and formats are apparent in the financial statements of large corporations, as are the financial footprints of their qualitative decisions. Within a particular industry or span of the value chain, companies make multiple strategic choices, including, for example, which customers will be targeted, what level of service will be maintained, and how to price products or services offered. Although many of these decisions are detailed and subtle, we can often categorize companies into either a low-price, high-volume or a high-price, low-volume strategy. The retail industry offers many examples of companies at either end of the price–volume spectrum. If you need a new pair of blue jeans, you can go to Wal-Mart, which sells Levi's® for as little as $25, or you can go to Nordstrom, which sells True Religion® jeans for about $200. Both Wal-Mart and Nordstrom are large retailers at the end of the value chain, but their strategies are otherwise different.

Wal-Mart, with the largest sales revenues of any U.S. company, sells a wide range of products, from apparel to electronics to groceries, and almost everything in between. The company has built its success on its slogan of "Everyday Low Prices" and targets the broadest possible customer base. The goal is to make a small profit on each pair of jeans, and then to sell many pairs of jeans, a classic low-price, high-volume strategy. Nordstrom, by contrast, is a much smaller company that focuses on high-end apparel and higher-income customers. Its goal is to make a higher profit on each pair of jeans, knowing that it will sell fewer than its low-price competitors, a classic high-price, low-volume, or niche, strategy. Even the physical appearance of these two companies' stores reflects their different strategic choices. Wal-Mart stores are enormous and functional, usually made of cinder block, on a floor plan similar to that of a traditional grocery store. Products are stacked on high shelves, and customers serve themselves with large carts. Nordstrom stores are well lit, with wide open spaces, many salespeople, and not a shopping cart or basket in sight. Products are arranged on tables to look appealing, not to maximize the use of square footage of displays, and some stores include a large seating area around a grand piano where a man in a tuxedo might be playing show tunes. The financial statements of these two companies are just as distinctive as their respective strategic choices and physical appearance. You may be able to buy blue jeans at both, but little else about them is similar.

The condensed financial statements for Wal-Mart and Nordstrom illustrate the connections between their strategic choices and their financial statements (Exhibit 1.9).

EXHIBIT 1.9	Income Statements for Fiscal Year 2014 (in millions of dollars)	
	Nordstrom	**Wal-Mart**
Sales revenue..	$13,110	$482,229
Cost of goods sold..	(8,406)	(365,086)
Gross profit..	4,704	117,143
Selling, general, and administrative expenses......................	(3,777)	(93,418)
Other operating revenue..	396	3,422
Operating income..	$ 1,323	$ 27,147
Interest expense...	(138)	(2,348)
Net income before income taxes....................................	$ 1,185	$ 24,799
Income tax expense..	(465)	(7,985)
Net income..	$ 720	$ 16,814

The income statement, also known as the profit-and-loss (P&L) statement, measures the total revenue the company earned through selling its products during a specific period, in this case during the 2014 fiscal year. In its simplest terms, sales revenue for a retailer equals the number of units sold times the price of each unit. Every time Nordstrom sells a $200 pair of blue jeans, its revenue increases by $200. At the same time, Nordstrom incurred a cost for each pair of jeans that must also be considered in measuring the firm's total financial performance. The **cost of goods sold** is, just as the name indicates, the cost of the units sold by the company. With each unit sold, the company records both the revenue it earned and the cost of the unit sold, and revenues minus cost of goods sold is **gross profit**, an important first step in evaluating the company's financial performance.

In comparing Nordstrom and Wal-Mart, the first thing we notice is the significant difference in size, as Wal-Mart's revenues are more than 40 times Nordstrom's. Given Wal-Mart's strategy to sell a wide variety of products in large stores, and given that it has almost 9,000 stores worldwide whereas Nordstrom has only 200 stores, the difference in dollar amounts is not surprising. Certainly Wal-Mart's operating profit of over $27 billion dwarfs Nordstrom's operating profit of just over $1 billion. But we need to consider these amounts within the context of each company. A **common-size income statement** recasts each item as a percentage of the company's revenue and allows us to compare the companies as if they were a "common" size (Exhibit 1.10).

EXHIBIT 1.10	Income Statements Common-Sized for Fiscal Year 2014 (as a percentage of sales revenue)	
	Nordstrom	**Wal-Mart**
Sales revenue.	100.0%	100.0%
Cost of goods sold.	(64.1)	(75.7)
Gross profit.	35.9	24.3
Selling, general, and administrative expenses.	(28.8)	(19.4)
Other operating revenue.	3.0	0.7
Operating income.	10.1	5.6
Interest expense.	(1.1)	(0.5)
Net income before income taxes	9.0	5.1
Income tax expense.	(3.5)	(1.6)
Net income.	5.5%	3.5%

Now we can see more clearly the financial consequences of the companies' strategic choices. With its focus on high-end apparel and higher-income customers, Nordstrom charges a proportionately higher selling price, relative to its cost, than Wal-Mart, and we see the results in its gross profit rate of 35.9%, significantly higher than Wal-Mart's 24.3%.

On the next line of the income statement, the companies report **selling, general, and administrative (SG&A) expenses**, an aggregation of the many costs of operating a retail company: compensation of salespeople and corporate executives, rent on stores and warehouses, fuel for trucks used to distribute goods, and utilities to keep everything running. In millions of dollars, Wal-Mart's SG&A expenses are, of course, much higher than Nordstrom's, but as a percentage of sales revenue, they are proportionately lower. Again, we can trace this difference back to the company's choices. Nordstrom's emphasis on customer service requires more salespeople, relative to revenue, and its decision to design stores that are attractive and decorative requires more expensive spaces and fixtures. It is not uncommon to find that companies with higher gross margin rates often incur proportionately higher SG&A rates, as the incremental selling costs are what support the premium price charged for the product.

Next we see that both companies have revenue streams aside from selling goods. For Nordstrom, its other operating revenue is generated by fees charged to customers who have charge accounts with the store. For Wal-Mart, the additional revenue is generated by membership fees earned by its Sam's Club warehouse stores. As a result of the companies' decisions and activities in 2014, Nordstrom's **operating margin**—operating income as a percentage of sales revenue—of 10.1%, was almost twice Wal-Mart's operating margin of 5.6%.

The balance sheets for the two companies as of the last day of fiscal 2014 illustrate that they both held the same kinds of assets—**cash**, **accounts receivable**, **inventories**, and **property, plant, and equipment**, as these are the resources needed to operate retail stores. They had similar liabilities, reporting **accounts payable**, the amounts owed to their suppliers of merchandise; **accrued liabilities**, the amounts owed for salaries and utilities, for example; and **short-term** and **long-term debt**, the amounts owed to banks and financial institutions (Exhibit 1.11).

EXHIBIT 1.11	Balance Sheets as of the End of Fiscal Year 2014 (in millions of dollars)	
	Nordstrom	**Wal-Mart**
Assets		
Current assets:		
Cash.	$ 827	$ 9,135
Accounts receivable.	2,306	6,778
Inventories	1,733	45,141
Other current assets.	358	2,224
Total current assets.	$5,224	$ 63,278
Property, plant, and equipment	3,340	116,655
Other long-term assets	681	23,773
Total assets.	$9,245	$203,706
Liabilities and shareholders' equity		
Current liabilities:		
Accounts payable.	$1,328	$ 38,410
Accrued liabilities	416	19,152
Other current liabilities	1,048	1,021
Short-term debt	8	6,689
Total current liabilities	$2,800	$ 62,300
Long-term debt	3,123	43,692
Other long-term liabilities.	882	8,805
Total liabilities	$6,805	$117,645
Shareholders' equity:		
Common stock and additional paid-in capital.	$2,338	$ 2,785
Retained earnings	166	85,777
Other shareholders' equity.	(64)	(2,625)
Total shareholders' equity.	$2,440	$ 85,937
Total liabilities and shareholders' equity.	$9,245	$203,706

As with the income statement comparison, however, Wal-Mart's size (over $200 billion in assets) overwhelms Nordstrom's ($9.2 billion in assets). And as with the income statement, we can compare the balance sheets more readily by using the **common-size balance sheet** in which we consider each component as a percentage of total assets (Exhibit 1.12).

EXHIBIT 1.12	Balance Sheets Common-Sized as of the End of Fiscal Year 2014 (as a percentage of total assets)		
		Nordstrom	Wal-Mart
Assets			
Current assets:			
Cash		9.0%	4.5%
Accounts receivable		24.9	3.3
Inventories		18.7	22.2
Other current assets		3.9	1.1
Total current assets		56.5%	31.1%
Property, plant, and equipment		26.1	57.2
Other long-term assets		7.4	11.7
Total assets		100%	100%
Liabilities and Shareholders' Equity			
Current liabilities:			
Accounts payable		14.4%	18.9%
Accrued liabilities		4.5	9.4
Other current liabilities		11.3	0.5
Short-term debt		0.1	3.2
Total current liabilities		30.3%	32.0%
Long-term debt		33.8	21.4
Other long-term liabilities		9.5	4.3
Total liabilities		73.6%	57.7%
Shareholders' equity:			
Common stock and additional paid-in capital		25.3%	1.4
Retained earnings		1.8	42.1
Other shareholders' equity		(0.7)	(1.2)
Total shareholders' equity		26.4%	42.3%
Total liabilities and shareholders' equity		100.0%	100.0%

Continuing our introduction to specific terms, we will next walk through these accounts individually, and we will discuss all of them in more detail in Chapter 2.

Cash is probably the most familiar of assets, and for corporations, as for individuals, is essential. Companies keep cash in the bank, but also may have investments in money market funds with financial institutions. The proportion of assets held in cash varies significantly from one company to another and from one date to another. Although all companies need cash, they would not want cash to be their only asset. Wal-Mart and Nordstrom earn revenue by selling goods in stores. Their essential assets are, therefore, inventory and property, plant, and equipment. Cash is necessary as the means to having the resources and services that enable the company to operate.

Accounts receivable are the amounts due to the company from its customers. When a customer uses a credit card to purchase goods at Wal-Mart, for example, Wal-Mart receives cash a day or two later when the credit card company processes the transaction. Nordstrom, however, offers some customers a Nordstrom credit card with payment terms that extend over several months. Consequently, Nordstrom may wait one or two months after a sale before it receives cash from the customer. This difference in strategic choice is reflected clearly in Nordstrom's much higher percentage of accounts receivable—24% in contrast to Wal-Mart's 3%. Offering credit directly to customers is one of the reasons that Nordstrom charges a higher price, relative to its cost, than Wal-Mart and thus contributes to its higher gross margin that we observed in comparing the common-size income statements.

Inventory is the cost of products that the company is holding to sell to customers. For a retailer like Nordstrom, inventory includes all of the apparel, shoes, and accessories in its stores and warehouses. Similarly, Wal-Mart's inventory includes all of its goods for sale, but unlike Nordstrom, Wal-Mart's range of products is much broader. Note that whereas companies account for inventory internally in detail, they report externally by aggregating across all products. As outsiders, we cannot know, for example, how much of Wal-Mart's ending inventory is groceries versus apparel versus home goods.

Property, plant, and equipment includes the company's land, buildings (stores and warehouses, for example), equipment (shelves, desks, and computers, for example), delivery trucks, and similar items needed to operate the business. Also known as *fixed assets*, these are tangible resources that the company owns and will use for more than one year. As we saw with the illustration of KW Bookkeeping, these assets are depreciated over their useful lives to reflect their use over time.

Accounts payable are the amounts that the company owes to its primary suppliers. Wal-Mart purchases many of its products (detergent and toothpaste, for example) from Procter & Gamble. When companies do business with other companies, they typically extend credit to one another, so that Procter & Gamble will ship goods to Wal-Mart before Wal-Mart is required to pay Procter & Gamble. Once the goods are shipped, Wal-Mart clearly has an obligation to its supplier, recorded in accounts payable.

Accrued liabilities are the amounts that the company owes to companies and individuals that have provided services used in operations. As of a specific balance sheet date, Wal-Mart and Nordstrom may owe their employees a week or two of salaries, or the companies may owe utilities providers for electricity and telephone service. Accrued liabilities and accounts payable are both trade credit accounts, as they are obligations to trade suppliers as opposed to financial institutions.

Short-term and Long-term debt reflect the amounts owed by the company to banks or other financial institutions. When companies need cash, like individuals, they often borrow from banks, incurring an interest charge during the period to compensate the lender. If the loan must be repaid within a year, it must be classified as short term, or current, whereas loans with a longer maturity date are classified as long term (or non-current).

Shareholders' equity (also known as stockholders' equity or owners' equity) accounts are inherently long term, as these claims do not have a due date. When a company issues stock in exchange for cash, the shareholders are contributing capital to the company, and that investment by shareholders is captured in the **common stock** and **additional paid-in capital** accounts. Together they represent the amount of capital that shareholders have contributed as of the balance sheet date.

The **retained earnings** account is the most abstract account on the balance sheet, and understanding it is essential to understanding the structure of financial reporting. When shareholders contribute capital to a company, they acquire a claim on the company's net income, also known as its earnings. As illustrated in KW Bookkeeping Services, every time the company earns net income, the owner's claim increases. Similarly, when Wal-Mart or Nordstrom sells a pair of blue jeans, it earns net income that belongs to its shareholders. Shareholders can demand that the company distribute earnings back to them, a return of their investment called a dividend. Alternatively, shareholders can reinvest the earnings, thus increasing their claim and increasing the size of the company. Retained earnings is the account that accumulates all of the net income earned by a company that shareholders have chosen to reinvest. For older, historically profitable companies, retained earnings constitute a substantial portion of total shareholders' equity. Remember that the retained earnings account is not a bank account. The company's cash in the bank is an asset, cash, whereas its retained earnings reflect the income accumulated and reinvested over the entire life of the firm. Wal-Mart, for example, over its long and profitable life, has accumulated over $85 billion in retained earnings, but its cash balance at the end of fiscal 2014 was only $9.1 billion. As Wal-Mart retains its earnings, it literally reinvests them so that it can continue to grow and earn more on behalf of its shareholders.

If we use Wal-Mart's balance sheet as of the end of 2014, we can see that the company had approximately $9.1 billion in cash on hand then. Its balance sheet at the beginning of fiscal 2014 disclosed that the company had $7.3 billion in cash when it started the year. So together, the two balance sheets indicate that during fiscal 2014, Wal-Mart's cash decreased by approximately $1.8 billion. The two balance sheets tell us nothing, however, about how much cash the company received and how much it disbursed during the year. As illustrated for KW Bookkeeping, because of the importance of cash, an entire statement is devoted to reporting where it came from and where it went. We will discuss the statement of cash flows in more detail in Chapter 4. Condensed versions of Wal-Mart's and Nordstrom's statements of cash flows are presented in Exhibit 1.13.

EXHIBIT 1.13	Statements of Cash Flows for Fiscal Year 2014 (in millions of dollars)		
		Nordstrom	**Wal-Mart**
Net cash flows from operating activities		$1,220	$ 28,564
Net cash flows used in investing activities.		(889)	(11,125)
Net cash flows used in financing activities		(698)	(15,585)
Net change in cash.		$ (367)	$ 1,854

The classification of cash flows into operating, investing, and financing activities is supported by further detail in the actual statements, but the categories are defined to organize cash collections and payments according to their purpose. Operating cash flows increase with collections from customers and decrease with payments to suppliers (as when Wal-Mart pays Procter & Gamble) and with payments to employees. Investing cash flows are payments to acquire property, plant, and equipment and investments offset by cash received for the sale of property, plant, and equipment and investments. Financing cash flows are amounts received from issuing stock or borrowing from financial institutions offset by cash paid to repay debt or for dividends. Unlike the income statement and balance sheet, we do not "common-size" the statement of cash flows, but use other analytical tools covered in Chapters 4 and 6. In simplest terms, we can see that during fiscal 2014, both Nordstrom and Wal-Mart generated positive cash flows from their operations, made investments in property, plant, and equipment, and paid out more than they received in managing their financing activities.

FINANCIAL STATEMENTS AND FINANCIAL FOOTPRINTS

Comparing Wal-Mart and Nordstrom is one context in which to see that different corporate strategies leave different financial "footprints." Let's consider some other examples. Kelly Services, Inc., is a global agency that provides temporary staffing to companies. While it places a wide range of personnel, from scientific researchers to chefs to paralegals, the company's core purpose is to connect its corporate clients with the temporary staffing they require. Think about the balance sheet for a company like Kelly Services: what kinds of assets does it need? With no manufacturing and no stores, Kelly has little in property, plant, and equipment and no inventory. However, because Kelly offers credit to its many clients, over 60% of its assets are current accounts receivable. By contrast, Carnival Cruise owns and operates more than 50 large ships offering cruises around the world. What kinds of assets does it need? As you might expect, over 80% of its assets are property, plant, and equipment, as it could not operate without those enormous Carnival and Princess boats. In a different industry, Gap, Inc., the specialty retailer that operates

Gap, Old Navy, Banana Republic, and Athleta, rents most of its store space, and therefore shows relatively little property, plant, and equipment on its balance sheet. Consequently, its most significant asset is inventory.

As you learn the details and terminology of financial statements, consider also the larger context of the company, its industry, and its strategic choices. What assets does it need? What liabilities must it carry? Does it target upper-end customers, like Nordstrom, so that it can generate a high gross margin rate? Or is it more about low prices and low markup, like Wal-Mart? How much of the industry value chain does the company span? Is it vertically integrated like American Apparel, and thus reporting significant property, plant and equipment on its balance sheet, substantial depreciation on its income statement, and major capital expenditures on the statement of cash flows? Or is it very focused, like a graphic designer, with very little in assets required to operate? Analyzing financial performance and condition requires a combination of qualitative understanding and technical skills, and you will learn and apply both throughout this course.

CONCLUSION

Whether the company is as small as KW Bookkeeping Services or as enormous as Wal-Mart, its financial statements for a month or a quarter or a year summarize the consequences of its decisions and transactions. This introduction to the primary financial statements—the statement of cash flows, income statement, and balance sheet—illustrates the formats of these statements and their connections to both the context and strategy of a company.

In Chapter 2, we will use the **balance sheet equation (BSE) format**—Assets = Liabilities + Shareholders' equity—to work through individual transactions, the building blocks of financial statements, to see the details that support each of the statements.

KEY CONCEPTS AND TERMS

accounts payable, 10, 12
accounts receivable, 10, 11
accrued liabilities, 10, 12
additional paid-in capital, 12
assets, 4
balance sheet, 3
balance sheet equation (BSE)
    format, 14
capital assets, 4
capital expenditure, 4
capital stock, 4
cash, 10, 11
common-size balance sheet, 10
common-size income
    statement, 9

common stock, 4, 12
cost of goods sold, 9
current assets, 4
current liabilities, 4
depreciation, 7
expenses, 3
financial statements, 1
gross profit, 9
income statement, 3
inventories, 10
inventory, 12
invested capital, 4
liabilities, 4
long-term debt, 10, 12
net income, 5

operating margin, 9
owners' equity, 4
property, plant, and
    equipment, 10, 12
retained earnings, 6, 12
revenues, 3
selling, general, and
    administrative (SG&A)
    expenses, 9
shareholders' equity, 4, 12
short-term debt, 10, 12
statement of cash flows, 3
working capital, 4

QUESTIONS

Q1-1. Describe the concept of an industry's value chain. (It may help to use a specific industry as an example.)

Q1-2. What is the fundamental accounting equation? Why must it be true?

Q1-3. What are the three primary financial statements?

Q1-4. Identify three reasons for the difference between net income and net cash flow during a given period.

Q1-5. Identify and describe three kinds of expenses.

Q1-6. Describe the proper format of a balance sheet. How are assets and liabilities classified?

Q1-7. Identify and describe three asset accounts.

Q1-8. Identify and describe three liability accounts.

Q1-9. How does the income statement connect to the balance sheet?

Q1-10. Describe the purpose of retained rarnings. Why is it a shareholders' equity account?

EXERCISES

E1-1. **Preparation of an Income Statement** The table below includes income statement accounts for **Tootsie Roll Industries, Inc.**, in alphabetical order for the year ending December 31, 2014.

Tootsie Roll Industries, Inc.

Required:
Prepare a multi-step income statement for the year ending December 31, 2014.

Cost of goods sold.	$341,880
Income tax expense.	28,434
Other income, net.	7,371
Sales and royalty revenue	543,525
Selling, marketing and administrative expenses	$117,722

E1-2. **Preparation of an Income Statement** **Dick's Sporting Goods, Inc.** is a full-line sports and fitness retailer offering a broad assortment of competitively-priced, brand-name sporting goods equipment, apparel, and footwear.

Dick's Sporting Goods, Inc.

Required:
Using the alphabetical list of accounts below, prepare a multi-step income statement for fiscal years 2014 and 2013.

	2014	2013
Cost of goods sold	$4,727,813	$4,269,223
Income tax expense	211,816	208,509
Interest expense	3,215	2,929
Net sales	6,814,479	6,213,173
Other income	5,170	12,224
Pre-opening expenses	30,518	20,823
Selling, general and administrative expenses	$1,502,089	$1,386,315

E1-3. **Preparation of a Statement of Retained Earnings** **Trail Mix, Inc.** was organized to do business on March 2, 2013 with an investment of $125,000 by each of its two shareholders. Net income for 2013 was $34,500. Net income increased to $56,400 in 2014 and to $94,250 in 2015. The company did not pay any dividends in 2013. However, Trail Mix distributed $5,000 dividends to each of the shareholders for both 2014 and 2015.

Trail Mix, Inc.

Required:
Prepare a statement of retained earnings for the year ended December 31, 2015.

E1-4. **Preparation of Income Statements** **NIKE, Inc.** is an athletic apparel and footwear company. Its annual report includes the following description: "Our principal business activity is the design, development, and worldwide marketing and selling of athletic footwear, apparel, equipment, accessories, and services. NIKE is the largest seller of athletic footwear and athletic apparel in the world. We sell our products to retail accounts, through NIKE-owned retail stores and internet websites (which we refer to as our "Direct to Consumer" or "DTC" operations), and through a mix of independent distributors and licensees throughout the world. Virtually all of our products are manufactured by independent contractors." The following accounts are taken from Nike's financial statements for the years ended May 31, 2014 and May 31, 2013.

NIKE, Inc.

Required:

a. Using the alphabetical list of accounts, prepare a multi-step income statement for the years ended May 31, 2014 and May 31, 2013.

b. What is the cause of the difference in net income between the two years?

	2014	2013
Cost of sales.	$15,353	$14,279
Demand creation expense	3,031	2,745
Income tax expense.	851	805
Interest expense (income), net	33	(3)
Operating overhead expense.	5,735	5,051
Other expense (income), net	103	(15)
Revenues	$27,799	$25,313

PROBLEMS

Staples, Inc. **P1-1.** **Preparation of a Balance Sheet** Staples, Inc. is a worldwide office supply company that is headquartered in Framingham, Massachusetts. Its most recent annual report says: "We add value to our customers through a combination of low prices, a broad selection of office products, convenient store locations, and excellent customer service. Our core competency lies in our ability to address customer groups with different needs and deliver our brand promise: we bring easy to your office." The table below includes balance sheet accounts for Staples, Inc. as of January 31, 2015, listed in alphabetical order.

Required:

Prepare a classified balance sheet for Staples, Inc. as of January 31, 2015, in good form.

Account Title	$000s
Accounts payable.	$1,866,545
Accounts receivable.	1,927,781
Accrued expenses and other current liabilities	1,332,308
Accumulated depreciation	4,314,421
Additional paid-in capital	4,943,721
Cash and cash equivalents	627,174
Common stock.	565
Debt maturing within one year	91,718
Equipment	2,824,877
Furniture and fixtures	1,015,737
Goodwill and intangible assets, net	3,015,046
Land and buildings.	947,999
Leasehold improvements.	1,230,740
Long-term debt, net of current maturities	1,023,997
Merchandise inventories	2,144,447
Other long-term assets	417,327
Other long-term liabilities.	685,795
Prepaid expenses and other current assets.	477,021
Retained earnings	$ 369,079

Tootsie Roll Industries, Inc. **P1-2.** **Preparation of a Balance Sheet** Tootsie Roll Industries, Inc., has manufactured and sold Tootsie Rolls, Junior Mints, and other candies since 1896. The table below includes balance sheet accounts for Tootsie Roll as of December 31, 2014.

Required:

Prepare a classified balance sheet for Tootsie Roll Industries, Inc., as of December 31, 2014.

Accounts payable.	$ 11,641
Accounts receivable.	46,830
Accrued liabilities	46,810
Accumulated depreciation	298,128
Bank loans, short-term.	124
Capital in excess of par value	599,513
Cash and cash equivalents	100,108
Common stock.	41,786
Deferred compensation and other long-term liabilities	146,597
Dividends payable	4,814
Goodwill.	73,237
Income taxes payable	1,070
Inventories	70,379
Investments, long-term	163,579
Investments, short-term.	39,450
Long-term debt	8,194
Other current assets.	1,794
Other long-term assets	43,844
Prepaid expenses.	6,060
Property, plant, and equipment, at cost.	488,209
Retained earnings	49,837
Trademarks.	$175,024

P1-3. **Preparation of a Balance Sheet** Again, for **Dick's Sporting Goods**, the alphabetical list of accounts appears below.

Dick's Sporting Goods, Inc.

Required:

Prepare a classified balance sheet as of the end of the reporting period for fiscal 2014.

Accounts payable.	$ 614,511
Accounts receivable.	80,292
Accrued expenses	283,828
Additional paid-in capital	1,015,404
Cash and cash equivalents	221,679
Common stock.	1,181
Current portion of long-term debt and leasing obligations	537
Deferred revenue and other liabilities, long-term.	479,227
Deferred revenue and other liabilities, short-term	172,259
Goodwill.	200,594
Income taxes payable	47,698
Income taxes receivable.	14,293
Intangible assets, net	110,162
Inventories	1,390,767
Long-term debt and leasing obligations	5,913
Other long-term assets	71,676
Prepaid expenses and other current assets.	143,353
Property and equipment, net	1,203,382
Retained earnings	$ 815,640

P1-4. **Preparation of Balance Sheets**

For **Nike, Inc.**, the alphabetical list of accounts appears below.

NIKE, Inc.

Required:

a. Prepare classified balance sheet accounts provided below in alphabetical order, prepare classified balance sheets as of May 31—the closing date—of 2014 and 2013.

b. Identify three accounts that changed between the beginning and end of the year and provide a likely reason for the change.

	2014	2013
Accounts payable.............................	$1,930	$1,669
Accounts receivable, net	3,434	3,117
Accrued liabilities.............................	2,491	2,054
Capital in excess of stated value	5,865	5,184
Cash and equivalents..........................	2,220	3,337
Common stock................................	3	3
Current portion of long-term debt	7	57
Goodwill.....................................	131	131
Identifiable intangible assets, net................	282	289
Income taxes payable	432	84
Inventories	3,947	3,484
Long-term debt	1,199	1,210
Notes payable, short-term......................	167	98
Other long-term assets	1,651	1,043
Other long-term liabilities......................	1,544	1,292
Prepaid expenses and other current assets........	1,173	1,064
Property, plant and equipment, net	2,834	2,452
Retained earnings	4,956	5,894
Short-term investments	$2,922	$2,628

Facebook, Inc.   **P1-5.**   **Preparation of Classified Balance Sheet and Multi-Step Income Statement**   Facebook, Inc., discloses in its 2014 annual report that its "top priority is to build useful and engaging products that enable people to connect and share through mobile devices and personal computers." Its products include Facebook, Instagram, and WhatsApp, and it generates most of its revenue through advertising.

Required:
The following is a list of accounts from Facebook's financial statements. Use this alphabetical list of accounts to prepare a classified balance sheet as of December 31, 2014 and a multi-step income statement for the year ended December 31, 2014. (*Hint:* Identify whether the account is a balance sheet or income statement account first.)

Account Title	Millions
Accounts payable..	$ 176
Accounts receivable, net	1,678
Accrued expenses and other current liabilities	1,068
Capital lease obligations, less current portion............	119
Cash and cash equivalents	4,315
Common stock and additional paid-in capital.............	29,997
Cost of revenue	2,153
Current portion of capital lease obligations	114
Deferred revenue and deposits	66
General and administrative expense	973
Goodwill and other intangibles...........................	21,910
Income tax expense.....................................	1,970
Interest expense, net	84
Marketable securities, short-term	6,884
Marketing and sales expense.............................	1,680
Other liabilities	2,545
Other long-term assets	637
Prepaid expenses and other current assets................	793
Property and equipment, net	3,967
Research and development expense.......................	2,666
Retained earnings	6,099
Revenue...	$12,466

P1-6. **Preparation of Classified Balance Sheet and Multi-Step Income Statement**   Incorpo-   3M Company
rated in 1929, the **3M Company** develops, manufactures, and markets a wide range of products that include industrial adhesives, commercial graphic inks and films, medical tapes, and
the ubiquitous Post-it note.

Required:
The following is a list of accounts from 3M's financial statements. Use this alphabetical list
of accounts to prepare a classified balance sheet as of December 31, 2014 and a multi-step
income statement for the year ended December 31, 2014.

Account Titles	Millions
Accounts payable.	$ 1,807
Accounts receivable, net	4,238
Accrued income taxes	435
Accrued payroll	732
Accumulated depreciation	14,352
Additional paid-in capital	4,412
Cash and cash equivalents	1,897
Common stock.	9
Cost of sales.	16,447
Finished goods.	1,723
Goodwill	7,050
Income tax expense.	2,028
Intangible assets, net	1,435
Interest expense, net	109
Investments	102
Long-term debt	6,731
Marketable securities—current	626
Marketable securities—non-current.	828
Net sales.	31,821
Other current assets.	1,298
Other current liabilities	2,918
Other long-term assets	1,554
Other long-term liabilities	1,555
Pension and postretirement benefits liability, long-term	3,843
Prepaid pension benefits, long-term	46
Property, plant and equipment, net	8,489
Property, plant and equipment, cost	22,841
Raw materials and supplies	902
Research, development and related expenses	1,770
Retained earnings	8,721
Selling, general and administrative expenses	6,469
Short-term borrowings and current portion of long-term debt	106
Total inventories	3,706
Work in process	$ 1,081

P1-7. **Reading an Income Statement**   Mattel, Inc. is a U.S.-based toy company with about half of   Mattel, Inc.
its revenues from sales outside North America. Its globally-recognized names include Barbie,
Fisher-Price, Hot Wheels, and American Girl, and because of its licensing arrangements with
Disney, Viacom, and Warner Brothers, many of its products are based on well-known characters, such as Winnie the Pooh, SpongeBob SquarePants, and Batman. Its income statements
for the years ended 2014, 2013, and 2012 appear in the exhibit below as the basis for the following questions. (Note that the company reports in thousands of U.S. dollars.)

Required:
a. What is Mattel's largest expense?
b. Calculate the gross margin percentage $\left(\frac{\text{Gross profit}}{\text{Total revenue}}\right)$ for each of the three years. Why
   might this ratio be useful?
c. What is Mattel's second largest expense? What kinds of specific costs might be
   included in that line of the income statement?

d. Although you don't have a balance sheet, how can you tell from the income statement that Mattel has borrowed from banks and other lenders?

e. Mattel's net income has increased over the three years. Has its profit margin $\left(\frac{\text{Net income}}{\text{Total revenue}}\right)$ changed?

MATTEL, INC. AND SUBSIDIARIES **CONSOLIDATED STATEMENTS OF OPERATIONS**			
	For the Year		
(In thousands, except per share amounts)	**2014**	**2013**	**2012**
Net sales.	$6,023,819	$6,484,892	$6,420,881
Cost of sales.	3,022,797	3,006,009	3,011,684
Gross profit.	3,001,022	3,478,883	3,409,197
Advertising and promotion expenses.	733,243	750,205	717,803
Other selling and administrative expenses	1,614,065	1,560,575	1,670,379
Operating income.	653,714	1,168,103	1,021,015
Interest expense.	79,271	78,505	88,835
Interest (income).	(7,382)	(5,555)	(6,841)
Other non-operating (income), net.	(5,085)	(3,975)	(6,024)
Income before income taxes	586,910	1,099,128	945,045
Provision for income taxes.	88,036	195,184	168,581
Net income.	$ 498,874	$ 903,944	$ 776,464

Southwest Airlines   **P1-8.**   **Reading a Balance Sheet**   Southwest Airlines is a U.S. passenger airline focused on domestic, point-to-point, low-fare, and short- to medium-haul routes. Its balance sheets as of December 31, 2014 and December 31, 2013 appear in the exhibit below as the basis for the following questions. (Note that the company reports in millions of U.S. dollars.)

Required:

a. What is Southwest Airlines' largest asset? What is its book value as of December 31, 2014?

b. Calculate the current ratio $\left(\frac{\text{Current assets}}{\text{Current liabilities}}\right)$ as of December 31, 2014 and December 31, 2013. Why might this ratio be helpful?

c. What might be the explanation for the company's air traffic liability?

d. What is Southwest Airlines' largest long-term liability as of December 31, 2014?

e. Calculate the total liabilities as of December 31, 2014.

f. Was Southwest Airlines profitable during 2014? How can you tell?

SOUTHWEST AIRLINES CO. Consolidated Balance Sheet (in millions, except share data)	December 31, 2014	December 31, 2013
Assets		
Current assets:		
Cash and cash equivalents..............................	$ 1,282	$ 1,355
Short-term investments	1,706	1,797
Accounts and other receivables........................	365	419
Inventories of parts and supplies, at cost.................	342	467
Deferred income taxes	477	168
Prepaid expenses and other current assets...............	232	250
Total current assets.................................	4,404	4,456
Property and equipment, at cost:		
Flight equipment.....................................	18,473	16,937
Ground property and equipment	2,853	2,666
Deposits on flight equipment purchase contracts	566	764
Assets constructed for others	621	453
	22,513	20,820
Less allowance for depreciation and amortization............	8,221	7,431
	14,292	13,389
Goodwill..	970	970
Other assets.......................................	534	530
	$20,200	$19,345
Liabilities and stockholders' equity		
Current liabilities:		
Accounts payable....................................	$ 1,203	$ 1,247
Accrued liabilities	1,565	1,229
Air traffic liability	2,897	2,571
Current maturities of long-term debt	258	629
Total current liabilities	5,923	5,676
Long-term debt less current maturities	2,434	2,191
Deferred income taxes.................................	3,259	2,934
Construction obligation	554	437
Other noncurrent liabilities	1,255	771
Stockholders' equity:		
Common stock, $1.00 par value: 2,000,000,000 shares authorized; 807,611,634 shares issued in 2014 and 2013	808	808
Capital in excess of par value...........................	1,315	1,231
Retained earnings....................................	7,416	6,431
Accumulated other comprehensive loss	(738)	(3)
Treasury stock, at cost: 132,017,550 and 107,136,946 shares in 2014 and 2013 respectively	(2,026)	(1,131)
Total stockholders' equity............................	6,775	7,336
	$20,200	$19,345

Chapter Two

Financial Statements and the BSE: Construction

LEARNING OBJECTIVES

When you complete this chapter you should be able to:

1. Understand and use transaction analysis to record business events in the Balance Sheet Equation (BSE) format.

2. Build financial statements from completed transactions analysis in BSE format.

3. Understand, discuss and calculate differences between cash flows and accrual based income measurement.

4. Understand, apply and discuss the matching principle used when recognizing revenues and expenses.

INTRODUCTION

The three primary financial statements—balance sheet, income statement, and statement of cash flows—are the core of a company's periodic disclosure of its financial performance and condition. Now that you have seen examples of those statements for both small and large companies, we will walk through the mechanics of how a company's individual transactions are captured and aggregated in its financial statements.

Balance Sheet Equation (BSE)

We begin with the fundamental accounting equation (Exhibit 2.1):

$$\text{Assets} = \text{Liabilities} + \text{Owners' Equity}$$

The balance sheet equation, or BSE, provides the framework for the balance sheet, and every transaction undertaken by a company affects components of the BSE. For example, when KW Bookkeeping Services borrowed $10,000 from the bank, cash—an asset—increased by $10,000 and short-term bank loan payable—a liability—increased by $10,000. The transaction changed both sides of the equation, but the equation still holds, and must always hold. The balance sheet as of a specific date aggregates the financial consequences of every transaction the company has undertaken through that date. As portrayed in Exhibit 2.1, two balance sheets—one as of the beginning of a period and the second as of the end of the period—form bookends that are connected by the statement of cash flows and income statement, which disclose, in the aggregate, the transactions that changed the BSE and, therefore, the balance sheet.

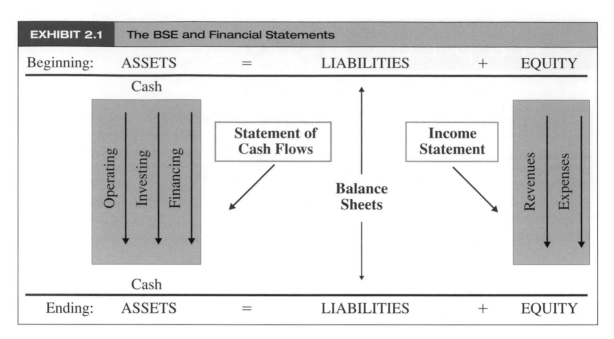

EXHIBIT 2.1 **The BSE and Financial Statements**

Transactions Analysis: A Simple Example

KW Bookkeeping, our small company introduced in Chapter 1, undertook the following transactions when it began:

1. Issued stock to its owner for $30,000 cash.
2. Borrowed $10,000 from the bank.

BSE analysis for each transaction would be as shown in Exhibit 2.2.

EXHIBIT 2.2 **KW Bookkeeping Services Transactions 1 and 2**

		ASSETS		LIABILITIES	OWNERS' EQUITY	
		Cash	Other Assets	Bank Loan Payable	Capital Stock	Retained Earnings
	Beginning balances	0	0	0	0	0
1	Issue stock to owner	30,000			30,000	
2	Borrow from bank.	10,000		10,000		
	Ending balances	40,000	0	10,000	30,000	0

The proper format for the balance sheet after these transactions were completed, as seen in Chapter 1 (Exhibit 1.2), is shown in Exhibit 2.3.

EXHIBIT 2.3 **KW Bookkeeping Services Balance Sheet as of January 1, 2012**

ASSETS		LIABILITIES & OWNERS' EQUITY	
Current assets		Current liabilities	
Cash	$40,000	Bank loan payable	$10,000
Total current assets.	$40,000	Total liabilities	$10,000
Long-term assets		Owners' equity	
		Contributed capital	30,000
Total assets.	$40,000	Total liabilities and owners' equity . . .	$40,000

Transactions Analysis: A Comprehensive Example

As a more comprehensive illustration, we'll consider John Palmer, an entrepreneur who combined his MBA education with his passion for cycling when he bought Local Cycle, a specialty retail store in suburban Boston. Although he acquired an existing business, we'll assume for the moment that he decided instead to start from scratch.

1. To get his business started, on January 1, 2014, John contributed $100,000 of his personal savings and decided to be the sole owner of Local Cycle.
2. With a local bank, John negotiated a *line of credit* for $25,000 to be borrowed as needed.
3. He found a vacant store available in a busy shopping center with plenty of parking, and he signed a lease for the space. The lease term began on March 1, when Palmer moved into the store and paid the landlord $5,000 in advance to cover rent for both March and April.
4. The company paid $48,000 for equipment with an expected useful life of 10 years.
5. The company also purchased computer equipment for $9,000 that it expects to use for five years.

BSE analysis for these transactions would be as shown in Exhibit 2.4.

EXHIBIT 2.4	Local Cycle Start-Up Transactions					
		ASSETS		**LIABILITIES**	**OWNERS' EQUITY**	
		Cash	Plant and Equipment	Bank Loan Payable	Capital Stock	Retained Earnings
	Beginning balances	*0*	*0*	*0*	*0*	*0*
1	Issue stock to owner	100,000			100,000	
4	Purchase equipment	(48,000)	48,000			
5	Purchase computer	(9,000)	9,000			
	Ending balances.	*43,000*	*57,000*	*0*	*100,000*	*0*

Note that the line of credit and the lease signing described in items 2 and 3 do not appear in Exhibit 2.4. They have no immediate effect on the balance sheet equation because no transaction of economic substance has occurred yet. If Local Cycle borrows money under the line of credit, its assets (specifically, cash) and liabilities (specifically, bank loan payable) will increase. Signing the lease, although important to the business, is not yet a formal transaction. Going forward, when Local Cycle moves into the store, it will incur rent expense each month to reflect the cost of using the space. As the company completed this first phase of its start-up activities on January 31, 2014, its proper balance sheet would be as shown in Exhibit 2.5.

EXHIBIT 2.5	Local Cycle Balance Sheet as of January 31, 2014		
ASSETS		**LIABILITIES & OWNERS' EQUITY**	
Current assets			
Cash	$ 43,000		
Total current assets.	$ 43,000	Total liabilities	$ 0
Long-term assets		Owners' equity	
Display equipment	48,000	Contributed capital.	100,000
Computers	9,000		
Plant and equipment.	$ 57,000		
Total assets.	$100,000	Total liabilities and owners' equity . . .	$100,000

In addition to hiring qualified salespeople, John had to find the right suppliers of bicycles, parts, and accessories. His strategy involves carrying two primary brands, which he purchases directly from the manufacturers. Both vendors were willing to extend credit to Local Cycle for 45 days after the shipment of any order.

Transaction: The company purchased $65,000 of bicycles and accessories, paid $20,000 immediately, and left the balance of $45,000 on account to be paid within 45 days (Exhibit 2.6). The BSE reflects the increase in inventory, the decrease in cash for the immediate payment, and the increase in current liabilities for the balance still owed to the supplier.

EXHIBIT 2.6	Local Cycle Start-Up Transactions, Continued						
	ASSETS			**LIABILITIES**		**OWNERS' EQUITY**	
	Cash	Inventory	Plant and Equipment	Accounts Payable	Bank Loan Payable	Capital Stock	Retained Earnings
Beginning balances	43,000	0	57,000	0	0	100,000	0
Purchase inventory.	(20,000)	65,000		45,000			
Ending balances.	23,000	65,000	57,000	45,000	0	100,000	0

The store opened for business on March 1, 2014. During the month of March, Local Cycle undertook the following transactions:

1. Sold cycles and accessories for $21,300. Collected $20,000 from customers. The remaining $1,300 will be collected during the first week of April. The cost of the goods sold was $11,700.
2. Paid vendors $13,400.
3. Paid rent for March and April: $2,500 per month = total payment of $5,000.
4. Paid salaries for March of $4,200.
5. Paid utilities for March of $800.
6. Used the display equipment. Because it is expected to be useful for 10 years, or 120 months, Local Cycle must allocate 1/120th of its cost to each month as depreciation expense: $48,000/120 = $350 per month.
7. Used computer equipment. As in transaction 6, this equipment must be depreciated over its useful life of 5 years, or 60 months: $15,000/60 = $250 per month.

Critical to the structure and content of the financial statements is the accrual basis of income measurement, which is required under generally accepted accounting principles (GAAP) and is built on two fundamental concepts: revenue recognition and the matching principle. First, revenue is recognized when the company completes its earnings process, as long as collection is reasonably certain. Consequently, revenue is recognized in the period when it is earned, which may not coincide with the period when the cash is collected. Second, expenses—the costs of goods and services used—are matched to the same period as the revenue. That is, we match accomplishment (revenue) with the effort (expenses) needed to generate revenue. Expenses are recognized in the period when goods and services are used, which may not coincide with the period when cash is paid for them. Some consequences of using an **accrual-based accounting** system are that in any given period:

- Revenues do not equal cash collected from customers;
- Expenses do not equal cash paid to suppliers, employees, landlords, and others; and
- Net income, revenue minus expenses, does not equal net cash flow or operating cash flow.

Local Cycle records revenue (sales) when the company completes the sale and the customer takes possession of the cycle and accessories, and it records expenses when it uses goods or services to generate that revenue. Recall that every transaction that affects net income must be captured in the retained earnings balance sheet account. As the company earns revenue, net income is increasing, and as the company incurs expenses, net income is decreasing. The effect on the BSE is the financial reporting consequence of the fundamental connection between net income and owners' equity.

In the value chain that begins with a bicycle designer's brilliant idea and ends with a satisfied rider, Local Cycle is the link between the manufacturer and the rider, as shown in Diagram 2.1.

DIAGRAM 2.1	**Value Chain for a Bicycle**

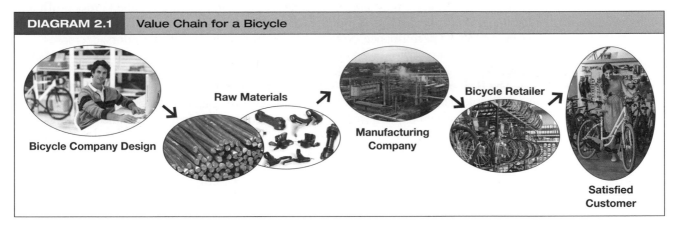

Each company in the value chain has to make a profit and generate a positive operating cash flow (OCF) to continue in business. Bicycle companies such as Specialized or Parlee have to make a profit based on design, reputation, and oversight of the entire bicycle development and sale processes. Raw materials mining companies (steel and aluminum) and carbon fiber producers must make profits to continue mining and creating new composite materials. Manufacturers of bikes, which for most major companies currently are located in Taiwan, must generate a profit on manufacturing operations. Finally, the bicycle retailer must make a profit on location, selection, availability, service, and customer satisfaction. More specifically for Local Cycle, every time that it sells a bike at a sales price higher than its cost from the bicycle company, it earns income that belongs to its owner. With each sale, the company increases the value of the owners' equity in the company, just as it delivers value to its customers. BSE analysis for Local Cycle's March transactions 1 through 7 is shown in Exhibit 2.7.

EXHIBIT 2.7	**Local Cycle Transactions, March 2014**								
		ASSETS				**LIABILITIES**		**OWNERS' EQUITY**	
	Cash	Accounts Receivable	Inventory	Prepaid Rent	Plant & Equipment	Accounts Payable	Bank Loan Payable	Capital Stock	Retained Earnings
Beginning balances ...	23,000	0	65,000	0	57,000	45,000	0	100,000	0
1-a Sell goods..........	20,000	1,300							21,300
1-b Cost of goods sold....			(11,700)						(11,700)
2 Pay vendors	(13,400)					(13,400)			
3 Pay rent	(5,000)			2,500					(2,500)
4 Pay salaries	(4,200)								(4,200)
5 Pay utilities	(800)								(800)
6 Depreciate store equipment.........					(350)				(350)
7 Depreciate computer ..					(250)				(250)
Ending balances......	19,600	1,300	53,300	2,500	56,400	31,600	0	100,000	1,500

The first transaction—selling cycles and accessories—reflects the central mission of this company. Note that sales revenue of $21,300 is recognized during the month, even though not all of it was collected in cash. The remaining $1,300 affects the BSE as an increase in accounts receivable, a current asset. The matching principle requires that the cost of the goods sold be recognized at the same time as the revenue. The BSE effects of selling cycles and accessories include both the recognition of the revenue earned and the recognition of the cost of goods sold, the expense of using inventory. Thus, the BSE effect for transaction 1 includes both the revenue of $21,300—an increase in retained earnings, and cost of goods sold of $11,700—a decrease in retained earnings, for a net change in retained earnings of $9,600 as a result of the sale of cycles and accessories in the month of March. Recall from Chapter 1 that sales revenue less cost of goods sold is called gross profit and that the gross profit rate (gross profit/revenue) is a common metric in evaluating and comparing corporate performance. Note that transaction 2, payment to vendors, decreases cash but has no effect on net income or retained earnings. The payment reduces the company's current liability—accounts payable—but does not involve an expense of the period.

The BSE effect of transaction 3, payment for March and April rent, reflects the matching principle. During the month of March, the cost of leasing the store was $2,500, which is recognized as rent expense, a decrease in net income and therefore retained earnings. The other $2,500 is an asset—prepaid rent—that the company will use in April. So although cash decreased by $5,000, half of the payment is for an asset, a resource with future value to the company. Transactions 4 and 5 involve cash payments for services that coincide with the period when the company used those services. Consequently, the payments equal the expenses in March, so that the effects on cash and retained earnings are the same.

Transactions 6 and 7 are slightly different from the first five transactions, as they do not involve an exchange with a customer or vendor. During the month, Local Cycle used its store equipment and computers to generate revenue, and it must recognize the cost of using those resources. The company's use of these resources is continuous, but we record the cost at the end of each reporting period as an adjustment to the balance sheet equation. The BSE effect, as shown in Exhibit 2.7, reflects the cost during March of using one month of the assets' capacity, and the decrease in retained earnings for depreciation expense equals the decrease in the book value of the assets. Depreciation never involves cash flow, as it reflects the allocation of the cost of long-term assets over their useful lives. For example, the periods in which Local Cycle uses the store equipment and computer system should show depreciation expense commensurate with the use of these assets. Depreciation does not necessarily match decreases or increases in asset value but is simply matching part of the cost of the asset to the specific periods used (i.e., depreciation expense). Over the last 10 years in Shanghai, China, real estate values have increased substantially. However, if a company purchased office space in Shanghai during 2003, although the market value of this space has increased, the amount shown as an asset on the company books (known as book value) would decrease between 2003 and 2013 because of depreciation expense taken over this decade.

The worksheet in Exhibit 2.7 is complete in the sense that it captures the BSE effect of all the transactions undertaken in March, and we can use it to construct the three primary financial statements for Local Cycle. The ending balances along the bottom row will be the components of the ending (March 31, 2014) balance sheet. The cash column includes all the components of a statement of cash flows, and the retained earnings column includes all the components of an income statement (Exhibit 2.8).

EXHIBIT 2.8	Local Cycle Balance Sheet as of March 31, 2014		
ASSETS		**LIABILITIES & OWNERS' EQUITY**	
Current assets		Current liabilities	
Cash	$ 19,600	Accounts payable	$ 31,600
Accounts receivable	1,300		
Inventory	53,300	Total liabilities	$ 31,600
Prepaid rent	2,500		
Current assets	$ 76,700	Owners' equity	
		Contributed capital	100,000
Long-term assets		Retained earnings	1,500
Plant and equipment, net	56,400	Total owners' equity	101,500
Total assets	$133,100	Total liabilities and owners' equity	$133,100

The Cash column of the worksheet includes all transactions that affected cash:

		Cash
	Beginning balances	23,000
1-a	Sell goods.	20,000
1-b	Cost of goods sold.	
2	Pay vendors	(13,400)
3	Pay rent	(5,000)
4	Pay salaries	(4,200)
5	Pay utilities.	(800)
6	Depreciate store equipment.	
7	Depreciate computer	
	Ending balances.	19,600

Looking at only the cash column highlights, again, that the recognition of the cost of goods sold (1-b) and the recognition of depreciation expense (6 and 7) are *not* associated with cash payments, even though they are expenses that reduce net income and, consequently, retained earnings. During March, all of the cash receipts and payments were the result of operating activities (Exhibit 2.9).

EXHIBIT 2.9	Local Cycle Statement of Cash Flows for the Month Ending March 31, 2014

Received from customers	$20,000
Paid for merchandise.	(13,400)
Paid for salaries	(4,200)
Paid for rent	(5,000)
Paid for utilities.	(800)
Net operating cash flows	($ 3,400)
Net change in cash.	($ 3,400)

The retained earnings column captures all of the transactions that affect net income:

		Retained Earnings
	Beginning balances	0
1-a	Sell goods.	21,300
1-b	Cost of goods sold.	(11,700)
2	Pay vendors	
3	Pay rent	(2,500)
4	Pay salaries	(4,200)
5	Pay utilities.	(800)
6	Depreciate store equipment.	(350)
7	Depreciate computer	(250)
	Ending balances.	1,500

Looking only at the retained earnings column highlights the components of Local Cycle's profitability: revenue earned and expenses incurred during the month. By rearranging the data into a standard format and using the vocabulary of accrual-basis income measurement, we can use these components to construct the March income statement (Exhibit 2.10).

Note that only in this first month does net income equal the ending balance in the retained earnings account because the beginning balance was zero. For any company at any point in its life, the *change* in retained earnings (ending balance minus beginning balance) equals net income for the period minus any dividends.

EXHIBIT 2.10	Local Cycle Income Statement for the Month Ending March 31, 2014	
Revenues		$21,300
Cost of goods sold		(11,700)
Gross profit		$ 9,600
Salaries expense		(4,200)
Rent expense		(2,500)
Utilities expense		(800)
Depreciation expense		(600)
Net income		$ 1,500

We observe also that while *net income* is a *positive* $1,500 in March, *operating cash flow* is a *negative* $3,400. With a cash balance of $19,600 (see Exhibit 2.8, balance sheet as of March 31, 2014), the negative $3,400 in operating cash flow is not too big of an issue. However, if this negative flow is repeated in subsequent periods, this would be a troubling sign. We will examine the impact of negative operating cash flows in more depth after we review April's results.

Transactions Analysis: Extension

During the month of April, Local Cycle undertook the following transactions:

1. Sold cycles and accessories for $28,700. Collected $27,000 from customers: $1,300 from March sales and $25,700 from April sales. The cost of the goods sold was $15,800.
2. Used the line of credit from the bank, and borrowed $20,000. Monthly interest expense will be $60, but will not be paid until the loan is repaid at the end of June. John plans to use much of the cash to pay the vendors that have offered him slightly lower costs if he pays more quickly.
3. Purchased merchandise costing $23,400 on account. Five days later, paid vendors $39,400.
4. Paid $2,400 for advertising in print and online to run evenly during April and May.
5. Paid salaries of $5,700. Because the month end did not coincide with the end of a pay period, Local Cycle owes its employees an additional $450 in salaries for the month.
6. Paid utilities for April of $840.
7. Used the display equipment, requiring depreciation expense of $350 per month.
8. Used computer equipment, requiring depreciation expense of $250 per month.
9. Used the leased space for the month. Rent was already paid in March.
10. On April 30, purchased equipment for the cycle service department for $5,000. Its expected useful life is five years.
11. Incurred and paid income tax expense at a rate of 35% of pretax income.

The BSE effects of transactions 1 through 11 are shown in Exhibit 2.11. As in March, sales revenue for April is recognized as earned, and the cost of goods sold is matched to revenue for the month. Local Cycle's gross profit of $12,900 ($28,700 revenue less $15,800 cost of goods sold) increased retained earnings and assets, as the increase in cash and accounts receivable exceeded the decrease in inventory. We can see that the balance of accounts receivable has increased, which is common when sales revenue increases.

John's decision to borrow from the bank is a financing decision with important consequences for operations, as he understands that paying vendors more quickly will lower the cost they charge on merchandise. On the other hand, he will have to incur the **interest expense** charged by the bank. Consequently, the company must adjust the BSE to recognize interest expense for the month because Local Cycle used the bank's funds for the month of April. Because no payment is required until June, the decrease in retained earnings equals the increase in the current liability, interest payable.

Transaction 4 is similar to Local Cycle's March 1st payment for two months of rent on the leased space. In this case, the payment is for two months of advertising. The company recognized $1,200 as advertising expense in April, while the other $1,200 is reflected as an asset, prepaid advertising. In transaction 5, total salaries expense for the month is $6,150, the total cost of employee salaries. Although Local Cycle paid its employees $5,700, the actual cost of the employees' salaries for the month was $6,150, with the difference of $450 reflected in higher liabilities.

EXHIBIT 2.11	Local Cycle, April 2014—Transactions 1–11											
			ASSETS					LIABILITIES				OWNERS' EQUITY	
		Cash	Accounts Receivable	Inventory	Prepaid Rent	Prepaid Advertising	Plant & Equipment	Accounts Payable	Salaries Payable	Interest Payable	Bank Loan Payable	Capital Stock	Retained Earnings
	Beginning balances	$19,600	$1,300	$53,300	$2,500	$ 0	$56,450	$31,600	$ 0	$ 0	$ 0	$100,000	$ 1,550
1-a	Sell goods.	27,000	1,700										28,700
1-b	Cost of goods sold.			(15,800)									(15,800)
2-a	Borrow from bank.	20,000									20,000		
2-b	Interest expense.									60			(60)
3-a	Purchase merchandise. . .			23,400				23,400					
3-b	Pay vendors	(39,400)						(39,400)					
4	Pay advertising.	(2,400)				1,200							(1,200)
5	Pay salaries	(5,700)							450				(6,150)
6	Pay utilities	(840)											(840)
7	Depreciate store equipment.						(400)						(400)
8	Depreciate computer						(150)						(150)
9	Use leased space.				(2,500)								(2,500)
10	Purchase equipment	(5,000)					5,000						
	Pretax balances	13,260	3,000	60,900	0	1,200	60,900	15,600	450	60	20,000	100,000	3,150
11	Paid income taxes	(542)											(542)
	Ending balances.	$12,718	$3,000	$60,900	$ 0	$1,200	$60,900	$15,600	$450	$60	$20,000	$100,000	$ 2,608

Depreciation on equipment continues, as in March, and we must adjust for another month of use of those long-term assets. Transaction 9 also requires an adjustment to the BSE; because the leased space was used in April, the company recognizes the month's rent expense and the use of the current asset, prepaid rent. Notice that we do not recognize depreciation on the equipment purchased on April 30, as the company has not begun to use it. Its monthly depreciation will, however, be recorded in preparing financial statements for May. In order to complete the transactions analysis and financial statements for April, we need to calculate the company's pretax income as the basis for its income tax expense. The worksheet shows that retained earnings has grown from $1,500 to $3,050, before considering income tax expense, and we can conclude that pretax income for the month was $1,550. Thus, income tax expense must be 35% × $1,550 = $542, which, we'll assume, was paid in cash at the end of the year, as reflected in the lower portion of Exhibit 2.11.

Using the worksheet, we can construct the three financial statements for Local Cycle for the month of April 2014 (Exhibits 2.12, 2.13, and 2.14).

As in March, although Local Cycle earned a profit of $1,008 in April, its operations during the same month used cash of $21,882. In Chapter 4, we will discuss the statement of cash flows in greater detail. For now, consider the importance of both net income and net operating cash flows to John Palmer as he evaluates the financial performance of his company. Net income, measured on an accrual basis, is a crucial indicator of the company's viability, and positive net income for a young or fast-growing business is a real accomplishment. From the income statement, we can see that Local Cycle generates revenue in excess of its product and periodic expenses. However, from the statement of cash flows, we can also see that the company's operations so far are requiring more cash than they generate, particularly as a result of the need to pay for inventory before the company sells goods and collects from customers. It is common for young and fast-growing firms to have negative operating cash flows (cash burn), but Palmer must monitor the company's cash flow carefully, as no company can survive without cash. As long as the operations use more cash than they generate, Palmer will have to find cash from other sources. Currently, his cash balance is not robust enough to cover an extended period of cash burn, that is, negative operating cash flows. Other sources to consider are family, friends, additional investors, and loans such as the bank loan taken in April. Both the income statement and the statement of cash flows are essential in evaluating and managing a company. Cash is necessary to continue operating and eventually to grow the business. Income measures success by matching accomplishment and effort to enable stakeholders to assess operations and make decisions to support the company's growth and financial success.

EXHIBIT 2.12	Local Cycle Balance Sheet as of April 30, 2014		
ASSETS		**LIABILITIES & OWNERS' EQUITY**	
Current assets		Current liabilities	
Cash	$ 12,718	Accounts payable	$ 15,600
Accounts receivable	3,000	Salaries payable	450
Inventory	60,900	Interest payable	60
Prepaid advertising	1,200	Bank loan payable	20,000
Current assets	$ 77,818	Current liabilities	$ 36,110
		Owners' equity	
		Contributed capital	100,000
Long-term assets		Retained earnings	2,508
Plant and equipment, net	60,800	Total owners' equity	102,508
Total assets	$138,618	Total liabilities & owners' equity	$138,618

EXHIBIT 2.13	Local Cycle Statement of Cash Flows for the Month Ending April 30, 2014	
Received from customers	$27,000	
Paid for merchandise	(39,400)	
Paid for salaries	(5,700)	
Paid for advertising	(2,400)	
Paid for utilities	(840)	
Paid for income taxes	(542)	
Net operating cash flows		($21,882)
Purchase equipment	(5,000)	
Net investing cash flows		($ 5,000)
Proceeds from bank loan	20,000	
Net financing cash flows		$20,000
Net change in cash		($ 6,882)

EXHIBIT 2.14	Local Cycle Income Statement for the Month Ending April 30, 2014	
Revenues		$28,700
Cost of goods sold		(15,800)
Gross profit		$12,900
Salaries expense		(6,150)
Rent expense		(2,500)
Advertising expense		(1,200)
Utilities expense		(840)
Depreciation expense		(600)
Operating income		1,610
Interest expense		(60)
Net income before income taxes		$ 1,550
Income tax expense		(542)
Net income		$ 1,008

The mechanics of transactions analysis using the BSE require systematic application of the concept of revenue recognition and the matching principle, as well as familiarity with the terminology of financial statements and accounts. For most students, the key to understanding is practice. Following is another illustration using Apple Inc., a large, fast-growing company best known for its innovative iPod, iPhone, and iPad. The numbers are derived from its fiscal 2014 financial statements, but for purposes of the illustration, we have simplified some of the transactions.

Transactions Analysis: Example—Large Company

Apple Inc. began fiscal 2014 with the balance sheet shown in Exhibit 2.15.

EXHIBIT 2.15	Apple Inc. Balance Sheet as of September 28, 2013 and September 27, 2014 (all amounts in millions of dollars)		
		2013	**2014**
Assets			
Cash		$ 14,250	$ 13,738
Marketable securities		26,287	11,087
Accounts receivable		20,641	27,936
Inventory		1,764	2,024
Other current assets		10,200	12,200
Total current assets		73,142	66,985
Long-term assets			
Investments		106,215	130,415
Property, Plant, and Equipment		16,597	19,368
Other long-term assets		10,800	14,400
Total long-term assets		133,612	164,183
Total assets		$206,754	$231,168
Liabilities			
Accounts payable		$ 22,367	$ 30,367
Accrued expenses		8,427	12,927
Deferred revenue		8,697	12,497
Other current		4,167	12,267
Total current liabilities		43,658	68,058
Long-term debt		39,076	53,976
Total liabilities		82,734	122,034
Owners' equity			
Capital stock		19,764	23,064
Retained earnings		104,256	86,070
Total owners' equity		124,020	109,134
Total owners' equity and liabilities		$206,754	$231,168

During the year a series of transactions took place and were recorded which not only reconcile the beginning and ending balances sheet in Exhibit 2.15 but also allow the construction of the income statement and statement of cash flows for fiscal 2014. Apple most likely undertook transactions similar to the following (000,000 omitted):

1. Through its website, retail stores, and other retail outlets worldwide, Apple sold products for $182,795. Cash collected from customers was $175,500 and the remainder increased accounts receivable.

2&3. Apple began the year with a deferred revenue balance of $8,697. Deferred or unearned revenue is a liability reflecting goods or services that the company owes to its customers who have paid Apple cash in advance. Every time Apple sells a gift card (e.g., for iTunes), it receives cash, but the company cannot recognize revenue at that time because it has not yet completed its earnings process. That is, it has not delivered a product or service to a customer. The BSE effect of selling a gift card is to increase cash and to increase the liability, deferred revenue (sometimes called unearned revenue, or advances from customers). For ease of this example, we separate the deferred revenue from other products ($1,300) from gift cards ($2,500—short-term) and ($3,000—long-term) and assume no deferred revenues were earned from these transactions.

4. During the year, Apple purchased components and assembled products. All direct costs of manufacturing goods are included in inventory and totaled $114,300 for the year. Of those costs, Apple paid $84,300 cash, with the remaining costs of $30,000 added to its accounts payable to vendors that offer Apple credit for as long as 90 days.

5. The company also paid its suppliers the total accounts payable beginning balance of $22,000.

6. Cost of goods sold for the fiscal year was $114,040.

7. Apple undertakes significant research and development (R&D) activities to support its ongoing innovation and new product lines. The total cash paid for R&D for the year was $3,041. Also a portion of R&D expense is depreciation and amortization from the equipment used in the research and development processes. See transaction numbers 9 & 11.

8. Apple purchased $9,571 in new equipment and paid cash for all of it.

9. During the year, Apple's use of its plant and equipment was recognized as depreciation expense of $6.800. In the income statement (Exhibit 2.17), $4,800 was included in SG&A expense and $2,000 in R&D expense.

10. Apple also purchased patents (included in other long-term assets) for $5,100 cash.

11. Its use of existing patents was recognized as amortization expense of $1,500. Amortization and depreciation are the same process of allocating the cost of a long-term asset over its useful life. Like equipment, patents do not last forever, and in the United States have a legal life of 20 years. We use the word depreciation in referring to tangible assets, such as equipment and buildings, and the word amortization in referring to intangible assets, such as patents. Of this amount, $1,300 was included in R&D expense and $200 in SG&A expense on the income statement.

12. Cash paid for Apple's selling, general, and administrative expenses (SG&A; for salespeople, corporate overhead, advertising, etc.) was $2,400 for the year as well as $4,500 included in the liability accrued expenses. Remember that SG&A also includes depreciation and amortization expenses of $4,800 and $200, respectively (transactions 9 and 11).

13. During fiscal 2014, the company sold $15,200 worth of marketable securities and with an additional $9,000 invested $24,200 in long-term investments during fiscal 2014.

14. Apple purchased miscellaneous current assets of $2,000 and made these purchases with other current liabilities.

15. Interest income net of minor interest expense was $1,400, all received in cash.

16. Apple's 2014 income tax expense was $13,900. Not only did they pay the $13,900 but an additional $200 of taxes payable which was included in other current liabilities.

17. Apple purchased and retired $45,000 of treasury stock. This transaction was essentially a subtraction from cash and from retained earnings.

18. During the year, Apple issued additional shares of stock in exchange for $3,300 cash.

19. The company paid a dividend of $11,200. Because dividends are a discretionary distribution by the company to its owners, they are reflected in the BSE through a

decrease in retained earnings. Dividends are not, however, an expense, as they do not reflect the cost of using goods or services to generate revenue.

20. Apple borrowed $18,200 by issuing short-term and long-term debt of $6,300 and $11,900 respectively.

These items walk through each of the transactions for Apple during fiscal 2014. The transactions are captured in the BSE, Exhibit 2.16.

| EXHIBIT 2.16 | Apple Inc. BSE Transactions Analysis: Fiscal, 2014 | | | | | | | | | | | | | | |

	ASSETS								LIABILITIES				OWNERS' EQUITY		
	Cash	Marketable Securities	Accounts Receivable	Inventory	Other Current Assets	Long-Term Investments	Plant and Equipment, Net	Other Long-Term Assets	Accounts Payable	Accrued Expenses	Deferred Revenue	Other Current Liabilities	Long-Term Liabilities	Capital Stock	Retained Earnings
Beginning balances	$ 14,250	$26,287	$20,641	$ 1,764	$10,200	$106,215	$16,597	$10,800	$22,367	$ 8,427	$ 8,697	$ 4,167	$39,076	$19,764	$104,256
1 Sales.....................	175,500		7,295												182,795
2 Deferred revenue	1,300										1,300				
3 Gift cards	5,500										2,500		3,000		
4 Produced goods...........	(84,300)			114,300					30,000						
5 Pay credit balance	(22,000)								(22,000)						
6 Cost of goods sold.........				(114,040)											(114,040)
7 Research and development ...	(3,041)														(3,041)
8 New equipment	(9,571)						9,571								
9 Depreciation...............							(6,800)								(6,800)
10 New patents...............	(5,100)							5,100							
11 Amortization...............								(1,500)							(1,500)
12 SG&A....................	(2,400)									4,500					(6,900)
13 Investments	(9,000)	(15,200)				24,200									
14 Purchased OCA with CL					2,000							2,000			
15 Interest income............	1,400														1,400
16 Income taxes..............	(14,100)											(200)			(13,900)
17 Treasury stock purchase	(45,000)														(45,000)
18 Stock issue................	3,300													3,300	
19 Dividend..................	(11,200)														(11,200)
20 Issue debt................	18,200												6,300	11,900	
Ending balances...........	$ 13,738	$11,087	$27,936	$ 2,024	$12,200	$130,415	$19,368	$14,400	$30,367	$12,927	$12,497	$12,267	$53,976	$23,064	$ 86,070

Beginning balance sheet balances are included in the first row of the BSE and the ending balance sheet developed from the last row balances in the BSE. Using the retained earnings column, we can construct Apple's income statement for the year (Exhibit 2.17) with the adjustments discussed for depreciation and amortization expenses as well as not including the treasury stock transaction (transaction 17) and dividend payment (transaction 19). Using the cash column, we can construct Apple's statement of cash flows for the year (Exhibit 2.18).

EXHIBIT 2.17	Apple, Inc. Income Statement for the Year Ending September 27, 2014 (all amounts in millions of dollars)

Income Statement (000,000 omitted)	2014
Revenues	$182,795
Cost of goods sold...	(114,040)
Gross profit...	$ 68,755
Operating expenses	
Selling, general, and administrative expense (SG&A)	(11,900)
Research and development expense (R&D)......................................	(6,341)
Operating income..	$ 50,514
Interest income..	1,400
Earnings before tax	$ 51,914
Income tax	(13,900)
Net income...	$ 38,014

Note:
R&D expense equals the cash paid of $3,041 plus $2,000 of depreciation expense and $1,300 of amortization expense.
SG&A (selling, general & administrative) expense equals $6,900 (transaction 12) plus depreciation expense of $4,800 and amortization expense of $200.

EXHIBIT 2.18	Apple, Inc. Statement of Cash Flows for the Year Ending September 27, 2014 (all amounts in millions of dollars)	
Statement of Operating Cash Flows		**2014**
Operating activities:		
Cash from customers..............................		$175,500
Paid to suppliers.................................	$(84,300)	
	(22,000)	(106,300)
Deferred revenue	1,300	
	$ 5,500	6,800
R&D paid.......................................		(3,041)
SG&A paid		(2,400)
Interest income.................................		1,400
Taxes paid.....................................		(14,100)
Operating cash flows		$57,859
Investing activities		
Purchase equipment............................		(9,571)
Purchase intangible assets......................		(5,100)
Purchase investments		(9,000) (23,671)
Financing activities.................................		
Purchase treasury stock........................		(45,000)
Issue common stock		3,300
Dividends paid		(11,200)
Issue debt.....................................		$ 18,200 (34,700)
Change in cash....................................		(512)
Beginning cash balance.............................		14,250
Ending cash balance		$13,738

To reinforce your understanding of the connection between the income statement and balance sheet, consider again the retained earnings column of Exhibit 2.16 which captures all of the components of the income statement. Together with the dividend paid and the treasury stock purchased and retired, we can tie together the beginning and ending retained earnings balance sheets amounts:

Retained earnings, beginning balance................................	$104,256
Plus net income for the period......................................	+ 38,014
Less dividends to owners during the period	(11,200)
Less treasury stock purchased	(45,000)
Retained earnings, ending balance	$86,070

It is also interesting to compare the net income and operating cash flows (OCF) for Apple, Inc. as we did with Local Cycle. As reported in Exhibit 2.17, Apple's income was $38.014 billion; from Exhibit 2.18, Apple's OCF was $57.859 billion. Both of these are incredibly large and frankly expected for a well-established, thriving company. Unlike our new venture Local Cycle, Apple has no issues with cash burn periods and can easily cover its investing activities with its cash on hand and its hugely positive OCF.

Before we conclude this chapter, we need to examine more in-depth the transaction that is unusual for new ventures but common for major companies: treasury stock purchases. Companies issue stock to shareholders to increase the company's resources, but companies can also buy back shares of the stock. **Treasury stock** is outstanding company stock repurchased by the company itself and held for reissue in the future. When shares are held by stockholders, they are called shares outstanding, but when repurchased by the company, they are no longer outstanding, as they do not trade and cannot be voted.

Let's look at an example to illustrate the definition of treasury stock and understand its treatment in the financial statements. The situation is as follows: Local Cycle is owned by its founder (John) and the founder's father-in-law (Tyler). Let's assume that instead of being a sole investor in this venture, John invested $100,000 and received 10,000 shares of common stock. The father-in-law, Tyler, invested $30,000 and received 3,000 shares of common stock. Tyler needs money and is tired of supporting his daughter's husband. He asks John to have the company buy back his stock. The company has done well in its start-up phase, and the stock is probably worth more than its original value of $1 per share. Because, however, this is family, the father-in-law asks only for the return of his original investment. And because Local Cycle is still in its start-up phase, accommodating Tyler's request is going to be difficult because this request takes cash. That is, Local Cycle has to write a check from its cash account for $30,000 and pay Tyler. In exchange, Tyler will return his stock to the company, and owners' equity is reduced because Tyler has "cashed out" and no longer has invested in the company. (It is worth noting that because of this action by the company, John is now 100% owner, whereas before he owned $100,000/$130,000 or 77%.) In theory, common stock needs to be reduced by $30,000. (The BSE transaction is: –$30,000 cash; –$30,000 common stock.) This transaction depicts what has happened: one owner has withdrawn his investment and the company has $30,000 less in cash to support its future. This transaction is, in fact, what is done if Local Cycle decides to destroy the stock certificates (the term is "retire") and never issue these shares again.

Local Cycle may not want to retire the shares but instead hold them temporarily and reissue them to new owners as additional investment is needed, as part of an employee stock option plan (ESOP) or for many other reasons. If the shares are held in expectation of reissuance, they are termed treasury stock. The BSE transaction then becomes −$30,000 cash; + treasury stock, which is a contra–owners' equity account and as such shown as a deduction in the owners' equity section of the balance sheet. (Note that treasury stock is a contra-equity account, just as accumulated depreciation is a contra-asset account.)

Following is an excerpt from the 2014 10-K Report (accessed on SEC/Gov/Archives/Edgar) of Home Depot, a well-known leader in the building supplies industry, showing the stockholder's equity section as of 2/3/2013 (left column) and 2/2/2014 (right column) (dollar amounts in millions). Home Depot has a substantial amount of treasury stock, 270 million shares, for which it paid a total of $10.694 billion in the year ending 2/2/2013. Treasury stock increased to approximately 374 million shares by 2/2/2014 and a total of $19.194 billion has been paid to buy treasury stock over the years. This was cash paid by Home Depot to existing stockholders to buy back their stock. These shares are no longer considered outstanding, no longer voting stock (i.e., votes cannot be cast to determine company policies), and no longer eligible for dividends; but they have not been retired and may be reissued by the company. That is why the shares are shown as the contra account treasury stock, which reduces stockholders' equity on the balance sheet.

Home Depot, Inc. (NYSE: HD)		
Stockholders' Equity	Feb. 3, 2013	Feb. 2, 2014
Common stock	$ 88	$ 88
Additional paid in capital	7,948	8,402
Retained earnings	20,038	23,180
Treasury Stock	(10,694)	(19,194)
Comprehensive Inc. and other	397	46
Total common equity	17,777	12,522
Total equity	$17,777	$12,522

In summary, although small corporations may repurchase issued stock and hold it for reissue, it is much more common for a large major company to have these transactions.

As can be seen in the Home Depot example, treasury stock can have a major impact on a company's balance sheet and needs to be understood in order to understand the stockholders' equity section of many publicly traded companies. Let's now briefly wrap up Chapter 2.

CONCLUSION

Whether the company is small and still in its early stages or large and public, the mechanics of transactions analysis remain the same. Every transaction affects the company's balance sheet equation, and by focusing on the specific accounts involved, we can see the underlying detail that generates the three primary financial statements.

We have also learned:

1. The balance sheet equation (BSE) and the BSE format must always be in balance.
2. Net income is *not* net cash flow or net operating cash flow.
3. Both net income and operating cash flows are important assessment tools for operations.

KEY CONCEPTS AND TERMS

accrual-based accounting, 26   interest expense, 30   treasury stock, 36

QUESTIONS

Q2-1. Explain why the balance sheet needs to balance.

Q2-2. List three types of transactions that impact the income statement and the statement of cash flows.

Q2-3. List three types of transactions that have no impact on the income statement.

Q2-4. Give an example of a transaction which when entered would not increase total assets.

Q2-5. A friend of yours thinks retained earnings represents cash that can be used by the owners. Explain to him what the retained earnings account represents and why his thinking is incorrect.

Q2-6. Explain the difference between an asset and an expense.

Q2-7. What are the major sources of funds to launch a business? How are these shown on a balance sheet?

Q2-8. Why are assets and liabilities classified into current and long term?

Q2-9. When a company pays interest on a loan, does this reduce the principal owed? Why or why not?

Q2-10. Which statement tells you how much cash you have at any time?

EXERCISES

E2-1. Discuss three major reasons why a company's income measured on an accrual basis will most likely differ from operating cash flow.

E2-2. During the month of March Gautam's had sales directly to customers of $50,000 (cash received immediately) and sales to distributors on credit of $100,000. The sales to distributors are expected to be collected in 45 days and certainly no later than April 30.

    a. Using the BSE enter the March sales transactions.
    b. Would these sales cause a difference between revenue reported on the income statement and operating cash flow? If so, how much of a difference?

E2-3.   Sabrina, at the end of June received a utility bill due in 30 days for the electricity used in her shop during June. The bill of $10,000 was due on July 15.

    a.   If needed in June, using the BSE record the receipt of the utility bill.
    b.   Using the BSE record the payment of the utility bill in July.
    c.   Will income and operating cash flow differ in June? If so, explain why.

E2-4.   On June 1, Debra purchased manufacturing equipment to more efficiently produce product and reduce her costs per unit. The equipment cost $30,000 with a useful life of ten years and no expected salvage value at the end of the useful life. To purchase the equipment, Debra paid cash of $10,000 and the equipment supplier gave her 90 days to pay the remaining $20,000.

    a.   Using the BSE format, enter the purchase of equipment transaction.
    b.   Is the $20,000 a short-term or long-term obligation?
    c.   How will the purchase of the equipment on June 1 impact the current year's income statement assuming year end is December 31?

E2-5.   On January 1, Zach opens a surf shop in Southern California. Before the opening he had invested $50,000 of cash in the business and used $30,000 of this money to purchase: surf boards from local shapers, board bags, leashes, wax and ding repair kits. At the end of January, Zach surveyed his product inventory and determined $10,000 of inventory had been sold, the customers using major credit cards.

    a.   Using the BSE, record the purchase of the inventory on January 1.
    b.   Using the BSE, record the fact that $10,000 of inventory had been sold during the month and $20,000 remained on hand. This entry should pertain to the flow of inventory. Do not record the revenue portion of this transaction.

E2-6.   Typically, Anna who has a high-end clothing and jewelry retail shop in a large U.S. city, requires 50% deposit on all custom clothing and jewelry. Once the order is taken, it typically takes Anna 60 days to purchase the raw materials, and craft the final project. The remaining 50% of the selling price is collected when the customer picks up the piece, always at the store. On November 15th, Anna received an order from a bride for her dress along with three dresses for her attendants. The order totaled $50,000 and 50% was paid on November 15. The promised date of delivery was January 5th of the following year.

    a.   Using the BSE, enter the receipt of cash on November 15. How did this affect income for the month of November?
    b.   On January 6th the customer picks up the dresses for her wedding and pays the final 50% of the $50,000. How should Anna record this event in the BSE?

E2-7.   Hector is a graphic designer who had his own firm working out of his apartment for the past 18 months. He decided to obtain his own office space in a renovating area of Santa Monica, California, and signed a lease for 12 months. Monthly rental was $2,500 and he had to pay first and last months' rent when he moved in to the rented space. Hector measures his income on a monthly basis.

    a.   Using the BSE, record the payment at the beginning of the month for the first and last months' rent amounts.
    b.   At the end of the first month, record any necessary adjusting entry.

E2-8.   When Hector moved into his newly leased space, he purchased office furniture and hung art, all of which cost him $5,000. He estimated the furniture and art would have a 5-year useful life before he would want to replace with new furniture and art. He was struggling because although the useful lives were 5 years, his lease was only for 1 year: over what time period should he depreciate his office furniture?

    a.   Discuss the options you see for Hector to depreciate his assets. Will these options impact his monthly income and operating cash flows? Over what period would you depreciate the assets?
    b.   Using the BSE, record the depreciation expense for the first month Hector is using the office.

E2-9.   Aman designed and sold iPad travel pouches with company and school logos. His sales to schools were typically through the alumni association and after four years he had successfully sold his product to colleges and universities throughout the United States. Recently he signed an agreement with a huge community college system in Florida which had in excess of 70,000 current students and an unimaginable number of alumni. His first sale was to the book stores on the community college campuses. Sales on account were for $3,000. His product margin was 55%; that is, the cost of goods sold (COGS) was $1,650.

a. Using the BSE enter the revenue part of this transaction.
b. Using the BSE enter the COGS part of this transaction.

E2-10.   Renee provided consulting services to help clients more effectively use social media. Once she had a contract, she lined up graphic designers, wrote her own copy, rolled out the campaign and trained the client's people to continue implementing the processes of advertising and brand building she had designed. For her last contract which was received and completed in June, Renee received an invoice of $1,000 for the graphic design work she had contracted to a freelance designer. Of this amount, she paid $200 and promised to pay the designer when she received her final payment.

a. Using the BSE, record Renee's receipt of the designer's invoice and her partial payment to the designer.
b. Renee as well as the graphic designer she employed had consistent cash flow problems. They did the work promptly but clients frequently would pay them in 60–90 days. What recommendations would you make to the two of them to improve their individual cash flows?

PROBLEMS

Tiffany & Company

P2-1.   **Revenue and Cost of Goods Sold for Tiffany**   Tiffany is a luxury store specializing in high-end jewelry. Prices and profits on individual items are high (approximately 60%). Besides cash and major credit cards, Tiffany also gives store credit (i.e., it has its own credit policy with terms given to selected customers). Assume on December 20, visiting the New York store of Tiffany, Tomas decides to purchase a necklace as a birthday present for his mother. The necklace costs $20,000 and Tomas asks if he can buy on credit. After a thorough credit check, the store agrees to give Tomas credit, Tomas signs the necessary forms and leaves the store with the necklace and the intent to pay for it in four months. Assume the following transactional timeline.

1. On December 20 Tiffany sells to Tomas on credit a necklace for $20,000.

2. The cost of the necklace to Tiffany was $8,000.

3. On January, 20, Tomas pays Tiffany $150 representing one month's interest on his outstanding receivable.

4. On February and March 20 Tomas pays Tiffany $150 as he did on January 20.

5. On April 20, Tomas sends Tiffany a check for $20,150 representing the payment for the necklace and the final interest payment due.

Required:
In the form below, enter the required BSE transactions.

Tiffany Jewelry													
	Cash	Accounts Receivable	Inventory	Property and Equipment	Accumulated Depreciation	Other Assets	Accounts Payable	Accrued Expenses	Unearned Revenue	Other	Long-Term Debt	Common Stock	Retained Earnings
Beginning balances													
Balance													
1 Sold necklace.													
2 COGS.													
3 January interest													
4 February interest													
5 March interest.													
6 April repay													

P2-2.   **Revenue Related Entries–Custom Furniture Maker**   Anna crafted custom furniture. When a customer wanted a piece of her furniture, Anna took the dimensions and they agreed upon the style of the piece. At this time she required 30% down. Once the cash was received, Anna completed three-dimensional drawings and after final approval by the customer, built the piece and notified the customer. Once the customer had paid Anna, Anna then delivered the furniture. The customer had 30 days to return the piece and would receive 75% of the retail price. With these policies in mind, record the following transactions for a dresser Anna made for a customer.

1. Anna contracted to build a custom dresser for a client's bedroom. The client and Anna agreed upon the style, wood (cherry and white maple), and the approximate dimensions. The price for the piece would be $15,000. Once Anna received the deposit of 30% she would complete the drawings on her Computer Assisted Drawing (CAD) system and send them to the client.
2. Anna received $4,500 from her client and began working on the drawings.
3. Anna sent the drawings to her client and after a SKYPE call and final approval, she began building the furniture.
4. She used $2,000 of wood and supplies to complete the furniture and paid $4,000 in direct labor to complete the dresser.
5. Anna received the final payment of $10,500 and immediately shipped the dresser to the client.
6. Thirty days had passed since the client received the dresser and thus the return period had expired.

Anna's Fine Furniture

Transactions	Cash	Accounts Receivable	Inventory	Property and Equipment	Accumulated Depreciation	Other Assets	Accounts Payable	Accrued Expenses	Unearned Revenue	Other	Long-Term Debt	Common Stock	Retained Earnings
Balance													

P2-3. Revenue Related Entries–Yoga Studio Entrepreneur Mary and Amir had traveled literally around the world studying yoga as well as Pilates. They decided to settle in the Midwest portion of the United States and open a studio in Wichita, Kansas. Although Wichita was not a "hot bed" of yoga, Mary thought they could change the culture in this city and have a unique and successful studio featuring yoga and Pilates instructions. Amir agreed with Mary and they invested $30,000 to create their studio.

Being creative, they devised several ways to create revenues and attract regular clients. For each of the transactions below, enter the events in the BSE format provided and be prepared to discuss your entries.

1. In the month of December, gift cards were sold entitling the recipient to 10 yoga sessions. The total sales were $12,000 representing 60 cards. The history for the industry is that these cards will be used fairly evenly in the three months following sales.
2. In December and the beginning of January, $72,000 of yearly memberships were sold for the year just beginning. These were non-refundable fees and all memberships would expire 12/31/current year. This entitled the members to unlimited yoga and Pilates sessions on a first-come, first-serve basis.
3. Pilates gift cards were sold for 20 sessions. These sessions included 10 minutes of warm up and cool down and 40 minutes of intense Pilates. Revenues were $30,000 representing 30 cards. Expectations were that the typical cardholder would complete two sessions per week and these gift cards would be entirely used by the end of March.
4. Yoga mats, workout clothing and DVDs were sold as well. Sales for the year were $10,000 and cost of those goods sold was $5,000.

Yoga & Pilates													
Transactions	Cash	Accounts Receivable	Inventory	Property and Equipment	Accumulated Depreciation	Other Assets	Accounts Payable	Accrued Expenses	Unearned Revenue	Other	Long-Term Debt	Common Stock	Retained Earnings
Balance													

P2-4. **Major Asset Purchases and Depreciation–Janitorial Services** Victoria decided to expand her janitorial service into adjacent cities and needed to purchase equipment and software systems. Below are the purchases she made.

1. Victoria purchased four vans for $20,000 each and had each painted with her company logo, company motto, website, email and telephone number. The cost to paint each van was $3,000.
2. Each van purchased in transaction 1 was expected to last 3 years and have essentially no salvage value at the end of that time. In actuality, Victoria planned to give these vans to her staff in order of seniority. She thought this would be a good reward for loyalty and motivation to keep the autos in good shape.
3. Victoria also purchased heavy-duty cleaning equipment, such as vacuum cleaners. Her total investment was $4,000.
4. The vacuum cleaners were estimated to have 2-year useful lives with no salvage value.
5. Victoria purchased other cleaning equipment including brooms, mops, dust brushes, and buckets. She spent $1,000 on these items and expected them to last one year.

Required:
For each transaction, enter the BSE entry in the form provided below. For the depreciation entries, enter the amount for a year's worth of depreciation.

Victoria's Janitorial Services													
Transactions	Cash	Accounts Receivable	Inventory	Property and Equipment	Accumulated Depreciation	Other Assets	Accounts Payable	Accrued Expenses	Unearned Revenue	Other	Long-Term Debt	Common Stock	Retained Earnings
Balance													

P2-5. **Major Asset Purchases and Depreciation–Furniture Maker** Anna was excited by the response to her new marketing plan. Besides a wider mailing of her beautiful brochure, she established storefronts in Dallas and Los Angeles, which resulted in a large increase in her orders. Anna had waited a year to make sure this new level of business was sustainable and now convinced that it was, she decided to expand her furniture producing facilities.

1. Luckily, Anna's shop was located in a rural region and she could afford to build an additional shop building for $100 per square foot on land she owned. She determined she needed an additional 10,000 feet of shop space to store wood and set up production

capabilities. To fund this $100,000 plant investment, Anna put $20,000 down and received a Small Business Administration (SBA) loan for the remainder of the purchase price.

2. Interest on the SBA was 5.5% annually and the principal was to be paid in equal, annual installments over the 8 years of financing.
3. The building was expected to last 20 years with no salvage value.
4. Anna purchased additional furniture-making equipment for $50,000. Some of this equipment was used but in excellent shape. Anna borrowed the entire amount from the SBA as well with a term loan.
5. Interest on the SBA equipment loan was 6% and the loan would be paid back in total at the end of 5 years. Interest was to be paid annually.
6. Anna with proper maintenance thought the equipment would last 10 years with a salvage value of $5,000.
7. Anna planned repairs and maintenance expense for the equipment to be $500 per year.

Required:

In the BSE form provided below enter the above asset-purchase transactions as well as the first year of the annual depreciation expense and required debt transactions, namely the payment of interest annually as well as the payment of principal (transaction 2 above) in the first year. Assume repairs and maintenance were $500.

Anna's Fine Furniture

Transactions	Cash	Accounts Receivable	Inventory	Property and Equipment	Accumulated Depreciation	Other Assets	Accounts Payable	Accrued Expenses	Unearned Revenue	Other	Long-Term Debt	Common Stock	Retained Earnings
Balance													

P2-6. **External Funding Entries** Peter needed additional funds to fund his projected growth and contemplated either loan or equity capital. These funds would be used to purchase raw materials inventory used to complete finished goods. These goods would be sold within the next 5 months. Using the BSE format provided below, enter the possible funding transactions that would secure the necessary funds needs to grow his business. Answer the questions that follow.

Transactions:

1. Peter, using a newly acquired bank line of credit, borrowed $50,000 of his $100,000 credit line. The per annum interest rate on this liability is 8%. Peter believes he will pay this liability in 6 months. Bank lines of credit typically must be paid within a year. With this money, he would buy raw materials inventory.
2. Not planning well, Peter used his business credit card and purchased $50,000 of raw materials inventory. The per annum interest rate is 16% if Peter does not pay back the $50,000 within 30 days. Peter does not think he will have the necessary cash to pay this liability within the next 6 months.
3. Peter could possibly purchase the raw materials on credit provided by his supplier with no interest rate. Although the supplier would only give 30-day terms, Peter would have to stretch his supplier for 5 additional months until he could pay this liability. No interest per annum is associated with this liability.
4. Peter could add a stockholder who would receive 1% of the company stock for a $50,000 investment. With this money, he would purchase raw materials inventory.

Questions:

a. Which funding method would most likely yield the most income in the current 12-month period?
b. Can you think of any reasons for Peter to not take on additional investors?
c. Can you think of a reason not to use the supplier's credit?
d. Which method of funding would you recommend and why?

BSE Format

Peter Needs Cash													
Transactions	Cash	Accounts Receivable	Inventory	Property and Equipment	Accumulated Depreciation	Other Assets	Accounts Payable	Accrued Expenses	Unearned Revenue	Other	Long-Term Debt	Common Stock	Retained Earnings
Line of credit													
Credit card													
Supplier													
Investor													

P2-7. **Cash Flows and Income Measurement—Nike** For this problem, Nike numbers were abridged and approximated to make the problem appropriate for an introductory text. The relationships and results closely approximate Nike reality for this year.

Nike, Inc.

Nike, Inc., designs, develops, and markets athletic footwear, apparel, equipment and accessories. In addition to the Nike brand with its well-known swoosh, the company's trademarks also include Converse® and Hurley®. Nike sells to many footwear and sporting goods retailers (e.g., Foot Locker), and it sells directly to consumers through its own retail stores and website. During the year, Nike undertook the transactions and adjustments listed below.

Required

For each of the following transactions indicate if it impacts the income statement (IS), the cash flow statement (CF), or both (B).

1. Purchased inventory costing $14,810 from manufacturers all initially on account.
2. Sold products for $25,300, of which $18,500 were sales to corporate customers on account and the remaining $6,800 were sales to individual customers for cash. The cost of the products sold was $14,230.
3. Used property, plant, and equipment, and recorded depreciation expense of $440.
4. Incurred selling and administrative expenses of $7,340 and paid $7,000 in cash. The remaining $340 is still owed to employees for salaries that will be paid in the first month of fiscal 2013.
5. Borrowed $1,000 from a local bank, which will be repaid in 2 years.
6. Incurred $24 interest expense and paid $20 in cash. The remaining $4 had been prepaid during fiscal 2011.
7. Purchased property, plant and equipment for $636 in cash.
8. Paid dividends of $703.
9. In the last month of the year, Nike received orders for $1,250 in products, which it will deliver during the first month of 2013.

Nike	IS	CF	Both	Neither
Transaction 1				
Transaction 2				
Transaction 3				
Transaction 4				
Transaction 5				
Transaction 6				
Transaction 7				
Transaction 8				
Transaction 9				

P2-8. **Income Statement Transactions Only—Service Company** Victoria is the Founder/CEO of a janitorial service focused on cleaning office buildings and other commercial buildings. Through the first quarter of the current year, she recorded the following transactions.

1. Q1 revenues were $175,000. Of these revenues, clients owed $30,000 in receivables which were due 30 days after the close of Q1.
2. Field wages for the quarter including payroll taxes were $18,000. Of these wages, $3,000 were yet to be paid at the end of Q1.
3. Cleaning supplies purchased during the quarter amounted to $8,000. In Q1, $5,000 of supplies were used on jobs.
4. Auto expenses were $9,000 for Q1. Of these expenses, $1,500 are depreciation expense and the remainder was paid in cash.
5. Technology related expenses were $2,500 and all paid in cash.
6. Insurance expense was $6,000 for the Q1. The one-year insurance policy costing $24,000 was paid at the end of the previous year and entered in the other asset account.
7. Marketing expenses for the period, all paid in cash, were $4,000.
8. Executive and supervisory salaries for the quarter equaled $90,000 and all paid during the Q1.
9. Occupancy expenses for home office were $25,000. Of these expenses, $3,000 was for depreciation, $5,000 remained unpaid and included in accrued expenses and the remainder was paid in cash.
10. Interest expense paid during the quarter was $3,500. Loan principal of $10,000 was also repaid in Q1. Both these transactions relate to long-term debt.

Required:
1. Enter the above transactions in the BSE provided below.
2. Construct an income statement in good form for Q1.
3. Why did you not need beginning balances to complete the income statement for Q1?

Victoria's Janitorial Services													
Transactions	Cash	Accounts Receivable	Supplies	Property and Equipment	Accumulated Depreciation	Other Assets	Accounts Payable	Accrued Expenses	Line of Credit	Other	Long-Term Debt	Common Stock	Retained Earnings
Balance													

P2-9. **Income Statement Only Transactions—Product Company** Tamantha created products with company logos. Companies used these products to enhance brands and reinforce company cultures. Her major products were shirts, jackets and hats followed closely by ball-point pens and other office oriented gifts. Tamantha has been in business for 10 years and below are her transactions for the most current year.

1. Sales for the year were $750,000 shipped evenly through out the year. Customers typically took 60 days to pay for their products. Of the $750,000 in sales $140,000 remained uncollected at year's end.
2. Tamantha needed to grow her inventory levels for expected increases in sales the following year. She purchased $450,000 of inventory receiving 30-day credit terms from her suppliers.
3. Cost of goods sold (COGS) for the revenues in transaction 1 were $300,000 for the products, $50,000 for labor to embroider or stencil on logos and $10,000 of depreciation expense. Of the $50,000 labor expense, $5,000 remained unpaid at the end of the year.
4. Tamantha paid $420,000 to her suppliers for the goods purchased in transaction 2.
5. Tamantha owned the building in which her office, production and shipping functions were housed. Depreciation expense, not included in the cost of goods sold was $30,000 and should be treated as general and administrative (G&A) expense.

6. Tamantha had very little advertising expense except for trade shows she attended. Otherwise most of her business was repeat business, referrals from customers and the networking she did within the Chambers of Commerce activities to which she belonged. Her expenses for these activities amount to $30,000 per year and are always paid in cash.
7. Tamantha was CEO/CFO and Vice President of Marketing. She paid herself a salary of $75,000 and she paid her head of operations and logistics $60,000.
8. Additional G&A expenses, all paid in cash were $45,000.
9. Interest expense paid on long-term debt was $15,000.
10. Tamantha's tax rate was 25%. Assume taxes would be paid Q1 of next year.

Required:
1. Enter the above transactions in the BSE provided below.
2. Construct an income statement in good form for the current year just ended.
3. Highlight the major differences between operating cash flows and net income in the above transactions.

Tamantha's Logos, Inc.

Transactions	Cash	Accounts Receivable	Inventory	Property and Equipment	Accumulated Depreciation	Other Assets	Accounts Payable	Accrued Expenses	Line of Credit	Other	Long-Term Debt	Common Stock	Retained Earnings
Balance													

P2-10. **Balance Sheet, Income Statement, and the BSE—Bicycle Company** At the end of the current year, Jen decided it would be best to establish forecasts for next year. Although she knew there were probably better methods, she decided she would frame everything in expected transactions and asked you as her accountant to pull together a forecasted income statement and balance sheet for next year using the Balance Sheet Equation (BSE). Using the expected transactions below given you by Jen and the attached BSE, enter the transactions and construct the expected income statement and balance sheet.

1. Sales are expected to increase slightly to $3,450,000. Fortunately Jen had decided to have no company credit policy and all transactions are either cash or major credit card. She assumes no accounts receivable; that is, all sales transactions are essentially cash.
2. Jen received exciting news that four new lines of cycles (one road-bike, two beach cruisers, and one urban/utility) have agreed to distribute their bikes through CycleForever. To gain these coveted accounts, Jen had to agree to carry company accessories and purchase a substantial amount of inventory in the fourth quarter of the current year. Because of these commitments she expected purchases to be $2,501,000 of which all but $266,500 was expected to be paid in cash by year's end.
3. Of the beginning inventory and purchases highlighted in transaction 2, cost of goods sold is expected to be $1,900,000 (a higher percentage of sales compared to previous years due to retail pricing pressures) and inventory is expected to increase to $1,254,000 from current levels of $653,000.
4. Jen planned to use a new company credit card to its maximum of $30,000 (+ cash & + credit card payable), loan the company $50,000 of her own funds and increase long-term borrowing by $149,000 to help finance this huge increase in inventory.
5. Selling & marketing expense was expected to be $560,000 and except for $45,000 of depreciation expense embedded in this number, all was expected to be paid in cash.
6. Similarly, general & administrative expense is expected to be $883,000 and all paid in cash except for the depreciation expense included in this number which was $25,000.
7. Fixed assets in total were expected to increase only $29,000 and depreciation expense Jen forecasted to be $70,000 (already included in transactions 5 and 6). For the purpose of this exercise, these will not be separated into the various categories but just listed as equipment/displays in the BSE.

8. Interest expense was estimated to be $58,000 and to be paid in cash.
9. Tax expense was estimated to be $12,500 and to be paid in cash.
10. Out of a sense of pride, Jen had expected to pay herself dividends of $5,000 at a minimum.

Required:
1. Using the BSE below with the beginning balances already in place, enter the forecasted transactions.
2. Prepare the forecasted income statement and balance sheet in good form.

Cycle Forever-3				Assets					Liabilities				Owners' Equity
Transactions	Cash	Inventory	Supplies	Equipment/ Displays	Intangible	Accumulated Depreciation	Other Assets	Accounts Payable	Credit Card	Notes Payable —ST	Long-Term Debt	Common Stock
Balance	$122,500	$653,000	$25,000	$399,000	$43,000	$(212,000)	$98,000	$321,000	$—	$544,000		$50,500
Sales												
Purchases												
CGS												
Line of credit												
NP—Officer												
NP—LT												
S&M												
G&A												
FA												
Interest expense												
Dividend												
Tax expense												
Balance												

P2-11. Balance Sheet and Income Statements—Pfizer 2014 (000,000 omitted) The balance sheet for **Pfizer, Inc.**, a global pharmaceutical firm for year 2013 is shown in Exhibit A. Although the amounts and relationships among these balance sheet accounts approximate the actual statements, data has been aggregated and amounts approximated to simplify this problem. Similarly, the accounts in the transactions presented below have been aggregated and the amounts approximated to further simplify this problem. *Pfizer, Inc.*

Transactions:
1. Sales for 2014 were $50,500 and were all on credit.
2. All beginning accounts receivable were collected.
3. Of the accounts receivable created in 2014, $40,000 was collected.
4. Pfizer wanted to maintain inventory levels evenly throughout the year. Inventory manufactured for the year was $9,100. For this problem, assume this amount was an increase to accounts payable.
5. Cost of goods sold for 2014 was $9,000.
6. Pfizer reduced its accounts payable by $9,400.
7. Selling, general & administrative expense for the year was $13,600. Of this amount, $1,000 was depreciation expense and the remaining amount was paid in cash.
8. Research & development expenses for the year were $6,700. $5,700 was paid in cash and the remaining $1,000 was depreciation expense.
9. Goodwill amortization expense was $4,200 for 2014.
10. Interest expense of $1,000 paid during the year was 2014 and should be expensed in 2014.
11. Restructuring charges for 2014 were estimated to be $2,500. These should be expensed and shown as an increase in other long-term liabilities.
12. Tax expense was $3,000. $2,000 will be paid later and is considered a long-term tax payable. The remaining $1,000 was paid in cash.
13. $6,000 of cash was used to buy treasury stock. To balance the decrease in cash, subtract the same amount from the treasury stock column.
14. Dividends of $8,000 were declared and paid for the year.
15. Other current assets for $2,200 were purchased during the year.
16. Long-term debt was reduced by $3,000.

Required:
a. Use the BSE format below to enter these 2014 transactions for Pfizer, Inc.
b. Construct the income statement, balance sheet and statement of cash flow for 2014.

Transactions	Cash	Short-Term Investment	Accounts Receivable	Inventory	Other CA	PPE	ADPPE	Long-Term Investments	Goodwill	Other Intangibles	Accounts Payable	Accrued Expenses	Short-Term Borrowings	Other CL	Long-Term Debt	Long-Term Taxes Payable	Other LTL	Common Stock	Retained Earnings	Treasury Stock
Balance...........	$2,500	$30,200	$9,600	$6,300	$5,300	$25,900	$(13,200)	$18,000	$43,000	$44,000	$3,200	$1,800	$6,500	$11,500	$38,000	$25,600	$8,500	$78,000	$66,500	$(68,000)
1. Sales............																				
2. Col. beg..........																				
3. Col. year..........																				
4. Buy inventory........																				
5. COGS...........																				
6. Pay suppliers.......																				
7. SGA																				
8. R&D																				
9. Amortization GW ...																				
10. Interest																				
11. Restryc...........																				
12. Income tax																				
13. TS................																				
14. Paid dividends.....																				
15. OCA																				
16. Pay debt..........																				

P2-12.   Balance Sheet and Income Statements—Whole Foods Market Inc. (WFMI) WFMI is a food retailer focused on healthy, organic products harvested or raised using sustainable practices. A national grocery chain in the United States, WFMI is known as a high-price/high-quality retailer. The stores are impeccably maintained and the stores serve prepared meals, sushi, sweets, and so on. The transactions below represent WFMI's activity in the most recent year. To simplify this problem, accounts have been aggregated and numbers simplified. However, the resultant financial statements will be a reasonable approximation of WFMI's results.

Transactions (000,000 omitted)

1. Sales for the year equaled $13,950. Because food retailing is largely a cash or major credit card business, only $100 of this amount was not received by year-end.
2. Receivables of $150 were collected from customers during the year.
3. Inventory was purchased of $8,950.
4. Cost of goods sold (COGS) for the year was $8,900.
5. Accounts payable (related to suppliers of inventory) of $9,100 total was paid during the year.
6. Selling, general & administrative expenses for the year were $4,100. Of this amount $675 was not paid and is accrued expenses, $300 was depreciation expense and the remaining $3,125 was paid in cash.
7. $15 was received in interest income.
8. Restructuring expenses were estimated to be $20 and to be paid the following year. These were listed in other current liabilities.
9. Tax Expense was $375. $325 was paid in cash and the remaining liability recorded in accrued expenses.
10. Dividends of $200 were paid.
11. Treasury stock of $500 was purchased for cash and kept in treasury to be used in the future.
12. WFMI expanded their number of stores and invested $800 in property, plant & equipment.

Required:
a.   Using the BSE format presented below, enter the transactions for 2014.
b.   Prepare the financial statements using the completed BSE format.

BSE FORMAT: WFMI

Transactions	Cash	Short-Term Investments	Accounts Receivable	Inventory	Prepaid Assets	Other CA	PPE	AD—PPE	Long-Term Investments	Goodwill	Other Long-Term Assets	Accounts Payable	Accrued Expenses	Other CL	Other Long-Term Liabilities	Common Stock	Retained Earnings	Treasury Stock
Balance—Beg. ...	$290	$730	$200	$420	$200	$100	$4,525	$(2,100)	$300	$680	$150	$250	$500	$300	$570	$2,750	$1,275	$(150)
1. Sales...........																		
2. Received 150....																		
3. Purchased inventory......																		
4. COGS..........																		
5. Pay suppliers																		
7. SG&A																		
10. Interest income...																		
11. Restructured charges.......																		
12. Taxes																		
14. Dividends.......																		
15. Treasury stock ...																		
14. Purchased PPE ..																		
16. Balance—End....																		

WHOLE FOODS MARKET INC.				
Balance Sheet				
Assets			**Liabilities**	
Cash........................	$ 255		Accounts payable................	$ 100
Short-term investments	730		Accrued expenses	1,225
Accounts receivable............	150		Other CL......................	320
Inventory.....................	470		Total current	1,645
Prepaid assets	200			
Other CA.....................	$ 100		Other long-term liabilities..........	$ 570
Total current		$1,905	Total liabilities..................	$2,215
PPE.........................	$5,325		Owners' equity	
Accumulated depreciation—PPE...	(2,400)		Common stock..................	2,750
Long-term investments	300		Retained earnings	1,645
Goodwill	680			
Other intangibles	$ 150		Treasury stock	$ (650)
Total long-term assets		$4,055	Total owners' equity	$3,745
Total assets...................		$5,960	Total liabilities and owners' equity ...	$5,960

P2-13. Balance Sheet and Income Statement   **Panera Bread** operates three business segments,   **Panera Bread**
including bakery-café operations, franchise operations, and fresh dough and other operations.
The following is some summary background information taken from their 2011 10-K.

> **Business:** Our bakery-cafés are located in urban, suburban, strip mall, and regional mall
> locations. We feature high quality, value priced food in a warm, inviting, and comfortable
> environment. With our identity rooted in handcrafted artisan bread we bake every day, we
> are committed to providing great tasting, quality food that people can trust. Nearly all of
> our bakery-cafés have a menu highlighted by antibiotic-free chicken, whole grain bread,
> and select organic and all-natural ingredients, with zero grams of artificial trans fat per
> serving, which provide flavorful, wholesome offerings. Our menu includes a wide variety of
> year-round favorites complemented by new items introduced seasonally with the goal of
> creating new standards in everyday food choices.

The following is the activity that took place during the year ended December 31, 2011
($ millions):

1. Sales made on account to the franchisees totaled $229. These amounts were expected to
   be collected within 35 days.
2. Cash and credit card sales at the retail locations were made totaling $1,593.
3. Purchased $108 in property and equipment on account for the locations expected to
   open later in the year. One vendor allowed $17 to be repaid in 15 months. The balance
   is due within 30 days.
4. Purchased $589 in dough and other related food products on account. Amounts are
   expected to be paid within 30 days.
5. The company issued $20 in shares of its company stock.
6. Payments of $218 were received from franchisees to pay previous amounts owed.
7. The cost of goods sold was $586.
8. The company reacquired certain intangible territory rights for a number of locations in
   the amount of $51.
9. The company prepaid 2012 rent for a number of locations totaling $17. They also paid
   $115 for rent associated with 2011.
10. Labor costs for the year totaled $484 of which all but $5 was paid by the end of the
    year.
11. Paid $671 related to amounts related to property and equipment and inventory
    purchases previously put on account.
12. Other operating expenses, primarily comprised of marketing costs totaled $298. Of this
    amount, $61 related to depreciation expense, $19 related to amortization expense, $205

was paid in cash and the remaining amount was included in accrued liabilities at the end of the year.

13. General and administrative expenses including corporate office salaries, travel and entertainment, professional fees, and so on were $118 and were paid in cash by the end of the year.

14. Given the financial results, the company decided to repurchase shares of their own stock (treasury stock purchase) totaling $97.

15. The Company paid $2 for interest expense and received $1 in other income during the year.

16. Income tax expense of $83 was paid during the year.

Required:

Using the balance sheet equation (BSE) format, enter each transaction and then construct the balance sheet and income statement for the year ended December 27, 2011. *Note:* The beginning balances are presented below, all amounts are in thousands and are included in the blank BSE template.

	Dec. 28, 2010
Cash.	$229
Accounts receivable.	20
Inventory.	14
Prepaid expenses.	66
Property and equipment.	823
Acc. depreciation	(378)
Intangible	143
Other long-term assets	7
Accounts payable.	7
Accrued liability and other current liability..	204
Other long-term liabilities.	117
Common stock.	130
Treasury stock	(78)
Retained earnings	$544

Panera BSE Activity		Assets								Liabilities			Owners' Equity		
Transactions	Cash	Accounts Receivable	Inventory	Prepaid Expenses	Property and Equipment	Accumulated Depreciation	Intangible	Other Long-Term Assets	Accounts Payable	Accrued Liabilities and Other Current Liabilities	Other Long-Term Liabilities	Common Stock	Treasury Stock	Retained Earnings
Beginning balances Dec. 28, 2010. . . .	$229	$20	$14	$66	$823	$(378)	$143	$7	$7	$204	$117	$130	$(78)	$544

CROCS   P2-14.   **Developing Financial Statements with the BSE**   This BSE exercise is abridged actual data and approximates **CROCS** financial accounts and operations at the end of 2012 and expectations for 2013. CROCS executives were forecasting a very modest increase of business in 2013. The market for CROCS was steady, new distribution channels were performing satisfactorily, and new product introductions might slightly expand market segments. Accordingly the transactions below capture the 2013 outlook as projected by CROCS executives. The CROCS' balance sheet at the beginning of 2013 before these expected transactions is shown in the top row of the BSE answer form provided. (All numbers in thousands except revenues which are expected to be $1,300,000,000.)

1. Revenues were projected to increase slightly to $1.3 billion. Assume receivables will be collected throughout the year and by year's end only $150,000 will remain uncollected and shown in accounts receivable.

2. The costs to manufacture CROCS (i.e., finished goods) were expected to be $570,000 and assumed to be incurred on credit (i.e., accounts payable). Assume all beginning accounts payable will be paid and all but $125,000 of this year's accounts payables will be paid in cash.
3. Cost of goods sold for 2013 is expected to be $560,000.
4. Selling, general and administrative expenses (SGA) will be $480,000. By year's end, $400,000 will be paid in cash, $50,000 will be depreciation expense and the remainder will remain in accrued expenses.
5. Amortization expense for intangible assets will be $5,000.
6. CROCS executives estimated restructuring expenses will be $7,500 and all will be paid in cash during 2013.
7. During 2013, CROCS planned to purchase $50,000 in property, plant and equipment. Of this, $10,000 would be paid in cash and $40,000 in common stock would be exchanged for the remainder of the purchase price.
8. Intangible assets (purchased rights to new manufactured technologies) will increase by $10,000 and be paid for in cash.
9. Interest expense is expected to be $1,000 and will be accrued during 2013 and paid in 2014.
10. CROCS executives expect to incur $100,000 of income tax expense in 2013. This entire amount will be paid in 2014.

Crocs Balance Sheet at the Beginning of 2013

CROCS Balance Sheet 12/31/2012				
Assets		**Liabilities**		
Cash.	$294,228	Accounts payable.	$155,900
Accounts receivable.	128,996	Accrued expenses	2,000
Inventory.	164,804		
Total current assets	$588,028	**Total current liabilities**	$157,900
Fixed assets	$132,241	Long-term debt	$ 54,300
Less: Accumulated assets	(40,000)	**Total liabilities**.	212,200
Net fixed assets	92,241	Owners' equity	
Intangible assets	59,931	Common stock.	337,000
Other assets	99,000	Retained earnings	290,000
		Total owners' equity	627,000
Total assets	$839,200	**Total liabilities and owners' equity** . . .	$839,200

Required:

a. Using the balance sheet equation format below which includes the above beginning balance sheet information, enter the impact of each transaction on the financial accounts. Note each instruction may have more than one entry.

Crocs—2013 (000s omitted)		Assets						Liabilities				Owners' Equity	
Transaction	Cash	Accounts Receivable	Inventory	Fixed Assets	Accumulated Depreciation	Intangible Assets	Other Assets	Accounts Payable	Accrued Expenses	Other Liabilities	Long-Term Debt	Common Stock	Retained Earnings
Beginning Balance													
1. Credit sales.													
2. Goods manufactured . . .													
3. COGS.													
4. SGA													
5. Amortization													
6. Restructuring													
8. Purchase fixed assets . .													
9. Intangible assets													
10. Interest													
11. Taxes													
Totals													

b. In generally accepted accounting principles (GAAP) format, develop a projected income statement for CROCS for the period ending 12/31/2013.

Under Armour **P2-15.** **Identify BSE Transactions Through Analysis of the Balance Sheet and Income Statement**
The following is some background business information about **Under Armour** taken from their 2011 10-K.

General: Our principal business activities are the development, marketing and distribution of branded performance apparel, footwear and accessories for men, women and youth. The brand's moisture-wicking fabrications are engineered in many designs and styles for wear in nearly every climate to provide a performance alternative to traditional products. Our products are sold worldwide and are worn by athletes at all levels, from youth to professional, on playing fields around the globe, as well as consumers with active lifestyles.

Our net revenues are generated primarily from the wholesale distribution of our products to national, regional, independent and specialty retailers. We also generate net revenue from product licensing and from the sale of our products through our direct to consumer sales channel, which includes sales through our factory house and specialty stores, website, and catalogs. Our products are offered in over twenty three thousand retail stores worldwide. A large majority of our products are sold in North America; however we believe that our products appeal to athletes and consumers with active lifestyles around the globe. Internationally, we sell our products in certain countries in Europe, a third party licensee sells our products in Japan, and distributors sell our products in other foreign countries.

The following includes the balance sheets and income statement for Under Armour, Inc.

UNDER ARMOUR, INC.
Income Statement
For the year ended December 31, 2010
(in millions)

Revenue	$1,064
Cost of sales	533
Gross profit	531
Operating expenses:	
SG&A expense	399
Depreciation expense	17
Amortization expense	2
Total operating expenses	418
Operating income	113
Interest expense	3
Income before taxes	110
Tax expense	42
Net income	$ 68

UNDER ARMOUR, INC.
Balance Sheets
December 31, 2010 and 2009
(in millions)

	2010	2009
Cash	$204	$187
Accounts receivable	102	79
Inventory	215	149
Prepaid expenses	34	33
Equipment	163	143
Accumulated depr. Equipment	(87)	(70)
Intangible assets	4	5
Other long-term assets	39	19
Total assets	$674	$545
Accounts payable	$ 85	$ 69
Accrued liabilities and other current liab.	57	42
Current portion of long-term debt	7	9
Long-term loans	9	11
Other long-term liabilities	20	15
Common stock	226	197
Retained earnings	270	202
Total liabilities and stockholders' equity	$674	$545

Required:
Based upon this information, prepare a listing of transactions that took place during the year ended December 31, 2010. State any assumptions that you are making. Use the following template for your answers:

Under Armour								Assets		Liabilities				Owners' Equity			Assumptions made
Transactions	Cash	Accounts Receivable	Inventory	Prepaid Expenses	Property and Equipment	Accumulated Depreciation	Intangible	Other Long-Term Assets	Accounts Payable	Accrued Liabilities and Other Current Liabilities	Current Portion of Long-Term Debt	Long-Term Debt	Common Stock	Retained Earnings		
Record revenue on account.															Revenue	All revenue was recorded on account. No cash sales.
Collect cash from customers.																
Purchased inventory on account.																All inventory purchase on account
Record cost of goods sold.															COGS	
Purchase property and equipment for cash. . . .																Purchased with cash. If you assumed it was put on account, the payment of payables row below would need to be modified.
Record depreciation expense															Depr.	
Record amortization expense															Amort.	
Record SG&A															SG&A	The increase in accrued liabilities relates to a portion of the SG&A expense and the remainder went through accounts payable.
Payment of payables																
Payment for current assets																
Pay and record interest															Interest	
Pay and record taxes															Tax	
Purchase other long-term assets																Purchased with cash. If you assumed it was put on account, the payment of payables number above would need to be modified.
Payment of debt.																
Cash received from borrowings																
Issuance of stock																
Ending total																

GAAP Variability, Financial Statement Construction, and Adjusting Entries: Some Complications

When you complete this chapter you should be able to:

1. Identify and explain the major differences between income as measured using accrual accounting principles and operating cash flows.

2. Apply revenue recognition criteria and calculate the impact of revenue recognition methods on financial statements.

3. Apply the matching principle used when recognizing revenues and expenses.

4. Calculate depreciation and warranty expenses and interpret related financial disclosures.

INTRODUCTION

Generally accepted accounting principles (GAAP) in the United States permit considerable variation in financial reporting across companies, in part because of the variability in substance across the myriad of business operations. Flexibility in rules and procedures is needed to capture these realities in financial statement formats. These flexibilities can be divided into two major categories: flexibility within measurement principles and flexibility within estimation procedures.

FLEXIBILITY WITHIN MEASUREMENT PRINCIPLES

Financial statements are based on the principles of accrual accounting, which are collected in a set of guiding principles and procedures termed *generally accepted accounting principles*, or GAAP. Because accrual accounting must measure continuous processes for discrete time periods, principles and procedures have been developed to capture the operating results for dynamic organizations during a specific period of time in an income statement and its financial position as of a specific date in a balance sheet. Examples of principles that have been developed are:

- Revenue recognition concepts that govern when to record a sale on the income statement;

- Cost of goods sold calculations to measure the expense of inventory when sold; and

- Depreciation methods to determine the pattern of expensing of long-term assets over their useful lives.

Understanding these principles is essential in grasping the differences between cash flow and accrual accounting, as well as in recognizing the imperfections of the data used in financial statement analysis. We will further discuss revenue recognition as an example of the comparability issues raised by a variety of principles—as an example of the comparability issues raised within the framework of GAAP.

Revenue Recognition

In Chapters 1 and 2, we saw income statements and observed that they always begin with revenue. We considered the BSE effect for Nordstrom of selling a pair of jeans or for Local Cycle of selling a bicycle in which an asset—cash or accounts receivable—increases and the company's retained earnings increase. This effect is called revenue recognition. Under GAAP, we recognize revenue and include it in income when two criteria are met: 1) the earnings process is substantially complete, and 2) the amount of revenue is measurable and reasonably certain of collection. These criteria govern the timing of revenue recognition, which is critical to companies and their reported profits.

The timing of revenue is a relatively simple decision for a restaurant, for example. The customer orders a meal, the meal is served, and the customer pays with either cash or a major credit card. The restaurateur meets the two criteria visibly and almost simultaneously: (1) the earnings process is essentially complete—the meal has been served and consumed, and (2) the amount of revenue is known and reasonably certain to be collected—the customer has paid with cash or a credit card. Revenue is recognized when the customer pays the bill.

> **Revenue Recognition BSE Entry: + Cash; + Retained Earnings (revenues)**

Now let's consider Local Cycle and its service contracts. When a customer buys a new bike, Local Cycle offers a two-year service contract for an additional $150, payable when the customer purchases the bike. Over the next two years, any routine maintenance, seasonal tune-ups, and minor repairs (listed in the contract) are provided for no additional charge. When should Local Cycle recognize the revenue for this service? The choices appear to be as follows:

1. When the cash ($150) is collected at the beginning of the two-year period—that is, when the bicycle is purchased and the customer pays for the service contract as well;
2. As the work is completed over the two-year period; or
3. Evenly over the two-year period—$75 per year.

The originating BSE effects for each of these alternatives at the time the customer pays for the service contract (with the bike sale in a different entry) are:

> **1. + $150 Cash; + $150 Retained Earnings (revenue)**
>
> **2. + $150 Cash; + $150 Unearned Revenue (a liability)**
>
> **3. + $150 Cash; + $150 Unearned Revenue (a liability)**

We can see that the cash portion of the transaction is the same in all three alternatives. However, Alternative 1 will recognize revenue for the entire contract in the current period, but no liability for the work yet to be performed over the next two years. Alternatives 2 and 3 will recognize the liability and reflect the contractual obligation of Local Cycle to perform repairs and maintenance for the customer over the next two years.

For Alternative 2, if no work is done during year 1, no revenue would be recognized and the entire amount would be recognized in year 2 when the work is complete or the contract expires. If work is done in year 1, revenue would be recognized according to the value of the work performed. Note that no more than $150 total revenue can be recognized over the two-year period no matter how much maintenance and minor repair work is completed on the bike.

For Alternative 3, revenue would be recognized evenly over the two years as $75 per year. To recognize revenue, the accountant for Local Cycle would make an **adjusting**

entry at the end of the year. Because both Alternatives 2 and 3 allocate service contract revenues over the period of the contract, let's focus on the BSE effects of Alternative 3. The balance sheet equation (BSE) entry at the end of the first year of the service contract would be:

– $75 Unearned Revenue; + $75 Retained Earnings (revenue)

The same entry would be made at the end of the second year of the service contract. The adjustment process is necessary to measure periodic income in the face of continuous business processes and is essential in using the accrual basis required by GAAP. At the end of any period for which income is measured, accounts must be adjusted to ensure that accomplishment and effort are properly matched to each other and recognized in the period in which income is earned. We will examine other revenue circumstances and expense estimations that necessitate adjusting entries throughout the remainder of this chapter.

How does Local Cycle decide when to recognize service contract revenues? The company receives cash up front, and the contracts are non-refundable, suggesting that the amount to be collected is reasonably certain. However, because Local Cycle will be providing a service over a two-year period, the work will not be complete until the two-year period is over. What would you decide?

Although most companies prefer to recognize revenue sooner rather than later, when we apply the two criteria for revenue recognition, we can see that the earnings process—providing routine maintenance and minor repairs over two years—is *not* complete when the company receives payment. Revenue should not be recognized at the time of sale but over the two-year process under Alternatives 2 or 3.

In fact, most companies recognize revenue for service contracts evenly over the life of the contract. Common examples include annual memberships in health and fitness centers, service contracts for electronics, retainers paid to lawyers for service over the next twelve months, and most other long-term revenue-generating agreements.

Revenue Recognition: Is the amount of revenue measurable and reasonably certain of collection?

Now let's examine a typical sales incentive program in the electronics industry that goes something like this: "Purchase a new TV and if you find the same model at a lower price within the next three months, we will send you a check for the difference!" Many retailers find this an effective incentive to combat the prevalent customer tendency to postpone electronics purchases in the hope of finding the absolute lowest price.

In this example we see a different issue about when to recognize revenue. The company has met the first criterion; clearly the earnings process is essentially complete because the sale has been made and the customer has the TV. In order to meet the second criterion, however, the company must be able to estimate the amount of revenue earned. Does the electronics retailer know how much it will refund over the next three months? If the retailer cannot reasonably estimate this amount, then it must wait three months after each sale before it recognizes revenue. If the retailer can reasonably estimate the amount to be refunded, then revenue may be recognized at the time the TV is delivered to the customer. Most companies can estimate these amounts and would recognize revenue at the time of sale, but would subtract the estimated refund from the sales price.

Electronics Retailer Income Statement for Period Ending December 31, Year XXXX	
Sales................................	$3,500
Less: Sales Allowances	($ 140)
Net Sales	$3,360

Revenue Recognition: How are product and service revenues allocated?

We consider one final example, a slightly more complex set of transactions.

Kush Rao and Max Martinez decided to begin a business selling a package of goods and services for college students. They contracted with an audio components manufacturer to supply components, and they planned to install and service dorm room entertainment systems for university students in major U.S. metropolitan areas. They promised their customers to supply the entertainment system, install it, and connect it to all other electronic devices owned by the customers, and then service the system through the four years the students were in school and living on campus. The typical package would be priced as follows:

1. Components:	$1,250
2. Installation:	$ 250
3. Service:.	$ 500
Total	$2,000

This price was calculated based on cost plus markup for the components and a reasonable fee for installation and service time. Kush and Max planned for this to be the base price with two package upgrades available, one with slightly better components totaling $2,500 and the top-of-the-line package at $3,000. The difference between the three price points was primarily due to better components; however, installation would also be a bit trickier and more expensive.

Over late-night coffees, Kush and Max discussed when to show sales revenue on the income statement and developed the following possibilities, using the base package as an example. Because the total amount was to be collected upfront and there was a "no-refund" policy, they wondered whether sales might be recognized at the beginning of the contract. After all, much of the work was done and cash was in the bank! They knew, though, that this alternative did not correctly reflect the timing of the work they would complete. The second possibility was to recognize the revenue at different points in time based on the rough pricing estimates they had used: 50% of the total price at time of sale, 25% when the installation was complete, and 25% evenly over the four years of the service contract. Finally, Kush and Max knew that the components in the base package would actually retail separately for $1,400 or 70% of the total price. Therefore, perhaps they should allocate the $2,000 package price as 70% at the time of sale, 15% when the installation was complete, and 15% over the four years of the service contract. The following shows the variability of the possible revenue amounts for the income statements.

Kush & Max: Entertainment Systems for Your Dorm							
	Year 1			Year 2	Year 3	Year 4	Total
	QTR 1	QTR 2	QTR 3	QTR 4			
Alternative 1	$2,000.00	$ —		$ —	$ —	$ —	$ —	$2,000.00
Alternative 2	$1,250.00	$250.00		$125.00	$125.00	$125.00	$125.00	$2,000.00
Alternative 3	$1,400.00	$300.00		$ 75.00	$ 75.00	$ 75.00	$ 75.00	$2,000.00

There are multiple possibilities, they thought (knowing they could develop others), but these three alternatives framed their decision: when they sell one standard package, in the first year they could recognize sales revenue of $2,000 (Alternative 1), $1,625 (Alternative 2: $1,250 + $250 + 125), or $1,775 (Alternative 3: $1,400 + $300 + $75). Perhaps more remarkably, years 2–4 could range from no revenue each year to $125 revenue per year. The BSE entries for each alternative for all four quarters are as follows:

BSE Entries			
Alternative 1	**Assets**	**Liabilities**	**Owners' Equity**
	Cash	Unearned Revenue	Retained Earnings
Year 1			
QTR 1	$2,000		$2,000
QTR 2			
QTR 3			
QTR 4			
Year 2			
Year 3			
Year 4			
Totals	$2,000 $—	$— $— $— $— $—	$— $— $2,000

BSE Entries			
Alternative 2	**Assets**	**Liabilities**	**Owners' Equity**
	Cash	Unearned Liabilities	Retained Earnings
Year 1			
QTR 1	$2,000	$ 750	$1,250
QTR 2			
QTR 3		$(250)	$ 250
QTR 4		$(125)	$ 125
Year 2		$(125)	$ 125
Year 3		$(125)	$ 125
Year 4		$(125)	$ 125
Totals	$2,000 $— $—	$— $ — $— $—	$— $— $2,000

BSE Entries			
Alternative 3	**Assets**	**Liabilities**	**Owners' Equity**
	Cash	Unearned Liabilities	Retained Earnings
Year 1			
QTR 1	$2,000	$ 600	$1,400
QTR 2		$(300)	$ 300
QTR 3			
QTR 4		$ (75)	$ 75
Year 2		$ (75)	$ 75
Year 3		$ (75)	$ 75
Year 4		$ (75)	$ 75
Totals	$2,000 $— $—	$— $ — $— $—	$— $— $2,000

Although the timing of cash collection is the same—at the beginning—for all three alternatives, the revenue recognized each year varies substantially. The first entry in which cash collection occurs is the originating entry. The entries that follow in Alternatives 2 and 3 are adjustments made at the end of the period (quarter or year) to adjust to accrual-based income measurement. Recall that the goal in this adjusting process is to match accomplishment and effort to the proper period—that is, when: (1) the earnings process is substantially complete, and (2) the amount of revenue is measurable and reasonably certain of collection.

This example illustrates the variability in the timing of revenue recognition within GAAP and its potential impact on financial statements. The principle is that revenue is recognized, that is, shown on the income statement, when the earnings process is complete and the revenue amount can be reasonably estimated, and its collection is reasonably certain. In this case, the principle would preclude Alternative 1, but either Alternative 2 or 3 would be acceptable.

Revenue recognition is a thorny issue, and misjudgments as well as abuses by companies are the most frequent causes for sanctions and fines imposed by the Securities and Exchange Commission (SEC). Although revenue recognition disclosure is required, it is difficult to quantify the impact of management judgment. The footnote shown below for Amazon is an example of revenue recognition disclosure. The disclosure makes the reader aware of the multiple revenue streams and revenue recognition methods used by Amazon, but does not make it easy to calculate the impact of these selections compared to other alternatives. A careful reading of the note, however, indicates then when Amazon sells its own products, such as the Kindle, it records revenue at the sales price, but when Amazon sells a product for a third party, it records only the commission as revenue.

Amazon Footnote—2014 SEC 10K Report:
Revenue

We recognize revenue from product sales or services rendered when the following four criteria are met: persuasive evidence of an arrangement exists, delivery has occurred or service has been rendered, the selling price is fixed or determinable, and collectability is reasonably assured. Revenue arrangements with multiple deliverables are divided into separate units and revenue is allocated using estimated selling prices if we do not have vendor-specific objective evidence or third-party evidence of the selling prices of the deliverables. We allocate the arrangement price to each of the elements based on the relative selling prices of each element. Estimated selling prices are management's best estimates of the prices that we would charge our customers if we were to sell the standalone elements separately and include considerations of customer demand, prices charged by us and others for similar deliverables, and the price if largely based on the cost of producing the product or service.

Sales of our digital devices, including Kindle e-readers, Fire tablets, Fire TVs, Echo, and Fire phones, are considered arrangements with multiple deliverables, consisting of the device, undelivered software upgrades and/or undelivered non-software services such as cloud storage and free trial memberships to other services. The revenue allocated to the device, which is the substantial portion of the total sale price, and related costs are generally recognized upon delivery. Revenue related to undelivered software upgrades and/or undelivered non-software services is deferred and recognized generally on a straight-line basis over the estimated period the software upgrades and non-software services are expected to be provided for each of these devices.

Sales of Amazon Prime memberships are also considered arrangements with multiple deliverables, including shipping benefits, Prime Instant Video, Prime Music, Prime Photo, and access to the Kindle Owners' Lending Library. The revenue related to the deliverables is amortized over the life of the membership based on the estimated delivery of services. Amazon Prime membership fees are allocated between product sales and service sales. Costs to deliver Amazon Prime benefits are recognized as cost of sales as incurred. As we add more benefits to the Prime membership, we will update the method of determining the estimated selling prices of each element as well as the allocation of Prime membership fees.

We evaluate whether it is appropriate to record the gross amount of product sales and related costs or the net amount earned as commissions. Generally, when we are primarily obligated in a transaction, are subject to inventory risk, have latitude in establishing prices and selecting suppliers, or have several but not all of these indicators, revenue is recorded at the gross sale price. We generally record the net amounts as commissions earned if we are not primarily obligated and do not have latitude in establishing prices. Such amounts earned are determined using a fixed percentage, a fixed-payment schedule, or a combination of the two.

Product sales represent revenue from the sale of products and related shipping fees and digital media content where we record revenue gross. Product sales and shipping revenues, net of promotional discounts, rebates, and return allowances, are recorded when the products are shipped and title passes to customers. Retail sales to customers are made pursuant to a sales contract that provides for transfer of both title and risk of loss upon our delivery to the carrier. Amazon's electronic devices sold through retailers are recognized at the point of sale to consumers.

> Service sales represent third-party seller fees earned (including commissions) and related shipping fees, digital content subscriptions, and non-retail activities such as AWS, advertising services, and our co-branded credit card agreements. Service sales, net of promotional discounts and return allowances, are recognized when service has been rendered.
>
> Return allowances, which reduce revenue, are estimated using historical experience. Allowance for returns was $147 million, $167 million, and $198 million as of December 31, 2014, 2013, and 2012. Additions to the allowance were $1.1 billion, $907 million, and $702 million, and deductions to the allowance were $1.1 billion, $938 million, and $659 million as of December 31, 2014, 2013, and 2012. Revenue from product sales and services rendered is recorded net of sales and consumption taxes. Additionally, we periodically provide incentive offers to our customers to encourage purchases. Such offers include current discount offers, such as percentage discounts off current purchases, inducement offers, such as offers for future discounts subject to a minimum current purchase, and other similar offers. Current discount offers, when accepted by our customers, are treated as a reduction to the purchase price of the related transaction, while inducement offers, when accepted by our customers, are treated as a reduction to purchase price based on estimated future redemption rates. Redemption rates are estimated using our historical experience for similar inducement offers. Current discount offers and inducement offers are presented as a net amount in "Total net sales."

Recently, Groupon, a company that earns revenues by offering coupons to entice new customers and increase sales for other businesses, showed amazing revenues because it recorded the total value of the coupon as revenue. When Groupon sells a coupon for $40 to be redeemed at a restaurant, it immediately remits approximately half of that amount to the restaurant. Groupon originally recognized all $40 as revenue and $20 as cost of goods sold. When the company filed its statements with the SEC, however, to issue shares publicly, it was required to show only the net of $20 as revenue.

Now we turn to the other major cause of variations in data presentation with GAAP: expense estimations. To illustrate the issues we will focus on the common practice of estimating the expenses associated with warranty programs offered at the time of sales and on the estimations needed to recognize the periodic expense of using long-lived assets.

FLEXIBILITY WITHIN ESTIMATION PROCEDURES

Accrual-based income measurement for an ongoing enterprise is focused on matching accomplishment and effort for a specific time period. The matching concept is a core principle of financial reporting, and it requires that the costs of generating revenue be recognized in the same period as the revenue. That is, expenses incurred are matched to revenues earned. Implementing this principle requires many estimates to capture the revenues and expenses in a discrete period in the continuous life of a dynamic company. The length of depreciable lives, product costs, bad debts associated with credit customers, and warranty costs are examples of expenses that must be estimated by companies to measure periodic income. We examine two of these estimates in depth: (1) the expense associated with warranty policies, and (2) the expense associated with depreciable assets.

Warranty Policies: An estimate within GAAP

Warranty policies can be classified into two major categories: those extended with the product at no apparent additional cost (e.g., standard three-year/36,000-mile warranty that accompanies any purchase of a Ford automobile) and those purchased by a customer at an additional cost (e.g., purchasing an extended warranty for a newly purchased automobile to extend the repair coverage past the standard three-year/36,000-mile policy). In this section we will discuss the first major category: warranties included with the product for no apparent additional cost. We will first look at the accounting for such a policy within a start-up company and then extend our discussion to warranties issued by Apple when it sells hardware.

Similar to Kush and Max, Ying Tsi and Daphne Cohen, as electrical engineers in a master's program, co-developed a new wireless audio speaker system and upon graduation partnered with a business undergraduate to create a start-up company (Y&D Audio) to produce and sell this new system. Unlike Kush and Max's product, this will be a "high-end" speaker set. Because it was new technology developed by young people and the management team had little business experience, Ying and Daphne decided to target their system to audiophiles and price the speaker system at $5,000, expecting each unit would cost $2,000 to produce. After speaking with numerous industry experts, they also decided to include a product warranty to encourage sales. Typical warranty periods were one year, but because Y&D is a new venture, Ying and Daphne decided on a two-year warranty period if the additional cost is not prohibitive. An examination of industry data revealed that the average cost of warranties for the first year after sale was typically 10%–15% of the cost of the system. Adding a second year to the warranty policy would increase the estimated total warranty expense over two years to between 15% and 25%.

Under accrual accounting, and specifically the matching principle, warranty expenses must be estimated at the time the revenue from the product sale is recognized. The reason for estimating the expense is the assumption that the warranty policy is critical to the successful sale at the designated price. The expense of the policy should be matched to the revenue earned in the period when the sales revenue is shown on the income statement, rather than waiting until the periods in which the warranty work is completed. The BSE entries for a typical sale and the related cost of goods sold (CGS) and a one-year warranty expense estimate of 10% of the cost are shown below:

Selected BSE Y&D Audio					
Event	**Assets**		**Liabilities**	**Owners' Equity**	
	Cash	Inventory	Warranty Liability	Retained Earnings	
Sale—One System	$5,000			$ 5,000	
CGS		$(2,000)		$(2,000)	
One-year Warranty			$200	$ (200)	

During the year following the sale of the audio system, the cost of actual warranty work would be recorded as a reduction in the warranty liability. For the example below, assume $80 in labor (paid immediately) and $50 in parts (from an inventory of spare parts) were used to complete warranty work. The BSE effect would be as follows:

Selected BSE Y&D Audio				
Event	**Assets**		**Liabilities**	**Owners' Equity**
	Cash	Inventory	Warranty Liability	Retained Earnings
Following year	$(80)	$(50)	$(130)	
Warranty work				

Note that the income statement column in the balance sheet worksheet, is unaffected by this transaction because the expense has already been estimated and included in the income calculation for the previous period. Because warranty expense estimates are an average for a large number of items sold, predicting the exact amount of warranty work is unlikely. The warranty liability is a function of the estimated expense net of the actual costs incurred. This liability is periodically analyzed by management (along with the expense), and the estimated warranty costs as a percentage of sales may be adjusted for future periods as the company becomes more experienced.

Although BSE entries clarify the mechanics and timing of accounting for warranty estimates and completed work, a more compelling issue is the range of the expense that may be estimated by management. In the earlier example, industry data show that warranty expenses connected to a one-year policy can range from $200 to $300 and for a two-year policy from $300 to $500. Selecting estimates at the extremes of this range can materially affect reported net income. Furthermore, if companies in the same industry select different percentages, comparative analysis of these companies might be difficult to interpret: that is, are operations substantively different or are differences a result of different percentage estimates?

For publicly traded companies, warranty estimates often are the basis for significant expenses included in general and administrative expenses on the income statement. Automotive companies such as Ford and Hyundai offer extensive warranties covering many periods post-sale. Some companies, such as L.L. Bean, a supplier of outdoor equipment and clothing, offer lifetime warranties on their goods sold. Here is an example of a typical warranty disclosure in a recent annual report from Apple Inc.:

Apple Footnote – 2014 SEC Form 10-K
Accrued Warranty and Indemnification
The Company offers a basic limited parts and labor warranty on its hardware products. The basic warranty period for hardware products is typically one year from the date of purchase by the end-user. The Company also offers a 90-day basic warranty for its service parts used to repair the Company's hardware products. The Company provides currently for the estimated cost that may be incurred under its basic limited product warranties at the time related revenue is recognized. Factors considered in determining appropriate accruals for product warranty obligations include the size of the installed base of products subject to warranty protection, historical and projected warranty claim rates, historical and projected cost-per-claim and knowledge of specific product failures that are outside of the Company's typical experience. The Company assesses the adequacy of its pre-existing warranty liabilities and adjusts the amounts as necessary based on actual experience and changes in future estimates.

The following table shows changes in the Company's accrued warranties and related costs for 2014, 2013 and 2012 (in millions):

	2014	2013	2012
Beginning accrued warranty and related costs	$2,967	$1,638	$1,240
Cost of warranty claims	(3,760)	(3,703)	(1,786)
Accruals for product warranty	4,952	5,032	2,184
Ending accrued warranty and related costs.	$4,159	$2,967	$1,638

As you can see from a review of this brief footnote, Apple's estimates are based on a number of factors, and any change in those factors or in Apple's weighting of those factors in its estimation procedures would change warranty expenses and net income for the period. Fortunately, all material changes in estimates must be disclosed in footnotes that are presented in the audited financial statements for a publicly traded company. Unfortunately, these footnotes can be vague and difficult to interpret. As an illustration of this lack of detail, we consider one more example of the impact of the variability of accounting estimates on financial data—depreciation estimates for long-term assets.

LONG-TERM ASSETS: DEPRECIATION EXPENSE

Assets are resources, owned or controlled by a company, that have reasonably quantifiable future benefits. In accrual accounting long-term assets must be expensed in the periods that benefit the company. For example, to test its audio systems before shipment, Y&D Audio purchased electronics equipment testers for $100,000. These assets were *expected* to be useful to the company for three to seven years, and therefore the $100,000 should be matched against revenues and proportionally expensed over three, four, five, six, or seven years.

Depreciation expense requires not only an estimate of the asset's useful life but also its salvage value, that is, the estimated value of the asset at the end of its useful life, or its scrap value. To keep this example simple, we will assume a salvage value of zero and focus on the estimated useful life assumption. With the estimated useful life ranging from three to seven years, depreciation expense could range from $33,333 ($100,000/3) to $14,286 ($100,000/7), and the useful life assumed could have a significant impact on a company's income statement. Experience may show these estimates to be incorrect, and if so, the company would change its useful life estimates for the remaining life of the asset.

For Y&D Audio, assume the electronics tester will have an estimated three-year life with no disposable value at the end of the three years. In other words, the tester equipment will provide benefit to Y&D for three years and help to generate income: the original cost of the equipment should be expensed over this three-year period. Let's use the BSE to see how this happens:

Y&D Audio Asset Purchase & Depreciation Expense					
	Assets		**=**	**Liabilities**	**+**	**Owners' Equity**
	Cash	Tester Equipment		Accumulated Depreciation		Retained Earnings
Originating Entry.						
1/1: Purchase Tester Equip.	$(100,000)	$100,000				
Adjusting entries.						
12/31/Year 1.		$ (33,333)				$ (33,333) Depreciation Expense
12/31/Year 2.		$ (33,333)				$ (33,333) Depreciation Expense
12/31/Year 3.		$ (33,334)				$ (33,334) Depreciation Expense
Totals	$(100,000) $—	$ —	$— $— $— $— $—			$(100,000)

As we can see, the original cost of the equipment is not expensed when it is purchased because it has estimable future value and is owned by the company: that is, it is an *asset*. Rather, the tester equipment is expensed over the period the asset is used to benefit business operations.

This example highlights the impact that depreciation estimates can have on income measurement for a new venture. Following is a recent disclosure from Willis Lease Finance Corporation, a public company, regarding its use of estimates and the impact of changing the estimates on net income. Note that the impact of lowering depreciation expense and the resulting increase in net income cannot be found on the income statement and is reported only in the footnote to the current year's financial statements. As you can see, if you are doing a time-series analysis of Willis Lease Finance Corporation and miss this footnote, your conclusions about year-over-year changes in operating performance could be incorrect.

Willis Lease Finance Corporation, 2013 10-K, Management Discussion and Analysis

On July 1, 2012 and again on July 1, 2013, we adjusted the depreciation for certain older engine types within the portfolio. It is our policy to review estimates regularly to accurately expense the cost of equipment over the useful life of the engines. The 2013 change in depreciation estimate resulted in a $3.9 million increase in depreciation for 2013. The net effect of the 2013 change in depreciation estimate is a reduction in 2013 net income of $2.3 million or $0.28 in diluted earnings per share over what net income would have otherwise been had the change in depreciation estimate not been made.

Examples of other common estimates required under GAAP are bad debts expense, sales returns, and losses due to inventory obsolescence. As users of corporate financial reports, we depend on standards under which independent auditors are required to make sure management includes in footnotes all material changes in estimates. Fundamentally, the purpose of all of these estimates is to recognize revenue and expenses—and, consequently, net income—in the proper period.

Before we conclude this chapter, let us examine one more example of a common situation that necessitates an adjustment at the end of periods to measure accrual-based income correctly paying for expenses before the periods in which the services are used. These are labeled **prepaid expenses** on the balance sheet and are typically listed as current assets.

Prepaid expenses occur when a company pays cash upfront for a service that covers multiple periods. For instance, it is common for a company to pay for insurance for the current as well as future periods. Let's assume that Kush and Max for their on-campus business are required by the college to have proof of insurance for as long as they are students and intend to operate their business on campus. Because they plan on launching their business from their dorm room and running it during their last two years of college, they take out a liability insurance policy for $4,000 for the two-year period. The originating and adjusting entries are as follows, assuming the policy was purchased and coverage began at the beginning of the two-year period:

Kush & Max Entries for Prepaid Insurance									
	Assets		**=**	**Liabilities**			**+**	**Owners' Equity**	
	Cash	Prepaid Assets						Retained Earnings	
Originating Entry.									
1/1: Purchase Insurance Policy . . .	−4,000	4,000							
Adjusting entries.									
12/31/Year 1.		−2,000						−2,000 Insurance Expense	
12/31/Year 2.		−2,000						−2,000 Insurance Expense	
Totals	−4,000	0	0	0	0	0	0	0	−4,000	

CONCLUSION

Throughout this chapter we have discussed the adjusting entries necessary to match accomplishment and effort in the proper period—that is, accrual-based income measurement.

Revenue recognition occurring after the collection of cash and estimated expenses, such as warranty and depreciation, typically involves originating entries followed by adjusting entries to measure and match revenues and expenses for discrete periods of time. In all of these adjustments there are some constants:

1. The adjustments are made at the end of a period in order to measure income properly; therefore, the adjustment is affected by the length of the period for which income is being measured (e.g., month, quarter, or year).
2. Cash is *not* involved in an adjustment.
3. Either an expense or revenue will be recognized in an adjustment.

Chapters 1, 2, and 3 have mainly focused on the income statement and balance sheet, with limited attention to the statement of cash flows. In Chapter 4, we turn our attention to the statement of cash flows, its different formats, the construction of these formats, and the information gained from examining this statement separately and in conjunction with the income statement and balance sheet.

KEY CONCEPTS AND TERMS

adjusting entry, 56   depreciation expense, 64   prepaid expenses, 65

QUESTIONS

Q3-1. What are the criteria for revenue recognition?

Q3-2. Provide an example of a company that would recognize revenue before it collects cash from its customer.

Q3-3. Provide an example of a company that would recognize revenue after it collects cash from its customer.

Q3-4. What is the matching concept? Why is it fundamental to measuring net income?

Q3-5. Describe deferred or unearned revenue. Provide three examples of deferred revenue.

Q3-6. Provide an example of an expense that is estimated. How should management make that estimate?

Q3-7. What is the BSE effect of estimating warranty expense for a given period?

Q3-8. What is the BSE effect of incurring the cost to repair a customer's warrantied product?

Q3-9. If a company changes an estimate of the useful life of equipment, will the effect of the change be apparent on the income statement?

Q3-10. Why are prepaid expenses recognized as assets?

EXERCISES

E3-1. **Business Model Revenue Recognition Timing**

Required:
Consider the following business descriptions and determine when revenue should be recognized by the bolded company.

1. **A retail store, such as Tiffany's,** displays merchandise; customers select items, pay with credit cards or cash, and take items. Customers are given 30 days to return items.
2. **A restaurant, such as Chipotle's,** sells food, beverages and gift cards which are paid for by the customers with cash or credit card.
3. **A grocery store, such as Whole Foods Markets,** sells food and related products. Whole Foods offers discounts that allow the customer to obtain a lower price on certain items.
4. **An online and store-front retailer, such as Apple,** sells an iPhone or iPad to consumers. The sale of these products includes the hardware, the software and the "free" right to obtain certain future software upgrades. For a separate fee, Apple will also provide a service and support contract that includes extended repair services and phone support.
5. **A magazine publisher, such as Sports Illustrated,** sells a year's subscription to one of its monthly magazines. The cash is paid in advance for the subscription.
6. **A service company, such as eBay,** charges a "listing" fee (similar to a newspaper ad, you need to pay this basic listing fee, even if your item doesn't sell) for certain items for display of your products on their site. In addition, if the eBay seller's item is bought, then that seller is also required to pay eBay a selling fee of 9.0% of the item's total sales price, not to exceed $100.
7. **A bio-technology company, such as Mylan,** enters into agreements with customers to license ("use for a fee") certain product rights or technology for a period of time. These agreements could include a non-refundable up-front payment, could be paid over a period of time or could be paid based upon the number of units the customer sells of their own product that "includes" the technology or product rights.
8. **A construction company, such as Suffolk Construction,** enters into a three-year construction contract for a building. The building is built according to plans, passes each inspection point, and project milestones are met during the three-year period. Progress payments are made during the construction period.

E3-2. **Timing of Revenue and Expense Recognition** For each of the following five independent transactions for J&D Bookkeeping Company, indicate whether revenue, expense, or neither should be recognized in the **October monthly** financial statements by placing an "**X**" within the appropriate box.

Transaction	Recognize Revenue in October	Recognize Expense in October	No revenue nor expense In October
J&D worked for clients during October and billed them for services rendered. J&D will receive cash from these clients in November.			
In September, J&D paid rent for its office space for the last four months of the year.			
During October, J&D used computer equipment which is estimated to have a 3-year useful life.			
J&D's employees worked during October and will be paid during the first week of November.			
During October, J&D collected cash from a client for work completed in September.			

E3-3. **Deferred Revenue** The Lynda.com Online Training Library teaches computer skills in video format to members through monthly and annual subscription-based plans. There are four types of membership plans as shown below:

	Basic (month-to-month)	Basic (Annual billing)	Premium (Month-to-month)	Premium (Annual billing)
Pricing	$25/month	$250/year	$37.50/month	$375/year

There is no cancellation policy once people sign up as members. More features are included as price goes up. For example, Premium (annual billing) allows members to download courses on iPhone and iPad, whereas other plans do not.

Required:
Describe how Lynda.com recognizes revenue for each sign-up under each plan.

E3-4. **Deferred Revenue** On January 1, 2015, the Fielder Company received $10,000 from a customer as an advance payment for consulting services that Fielder will provide in March 2015.

 a. What is the effect on the balance sheet equation of the transaction on January 1, 2015?
 b. What is the effect on the balance sheet equation of the necessary adjustment on **March 31, 2015**, when Fielder prepares its **quarterly** financial statements?

E3-5. **Prepaid Rent** On January 1, 2015, the Griffin Company paid $40,000 to rent office space for the next four months (i.e., through April 30, 2015).

 a. What is the effect on the balance sheet equation of the payment on January 1, 2015?
 b. What is the effect on the balance sheet equation of the necessary adjustment on **January 31, 2015**, when Griffin prepares its **monthly** financial statements?
 c. What is the balance in prepaid rent as of March 31, 2015?

E3-6. **Prepaid Insurance** On December 1, 2015, Morton Corporation purchased insurance for the next 12 months and paid $54,000.

 a. What is the effect on the balance sheet equation of the transaction on December 1, 2015?
 b. What is the effect on the balance sheet equation of the necessary adjustment on **December 31, 2015**, when Morton prepares its **monthly** financial statements?

E3-7. **Depreciation** On January 1, 2015, the Nelson Corporation purchased equipment for $10,000 cash. Nelson expects to use the equipment for 5 years and estimates that the equipment will have no salvage value.

    a. What is the effect on the balance sheet equation of the purchase on January 1, 2015?

    b. What is the effect on the balance sheet equation of the necessary adjustment on **December 31, 2015**, when Nelson prepares its **annual** financial statements?

E3-8. **Amortization** On January 1, 2015, the Reddick Corporation purchased a patent for $100,000. Reddick estimates that it will use the patent for its entire legal life of 20 years.

    a. What is the effect on the balance sheet equation of the purchase on January 1, 2015?

    b. What is the effect on the balance sheet equation of the necessary adjustment on **December 31, 2015**, when Reddick prepares its **annual** financial statements?

E3-9. **Warranty Liability** The Jackson Corporation sells home appliances and offers a two-year warranty as a standard feature of the sale. It estimates the cost of the warranties as 2% of revenues. During the first quarter of 2015, Jackson earned revenue of $36,000.

    a. What is the effect on the balance sheet equation of the necessary adjustment on March 31, 2015, when Jackson prepares its quarterly financial statements?

    b. In April 2015, Jackson pays $95 to repair a customer's washer under the warranty. What is the effect on the balance sheet equation of this transaction?

E3-10. **Warranty Liability** The Perrine Corporation extends a two-year warranty on all of its products. It reports a warranty liability balance of $18,500 at the beginning of 2015 and $21,875 at the end of 2015. During 2015, Perrine earned revenue of $2,240,000 on product sales, and it estimates warranty expense as 2% of revenue. Calculate the cost to Perrine of fulfilling its warranty obligation in 2013.

PROBLEMS

P3-1. **Revenue Recognition** A Babson student, Jessica, decides she is going to open her own yoga studio. She is going to open the studio on July 1, 2015 and is considering various ways to price her services and the way these may impact revenue recognition and cash flow. The following are the options that she is considering:

    a. Charge an upfront non-refundable fee of $150 to become a member of the studio for one year and then charge $40/month for unlimited yoga classes. Jessica expects that the average person is going to attend 8 yoga classes per month.

    b. Charge an upfront non-refundable fee of $100 to become a member of the studio for one year and then charge $50/month for unlimited yoga classes.

    c. Charge an upfront non-refundable fee of $600 for a one-year membership.

    d. Charge an upfront non-refundable fee of $200 to become a member of the studio for one year and then charge $8 per yoga class.

Required:

    1. How should the non-refundable fee be recognized as revenue?

    2. Which option would you expect would provide Jessica the most revenue in 2012? Show this by calculating the revenue under each scenario for 2012.

    3. Which option would you expect would provide Jessica the most cash flow in 2012? Show this by calculating the cash flow for each scenario for 2012.

P3-2. **Revenue Recognition** The following are transactions that took place at a coffee shop during the month August.

- Customers purchased and paid cash for coffee and pastries totaling $4,000.
- Customers purchased $1,000 in gift cards.
- Several corporate customers had breakfast events in which the coffee shop provided the coffee and food for a price of $3,000. The corporate customers put these amounts on account and will pay in September.
- Corporate customers who had breakfast events in July paid the coffee shop $400 in August.
- Customers purchased coffee and pastries using gift cards in the amount of $300.

Required:
Based upon the information above, how much revenue should be recognized in August?

P3-3. **Depreciation** The Albert Corporation purchased manufacturing equipment on January 1, 2015, for $750,000. It estimates that it will use the equipment for 10 years and that it will have no salvage value.

Required:
a. Record the effect on the balance sheet equation of the purchase.
b. Calculate depreciation expense for 2015.
c. Record the effect on the balance sheet equation of the adjustment necessary on December 31, 2015, to record depreciation for the year.
d. What is the book value of the equipment on the balance sheet as of December 31, 2015?
e. What is the book value of the equipment on the balance sheet as of December 31, 2016?

P3-4. **Interest Accrual** On July 1, 2015, Alvarez Company borrowed $100,000 from its local bank at a 10% annual interest rate. Under the terms of the loan, Alvarez will repay the principal and all of the interest in one year (i.e., on July 1, 2016).

Required:
a. Record the effect on the balance sheet equation of the origination of the loan on July 1, 2015.
b. Record the effect on the balance sheet equation of the necessary adjustment on December 31, 2015, when Alvarez prepares its annual financial statements.
c. What is the balance of interest payable on the loan as of June 30, 2016?
d. Record the effect on the balance sheet equation of the payment of the loan and all accrued interest on July 1, 2016.

P3-5. **Warranty Accrual** Randolph Corporation begins 2015 with a balance of $36,200 in its warranty liability account. The company sells washing machines with a 2-year warranty and estimates that total warranty costs are 8% of sales. During 2015, Randolph earns revenue of $500,000 and spends $44,000 to fulfill warranties.

Required:
Calculate the balance of Randolph's warranty liability at December 31, 2015.

P3-6. **Warranty Liability Disclosure** Hewlett-Packard (HP) Company reported the following information regarding its warranty liability in a recent annual report: **Hewlett-Packard**

Balance at beginning of year	$2,170
Accruals for warranties issued	2,007
Settlements made	(2,146)
Balance at end of year	$2,031

Required:
a. How much warranty expense did HP recognize during the year?
b. What was the cost to HP of fulfilling warranties during the year?

P3-7. **Warranty Liability Disclosure** (all amounts in millions) **Cisco Systems, Inc.**, designs and manufactures networking products for the telecommunications industry and reported revenue of $47,142 in its most recent fiscal year ending July 26, 2014. The company included the following note to its financial statements: **Cisco Systems, Inc.**

Product Warranties
The following table summarizes the activity related to the product warranty liability (in millions):

	July 26, 2014	July 27, 2013	July 28, 2012
Balance at beginning of fiscal year	$402	$373	$340
Provision for warranties issued	704	649	617
Payments	(660)	(620)	(584)
Balance at end of fiscal year	$446	$402	$373

The Company accrues for warranty costs as part of its cost of sales based on associated material product costs, labor costs for technical support staff, and associated overhead. The Company's products are generally covered by a warranty for periods ranging from 90 days to five years, and for some products the Company provides a limited lifetime warranty.

Required:
a. How much warranty expense did Cisco recognize during the most recent year?
b. Calculate warranty expense as a percentage of revenues for the most recent year.
c. What was the cost to Cisco of fulfilling warranties during the year?

Harley Davidson **P3-8.** **Analysis of Warranty Footnote** (all amounts in thousands) The following is the warranty footnote from the **Harley Davidson** 2014 10-K:

> *Product Warranty and Safety Recall Campaigns*—The Company currently provides a standard two-year limited warranty on all new motorcycles sold worldwide, except for Japan, where the Company provides a standard three-year limited warranty on all new motorcycles sold. In addition, the Company started offering a one-year warranty for Parts & Accessories (P&A) in 2012. The warranty coverage for the retail customer generally begins when the product is sold to a retail customer. The Company maintains reserves for future warranty claims which are based primarily on historical Company claim information. Additionally, the Company has from time to time initiated certain voluntary safety recall campaigns. The Company reserves for all estimated costs associated with safety recalls in the period that the safety recalls are announced.
>
> Changes in the Company's warranty and safety recall liability were as follows (in thousands):
>
> | | 2014 | 2013 | 2012 |
> |---|---|---|---|
> | Balance, beginning of period | $64,120 | $60,263 | $54,994 |
> | Warranties issued during the period | 60,331 | 59,022 | 54,394 |
> | Settlements made during the period | (74,262) | (64,462) | (67,247) |
> | Recalls and changes to pre-existing warranty liabilities | 19,061 | 9,297 | 18,122 |
> | Balance, end of period | $69,250 | $64,120 | $60,263 |
>
> The liability for safety recall campaigns was $9.8 million, $4.0 million and $4.6 million at December 31, 2014, 2013 and 2012, respectively.

Required:
Respond to the following questions:

a. How much expense did Harley Davidson record in 2014 relating to revenue generated in 2014?
b. What were the total payments made in 2014 for warranty related matters?
c. What impact did the $19,061 recalls and changes to pre-existing warranty-liabilities have on the income statement for 2014?

P3-9. **Revenue and Expense Recognition** The following activities took place relating to the month of November at one location of a large Mexican restaurant chain:

- The restaurant sold $900 in gift cards in November.
- Customers used gift cards totaling $1,500. Of this amount, $1,200 were purchased in the month of October and $300 were purchased in the month of November.
- The restaurant received $8,000 in cash from customers for meals provided during the month.
- The restaurant received $3,500 in cash for catering services provided in the previous month.
- Corporate customers purchased $5,000 of meals on account. Of this amount, $2,000 had been collected by the end of the month.

- Employee salaries for the month were $6,400. Of this amount, the restaurant paid $5,600 during the month.
- Rent of $3,400 was paid on October 25 for the month of November.
- The restaurant paid $1,500 on October 1 for advertising in local newspapers for the last three months of the year.
- The cost of utilities from November 1–November 30 was $2,100, which the restaurant will pay in December.

Required:

Prepare a simple income statement for the month of November.

P3-10.   **Revenue and Expense Recognition**   During September 2015, Alexander Company undertook the following transactions on the dates specified:

Sept. 1   Paid $400 for insurance for the next four months.

Sept. 1   Borrowed $6,000 from the local bank at an annual rate of 4%. The loan and interest will be repaid in one year (on Sept. 1, 2016).

Sept. 1   Purchased equipment for $15,000 cash. The estimated useful life of the equipment is 10 years.

Sept. 2   Purchased inventory from suppliers for $8,500 on account.

Sept. 2   Paid employees $3,200 for their August salaries.

Sept. 5   Sold goods to customers for $7,600 on account. The cost of the goods to Alexander was $4,400.

Sept. 8   Received an order from a customer for $350 of goods that will be delivered in October.

Sept. 15   Paid suppliers $8,500 cash for goods purchased on the 2nd.

Sept. 26   Collected $5,800 from customers for goods sold on the 5th.

Sept. 26   Sold goods to customers for $1,000 cash. The cost of the goods to Alexander was $550.

Sept. 29   Collected $670 cash from a customer for goods that will be delivered in October.

Sept. 30   Employees earned $3,240 during September, which Alexander will pay in October.

Required:

Prepare a simple income statement for the month of September 2015.

Chapter Four

The Statement of Cash Flows: Direct and Indirect Formats

LEARNING OBJECTIVES

When you complete this chapter you should be able to:

1. Understand and discuss the importance of analyzing both cash flows and accrual-based net income.
2. Know the three sections and format of the statement of cash flows.
3. Understand and prepare the operating section of the statement of cash flows using the indirect and direct methods.
4. Understand, construct, and analyze the statement of cash flows.

THE STATEMENT OF CASH FLOWS: THE TALE OF TWO FORMATS

In our Chapter 1 discussion of financial statements, we followed KW Bookkeeping Services from its origins through its second year of operations. We used income statements to evaluate KW's profitability in 2015 and 2016, and we used statements of cash flows to evaluate the company's management of cash over the same period. We will return to the KW example to illustrate the statement of cash flows and to introduce the indirect format of the operating section of the statement.

Example: KW Bookkeeping Services

KW Bookkeeping Services was created when the company issued stock to its sole owner, Kate Williams, in exchange for $30,000 cash. The company also borrowed $10,000 from a local bank, so that its start-up cash flows were all inflows that were the result of financing activities.

KW was ready to begin operations on January 1, 2015, when it reported the balance sheet shown in Exhibit 4.1.

EXHIBIT 4.1	KW Bookkeeping Services Balance Sheet as of January 1, 2015		
ASSETS		**LIABILITIES & OWNERS' EQUITY**	
Current assets		Current liabilities	
Cash	$40,000	Bank loan payable	$10,000
Total current assets.	$40,000	Total liabilities	$10,000
Long-term assets		Owners' equity	
		Contributed capital	30,000
Total assets.	$40,000	Total liabilities and owners' equity . . .	$40,000

During 2015, KW provided bookkeeping services to its customers and collected cash from them, and paid its employees, its landlord, and providers of utilities, all as part of the process of fulfilling its core operations. The operating activities portion of the statement of cash flows (SCF) reports the company's collections from customers and its payments for operating costs during the period. Although new companies often report payments in excess of collections, as they mature, they must generate positive cash flows from operations to support their ongoing growth.

The operating section may be prepared under either of two formats: the direct or the indirect format. When the operating activities section of the SCF is prepared using the **direct format**, it lists the cash inflows from revenue streams and outflows for the major cost categories. KW Bookkeeping's cash flows related to operations, as presented in Chapter 1, are shown in Exhibit 4.2 using the direct format.

EXHIBIT 4.2	KW Bookkeeping Services Statement of Cash Flows—Operating Section, Direct Format for the Year Ending December 31, 2015
Received from customers	$112,000
Paid for salaries	(58,000)
Paid for rent	(30,000)
Paid for utilities	(5,400)
Paid for interest	(600)
Net operating cash flows	$ 18,000

For the year, there was a net operating cash flow of $18,000, an accomplishment for a start-up, as many businesses use more cash than they generate during the early phase of operations. The cash flows shown in Exhibit 4.2 exclude any principal payments on KW's bank loan, as those payments are classified as financing (not operating) cash flows. This format of the operating section shows directly the inflows of cash from customer collections and the outflows of cash for specific operating functions, such as food, salaries, and rent. Like many new companies, KW's operating cash flows and net income were the same in its first year, as it neither extended credit to its customers nor used credit from its suppliers. KW's income statement for 2015 is shown in Exhibit 4.3.

EXHIBIT 4.3	KW Bookkeeping Services Income Statement for the Year Ending December 31, 2015
Revenues	$112,000
Salaries expense	(58,000)
Rent expense	(30,000)
Utilities expense	(5,400)
Interest expense	(600)
Net income	$ 18,000

Aside from its operating cash flows, KW's only other cash transaction during the year was to repay the bank loan of $10,000, a financing activity (Exhibit 4.4). KW did not undertake any investing activities during 2015.

EXHIBIT 4.4	KW Bookkeeping Services Statement of Cash Flows for the Year Ending December 31, 2015
Received from customers	$112,000
Paid for salaries	(58,000)
Paid for rent	(30,000)
Paid for utilities	(5,400)
Paid for interest	(600)
Net operating cash flows	$ 18,000

EXHIBIT 4.4	Continued

Financing cash flows:

Paid bank loan .... (10,000)

Change in cash. .... $ 8,000
Cash, beginning balance .... $ 40,000

Cash, ending balance. .... $ 48,000

Finally, we prepared the balance sheet for KW Bookkeeping as of December 31, 2015 (Exhibit 4.5).

EXHIBIT 4.5	KW Bookkeeping Services Balance Sheet as of December 31, 2015

ASSETS		LIABILITIES & OWNERS' EQUITY	
Current assets		Current liabilities	
Cash	$48,000	Bank loan payable	$ 0
Total current assets.	$48,000	Total liabilities	$ 0
Long-term assets		Owners' equity	
		Contributed capital.............	$30,000
		Retained earnings..............	18,000
		Total owners' equity	$48,000
Total assets.	$48,000	Total liabilities and owners' equity ...	$48,000

Cash increased by $8,000 because the company's operations generated more cash than it needed to repay its bank loan. The company's liabilities decreased as a result of the loan repayment, and its owners' equity increased because the company earned net income and did not distribute any dividends to its owner.

In 2016, KW's business became more complicated as it extended credit to its small business customers and invested in office and computer equipment. During the company's second year, we saw that its operating cash flows differ from its net income: (1) because cash collections from credit customers occur after the company earns revenue for its services, and (2) because depreciation of the equipment does not involve any operating cash payments.

Exhibits 4.6 and 4.7 show KW's statement of cash flows (using the direct format in the operating section) and income statement for 2016, which portray a growing venture with an increasing number of transactions causing cash flows and net income to diverge. Exhibit 4.8 is KW's balance sheet as of the end of 2016, its second year of operations.

EXHIBIT 4.6	KW Bookkeeping Services Statement of Cash Flows for the Year Ending December 31, 2016

Received from customers $123,000
Paid for salaries .... (64,000)
Paid for rent .... (24,000)
Paid for utilities. .... (5,900)
Paid for interest .... (300)

Net operating cash flows .... $ 28,800

Investing cash flows:
Purchase of equipment .... (21,000)
Financing cash flows:
Proceeds from bank loan .... $ 5,000

Change in cash .... $ 12,800

EXHIBIT 4.7	KW Bookkeeping Services Income Statement for the Year Ending December 31, 2016
Revenues	$133,500
Salaries expense	(64,000)
Rent expense	(24,000)
Depreciation expense	(7,000)
Utilities expense	(5,900)
Interest expense	(300)
Net income	$32,300

EXHIBIT 4.8	KW Bookkeeping Services Balance Sheet as of December 31, 2016		
ASSETS		**LIABILITIES & OWNERS' EQUITY**	
Current assets		Long-term liabilities	
Cash	$60,800	Bank loan payable	$ 5,000
Accounts receivable	10,500		
Total current assets	$71,300	Total liabilities	$ 5,000
Long-term assets		Owners' equity	
Equipment (cost)	$21,000	Contributed capital	$30,000
Accumulated depreciation	(7,000)	Retained earnings	50,300
Equipment (net)	$14,000	Total owners' equity	$80,300
Total assets	$85,300	Total liabilities and owners' equity	$85,300

In 2015, KW's net income and net operating cash flows were both $18,000. In 2016, however, net income and net operating cash flows diverge, as cash flows from operating activities were $28,800, while net income was $32,300. We know this is caused by credit sales and depreciation expense, but how much is caused by each? To focus on the differences between net income and net operating cash flows, we use an alternative approach to the operating section of the statement of cash flows: the indirect format.

Only the operating activities section of the statement of cash flows has two possible formats; the investing and financing activities sections do not vary in their formats. The **indirect format** begins with net income and highlights each of the differences between net income and net operating cash flows. Exhibit 4.9 presents the operating activities section for 2016 for KW Bookkeeping using the indirect format.

EXHIBIT 4.9	KW Bookkeeping Services Statement of Cash Flows—Operating Section, Indirect Format for the Year Ending December 31, 2016
Net income	$ 32,300
+ Depreciation expense	7,000
− Increase in accounts receivable	$(10,500)
Net operating cash flows	$ 28,800

First note that the operating activities sections of both the direct format in Exhibit 4.6 and the indirect format in Exhibit 4.9 show the same net amount, a positive operating cash flow of $28,800. These amounts will always be exactly the same; only the presentation format differs. Next we consider the logic underlying each of the line items so that we can develop some general rules for creating the indirect format for the operating activities section of the statement of cash flows (SCF).

We begin with net income, the last number on the income statement (also known informally as the "bottom line"). In this case we are given the net income number of $32,300 in Exhibit 4.7. Because we know that the owner did not withdraw a dividend from the company, we can also calculate net income by calculating the change in retained earnings: $50,300 (end of 2016) − $18,000 (beginning of 2016) = $32,300.

Depreciation and amortization expenses, as discussed in Chapter 3, are noncash expenses. The cash outflows to purchase long-term assets, such as equipment and patents, are reported in the investing section of the SCF, and occur in one period, while the asset's cost is allocated as depreciation or amortization expense over subsequent periods when it is used. Depreciation relates to tangible assets such as buildings and equipment; amortization relates to intangible assets such as patents. Companies must report depreciation and amortization expenses each year, and KW's income statement (Exhibit 4.7) includes depreciation expense of $7,000. Note also that in this case, the change in **accumulated depreciation**— $7,000 (end of 2016) − 0 (beginning of 2016)—equals $7,000, depreciation expense during 2016. Depreciation expense was subtracted, like any other expense, in calculating net income. Consequently, to derive net operating cash flow with net income as our starting point (as required under the indirect format), we must add back depreciation expense, amortization expense, and any other "noncash" expenses.

For KW, the other difference between net income and operating cash flows is the result of its decision to extend credit to some of its customers. Revenue for the company is reported on the income statement when bookkeeping services are provided. If the company earns revenue in one period and extends credit to the customer, accounts receivable will increase. Thus, by examining the change in accounts receivable during 2016—from a 0 balance at the beginning to $10,500 at the end—we can see that of the $133,500 revenue recognized for the year, $10,500 has not yet been collected. The decision to extend credit to some customers permitted KW to expand its client base to include small companies and supported the company's growth in 2016. However, the same decision means that the cash collected from customers during 2016 was less than the revenue earned and recognized in net income during 2016. Thus, the increase in accounts receivable is subtracted from net income, as net operating cash flows for the year were *less* than net income by $10,500 due to the extension of credit to some customers. The indirect format highlights these differences between net income and net operating cash flows, whereas the direct format reports the actual cash collections and payments undertaken for operations.

Tale of Two Formats: Local Cycle, March 2014

In Chapter 2 we walked through the balance sheet equation (BSE) effect of Local Cycle's transactions during March 2014. Local Cycle began the month with the balance sheet shown in Exhibit 4.10.

EXHIBIT 4.10	Local Cycle Balance Sheet as of March 31, 2014		
ASSETS		**LIABILITIES & OWNERS' EQUITY**	
Current assets		Current liabilities	
Cash	$ 23,000	Accounts payable	$ 45,000
Inventory	65,000		
Total current assets	$ 88,000	Total liabilities	$ 45,000
Long-term assets		Owners' equity	
Display equipment	48,000	Contributed capital	100,000
Computers	9,000		
Plant and equipment	57,000		
Total assets	$145,000	Total liabilities and owners' equity . . .	$145,000

During March, the company undertook the following transactions:

1. Sold cycles and accessories for $21,300. Collected $20,000 from customers. The remaining $1,300 will be collected during the first week of April. The cost of goods sold was $11,700.
2. Paid vendors $13,400.
3. Paid rent for March and April: $2,500 per month = total payment of $5,000.
4. Paid salaries for March of $4,200.
5. Paid utilities for March of $800.
6. Used the display equipment. Because it is expected to be useful for 10 years, or 120 months, Local Cycle must allocate 1/120th of its cost to each month as depreciation expense: $48,000 / 120 = $350 per month.
7. Used computer equipment. As in transaction 6, this equipment must be depreciated over its useful life of 5 years, or 60 months: $15,000 / 60 = $250 per month.

Exhibit 4.11 is the completed BSE from Chapter 2 capturing the March 2014 transactions (Exhibit 2.7) just listed. From this information we can construct the statement of cash flows (SCF) using either the indirect or direct format for the operating activities section.

EXHIBIT 4.11	Local Cycle Transactions, March 2014								
			ASSETS			LIABILITIES		OWNERS' EQUITY	
	Cash	Accounts Receivable	Inventory	Prepaid Rent	Plant & Equipment	Accounts Payable	Bank Loan Payable	Capital Stock	Retained Earnings
Beginning balances . . .	*23,000*	*0*	*65,000*	*0*	*57,000*	*45,000*	*0*	*100,000*	*0*
1-a Sell goods.	20,000	1,300							21,300
1-b Cost of goods sold. . . .			(11,700)						(11,700)
2 Pay vendors	(13,400)					(13,400)			
3 Pay rent	(5,000)			2,500					(2,500)
4 Pay salaries	(4,200)								(4,200)
5 Pay utilities	(800)								(800)
6 Depreciate store equipment.					(350)				(350)
7 Depreciate computer . .					(250)				(250)
Ending balances	*19,600*	*1,300*	*53,300*	*2,500*	*56,400*	*31,600*	*0*	*100,000*	*1,500*

Using the direct format for the operating activities section, for March 2014 we use the entries in the cash column, 1-a, 2, 3, 4, and 5, to develop the SCF shown in Exhibit 4.12. Note that entries 1-b, 6, and 7 had no effect on cash and thus are not included in the direct format.

EXHIBIT 4.12	Local Cycle Statement of Cash Flows for the Month Ending March 31, 2014
Received from customers	$20,000
Paid for merchandise	(13,400)
Paid for salaries	(4,200)
Paid for rent	(5,000)
Paid for utilities.	(800)
Net operating cash flows	($ 3,400)
Net change in cash	($ 3,400)

Because there were no cash transactions affecting long-term assets, there is no **cash flow from investing activities**. Similarly, because no cash transactions affected debt or owners' contributed capital, there is no **cash flow from financing activities**. In this simple example, all cash flows were **cash flows from operating activities**, and this section explains the entire change in cash from the beginning of the month to the end of the month.

Alternatively, we can construct the operating activities section of the SCF using the indirect format. As with KW Bookkeeping, note first that the two formats—direct (Exhibit 4.12) and indirect (Exhibit 4.14) arrive at the same amount; in March 2014, Local Cycle's operations generated negative cash flows, indicating that cash payments exceeded cash collections by $3,400 during the month. Using the indirect format, we begin with net income and highlight each of the reasons for the overall difference between net income and operating cash flows.

The indirect format is typically organized into two sections: (1) noncash expenses, beginning with depreciation expense; and (2) working capital changes, where working capital accounts are operating assets—excluding cash—and operating liabilities. In this example, operating assets are accounts receivable, inventory, and prepaid rent. Operating liabilities are accounts payable. Note that most operating assets and liabilities are current.

To construct the operating section of the statement of cash flows using the indirect method, we begin with net income as reported in Exhibit 4.13.

EXHIBIT 4.13	Local Cycle Income Statement for March 31, 2014	
Revenues		$21,300
Cost of goods sold.		(11,700)
Gross profit.		$9,600
Operating expenses:		
Rent	2,500	
Salaries.	4,200	
Utilities	800	
Depreciation—store equipment	350	
Depreciation—computer.	250	(8,100)
Net income.		$ 1,500

Clearly, the net income of $1,500 differs from the ($3,400) operating cash flows we calculated using the direct format for the operating activities section of the SCF shown in Exhibit 4.12. We can explain the difference using the indirect format, as shown in Exhibit 4.14.

EXHIBIT 4.14	Local Cycle Statement of Cash Flows—Operating Section, Indirect Format for the Month Ending March 31, 2014
Reconciliation from net income to net operating cash flows:	
Net income.	$ 1,500
+ Depreciation expense.	600
− Increase in accounts receivable.	(1,300)
+ Decrease in inventory.	11,700
− Increase in prepaid rent	(2,500)
− Decrease in accounts payable.	(13,400)
Net operating cash flows	($ 3,400)

The indirect format lists the reasons for the difference between net income of $1,500 and net operating cash flows of ($3,400).

First, the total noncash expenses of depreciation on the store equipment and the computer are added back to net income (+ $600). Although depreciation expense must be subtracted in net income calculations to reflect the periodic cost of using long-term assets, the recognition of this expense has no effect on cash flow. (BSE entry = − $600 accumulated depreciation and − $600 retained earnings.)

The remaining items are working capital changes that capture differences between accruals and cash flows. In this case, these are accounts receivable, inventory, prepaid rent, and accounts payable. Accounts receivable for Local Cycle increased from 0 to $1,300 during the month, indicating that $1,300 of the company's revenues earned had not yet been collected in cash. Consequently, operating cash flows were lower than net income by $1,300. By contrast, the balance of inventory decreased by $11,700, from $65,000 to $53,300, as the company sold goods that it already owned. This decrease in inventory is added to net income to calculate operating cash flow. That is, operating cash flow was higher than net income by $11,700. By contrast, once more, the increase in prepaid rent from 0 to $2,500 is the direct result of a cash outflow—to pay for rent in April—which does not have a corresponding expense in the March period. The $2,500 increase in prepaid rent is subtracted from net income to get another step closer to net operating cash flows.

Now we can make our first general calculation rule:

> If working capital assets increase in a specific period, net cash flow is lower in that period (as increases in assets require cash outflow), and those increases should be subtracted from net income to calculate operating cash flows. Conversely, decreases in operating assets should be added to net income to calculate cash from operations, because we are using assets or converting them into cash in the current period, having paid for them in a previous period.

We now turn to the operating liability side of the balance sheet, specifically to accounts payable. Accounts payable decreased from a beginning balance of $45,000 to $31,600, reflecting Local Cycle's payment of $13,400 to its vendors. The use of credit to purchase inventory as it prepared to begin operations allowed Local Cycle to acquire goods for resale without an immediate cash outflow, but it must repay its vendors eventually, requiring cash outflows—reflected in the decrease in accounts payable—in subsequent periods.

We can now make our second general calculation rule:

> If working capital liabilities increase in a specific period, net cash flow is higher for that period because the firm has postponed the payment of cash, and those increases must be added to net income to calculate net operating cash flows. Decreases in working capital liabilities reflect incrementally greater payments of cash, and therefore lower cash flows during the period, and those decreases must be subtracted from net income to calculate net operating cash flows.

Returning to Exhibit 4.14, we see that the indirect format highlights the reasons for the difference between net income and operating cash flows. In this case, Local Cycle's payments to vendors and for April's rent in advance, as well as the delay in its collections from customers, exceeded the effects of depreciation expense and the use of inventory already on hand. Consequently, its operating cash flows for the month were less than net income.

Tale of Two Formats: Local Cycle, April 2014

As one more example of the process for preparing a statement of cash flows using the indirect method, refer to Local Cycle's activities during April 2014, as described in Chapter

2. Exhibit 4.15 shows the company's balance sheet at the beginning and end of the month, with a third column indicating the change in each balance.

Using these changes, we will walk through the construction of Local Cycle's SCF using the indirect format for the operating activities section for April 2014. As required by the indirect format, we must begin the operating activities section with net income for the month, which was $1,008—as reported in the income statement in Exhibit 2.14. Knowing that the company did not return a dividend to its owner, we can also see from the change in the retained earnings account ($2,508 − $1,500) that net income for the month was $1,008. Exhibit 4.16 shows Local Cycle's SCF, using the indirect format, for April 2014.

EXHIBIT 4.15	Local Cycle Balance Sheets and Changes		
	April 30, 2014	**March 31, 2014**	**Change**
Cash	12,718	19,600	(6,882)
Accounts receivable	3,000	1,300	1,700
Inventory	60,900	53,300	7,600
Prepaid rent	0	2,500	(2,500)
Prepaid advertising	1,200	0	1,200
Current assets	77,818	76,700	
Property, plant, and equipment (PP&E)—cost	62,000	57,000	5,000
Accumulated depreciation	(1,200)	(600)	(600)
PP&E—net	60,800	56,400	
Total assets	138,618	133,100	
Accounts payable	15,600	31,600	(16,000)
Salaries payable	450	0	450
Interest payable	60	0	60
Bank loan payable	20,000	0	20,000
Current liabilities	36,110	31,600	
Capital stock	100,000	100,000	0
Retained earnings	2,508	1,500	1,008
Owners' equity (OE)	102,508	101,500	
Total liabilities & OE	138,618	133,100	

EXHIBIT 4.16	Local Cycle Statement of Cash Flows—Indirect Format for the Month Ending April 30, 2014

Reconciliation from net income to net operating cash flows:

Net income	$ 1,008
+ Depreciation expense	600
− Increase in accounts receivable	(1,700)
− Increase in inventory	(7,600)
+ Decrease in prepaid rent	2,500
− Increase in prepaid advertising	(1,200)
− Decrease in accounts payable	(16,000)
+ Increase in salaries payable	450
+ Increase in interest payable	60
Net operating cash flows	($21,882)
Purchase equipment	(5,000)
Net investing cash flows	($ 5,000)
Proceeds from bank loan	20,000
Net financing cash flows	$20,000
Net change in cash	($ 6,882)

As in the earlier examples, we list each item that has caused net operating cash flow and net income to differ, beginning with noncash expenses—specifically, depreciation expense of $600, which, as per Exhibit 2.14, was correctly subtracted in the calculation of net income and is reflected in the change in accumulated depreciation. Because depreciation expense reduces net income, but has no corresponding cash outflow, net operating cash flows are higher than net income by $600.

Next we turn to the current operating assets and current operating liabilities, which in this case are accounts receivable, inventory, prepaid rent, prepaid advertising, accounts payable, salaries payable, and interest payable. We created the following two general rules for calculating the impacts of current assets and liabilities on operating cash flows:

> If working capital assets increase in a specific period, cash decreases in that period (with the assumption that increases in these assets require outflows of cash), and those increases should be subtracted from net income to calculate operating cash flows. Conversely, decreases in assets should be added to net income to calculate cash from operations because these operating assets used in the current period were actually paid for in a previous period.
>
> If working capital liabilities increase in a specific period, cash increases in that year, as cash outflows are postponed until a future period, and those increases should be added to net income to calculate cash from operations. Conversely, decreases in liabilities mean cash was used pay those liabilities in the current period, and thus should be subtracted from net income to calculate cash from operations.

If we apply these rules, the increases in accounts receivable, inventory, and prepaid advertising are subtractions from net income to calculate operating cash flows, as is the decrease in accounts payable; the decrease in prepaid rent and the increases in salaries payable and interest payable are additions to net income in this indirect derivation of operating cash flows.

The format of the investing activities section is always the same (as in Exhibits 2.13 and 4.16), and its components are typically calculated from the BSE by subtracting beginning balances from ending balances. Because the balance of PP&E—cost increased by $5,000, we assume (and know from Chapter 2) that Local Cycle purchased additional equipment for $5,000, an investing activity requiring a cash outflow. The financing activities section shows Local Cycle's short-term borrowing in April, which is reflected in the increase in bank loan payable from 0 to $20,000. Note that most current liabilities are assumed to be working capital liabilities, and the changes in these accounts are used to calculate operating cash flows. The exceptions to this general rule are short-term borrowings represented in the balance sheet as notes payable, bank loan payable, and business credit card liability. All of these short-term liabilities are obligations to financial institutions rather than trade suppliers, and are therefore classified in the financing activities section of the SCF. Note, too, that although the repayment of principal is a financing activity, the payment of interest is classified as an operating activity under U.S. rules.

If we compare the direct and indirect formats, Exhibits 2.13 and 3.16, respectively, we can make the same observations as in the first section of this chapter: the operating cash flow amounts are the same using either format; the direct format discloses actual cash collections into and cash payments out of the business, whereas the indirect format discloses why net operating cash flows differ from net income. The investing and financing sections are exactly the same in formatting and amounts.

The statement of cash flows offers insight into a company's cash **operating cycle**. Any business starts with cash, which it uses to purchase goods and services that allow the company to earn revenue. When revenue is earned and then collected from customers, the cash operating cycle is complete, and it begins again. For some businesses, the cash operating cycle is short. For example, suppose that you go to the grocery store on a summer morning and purchase a cooler, ice, and a case of iced tea for $35 cash. You have just initiated a cash operating cycle. You drive to the beach, set up the cooler, and by 2:00 in the afternoon, you have sold all 24 bottles for $2 each, collecting $48 in cash. In this case, the cash cycle is complete within a single day. The $13 ($48 collected less $35 paid out) is both the net cash flow and the net income for this very simple business.

By contrast, consider a homebuilder. He buys land and purchases building materials for cash. He needs four months to complete the house, with additional cash payments to employees, and the house goes on the market. Two months later, the builder sells the house, and one month after that, collects from the buyer, for a total of seven months in the cash operating cycle. For KW Bookkeeping Services, the cash operating cycle includes monthly payments for rent, utilities, and salaries to generate revenue, which is collected either immediately or within one month: pay rent for space and equipment → pay employees → provide bookkeeping services → collect cash from clients. For Local Cycle, the cash operating cycle is more complicated, as it involves the purchase of inventory: pay rent for space → purchase and hold inventory → pay for inventory → pay employees and utilities → sell goods → collect from customers. When we discuss the details of financial statement analysis later in this text, we will define the calculations that permit us to measure a company's cash operating cycle in number of days.

Another metric used in evaluating a company's cash position is the **run rate**, or **burn rate**, for companies like Local Cycle whose net operating cash flows in March and April were negative. Like most start-ups and other companies that are growing quickly, Local Cycle's operations were "burning" cash, that is, using more cash than the company received in both months. Typically we define the burn rate on a monthly basis by calculating the excess of recurring operating cash payments—for rent and salaries, for example—over recurring operating cash collections from customers. Suppose a new software venture is collecting $2,000 each month from customers, but needs to pay $3,000 each month for its operating costs. Its monthly burn rate is $1,000. If the company has $24,000 of cash in the bank, we would estimate that it has 24 months, or two years, until it runs out of cash. Monitoring operating cash flows is critical for any business, large or small, and the statement of cash flows using either the indirect or direct format offers essential information in that analysis.

The Tale of Two Formats: A Public Company Example

We have now introduced and explained the two SCF formats for presenting operating activities, direct and indirect, using new ventures. We focus now on the SCF for a large company, Cracker Barrel Old Country Store (CBRL), a publicly traded U.S. company that owns and operates full-service restaurants emphasizing home-style country cooking. See CBRL's financial statements for 2014 in Exhibits 4.17, 4.18, and 4.19. During 2014, CBRL reported (in thousands of dollars) total revenues of $2,683,677, net income of $132,128 (as per the income statement), and net operating cash flows of $177,625. The indirect format of the statement of cash flows explains the specific reasons for the noticeable difference between net income and net operating cash flows.

EXHIBIT 4.17	CBRL Comparative Balance Sheets

CRACKER BARREL OLD COUNTRY STORE, INC.
CONSOLIDATED BALANCE SHEETS

(In thousands except share data)	August 1, 2014	August 2, 2013
ASSETS		
Current assets:		
Cash and cash equivalents	$ 119,361	$ 121,718
Property held for sale	—	883
Accounts receivable	22,704	15,942
Income taxes receivable	2,973	—
Inventories	165,426	146,687
Prepaid expenses and other current assets	11,997	12,648
Deferred income taxes	7,188	4,316
Total current assets	329,649	302,194
Property and equipment:		
Land	303,933	299,995
Buildings and improvements	767,149	746,764
Buildings under capital leases	3,289	3,289
Restaurant and other equipment	506,323	484,013
Leasehold improvements	271,049	255,058
Construction in progress	15,378	8,704
Total	1,867,121	1,797,823
Less: Accumulated depreciation and amortization of capital leases	823,837	771,454
Property and equipment—net	1,043,284	1,026,369
Other assets	59,315	59,743
Total	$1,432,248	$1,388,306
LIABILITIES AND SHAREHOLDERS' EQUITY		
Current liabilities:		
Accounts payable	$ 98,477	$ 110,637
Current maturities of long-term debt	25,000	—
Taxes withheld and accrued	36,261	35,076
Accrued employee compensation	60,933	62,780
Accrued employee benefits	26,050	24,477
Deferred revenues	49,825	44,098
Dividend payable	23,838	17,847
Current interest rate swap liability	4,704	—
Other current liabilities	19,350	21,152
Total current liabilities	344,438	316,067
Long-term debt	375,000	400,000
Long-term interest rate swap liability	3,239	11,644
Other long-term obligations	123,221	120,073
Deferred income taxes	57,709	56,496
Commitments and Contingencies (Notes 9 and 15)		
Shareholders' equity:		
Preferred stock—100,000,000 shares of $.01 par value authorized; 300,000 shares designated as Series A Junior Participating Preferred Stock; no shares issued	—	—
Common stock—400,000,000 shares of $.01 par value authorized; 2014—23,821,227 shares issued and outstanding; 2013—23,795,327 shares issued and outstanding	238	237
Additional paid-in capital	39,969	51,728
Accumulated other comprehensive loss	(4,733)	(6,612)
Retained earnings	493,167	438,673
Total shareholders' equity	528,641	484,026
Total	$1,432,248	$1,388,306

EXHIBIT 4.18	CBRL Comparative Income Statements		

CRACKER BARREL OLD COUNTRY STORE, INC.
CONSOLIDATED STATEMENTS OF INCOME

Fiscal years ended (In thousands except share data)	August 1, 2014	August 2, 2013	August 3, 2012
Total revenue	$2,683,677	$2,644,630	$2,580,195
Cost of goods sold	872,758	854,684	827,484
Gross profit	1,810,919	1,789,946	1,752,711
Labor and other related expenses	966,593	962,559	951,435
Other store operating expenses	506,533	482,601	464,130
Store operating income	337,793	344,786	337,146
General and administrative expenses	129,387	143,262	146,171
Operating income	208,406	201,524	190,975
Interest expense	17,557	35,742	44,687
Income before income taxes	190,849	165,782	146,288
Provision for income taxes	58,721	48,517	43,207
Net income	$ 132,128	$ 117,265	$ 103,081
Net income per share—basic	5.55	$4.95	$4.47
Net income per share—diluted	5.51	$4.90	$4.40
Basic weighted average shares outstanding	23,817,768	23,708,875	23,067,566
Diluted weighted average shares outstanding	23,966,015	23,948,321	23,408,126

Although the indirect format is not intuitive to most people at first, most corporations use the indirect format in their published financial reports. As the format requires, CBRL's operating activities section begins with its net income of $132,128. The statement then lists the "adjustments to reconcile net income to net cash provided by operating activities." Remember that the indirect method does not disclose actual cash inflows and outflows (as in the direct format), but instead shows the derivation of operating cash flows, one step at a time, from the required starting point of net income (or loss).

1. The first step is to add $68,389 of depreciation and amortization expense to net income. CBRL included exactly this amount of depreciation and amortization expense in other store operating expenses on the income statement. CBRL owns stores and equipment that must be depreciated (as well as trademarks that must be amortized) to recognize the expense of using those assets in generating revenues each year. In calculating net income, depreciation expense, like all expenses, is subtracted from revenue. Depreciation expense, as we discussed earlier, does not involve any cash payment. In fact, it has no effect at all on cash flows. So why does it appear prominently, first on the list, in a statement of cash flows? Its addition to net income is essential in the reconciliation to net operating cash flows, as it is a significant reason— in CBRL's case, the most significant reason—for the difference between net income and net operating cash flows. Consequently, the first step in the process of deriving net operating cash flows from net income is to add depreciation expense.

2. Another noncash expense involves compensation of employees using shares of stock. Just as with depreciation expense, this amount represents a cost incurred to operate the business, which was appropriately expensed in the calculation of net income, but it does not require any cash payment to employees (who receive company stock instead of cash). Thus net operating cash flows are higher than net income by $7,924 of noncash share-based compensation expense.[1]

---

[1] The excess tax benefit must be reclassified to the financing section, and is beyond the scope of an introductory course.

EXHIBIT 4.19	CBRL Comparative Statements of Cash Flows

CRACKER BARREL OLD COUNTRY STORE, INC.
CONSOLIDATED STATEMENTS OF CASH FLOWS

Fiscal years ended (In thousands)	August 1, 2014	August 2, 2013	August 3, 2012
Cash flows from operating activities:			
Net income	$132,128	$117,265	$103,081
Adjustments to reconcile net income to net cash provided by operating activities:			
Depreciation and amortization	68,389	66,120	64,467
Loss on disposition of property and equipment	5,163	4,057	2,702
Share-based compensation	7,924	17,839	14,420
Excess tax benefit from share-based compensation	(1,248)	(2,332)	(4,502)
Changes in assets and liabilities:			
Accounts receivable	(6,762)	(1,333)	(2,330)
Income taxes receivable	(1,725)	—	7,898
Inventories	(18,739)	(3,420)	(1,720)
Prepaid expenses and other current assets	651	(1,243)	(2,405)
Other assets	(1,701)	(1,033)	(4,725)
Accounts payable	(12,160)	9,366	1,592
Taxes withheld and accrued	1,185	(4,628)	7,369
Accrued employee compensation	(1,847)	(4,143)	17,729
Accrued employee benefits	1,573	(2,069)	(2,701)
Deferred revenues	5,727	6,402	5,066
Other current liabilities	(1,960)	6,628	2,651
Other long-term obligations	3,865	5,895	9,973
Deferred income taxes	(2,838)	(4,872)	1,257
Net cash provided by operating activities	177,625	208,499	219,822
Cash flows from investing activities:			
Purchase of property and equipment	(91,646)	(74,417)	(80,922)
Proceeds from insurance recoveries of property and equipment	1,082	456	752
Proceeds from sale of property and equipment	1,749	555	623
Net cash used in investing activities	(88,815)	(73,406)	(79,547)
Cash flows from financing activities:			
Proceeds from issuance of long-term debt	—	—	92,600
(Taxes withheld) and proceeds from issuance of share-based compensation awards, net	(8,457)	6,454	17,602
Principal payments under long-term debt and other long-term obligations	(1)	(125,153)	(117,733)
Purchases and retirement of common stock	(12,473)	(3,570)	(14,923)
Deferred financing costs	—	—	(263)
Dividends on common stock	(71,484)	(45,400)	(22,372)
Excess tax benefit from share-based compensation	1,248	2,332	4,502
Net cash used in financing activities	(91,167)	(165,337)	(40,587)
Net (decrease) increase in cash and cash equivalents	(2,357)	(30,244)	99,688
Cash and cash equivalents, beginning of year	121,718	151,962	52,274
Cash and cash equivalents, end of year	$119,361	$121,718	$151,962
Supplemental disclosure of cash flow information:			
Cash paid during the year for:			
Interest, net of amounts capitalized	$15,856	$29,959	$50,357
Income taxes	$66,444	$47,550	$18,768

3. During 2014, CBRL sold some of its property and equipment at a loss. The cash received when property and equipment are sold must be classified as an investing activity. If the cash received is less than the book value of the asset sold, then the loss must be recognized as a decrease in net income. Thus, operating cash flows are higher than net income by this loss, and CBRL added $5,163 back as an adjustment necessary to derive operating cash flows.

4. The remaining adjustments needed to derive net operating cash flows from net income (loss) all come under the heading *changes in assets and liabilities* (also known as *working capital assets and liabilities*). Consider again why changes in certain balance sheet accounts are steps in the process of reconciling from net income to net operating cash flow. The accrual basis underlying the financial reporting framework recognizes revenues when earned, which may not occur in the same reporting period as the cash collection from the customer. If the company earns revenue before it collects cash, the operating asset *accounts receivable* will increase. If the company collects cash before it earns revenue, the operating liability *deferred revenues* will increase. So the balance sheet account changes capture the difference between the revenue accrued and the cash collected during the period. The indirect method uses this framework as part of the process of deriving net operating cash flows.

   a. During 2014, CBRL's receivables increased from $15,942 to $22,704. It must therefore be true that the company collected $6,762 less in cash than it earned in revenue included in net income. Thus, CBRL's net operating cash flows for 2014 were $6,762 lower than net income as a result of this difference, and the statement shows the subtraction of the $6,762 increase in receivables.

   b. During 2014, CBRL's inventories increased from $146,687 to $165,426. The inventory buildup indicates that the company must have purchased more food, beverages, and paper supplies, as well as items sold in its gift shops, than it sold during the year. If the purchases were for cash, then the company's cash payments for inventories exceeded the corresponding expenses so that the net operating cash flows were lower than net income by the $18,739 difference. CBRL thus shows the subtraction of $18,739 in deriving net operating cash flow.

   c. Prepaid expenses decreased in 2014 from $12,648 to $11,997, indicating that CBRL paid incrementally less for services such as rent and insurance during the year than it expensed. Prepaid rent, for example, increases when a company pays cash before using the space, and prepaid rent decreases as the company uses the space. So, a net decrease reflects lower cash payments in the current year, and therefore higher net operating cash flow for the year. CBRL has aggregated that change with changes in other operating assets in its addition of $651 in the statement.

   d. Accounts payable indicate that in its purchases of inventory (see part b), CBRL does not pay immediately for those purchases but uses credit from its suppliers. During 2014, accounts payable decreased by $12,160, reflecting CBRL's decision to pay its suppliers more than it purchased. Thus, in the current year, CBRL's operating cash flows are lower, and the decrease in accounts payable is subtracted in the process of calculating net operating cash flows.

   e. Like many restaurants and retailers, CBRL offers gift cards, a business practice that generates cash for the company before the company earns revenue. Recall that the balance sheet effect of selling a gift card is to increase cash and increase a deferred revenue liability. When the gift cards are redeemed, the liability decreases and CBRL recognizes revenue. During 2014, CBRL's deferred revenues liability increased by $5,727, indicating that the company collected incrementally more in cash from the issuance of new gift cards than it earned in revenue from the redemption of existing gift cards. Thus, net operating cash flows are higher than net income, and the statement shows an addition of the decrease in the account.

After adjusting one piece at a time for each of the material differences between net income and net operating cash flows, CBRL arrives at the total net operating cash flows of $177,625 for 2014. The investing and financing sections that follow are more straightforward, as they disclose actual cash flows for specific kinds of transactions. CBRL's primary investing activity is capital expenditures, the purchase of property, plant, and equipment (PP&E) needed to maintain its productive capacity. In 2014, CBRL paid $91,646 for those purchases, an increase over 2013 and 2011. A common metric used in assessing a company's cash flow is **free cash flow**, which is usually defined as operating cash flows net of capital expenditures. In 2014, CBRL's operations generated cash flows of $177,625, which were sufficient to cover its $91,646 capital expenditures, leaving $85,979 free or available to be used for other purposes. An alternate version of this metric is the ratio of operating cash flow to capital expenditures, which for CBRL would be $177,625/$85,979 = 2.07 in 2014. If this ratio is greater than 1.0, then the company has generated positive free cash flow.

In the financing activities section, CBRL discloses that it did not increase its long-term borrowing. We can see on the balance sheet that its long-term debt decreased from $400,000 to $375,000 because $25,000 of the debt became current and is due within the next year. The company purchased shares of its common stock with total payment of $12,473. When a company purchases its own shares, it is removing them from the public market and decreasing its shareholders' equity. As noted earlier, the shares are called *treasury stock* and can be re-issued at a later date. Companies often repurchase their own shares and then issue them to employees as compensation. CBRL also paid $71,484 in dividends to shareholders, for a net cash outflow from financing activities of $91,167. When operating, investing, and financing cash flows are summed, we see that CBRL's net change in cash was a decrease of $2,357, which explains the change in the balance of cash from $121,718 at the beginning to $119,361 at the end of the year.

Like most public companies, CBRL does not provide a complete direct-format version of its operating activities in the statement of cash flows. The supplemental disclosure at the bottom of its statement of cash flows is required and reports its actual cash payments for income taxes and for interest during each year. (Some companies disclose these amounts in a separate note.) Payments for income taxes and for interest would be components of an operating activities section prepared using the direct format. Although we usually lack the specific details to prepare a complete version of the section in the direct format, we can estimate several other components.

For example, we know from CBRL's income statement that revenues earned in 2014 totaled $2,683,677. And we know from the balance sheets that receivables increased by $6,762, while the gift card liability increased by $5,727. Thus, we can see that cash collections from customers who purchased on credit were less than sales revenue (as revealed in the increase in receivables) and that cash collections from gift cards were greater than the revenue earned (as revealed in the increase in the gift card liability). Putting this together:

Total revenues	$2,683,677
− Increase in receivables	(6,762)
+ Increase in gift card liability	5,727
Cash collections from customers	$2,682,642

Cash collections from customers would be the first line of the operating activities section using the direct format.

Our ability to calculate CBRL's payments for specific operating costs is limited by the nature of the information provided. The fact that inventory increased by $18,739 indicates that CBRL purchased $18,739 more in food, beverages, paper supplies, and items for sale in its gift shops than it used or sold, and we could conclude that its total purchases for those items were ($872,758 in cost of goods sold + $18,739) = $891,497. To calculate the amount paid in cash for those purchases in 2014, however, we must assume that accounts payable reflect amounts owed to those suppliers, and not to suppliers of other items used in operations. If we make that assumption, then the decrease in accounts payable would indicate that CBRL's cash payments were more than its purchases, and we would calculate cash payments to suppliers of ($891,497 + $12,160) = $903,657 in 2014. However, because of the uncertainty of the ties between particular balance sheet accounts and particular expenses, our calculations can only be estimates.

Current discussions among financial reporting regulators suggest that in a few years, companies issuing public financial statements will likely be required to present the operating activities section of the statement of cash flows using both the indirect and the direct formats, as both are useful in evaluating a company's operating activities. Remember, though, that the format choice affects only the presentation, not the amount of the company's net operating cash flows.

KEY CONCEPTS AND TERMS

accumulated depreciation, 77

burn rate (or run rate), 83

cash flow from financing
   activities, 79

cash flow from investing
   activities, 79

cash flows from operating
   activities, 79

direct format, 74

free cash flow, 88

indirect format, 76

operating cycle, 83

run rate (or burn rate), 83

QUESTIONS

Q4-1. Identify three transactions that involve operating cash flows.

Q4-2. Explain why depreciation expense appears as an addition in the operating section of the statement of cash flows using the indirect method.

Q4-3. Explain why depreciation expense does not appear at all in the operating section of the statement of cash flows using the direct method.

Q4-4. Explain why an *increase* in accounts receivable is *subtracted* in the operating section of the statement of cash flows using the indirect method.

Q4-5. Provide three examples of *working capital changes* that would appear in the operating section of the statement of cash flows using the indirect method.

Q4-6. Identify three transactions that involve investing cash flows.

Q4-7. Explain the concept of *free cash flow*.

Q4-8. Identify three transactions that involve financing cash flows.

Q4-9. Describe how you would use a company's *cash burn rate*.

Q4-10. What two specific cash payment amounts must a company provide as supplemental information to the statement of cash flows if it uses the indirect format?

EXERCISES

E4-1. **Statement of Cash Flows Classification**

Required:

For each of the following transactions, determine the appropriate classification in the operating (O), investing (I), or financing (F) section of the statement of cash flows. If it is a transaction that does not impact cash and needs to be disclosed as supplementary information, denote with NC.

Classification

_____ A piece of equipment is purchased for cash

_____ Sold product to a customer on account

_____ Issuance of common stock for cash

_____ Advertising bill is paid

_____ Issuance of bonds

_____ Purchased supplies for cash

_____ Paid dividends

_____ Acquired shares in another company in exchange for cash

_____ Purchased a 180-day certificate of deposit

_____ Cash received from customer recorded as a deposit

_____ Purchase of intangible assets

_____ Paid income taxes

_____ A nine-month loan is obtained

_____ Paid employees

_____ Cash received for sale of equipment

_____ Purchased equipment in exchange for note payable

_____ Depreciation and amortization

_____ Repayment of bonds

_____ Cash payment made for 12-month insurance policy

_____ Issuance of common stock in exchange for promissory note

_____ Acquired 100% of the stock of a company in exchange for common stock

_____ Gain on sale of equipment

_____ Repurchase of common stock

NIKE, Inc. **E4-2.** **Selected Cash Flow Calculations** NIKE is a worldwide athletic apparel company that was incorporated in Oregon in 1968. The following is a summary of business from their 2013 10-K.

> General—Our principal business activity is the design, development and worldwide marketing and selling of athletic footwear, apparel, equipment, accessories and services. NIKE is the largest seller of athletic footwear and athletic apparel in the world. We sell our products to retail accounts, through NIKE-owned retail stores and internet websites (which we refer to as our "Direct to Consumer" operations) and through a mix of independent distributors and licensees, in virtually all countries around the world. Virtually all of our products are manufactured by independent contractors. Virtually all footwear and apparel products are produced outside the United States, while equipment products are produced both in the United States and abroad.

Below are the balance sheets and income statements from NIKE, Inc. for the years ending May 31, 2013, and May 31, 2012. Selected data for the two years are:

NIKE, Inc. (in millions)	May 31, 2013	May 31, 2012
Long-Term Assets		
Equipment	$ 5,500	$ 5,057
Accumulated depreciation	$ (3,048)	$ (2,848)
Equipment, net	$ 2,452	$ 2,209
Intangible	$ 513	$ 501
Other long-term	$ 993	$ 910
Total assets	$ 3,958	$ 3,620
Stockholders' Equity		
Common stock	$ 5,187	$ 4,644
Retained earnings	$ 5,695	$ 5,588
Accumulated other comprehensive income	$ 274	$ 149
Total Stockholder's Equity	$11,156	$10,381

2013: Net Income $2,485

2013: Depreciation Expense $200

2013: Amortization Expense $13

Required:

a. Calculate the amount Nike purchased in property, plant and equipment.

b. Calculate how much Nike purchased in intangible assets.

c. Calculate dividends paid.

E4-3. **Operating Section of Statement of Cash Flows (indirect method)** Partial balance sheets for the Davis Corporation are presented below.

	2015	2014
Assets		
Cash.	$ 65	$ 50
Accounts receivable.	105	120
Prepaid insurance.	32	40
Current assets	$202	$210
Liabilities and shareholders' equity		
Salaries payable.	$ 59	$ 54
Unearned revenue	46	85
Interest payable	18	12
Current liabilities.	$123	$151

During 2015 Davis earned net income of $130 and recognized depreciation expense of $42.

Required:

Prepare the operating section of the statement of cash flows using the indirect method.

E4-4. **Operating Section of the Statement of Cash Flows (indirect method)** Partial balance sheets for the Ward Corporation are presented below.

	2015	2014
Assets		
Cash.	$ 520	$420
Accounts receivable.	342	385
Office supplies	80	50
Prepaid interest	74	94
Current assets	$1,016	$949
Liabilities and shareholders' equity		
Accounts payable.	$ 403	$370
Advances from customers	118	156
Current liabilities.	$ 521	$526

During 2015 Ward earned income of $4,500 and recognized depreciation expense of $585.

Required:

Prepare the operating section of the statement of cash flows using the indirect method.

E4-5. **Operating Section of the Statement of Cash Flows (indirect and direct methods)** Presented below are partial balance sheets and an income statement for the Morrison Corporation.

MORRISON CORPORATION Balance Sheets As of December 31		
(All amounts in thousands)	2015	2014
Assets		
Cash.	$ 16	$ 12
Accounts receivable.	130	118
Prepaid insurance.	5	30
Total current assets	$151	$160
Liabilities and shareholders' equity		
Salaries payable.	$ 60	$ 48
Current note payable to bank.	37	30
Interest payable	10	6
Total current liabilities.	$107	$ 84

MORRISON CORPORATION	
Income Statements	
For the Year Ending December 31, 2015	
(All amounts in thousands)	
Sales revenue.	$1,250
Salaries expense	600
Depreciation expense.	350
Insurance expense	60
Interest expense.	40
Net income.	$ 200

Required:

a. Prepare the operating section of the statement of cash flows using the indirect method.

b. Prepare the operating section of the statement of cash flows using the direct method.

Tom's Fence, Inc. **E4-6.** **Operating Section of Statement of Cash Flows (indirect method)** Below are the balance sheets and income statements for **Tom's Fence, Inc.**

TOM'S FENCE, INC.	
Income Statement	
For the year ended December 31, 2015	
Revenue	$110,000
Cost of sales.	65,000
Gross profit.	45,000
Operating expenses:	
Salary expense	20,000
Depreciation expense.	7,000
General & admin. expense . .	8,000
Total operating expenses	35,000
Operating income.	10,000
Interest expense	3,000
Income before taxes.	7,000
Tax expense	2,000
Net income.	$ 5,000

TOM'S FENCE, INC. Balance Sheets December 31, 2015	2015	2014	Change
Cash	$35,000	$24,000	$11,000
Accounts receivable.	30,000	25,000	5,000
Inventory.	36,000	40,000	(4,000)
Equipment	40,000	10,000	30,000
Accumulated depr. equipment.	(9,000)	(2,000)	(7,000)
Total assets.	$132,000	$97,000	$35,000
Accounts payable.	$35,000	$32,000	$3,000
Interest payable	1,000	3,000	(2,000)
Loans payable (due in 2017)	42,000	30,000	12,000
Common stock.	30,000	11,000	19,000
Retained earnings	24,000	21,000	3,000
Total liabilities and stockholders' equity. .	$132,000	$97,000	$35,000

Note: A dividend was paid during the year.

Required:

Prepare the operating section of the statement of cash flows in good form using the indirect method.

E4-7. **Preparation of Indirect Statement of Cash Flows (indirect method)** Below are the bal-   Sarah's Catering,
ance sheet and income statements for **Sarah's Catering, Inc.**   Inc.

SARAH'S CATERING Income Statement For the year ended December 31, 2015		
Revenue		$249,000
Cost of sales.		119,000
Gross profit.		130,000
Operating expenses:		
Salary expense	63,500	
Depreciation expense.	5,200	
Advertising expense	6,600	
Total operating expenses		75,300
Operating income.		54,700
Interest expense		4,800
Income before taxes.		49,900
Tax expense		19,800
Net income		$ 30,100

SARAH'S CATERING Balance Sheets December 31, 2015 and 2014		
	2015	**2014**
Cash	$ 16,800	$ 13,100
Accounts receivable.	39,200	32,300
Inventory.	26,300	29,400
Prepaid advertising.	2,100	1,300
Equipment	75,600	68,700
Accumulated depr. equipment	(17,700)	(12,500)
Total assets.	$142,300	$132,300
Accounts payable.	$ 14,400	$ 12,900
Wages payable.	1,900	3,500
Unearned revenue	4,200	8,200
Long-term loans	47,200	53,200
Common stock.	7,300	6,800
Retained earnings	67,300	47,700
Total liabilities and stockholders' equity . .	$142,300	$132,300

Required:
Prepare a statement of cash flows in good form using the indirect method.

E4-8. **Preparation of Statement of Cash Flows (indirect method)** Presented below are balance sheets for the Baldwin Corporation as of the beginning and end of 2015 (all amounts in
thousands).

	2015	2014
Assets		
Cash	$ 521	$ 500
Accounts receivable.	92	80
Inventory.	489	432
Prepaid interest	10	16
Current assets.	1,112	1,028
Property, plant and equipment (at cost)	1,246	1,026
Less accumulated depreciation	(533)	(478)
Net property, plant and equipment.	713	548
Patent.	36	0
Total assets.	$1,861	$1,576
Liabilities and shareholders' equity		
Accounts payable.	$ 391	$ 317
Unearned revenue	118	96
Short-term bank loan payable	0	27
Current liabilities	509	440
Long-term bank debt payable	388	321
Total liabilities	897	761
Capital stock	318	280
Retained earnings	646	535
Shareholders' equity.	964	815
Total liabilities and shareholders' equity.	$1,861	$1,576

Additional information:

- Net income for 2015 was $150. Depreciation expense for 2015 was $55.
- During 2015, the company purchased equipment for $220 cash.
- During 2015, the company paid dividends in cash to shareholders.

Required:

Prepare a statement of cash flows (all three sections) for 2015 using the indirect method for the operating section.

E4-9.   **Preparation of Statement of Cash Flows (indirect and direct methods)**   Presented below are the balance sheet and income statement for Ortiz Corporation:

ORTIZ CORPORATION Balance Sheet		
(all amounts in thousands)	Dec. 31, 2015	Dec. 31, 2014
Assets		
Cash.	$100	$ 80
Accounts receivable (net).	210	175
Inventory.	135	152
Property, plant and equipment (at cost).	575	520
Accumulated depreciation	(185)	(155)
Total assets.	$835	$772
Liabilities and shareholders' equity		
Accounts payable.	$ 98	$107
Interest payable	15	12
Long-term debt payable.	230	209
Common stock.	300	300
Retained earnings	192	144
Total liabilities and shareholders' equity.	$835	$772

ORTIZ CORPORATION Income Statement for 2015	
Sales revenue.	$800
Cost of goods sold.	(500)
Gross margin	300
Wages and salaries expense	(150)
Depreciation expense.	(30)
Interest expense.	(23)
Net income before taxes	97
Income tax expense.	(34)
Net income.	$ 63

The firm did not sell any property, plant or equipment during the year. The firm paid dividends of $15 to shareholders.

Required:

a.   Prepare a statement of cash flows for Ortiz Corporation using the indirect format for the operating section.

b.   Prepare the operating section of the statement of cash flows for Ortiz Corporation using the direct format.

E4-10.   **Analysis of Changes in Property, Plant, and Equipment**   During 2015, the Stoddard Corporation sold equipment for $63 and recognized a gain of $15. The original cost of the equipment was $400. During 2015, Stoddard purchased new equipment to increase its productive capacity. Stoddard reported the following amounts on its balance sheets at the beginning and end of 2015.

	December 31, 2015	December 31, 2014
Property, plant and equipment, at cost	$8,626	$8,100
Accumulated depreciation	(4,220)	(4,045)
Property, plant and equipment, net	4,406	4,255

Required:
a. Calculate the accumulated depreciation on the equipment sold.
b. Calculate depreciation expense recognized during 2015.
c. Calculate capital expenditures during 2015.
d. If Stoddard did not engage in any other investing activities during 2015, prepare the investing section of its statement of cash flows for 2015.

PROBLEMS

P4-1. **Preparation of Statement of Cash Flows (indirect method)** Presented below are the balance sheets and income statement for the Hopkins Company.

Required:
Prepare a statement of cash flows using the indirect method for the operating section.

HOPKINS COMPANY Balance Sheets As of December 31		
	2015	2014
Cash.	$ 80	$ 95
Accounts receivable.	168	140
Inventory.	284	253
Prepaid insurance.	18	28
Current assets.	550	516
Property, plant and equipment (at cost).	868	790
Accumulated depreciation	(295)	(240)
Property, plant and equipment (net).	573	550
Total assets.	$1,123	$1,066
Accounts payable.	$ 187	$ 155
Salaries payable.	115	127
Short-term bank loan payable	50	0
Current liabilities.	352	282
Long-term bank debt payable	210	245
Common stock.	280	280
Retained earnings	281	259
Stockholders' equity	561	539
Total liabilities and stockholders' equity.	$1,123	$1,066

HOPKINS COMPANY Income Statement As of December 31	
Sales revenue.	$1,000
Cost of goods sold.	670
Gross profit.	330
Selling, general and administrative expense	185
Depreciation expense.	55
Operating income.	90
Interest expense.	22
Net income before taxes	68
Income tax expense.	20
Net income	$ 48

P4-2.   **Preparation of Statement of Cash Flows (indirect method)**   Presented below are the balance sheets and income statement for the Morgan Corporation.

MORGAN CORPORATION Balance Sheets As of December 31			
	2015	**2014**	**Change**
Assets			
Cash.	$ 18,000	$ 12,000	$ 6,000
Accounts receivable.	40,000	36,000	4,000
Inventory.	26,000	29,000	(3,000)
Prepaid rent	3,000	1,000	2,000
Total current assets.	$ 87,000	$ 78,000	$ 9,000
Property, plant and equipment (at cost).	410,000	360,000	50,000
Less: accumulated depreciation	(180,000)	(155,000)	(25,000)
Total assets.	$317,000	$283,000	$34,000
Liabilities and Shareholders' Equity			
Accounts payable to suppliers.	$ 18,000	$ 13,000	$ 5,000
Taxes payable.	1,000	2,000	(1,000)
Total current liabilities	19,000	15,000	4,000
Long-term notes payable.	205,000	220,000	(15,000)
Total liabilities	224,000	235,000	(11,000)
Common stock.	25,000	15,000	10,000
Retained earnings	68,000	33,000	35,000
Shareholders' equity	93,000	48,000	45,000
Total liabilities and shareholders' equity.	$317,000	$283,000	$34,000

MORGAN CORPORATION Income Statement For the year ending December 31, 2015	
Sales revenue.	$400,000
Cost of goods sold.	(225,000)
Gross profit.	175,000
Rent expense.	(12,000)
Depreciation expense.	(25,000)
Salary expense.	(70,000)
Operating income.	$ 68,000
Interest expense.	(11,000)
Net income before taxes	57,000
Income tax expense.	(17,000)
Net income	$ 40,000

No property, plant or equipment was sold during 2015.

Required:

a. Prepare a **statement of cash flows** (all three sections) for 2015 using the **indirect** method in the operating activities section.

b. Calculate cash collected from customers during 2015. (*Hint:* Assume that all sales were initially on account.)

c. Calculate cash paid to suppliers of inventory during 2015.

P4-3. **Preparation of the Statement of Cash Flows (indirect method)** Presented below are the income statement and balance sheets for Lakeview Associates, Inc.

LAKEVIEW ASSOCIATES, INC. Balance Sheets For the year ending December 31			
	2015	**2014**	**Change**
Cash.	$ 300	$ 200	$ 100
Marketable securities	105	135	(30)
Accounts receivable.	750	830	(80)
Inventory.	640	600	40
Current assets.	1,795	1,765	30
Equipment (cost)	2,100	1,800	300
Accumulated depreciation	(840)	(600)	(240)
Equipment, net.	1,260	1,200	60
Intangibles, net.	300	200	100
Total assets.	$3,355	$3,165	$190
Accounts payable.	$ 600	$ 755	$(155)
Taxes payable.	200	150	50
Short-term debt	1,000	900	100
Accrued interest.	30	40	(10)
Current liabilities.	1,830	1,845	(15)
Common stock.	1,400	780	620
Retained earnings	525	540	(15)
Treasury stock	(400)	0	(400)
Total shareholders' equity	1,525	1,320	205
Total liabilities and shareholders' equity.	$3,355	$3,165	$190

LAKEVIEW ASSOCIATES, INC. Income Statement For the year ending December 31, 2015	
Revenue	$6,500
Cost of goods sold.	3,360
Gross profit	3,140
Sales and marketing expense	1,200
General and administrative expense	700
Depreciation expense.	240
Amortization expense.	110
Operating income	890
Interest (income).	(108)
Interest expense.	53
Income before income taxes	945
Income tax expense.	319
Net income	$ 626

Required:

a. Prepare the statement of cash flows for 2015 using the indirect method for the operating section.

b. Calculate cash collected from customers in 2015.

c. Calculate interest paid during 2015.

P4-4. **Preparation of the Statement of Cash Flows (indirect method)** Presented below are the balance sheets and income statement for the Mayfield Trucking Company for 2015.

Additional information:

- On January 1, 2015, Mayfield sold equipment for $200 cash. The equipment originally cost $212 and had accumulated depreciation of $54.
- During the year, Mayfield repurchased its own stock with cash.
- During the year, Mayfield paid dividends of $47 cash.

Required:

Prepare a statement of cash flows (all three sections) for 2015 for Mayfield Trucking Company using the indirect method for the operating section.

MAYFIELD TRUCKING COMPANY Balance Sheets as of December 31			
	2015	**2014**	**Change**
Assets			
Cash	$ 1,803	$ 2,779	(976)
Accounts receivable (net)	209	279	(70)
Inventories of parts and supplies	203	259	(56)
Prepaid rent	313	57	256
Other current operating assets.	740	2,524	(1,784)
Current assets	$ 3,268	$ 5,898	
Property, plant and equipment (at cost)	15,871	15,160	711
Less accumulated depreciation	(4,831)	(4,286)	(545)
Property, plant and equipment (net).	11,040	10,874	
Total assets.	$14,308	$16,772	

continued

MAYFIELD TRUCKING COMPANY Balance Sheets as of December 31			
	2015	2014	Change
Liabilities and Shareholders' Equity			
Accounts payable.	$ 831	$ 800	31
Accrued expenses	1,975	4,038	(2,063)
Current liabilities.	2,806	4,838	
Bonds payable	6,549	4,993	1,556
Total liabilities	9,355	9,831	
Common stock, no par value.	2,215	2,215	0
Retained earnings	4,919	4,788	131
Treasury stock	(2,181)	(62)	(2,119)
Shareholders' equity	4,953	6,941	
Total liabilities and shareholders' equity.	$14,308	$16,772	

MAYFIELD TRUCKING COMPANY Income Statement For the year ending December 31, 2015	
Sales revenue.	$11,023
Salaries and wages expense	3,340
Fuel and oil expense	3,713
Depreciation expense.	599
Other operating expenses	2,922
Operating income.	449
Gain on sale of equipment	(42)
Interest expense.	213
Income before income taxes	278
Income tax expense.	100
Net income.	$ 178

P4-5.   **Preparation of the Statement of Cash Flows (indirect method)**   Bed Bath & Beyond,   Bed Bath & Beyond,
Inc., sells a wide assortment of home furnishings through its retail stores (including Christmas   Inc.
Tree Shops) and websites. Below are the balance sheets and income statement for Bed Bath &
Beyond, Inc., for the fiscal year ending February 28, 2015.

    Depreciation and amortization expense for the year was 239,193. The company did not
sell property and equipment during the year, nor did it pay dividends.

Required:

Prepare a statement of cash flows for the year using the indirect method for the operating
section.

(amounts in thousands)	February 28, 2015	March 1, 2014
Assets		
Cash and cash equivalents	$ 875,574	$ 366,516
Short-term investments	109,992	489,331
Merchandise inventories	2,731,881	2,578,956
Other current assets.	366,156	354,184
Total current assets.	4,083,603	3,788,987
Long-term investments	97,160	87,393
Property and equipment, net	1,676,700	1,579,804
Goodwill	486,279	486,279
Other assets.	415,251	413,570
Total assets.	$6,758,993	$6,356,033

continued

continued from previous page

(amounts in thousands)	February 28, 2015	March 1, 2014
Liabilities and Shareholders' Equity		
Accounts payable..........................	$1,156,368	$1,104,668
Accrued expenses and other current liabilities	403,547	385,954
Merchandise credit and gift card liabilities........	306,160	284,216
Current income taxes payable................	76,606	60,298
Total current liabilities.....................	1,942,681	1,835,136
Long-term operating liabilities	573,122	579,610
Long-term debt	1,500,000	0
Total liabilities	4,015,803	2,414,746
Shareholders' equity:		
Common stock—$0.01 par value..............	3,367	3,350
Additional paid-in capital	1,754,379	1,659,370
Retained earnings	9,553,376	8,595,902
Treasury stock, at cost....................	(8,567,932)	(6,317,335)
Total shareholders' equity.................	2,743,190	3,941,287
Total liabilities and shareholders' equity.........	$6,758,993	$6,356,033

	February 28, 2015
Net sales..	11,881,176
Cost of sales..	7,261,397
Gross profit...	4,619,779
Selling, general and administrative expenses	3,065,486
Operating profit.......................................	1,554,293
Interest expense, net	50,458
Earnings before provision for income taxes.....................	1,503,835
Provision for income taxes....................................	546,361
Net earnings	957,474

Amazon.com, Inc. **P4-6.** **Preparation of the statement of cash flows (indirect method)** Amazon.com, Inc., is the well-known online retailer of consumer products selling a wide range of goods all over the world. Below are the balance sheets for its year ending December 31, 2014. During 2014, Amazon.com reported a net loss of $241 million and depreciation and amortization expense of $4,746 and stock-based compensation expense of $1,497. The company did not sell property, plant and equipment, nor did it pay dividends.

Required:

Prepare a statement of cash flows for the year using the indirect method for the operating section.

| (amounts in millions) | December 31 | |
	2014	2013
ASSETS		
Current assets:		
Cash and cash equivalents	$14,557	$ 8,658
Marketable securities....................................	2,859	3,789
Inventories	8,299	7,411
Accounts receivable, net and other	5,612	4,767
Total current assets	31,327	24,625
Property and equipment, net	16,967	10,949
Goodwill	3,319	2,655
Other assets...	2,892	1,930
Total assets...	$54,505	$40,159

continued

(amounts in millions)	December 31	
	2014	2013
LIABILITIES AND STOCKHOLDERS' EQUITY		
Current liabilities:		
Accounts payable...	$16,459	$15,133
Accrued expenses and other............................	9,807	6,688
Unearned revenue	1,823	1,159
Total current liabilities.....................................	28,089	22,980
Long-term debt	8,265	3,191
Other long-term liabilities................................	7,410	4,242
Stockholders' equity:		
Common stock...	5	5
Treasury stock, at cost.................................	(1,837)	(1,837)
Additional paid-in capital	10,624	9,388
Retained earnings	1,949	2,190
Total stockholders' equity	10,741	9,746
Total liabilities and stockholders' equity....................	$54,505	$40,159

P4-7. **Preparation of the Statement of Cash Flows (indirect method)** **Chipotle Mexican Grill, Inc.**, operates over 1,700 restaurants in North America with "a focused menu of burritos, tacos, burrito bowls (a burrito without the tortilla) and salads, made using fresh ingredients," according to the company's 2014 annual report. Presented below are its balance sheets and income statement for the year ending December 31, 2014. During 2014, Chipotle recognized stock-based compensation expense of 96,440.

Chipotle Mexican Grill, Inc.

Required:

Prepare the statement of cash flows using the indirect method for the operating section.

(amounts in thousands)	2014	2013
Cash and cash equivalents	$ 419,465	$ 323,203
Accounts receivable, net	34,839	24,016
Inventory..	15,332	13,044
Prepaid expenses and other current assets..............	53,763	47,416
Income tax receivable	16,488	3,657
Investments, short-term..............................	338,592	254,971
Total current assets.................................	878,479	666,307
Property and equipment, net	1,106,984	963,238
Long-term investments	496,106	313,863
Other assets..	42,777	43,933
Goodwill	21,939	21,939
Total assets..	$2,546,285	$2,009,280
Liabilities and shareholders' equity		
Current liabilities:		
Accounts payable....................................	$ 69,613	$ 59,022
Accrued payroll and benefits	73,894	67,195
Accrued liabilities	102,203	73,011
Total current liabilities..............................	245,710	199,228
Deferred rent	219,414	192,739
Other long-term operating liabilities....................	68,792	79,025
Total liabilities.....................................	533,916	470,992
Shareholders' equity:		
Common stock $0.01 par value........................	354	352
Additional paid-in capital	1,038,503	921,460
Treasury stock, at cost...............................	(748,759)	(660,421)
Retained earnings	1,722,271	1,276,897
Total shareholders' equity...........................	2,012,369	1,538,288
Total liabilities and shareholders' equity.................	$2,546,285	$2,009,280

	2014
Revenue	$4,108,269
Restaurant operating costs:	
Food, beverage and packaging	1,420,994
Labor	904,407
Occupancy.	230,868
Other operating costs.	441,220
General and administrative expenses	273,897
Depreciation and amortization	110,474
Pre-opening costs	15,609
Total operating expenses	3,397,469
Income from operations	710,800
Interest and other income (expense), net.	3,503
Income before income taxes	714,303
Provision for income taxes.	(268,929)
Net income.	$ 445,374

Kellogg Company **P4-8.** **Preparation of Statement of Cash Flows (indirect method)**   Founded in 1906, **Kellogg Company** manufactures and distributes ready-to-eat cereal and other convenience foods. Its well-known trademarks include Kellogg's Corn Flakes, Rice Krispies, and Fruit Loops. Presented below are its balance sheets for the year ending December 31, 2014. Kellogg reported net income of $633 million, depreciation and amortization expense of $503 million, and other non-cash expenses of $549 million.

Required:

Prepare a statement of cash flows for the year using the indirect method for the operating section.

(amounts in millions)	2014	2013
Cash and cash equivalents	443	273
Accounts receivable, net	1,276	1,424
Inventories	1,279	1,248
Other current assets.	342	322
Total current assets	3,340	3,267
Property, net.	3,769	3,856
Goodwill	4,971	5,051
Other intangibles, net.	2,295	2,367
Other assets.	778	933
Total assets.	15,153	15,474
Current maturities of long-term debt	607	289
Notes payable	828	739
Accounts payable.	1,528	1,432
Other current liabilities	1,401	1,375
Total current liabilities.	4,364	3,835
Long-term debt	5,935	6,330
Other liabilities	2,003	1,702
Common stock, $.25 par value	105	105
Capital in excess of par value	740	688
Retained earnings	6,689	6,749
Treasury stock, at cost.	(3,470)	(2,999)
Accumulated other comprehensive income (loss)	(1,213)	(936)
Total equity.	2,851	3,607
Total liabilities and equity	15,153	15,474

P4-9. **Preparation of the Statement of Cash Flows (indirect method)** Presented below are the balance sheets and income statement for the Newfoundland Corporation.

Additional information:

- On January 1, 2015, Newfoundland sold equipment at a loss of $1,200. The equipment originally cost $39,500.
- During 2015, Newfoundland issued an additional 8,000 shares of common stock.

Required:
Prepare a statement of cash flows for the year using the indirect method for the operating section.

NEWFOUNDLAND CORPORATION Balance Sheets as of December 31		
	2015	**2014**
Assets		
Cash..	$ 87,500	$ 44,000
Accounts receivable (net)......................	65,000	51,000
Inventory......................................	63,800	86,500
Prepaid expenses.............................	4,400	5,400
Current assets..............................	220,700	182,900
Property, plant and equipment (at cost)...........	124,000	115,000
Less accumulated depreciation.................	(27,000)	(9,000)
Property, plant and equipment (net).............	97,000	106,000
Total assets...............................	$317,700	$292,900
Liabilities and Shareholders' Equity		
Accounts payable.............................	$ 25,000	$ 30,000
Wages payable...............................	6,000	15,000
Income taxes payable	3,400	3,800
Current liabilities...........................	34,400	48,800
Notes payable to banks	30,000	60,000
Total liabilities	64,400	108,800
Common stock, $1 par value...................	28,000	20,000
Additional paid-in capital	192,000	140,000
Retained earnings	33,300	24,100
Shareholders' equity.......................	253,300	184,100
Total liabilities and shareholders' equity........	$317,700	$292,900

NEWFOUNDLAND CORPORATION Income Statement for the year ending December 31, 2015	
Sales revenue..	$678,000
Cost of goods sold....................................	(411,000)
Gross profit..	267,000
Depreciation expense...............................	(28,600)
Other operating expenses	(91,000)
Operating income...................................	147,400
Loss on sale of equipment............................	(1,200)
Interest expense....................................	(2,800)
Income before income taxes	143,400
Income tax expense.................................	(43,890)
Net income	99,510

P4-10. **Preparation of the Statement of Cash Flows (indirect method)** Presented below are balance sheets and additional information for the Tyler Corporation for the year ending December 31, 2014.

Additional information:

- All short-term investments were purchased on December 31, 2014 (just before closing of the previous year) and sold during 2015 at cost.
- Equipment costing $28 with accumulated depreciation of $13 was sold during 2015 for $12 cash.
- Dividends of $6 were declared and paid during 2015.

Required:

a. Prepare a statement of cash flows using the indirect method for the operating section.
b. Calculate sales revenue for 2015.
c. Calculate cost of goods sold for 2015.

TYLER CORPORATION Balance Sheets As of December 31		
(all dollar amounts in thousands)	2015	2014
Assets		
Cash.	$ 45	$ 54
Short-term investments	0	95
Accounts receivable.	85	45
Inventory.	90	63
Property, plant and equipment.	339	265
Accumulated depreciation	(111)	(100)
	448	422
Liabilities and shareholders' equity		
Accounts payable.	48	38
Wages payable.	19	12
Income taxes payable	5	3
Long-term debt	196	193
Common stock.	150	150
Retained earnings	30	26
	$448	$422

TYLER CORPORATION Statement of Cash Flows—Operating Section (Direct Method) For the year ending December 31, 2015	
Cash collected from customers	398
Cash paid to suppliers of inventory	(327)
Cash paid for wages	(67)
Cash paid for interest.	(12)
Cash paid for taxes	(3)
Cash flow from operations	(11)

Chapter Five

Opportunity Assessment and Introduction to Forecasting

When you complete this chapter you should be able to:

1. Understand the use of forecasts in strategic decision-making processes.

2. Forecast future operations using selected ratios in spreadsheets.

3. Use forecasting models, break-even analysis and ROI to assess growth opportunities.

4. Perform and interpret basic sensitivity analysis.

INTRODUCTION

In the first section of this textbook we introduced you to financial statement construction and formats. Within these chapters, we discussed industry and business model impacts on financial statements, and we introduced the implications of these analyses. The second section of this book examines the use of financial data in **assessing** operations (financial statement analysis) and **forecasting** operations (financial statement forecasting and strategy assessment). To introduce the latter half of the text, we will introduce the basics of forecasting within the context of an entrepreneur exploring whether or not she has a cool idea or a real business opportunity. To understand if a cool idea is a business opportunity, she needs to be able to estimate the initial investment, how long she needs to operate until profitability, how quickly she will generate positive operating cash flow, and whether she can acquire the needed resources to execute this opportunity. We begin with a description of the business and idea/opportunity and then introduce forecasting as the entrepreneur/CEO undertakes the analysis.

THE BUSINESS: ON THE EDGE SHOES (ONES)

Jennifer had always been interested in fashion, specifically high-fashion, and she always wanted to own her own business. When she got married, shortly after college graduation, she was appalled at the dearth of fashionable wedding shoes. Everything she saw was an afterthought dyed to match the bridesmaids' dresses. For her own wedding, she designed her own shoes, with sewn-on gems (manufactured not mined), sequins, and silver and gold chains bringing life to her designs. Over 400 people attended her wedding, located in a major Texan city, and several of her guests inquired about her shoes.

About three months after returning from her honeymoon, one of her wedding guests called and asked her if she would design wedding shoes for her wedding and if so, what it would cost. Jennifer knew her costs of materials, roughly estimated her time at $30/hour, and calculated the cost of her shoes to be $1,000. She quoted the potential customer a price of $2,500 for her shoes and $1,500 per pair for her bridesmaids' shoes. The potential customer became an actual customer and ordered one pair of shoes for herself and five pair of shoes for her bridesmaids, a $10,000 first order. Jennifer was an entrepreneur!

Now, four years and many hard-learned lessons later, Jennifer reviewed her four years of income statements and balance sheets. (See Exhibits 5.1–5.3.) After two years of struggling, years 3 and 4 were profitable and the operating cash flow was positive. Note that Jennifer's annual operating cash flows were approximated as income before tax + depreciation expense. For example, in year 4, operating cash flow equaled income before tax of $34,000 + depreciation expense of $8,000, for a total of $42,000.[1] She had figured out how to control her inventory levels and her production costs (i.e., minimize waste), and where to effectively advertise (see specifically Exhibit 5.2).

EXHIBIT 5.1	ONES Income Statements: Years 1–4			
ONES Income Statement	**Year 1**	**Year 2**	**Year 3**	**Year 4**
Revenues	$ 660,000	$ 748,000	$ 836,000	$ 880,000
COGS (Basic shoe + add-ons)	(343,200)	(374,000)	(401,280)	(396,000)
Gross profit.	316,800	374,000	434,720	484,000
Operating expenses				
Wages: shoes	160,000	194,480	225,720	220,000
Rent	20,000	20,000	20,000	20,000
Insurance	10,000	10,000	10,000	10,000
Utilities	12,000	12,000	12,000	12,000
Marketing	10,000	10,000	5,000	5,000
Depreciation	8,000	8,000	8,000	8,000
Founder's salaries.	80,000	100,000	120,000	150,000
Total operating expenses	300,000	354,480	400,720	425,000
Operating income.	16,800	19,520	34,000	59,000
Interest expense.	(25,000)	(25,000)	(25,000)	(25,000)
Income before tax	$ (8,200)	$ (5,480)	$ 9,000	$ 34,000

EXHIBIT 5.2	ONES Income Statements in Common-Size Format: Years 1–4			
ONES Income Statement	**Year 1**	**Year 2**	**Year 3**	**Year 4**
Revenues	100%	100.0%	100.0%	100.0%
COGS (Basic shoe + add-ons)	−52	−50.0	−48.0	−45.0
Gross profit.	48	50.0	52.0	55.0
Operating expenses		0.0	0.0	0.0
Wages: shoes	24	26.0	27.0	25.0
Rent	3	2.7	2.4	2.3
Insurance	2	1.3	1.2	1.1
Utilities	2	1.6	1.4	1.4
Marketing	2	1.3	0.6	0.6
Depreciation	1	1.2	1.2	1.2
Founder's salaries.	12	13.4	14.4	17.0
Total operating expenses	45	47.4	47.9	48.3
Operating income.	3	2.6	4.1	6.7
Interest expense.	−4	−3.3	−3.0	−2.8
Income before tax	−1%	−0.7%	1.1%	3.9%

---

[1] A typical surrogate for operating cash flow is EBITDA, Earnings Before Interest, Taxes, Depreciation and Amortization. Jennifer, because interest expense was a required annual payment, subtracted interest expense to estimate her operating cash flow and better understand cash generated through operations to implement her strategic plans based on her current capital structure (combination of debt and equity financing).

EXHIBIT 5.3	ONES Balance Sheet at End of Year: Years 1–4			
ONES Balance Sheet	Year 1	Year 2	Year 3	Year 4
Cash.	$ 40,000	$ 39,920	$ 54,192	$ 96,720
Inventory.	34,800	37,400	40,128	39,600
Equipment	80,000	80,000	80,000	80,000
Accumulated depreciation	(8,000)	(16,000)	(24,000)	(32,000)
Total assets.	146,800	141,320	150,320	184,320
Accounts payable.	10,000	10,000	10,000	10,000
Long-term notes payable.	100,000	100,000	100,000	100,000
Total liabilities.				
Owners' investment	45,000	45,000	45,000	45,000
Retained earnings	(8,200)	(13,680)	(4,680)	29,320
Total liabilities and owners' equity . .	$146,800	$141,320	$150,320	$184,320

Jennifer had created two custom lines for which she was known, Contemporary and Traditional. The Contemporary line included any design she could imagine once she interviewed and understood the bride and her wedding plans. She used new-age materials and matched the gems and precious metals to the tastes and budget of the bride. She loved this market segment because there were no rules, and many times her shoes would be featured in national bride magazines and twice had been highlighted in *Marie Claire*.

The Traditional line was begun because of several customer requests and had proven to be profitable, if not as creatively rewarding. Her basic design elements were taken from estate jewelry, and the shoes always had an antique quality about them. Frequently an old movie would be her designing "center" for one of these projects. Recently, the classic film *Top Hat* with Fred Astaire and Ginger Rogers was her source of inspiration, and these shoes were featured in the fashion section of the *New York Times Sunday Magazine*.

As Jennifer reflected on her business, she could see that the major constraint to growth was her core strategy—not a good position in which to find oneself. She was a custom designer and only had so much time in the day. Furthermore, there was a limit to this market segment. In reality, how many women would pay $3,000 for a pair of custom wedding shoes (her current price point)? This realization led her to consider exploring the business opportunity contained in the idea she had had for some time: mass customization. That is, could she design three to five versions of unique shoes, sell them for $800/pair retail, and make a profit? We now join Jennifer as she proceeds through a very rough analysis including forecasting the basics to understand if it is worth pursuing this business segment in depth.

IDEA OR OPPORTUNITY—ASSESSMENT STEPS (AS)

This section of the chapter is based on the following six assessment steps to initially analyze a possible business opportunity. A detailed discussion of each step follows.

AS1. Scoping the market including understanding the customer pain and customer value proposition, market size, growth rate and competitors

AS2. Assessing fit for company and for owner

AS3. Running the numbers including forecasts and initial investment calculations

AS4. Assessing the opportunity using ratios and scenario planning

AS5. Identifying financing needs and sources

AS6. Initial decision: Is it an idea or a business opportunity?

AS1. SCOPING THE MARKET

Weddings, a clothing industry staple, were expected to increase over the next three to five years as the Millennium generation was now entering their 30s and beginning to get married. Furthermore, people were once again spending money on weddings as lavish celebrations. Bridal publications consistently supported the soundness of the industry, especially in the largest U.S. cities (e.g., New York City, Los Angeles, Chicago, Houston, Miami, etc.).

Jennifer had evidence that some upscale department stores were considering adding or increasing their bridal offerings, including shoes and accessories. As an example, one jewelry designer she knew was developing bridal lines to sell in selected Macy's stores. But the most exciting piece of information came from a meeting she had with one of the major buyers for a competitor of Macy's. This buyer had followed Jennifer's designs over the last three years and had pitched to her supervisors the possibility of carrying high-end bridal shoes (for brides only to begin) in 10 of the buyer's stores in major cities, one located in the Texas city in which Jennifer worked and designed. The buyer identified the customer pain point as the desire to have a unique wedding gown and accessories but attainment of this desire was currently beyond reach for all but the wealthiest brides to be. The customer value proposition was selective and limited shoe designs by a noted designer at one-third the price of custom bridal shoes.

The numbers for this market segment were staggering. If the chain decided to launch, it would purchase 1,000 pairs of shoes in the first order. Jennifer now sold 400 pair of shoes per year (80 for brides and 320 for bridesmaids). If the retailer decided to expand to more stores, orders could reach 5,000 pairs per year as early as the end of year 2. Better yet, Jennifer was invited to the company's New York headquarters to present her company and explore with company representatives the possibility of designing and supplying a uniquely designed bride's shoe but producible in large lots.

The meeting went well. Jennifer presented her company, including information on her supply chain and its capacity, her costs per pair of shoes, and her margins and the financial position of her operations. Meanwhile, the retailer had already done extensive research in this market and had some price points and order qualities it wanted to explore.

The company's market research indicated that its customers would be willing to spend between $1,000 and $1,200 per pair of shoes, and in the 10 pilot cities (one store in each city), sales were expected to be 100 units per city in the first year the shoes would be offered. After the initial offering, assuming customer satisfaction, they forecasted anywhere from 200 to 500 pairs of shoes per year per city. (Here Jennifer had made a note that they were not even considering bridesmaid shoes—which would be an additional 800 to 2,000 pairs of shoes per year per location.) The major customer benefits the store provided were a reputation of quality; one-stop shopping for dresses, shoes, and jewelry; and a promised delivery of the dress, shoes, and other accessories within one month from the order point. Although Jennifer was a well-recognized designer, she was a small shop, and because of her business size, the retailer wanted all shoes in inventory before its stores began selling the product. The retailer would require delivery of 1,000 pairs of shoes almost immediately if the deal went forward. The retailer wanted four styles of shoes: two Contemporary styles and two Traditional styles. The final condition was the difficult one for Jennifer to hear: The store would pay only $500 per pair delivered. This was far under the current cost of producing her shoes, which ranged from $1,200 to $2,500. She was not sure she could meet the target price and make a profit!

The retailer and Jennifer agreed on the next steps in exploring this opportunity. Jennifer was to return in three weeks with designs, the supply chain confirmed, and proof that she could deliver 1,000 pairs of shoes two months after the order and eventually 5,000 pairs of shoes in two orders of 2,500 per year. Finally, her company had to be healthy within the outlined financial parameters, and she hoped she could sensibly forecast profitable operations and a solid balance sheet for this project.

The retailer would hone its market research study more thoroughly to examine the market size, likely demand, and price points for brides' and bridesmaids' shoes (at Jennifer's request). As noted, the Macy's-like possibility would substantially increase Jennifer's ONES business and move it in a different strategic direction from custom-designed wedding shoes to high-end, limited-production shoes with four standard styles available.

Jennifer knew she had to gather information through calls or visits and make some quick decisions. However, before she gathered more information and ran numbers, she reflected on whether or not she really wanted to shift the focus of her business.

AS2. FIT FOR BUSINESS AND OWNER

For the business, strategic considerations include answering the questions: Does she want to drastically change her strategy from a high-margin, low-volume product to a relatively low-margin, high-volume product? If the market segments are not as different as she thinks—that is, if there is a significant customer overlap in these market segments—will she cannibalize her current business? Can she deal with a major customer that has more power in the relationship?

For the owner, skill sets, lifestyle and personal motivations need to be examined. Can she run a company with two completely different market strategies? Does she have the skills to run a rapidly growing company and the personal risk capacity to sleep at night as she extends herself out of her comfort zone? She now has to complete a series of assessment steps, most of which are related to the numbers she was about to calculate. Could she forecast her future well enough to risk her reputation as well as her business? These were tough issues with which to grapple.

From a more personal perspective, Jennifer had begun this company because of a love for design and an opportunity she correctly recognized. Will she be able to continue to devote time to designs for individual clients or will she be occupied by the large retailer and similar customers when this new market is successfully launched? Is she satisfied with her current lifestyle and the size of the company? Does she have the energy and drive to go for a hyper-growth strategy?

As Jennifer thought about these questions, she realized she enjoyed the notion of becoming the entrepreneurial leader of a rapidly growing company. She wanted to create a sustainable business that encompassed much more than just being a shoe designer. After discussing this apparent opportunity with her advisory board and family, Jennifer thought it would be an interesting, fun and life-altering challenge, if a bit chaotic. She would continue exploring this possible opportunity.

AS3. RUNNING THE NUMBERS

Jennifer developed four new designs based on preliminary sketches she had been working on for months (deadlines often enable amazing productivity). She was pleased with the designs and knew they would be unique as well as easier to produce.

She called and made an appointment with her current finished shoes inventory supplier and also identified possible new suppliers if her meeting did not go well. She hoped to negotiate a satisfactory price and possible credit terms on this major contract. If not, she would schedule a meeting with her back-up manufacturer.

With sketches in hand, she visited first with her current supplier. After describing the opportunity, he quickly estimated production costs per unit based on a minimum order of 300 pairs per model and the per-unit cost was $350 per pair. Four shoe styles meant 1,200 pairs would be produced. The extra shoes (1,200 − 1,000 = 200) would be shipped to ONES for Jennifer to store and use these to replaced damaged shoes. Furthermore, the manufacturer would extend 15-day credit terms—n/15. If things went well for the first 12 months, the supplier would extend her credit terms to n/30.

Next, Jennifer connected with her local shipper, DLM Shipping. This was a small regional trucking firm; she had known the CEO, Eric, all her life and trusted him. She treated Eric to coffee and described the job. He was excited for her and said he would pick up the shoes from her manufacturer and deliver them to each of the 10 stores as well as deliver the excess models to her inventory storage space as finished goods inventory. The shoes would be insured by Eric from the moment the manufacturer loaded them on the truck to the time the stores offloaded them at their shipping docks. Eric felt that he could deliver between 1,000 and 1,500 pair of shoes for approximately $30,000. Eric said his estimates were based on 6% of estimated revenues. Jennifer and Eric shook on the deal, and Jennifer was close to beginning her forecasts.

Because Jennifer did not manufacture her shoes, she did not expect a large initial investment. The cost of significant web redesign to feature this new market segment and an increase in inventory storage space to carry excess shoes in case sales went well were about the only investments that she could foresee. She planned to lease the storage space.

However, her operations had to change immediately. She would need a person to be the product manager, and that person would need office space and administrative assistance. Gulp. How would she pay for her inventory as well as salaries until the new client paid? She had completed her critical visits to her supplier and a freight company, and now it was time to list her critical growth and forecast assumptions (Exhibit 5.4).

EXHIBIT 5.4	Base Case Assumptions

Selling price per unit: $500
Manufacturing costs per unit (inventory costs and costs of goods sold): $350 per pair
Shipping costs: $30,000 for year 1 and $70,000 ($30,000 + (4 × $10,000)) − $130,000 ($30,000 + (10 × $10,000)) for year 2
Product manager: $50,000 salary + $15,000 benefits annually
Administrative assistant—part time: $20,000 annually (1/2 time, no benefits)
Additional rent expense—$1,200 annually
Web redesign: one-time investment of $5,000

Base Case Scenario: Exhibit 5.5 represents the assumptions portion of the Excel spreadsheet for Jennifer's Base Case Scenario. Let's go through each line and match the entry to Jennifer's assumptions.

Now she thought she was ready to forecast.

EXHIBIT 5.5	Base Case Scenario Assumption Set in Excel						
ONES-Base Case Assumptions	**Q1**	**Q2**	**Q3**	**Q4**	**Year 1**	**Year 2**
Orders/quarter	0	1,000	0	0	1,000	2,000
$/order	$500.00	$500.00	$500.00	$500.00	$500.00	$500.00
COGS (% of revenue)	70%	70%	70%	70%	70%	70%
Shipping costs	6%	6%	6%	6%	6%	7%
Incremental product manager expense . . .	$16,250	$16,250	$16,250	$16,250	$65,000	$65,000
Incremental operating expenses	$ 5,300	$ 5,300	$ 5,300	$ 5,300	$21,200	$21,200

Orders per quarter: Jennifer thought that orders in year 2 would be distributed in at least two and most likely three quarters. However, she understood that the retailer was concerned about her ability to ramp up her supply chain and wanted to minimize stock-out possibilities. Furthermore, with her supply chain more robust, she could meet the possible demand of 5,000 pairs rather than the 2,000 pairs in the Base Case Scenario if a "best-case" scenario occurred.

$/Order: This amount was established by the retail store chain and was non-negotiable. Jennifer hoped she could renegotiate this upward for year 2. After all, this was a high-end department store charging premium prices, and she was an in-demand wedding shoe designer.

COGS (% of Revenue): The price of $350/pair had been negotiated with her suppliers. For ease of planning and because most companies talked about "gross margin," she converted this cost into a percentage of revenue (COGS/Revenue = $350/$500 = 70%). She also noted that this left her an expected gross margin of 30% ((Gross Margin = (Revenue − COGS)/Revenue)). Compared to her usual gross margins of 55%, 30% was quite small. She planned to make up in volume what she lost in gross margin. She thought (actually, hoped) that the $350 cost could be negotiated down to $325/pair (perhaps even less) in year 2 if all things went as planned.

Shipping Costs (% of Revenue): Eric had quoted her a dollar amount that increased in 500-pair increments as her shipping volume increased. She realized that this was a fixed amount, but as with COGS, converted it into a percentage of revenue for predictive purposes. Six percent in year 1 (6%) and 7% in year 2 were approximations, but the estimates were close enough. In a best-case scenario, the year 1 percentage would be close to 6%, but the year 2 percentage could be as low as 3% to 4%.

Incremental Product Manager Expense: She had discussed with a human resources firm the salary levels and benefits range necessary to attract the type of individual needed. The estimated salary and benefits of $65,000 was the average of that range and was allocated to each quarter ($65,000/4).

Incremental Operating Expenses: The amount of $5,300/quarter included the additional part-time administrative person plus the additional rent to house finished shoes inventory allocated to each quarter ((salary + rent)/4 = ($20,000+$1,200)/4 = $5,300). These amounts and this total were fixed expenses and would not vary with the year 1 sales levels. Therefore, she did not convert this additional expense into a percentage of revenues but kept it at a fixed amount because it could not vary with sales activity. Expenses like rent and salaries are termed **fixed costs** (or expenses) because they are fixed for a period of time. Contrast this type of cost with COGS and shipping, which do vary with sales activities and because of this variation are termed **variable costs** (or expenses). One last term we need to introduce is the term **contribution margin**, which is defined as (Sales – Variable Costs)/Sales in percentage terms. This calculation is labeled *contribution margin* because it is the amount of every sales dollar left after covering the expenses to pay fixed costs and yield a profit. This term and formula will be discussed further in our example when Jennifer evaluates this opportunity using a calculation known as break-even analysis.

We have now explored Jennifer's development of her assumption set for her Base Case Scenario. Exhibit 5.6 represents the forecasts for year 1 by quarter and years 1 and 2 by year. Let's examine what these forecasted numbers tell Jennifer about her opportunity.

Exploring the forecasted income statements shown in Exhibit 5.6, Jennifer notes the following important observations:

1. There is a projected income of $33,800 in year 1, and better than quadruple that amount in year 2, $153,800—that is a good thing!
2. Things look pretty bleak in quarters Q1, Q2, and Q4, but great in Q3, a result of only one order for this opportunity. It looked like an all-or-nothing scenario.

When she examined the forecasted operating cash flows, she gulped big time. Although both years 1 and 2 showed positive operating cash flows (which would make any entrepreneur happy), Q1 and Q2 were shocking. She had to begin ramping up immediately to meet her supply obligations, she had a one-time web redesign expense of $5,000 and the timing of these cash outflows were such that she went $423,100 in the hole—that is, a big, fat, red, negative, in-the-hole amount of ($423,100)—before she went back to positive. Could this be correct? She went back to write down and reexamine her cash flow assumptions:

Pay to Supplier: Her supplier for the first time gave her 15 days to pay for finished shoes. To ensure she had the shoes ready for the retailer, she absolutely needed to order the shoes in Q1, and with only 15 days of credit, she would have to pay for them at the end of Q1. The outflow of ($350,000) is correct.

Pay to Freight Company: Eric had given her a credit period, but because the shoes had to be shipped in early to mid-Q2, she would need to pay his bill of $30,000 in Q2. Yep, the ($30,000) outflow in Q2 was spot on.

Incremental Operating Expenses: In Q1, she had to ramp up and immediately hire her employees and have the space to store the additional shoes that were not drop shipped directly to the customer. These payments essentially happened each month, and thus cash outflows of ($5,300) per quarter matched the activity. Again, her assumption was

EXHIBIT 5.6	Base Case Scenario Forecasts: Incremental Income Statements and Operating Cash Flows					

ONES-Base Case Assumptions	Q1	Q2	Q3	Q4	Year 1	Year 2
Orders/quarter	0	1,000	0	0	1,000	2,000
$/order	$500.00	$500.00	$500.00	$500.00	$500.00	$500.00
COGS (% of revenue).	70%	70%	70%	70%	70%	70%
Shipping costs	6%	6%	6%	6%	6%	7%
Incremental product manager expense . . .	$16,250	$16,250	$16,250	$16,250	$65,000	$65,000
Incremental operating expenses	$ 5,300	$ 5,300	$ 5,300	$ 5,300	$21,200	$21,200

Income Statement	Q1	Q2	Q3	Q4	Year 1	Year 2
Revenue	$ —	$ 500,000	$ —	$ —	$ 500,000	$1,000,000
COGS.	$ —	$(350,000)	$ —	$ —	$(350,000)	$ (700,000)
Shipping costs		$ (30,000)			$ (30,000)	$ (60,000)
Gross profit.	$ —	$ 120,000	$ —	$ —	$ 120,000	$ 240,000
Wage expense	$(16,250)	$ (16,250)	$(16,250)	$(16,250)	$ (65,000)	$ (65,000)
Other operating expenses	$ (5,300)	$ (5,300)	$ (5,300)	$ (5,300)	$ (21,200)	$ (21,200)
Operating profit	$(21,550)	$ 98,450	$(21,550)	$(21,550)	$ 33,800	$ 153,800

Operating Cash Flow	Q1	Q2	Q3	Q4	Year 1	Year 2
Collect from customer			$500,000		$ 500,000	$1,000,000
Pay to supplier	$(350,000)				$(350,000)	$ (700,000)
Pay to freight company		$ (30,000)			$ (30,000)	$ (60,000)
Pay to PM.	$ (16,250)	$ (16,250)	$ (16,250)	$(16,250)	$ (65,000)	$ (65,000)
Additional operating expenses.	$ (5,300)	$ (5,300)	$ (5,300)	$ (5,300)	$ (21,200)	$ (21,200)
Net operating cash flow	$(371,550)	$ (51,550)	$478,450	$(21,550)	$ 33,800	$ 153,800
One-time investments			$ (5,000)			
Incremental cash flow	$(371,550)	$ (51,550)	$473,450	$(21,550)	$ 33,800	$ 153,800
Cumulative cash flow	$(371,550)	$(423,100)	$ 50,350	$ 28,800	$ 28,800	$ 153,800

correct—this is depressing. Maybe the assumption about when the cash was to be received from the customer was incorrect.

Customer Collections: The $500,000 amount was reassuring, but did she really have to wait until Q3 to receive it? She contracted to drop ship the shoes to the stores in Q2, but toward the end of the quarter. She assumed the department stores would each receive 100 pair of shoes in the third month of Q2. The stores then would begin sales to brides in Q3. Jennifer had called the department store buyer and asked when she would be paid. The store said its normal credit terms were n/60. That meant that even though the store received the final product in Q2 and even if it did not sell a single pair of shoes, it owed $500,000 to Jennifer, and yet would not pay her until two months after receiving the shoes. In fact, the retailer would receive cash from its customers before it paid Jennifer. Jennifer thought this policy unfair, but she was a small supplier and had little power or influence to negotiate better collection terms. Q3 collection was a reasonable if dissatisfying assumption. In fact, Jennifer had called a number of other small suppliers who had a history with this retailer and found that the company sometimes stretched the pay period to 90+ days.

In sum, as we have seen in the first four chapters of this text, net income and operating cash flow seldom are equal. For Jennifer, although they are almost equal when viewed annually and in fact are projected to be equal in year 2, for year 1, quarter over quarter, they are quite different. That is because product supply and payment for production must happen significantly before the sale happens, and then there is a lag between the customer's receipt of the product and the payment to Jennifer.

The conclusion: Jennifer needs at least $423,100 for six months (Q1 and Q2) to be able to launch this opportunity, probably more to give her a cash safety cushion. She asked two questions: Is the opportunity worth it? Can she get the money?

AS4. ASSESSING THE NUMBERS USING RATIOS AND SCENARIO PLANNING

Is the Opportunity Worth It?

Jennifer should consider multiple factors in her decision process: strategic fit, long-run implications for her entire business, and risk versus profitability. We will use three calculations to inform Jennifer's decision making in assessing risk versus profitability: return on investment, break-even analysis, and payback period. Remember, this is just a first-cut, big-picture assessment. If Jennifer thinks the opportunity is a "go," she will then delve into a more thorough analysis—techniques and tools covered later in this text and in more advanced courses. For example, she would do monthly forecasts for the first year and most likely forecast three to five years out. Also, she needs to include interest in her profit and cash flow calculations if she borrows the needed money.

Ratios

Return on investment (ROI) is basically: Income from an opportunity/Investment to launch an opportunity or **ROI = Income/Investments**. The initial amount of **investment** typically comprises the one-time costs and long-term asset investments required to execute the opportunity. In this opportunity, the investment is limited to two costs: carrying inventory and the web redesign. The web redesign will cost $5,000. The inventory-carrying costs will equal the number of pairs between the minimum run size for the manufacturer (1,200) and the order from the department store (1,000) multiplied by the cost of $350/pair: 200 × $350 = $70,000. Jennifer decided to include the entire investment in inventory because if the shoes didn't sell in the department stores, she could not redesign the shoes into custom models—that is, they would be useless to her. The total investment for this opportunity equals $70,000 + $5,000 = $75,000.

Return, a measure of profit, is the incremental increase (or decrease) in profit generated by the specific opportunity.

For Jennifer, the forecasts show profit of $33,800 in year 1 and $143,000 in year 2, and we assume for every year after. ROI = $33,800/$75,000 in year 1 = 45%; and $153,800/$75,000 = 205% in year 2. These are large numbers, and even with an untrained eye the rewards from this opportunity are clearly quite good.

Break-even Analysis

Break-even analysis calculates the level of sales required to show no profit or loss and helps assess the risk of a venture. If break-even happens at a low level of sales, the venture is considered less risky; and at a high level of sales, more risky. In Jennifer's case, break-even at less than the first customer order would demonstrate very little financial risk in year 1. If break-even occurs at greater than the 1,000 pairs ordered, then financial risk would be considered high. Of course, there is reputational risk of business discontinuance if the retailer store is dissatisfied, whether or not break-even sales are achieved.

The break-even formula is **Fixed Expenses/Contribution Margin**. As previously noted, *fixed expenses* are those expenses unaffected by changes in sales volume and were discussed earlier in this chapter when developing the Base Case Scenario assumption set (Exhibit 5.4). For ONES, these were the additional compensation for the product manager and part-time administrative assistant plus the increased rent to store inventory: $65,000 + $20,000 + $1,200 = $86,200. A good way to interpret this number is that every year, $86,200 in fixed expenses must be paid before the company can make a profit.

As previously defined, the *contribution margin* equals (Sales Price − Variable Expenses)/Sales Price. Out of every sale, a portion of the price has to cover the variable expenses necessary to generate the sale. The remainder, the contribution, goes to cover the fixed expenses, and once those are covered, the company yields a profit. The contribution for Jennifer's opportunity is $500 - $380 (cost + shipping) = $120. The contribution margin is $120/$500 = 24%. In other words, 24 cents out of every sales dollar contributes to covering fixed costs and making a profit.

Break-even sales for Jennifer equal: $86,200/0.24 = $359,167, or roughly $360,000, in year 1, far below the minimum sales level stated in the contract of $500,000! Break-even is not an issue in year 1, as the venture will be profitable immediately. Again, financially this appears to be a low-risk opportunity.

Payback Period

Payback period is the length of time it takes a venture to return its initial investment. Sometimes this is referred to as "covering" one's initial investment. Only after Jennifer's investment is returned can she truly make a profit on the deal. This calculation also helps assess risk: the longer the payback period, the riskier the opportunity. Remember that in this case Jennifer's initial investment was simple to calculate: $70,000 in inventory plus $5,000 for the web redesign, a total of $75,000. In what period of time will this investment be returned or covered? **Payback = Original Investment/Profit per period.**

<u>Original Investment</u>   As calculated earlier, the original investment is forecasted to be $75,000. Other items that could possibly occur and would be considered in this calculation are equipment to be purchased, such as computers and office equipment for the product manager, one-time branding efforts, and investment in shoe molds if required by the manufacturer.

<u>Profit per Period</u>   The period selected could be monthly, quarterly, or yearly. Because Jennifer's opportunity has only one order point in year 1 and such uneven profits per quarter, we will use the year 1 forecasted profit of $33,800.

Payback

The Payback Period calculation for Jennifer is Original Investment/Annual Profit = $75,000/$33,800 = 2.2 years. Although this may seem short, to Jennifer, 2.2 years is a bit disconcerting because this opportunity is essentially a one-year contract with a potential for much more. However, if the contract is not renewed for year 2, Jennifer not only earns *no* return, she loses money. Let's take a look at the following calculations:

Forecasted profit year 1	$33,800
Inventory write-off	($70,000)
Wasted web redesign.	($ 5,000)
Projected loss if only year 1	($41,200)

This is the first calculation signaling possible problems and caused Jennifer to pause. She did not make that much money now—is it worth the risk of a loss of $41,200 to pursue this opportunity? The next section of this chapter focuses on all the factors Jennifer needs to weigh before making her decision and exploring answers to the first question posed earlier: Where would she get the money? Jennifer thought she should go for it but wanted to make one more set of calculations to get a better sense of the upside.[2]

Scenario Planning

In the Base Case Scenario, Jennifer assumed the retailer's initial proposal for price and units and had firm numbers from her manufacturer and shipping agent. She felt she was probably on the low side with her estimate of the product manager's compensation

---

[2] Note that because forecasted profit increases in year 2 Jennifer would actually achieve payback in year 2 but only IF she makes it to year 2!

expense as well as that for the office manager. She also realized she didn't consider the additional office furniture and computers they might need, although it was entirely reasonable to assume they could get by on her current computer system and office arrangement. She felt in Scenario 2, she should change the assumption about price, as she thought she could push the $500 to $525 in year 1. She also thought in year 2, she could get the retailer to agree to introduce matching bridesmaids' shoes. She was fairly certain bridesmaids' shoes would sell for 80% of the brides' shoes and cost about 70% of the manufacturing cost quoted to her for the brides' designs. Based on her experiences, four pairs of bridesmaids' shoes would sell for every pair of brides' shoes sold. Finally, she spoke with Eric, who told her that shipping costs would decrease to 4% and possibly 3% of revenues. Her Scenario 2 assumption set is shown in Exhibit 5.7, and the assumption set and income statement forecasts are shown in Exhibit 5.8.

EXHIBIT 5.7	Scenario 2 Assumption Set

Selling price: Brides' shoes $525
  Bridesmaids' shoes $405
Manufacturing costs per unit (Inventory costs and Costs of Goods Sold):
  Brides' shoes . . . . $350 per pair
  Bridesmaids' shoes . . . . . $245 per pair
Shipping costs: $31,500 (6% of revenue, for ease of forecasting) for year 1; $171,600 (4% of revenue of $4.29M) for year 2
Product manager: $60,000 salary + $20,000 benefits annually
Administrative assistant—part time: $30,000 annually (2/3 time, no benefits)
Additional rent expense: $1,200 annually
Web redesign: one-time investment of $5,000
Additional computer equipment: $10,000
Additional office furniture: $6,000

EXHIBIT 5.8	Scenario 1 Assumption Set and Income Statement Forecasts

ONES-Scenario 1 Assumption Set

Assumptions	Q1	Q2	Q3	Q4	Year 1	Year 2
Orders/quarter: Bride	0	1,000	0	0	1,000	2,000
Orders/quarter: Bridesmaid						8,000
$/order: Bride	$525	$525	$525	$525	$525	$525
$/order: Bridesmaid	$405	$405	$405	$405	$405	$405
COGS (% of revenue): Bride	$350	$350	$350	$350	$350	$350
COGS (% of revenue): Bridesmaid.	$245	$245	$245	$245	$245	$245
Shipping expenses.	6%	6%	6%	6%	6%	4%
Incremental supervisory expense.	$20,000	$20,000	$20,000	$20,000	$80,000	$80,000
Incremental operating expenses	$ 7,800	$ 7,800	$ 7,800	$ 7,800	$31,200	$31,200
Additional investments.						
Web redesign (expense).			$ 5,000			
Office furniture	$10,000					
Computer equipment	$ 6,000					

Income Statement	Q1	Q2	Q3	Q4	Year 1	Year 2
Revenue	$ —	$ 525,000	$ —	$ —	$ 525,000	$ 4,290,000
COGS.	$ —	$(350,000)	$ —	$ —	$(350,000)	$(2,660,000)
Shipping costs	$ —	$ (31,500)	$ —	$ —	$ (31,500)	$ (171,600)
Gross profit.		$ 175,000	$ —	$ —	$ 175,000	$ 1,630,000
Wage expense	$(20,000)	$ (20,000)	$(20,000)	$(20,000)	$ (80,000)	$ (80,000)
Web design expense		$ (5,000)				
Additional depreciation expense	$ (800)	$ (800)	$ (800)	$ (800)	$ (3,200)	$ (3,200)
Other operating expenses	$ (7,800)	$ (7,800)	$ (7,800)	$ (7,800)	$ (31,200)	$ (31,200)
Operating profit	$(28,600)	$ 141,400	$(28,600)	$(28,600)	$ 60,600	$ 1,515,600

Jennifer was buoyed by this scenario's results. In year 1, if she could negotiate selling price up, that additional $25,000 in revenue would add substantially to her operating profit for this opportunity, as projected operating income rises from $33,800 to $60,000. The results of year 2 if bridesmaids' shoes are added was near breath-taking: an increase from $143,800 to $1,515,600—an upside that made the potential risks seem more reasonable to assume. She wanted to calculate the cash flow and the ratios for Scenario 2 as she had calculated for the Base Case Assumption Set before she made her decision to discard or continue with her decision process.

THE RATIOS FOR SCENARIO 2

Exhibit 5.9 shows the three ratios previously introduced to evaluate the Base Case Scenario—ROI, break-even analysis, and payback period—for years 1 and 2. Jennifer immediately noticed a significantly higher return for Scenario 2 in year 1 (67%) compared to the Base Case calculation (45%), even with the additional amount invested for office furniture and computer systems. However, the "wow" factor was contained in the year 2 ROI, which equaled 1,665%. She understood this was before any other expenses associated with this opportunity, such as interest expense and tax considerations, but this was still a phenomenal number.

EXHIBIT 5.9	ONES Alternative Scenario 2 Ratios: ROI, Break-Even, and Payback Period	
Return on investment		
Investment	$ 91,000	$ 91,000
Operating income.	$ 60,600	$ 1,515,600
Return on investment.	67%	1665%
Break-even		
Contribution margin		
Selling price	$ 525.00	$ 429.00
Variable cost.	$ 350.00	$ 266.00
Average contribution margin	33%	38%
Fixed costs		
Product manager	80,000	80,000
Operational expense	$ 31,200	$ 31,200
Total fixed costs	$111,200.00	$111,200.00
Break-even sale $.	$333,600.00	$292,667.48
Payback period		
Investment	$ 91,000	
Operating profit	$ 60,600	
Payback period	1.83 years	

Looking at break-even sales in year 1, it was about the same under both scenarios ($359,167 v. $333,600) and even dropped a bit in year 2 because of the improved contribution margin on the bridesmaids' shoes. Note that the year 2 break-even sales calculation was a little less straightforward than in year 1 because of the existence of two products. A weighted-average contribution margin was calculated by weighting the individual product contribution margins by the expected sales amounts. In this scenario, sales were forecasted at four bridesmaids' pairs for every one bride's pair—80% of units sold would be bridesmaids' shoes at a 39.5% contribution margin, and 20% of units sold would be brides' shoes at a 33.3% contribution margin. The weighted-average calculation was 38%, which is the number she used in the break-even formula denominator. She knew this was not an exact margin but reasoned it was close enough to give her a good idea of the sales needed to break even.

Payback period was nearly the same at 1.83 year versus slightly over two years, and the concern here is the possibility of a "one-and-done" order. Her loss would be greater if the retailer cancelled after year 1 because then she would also have invested in the furniture and the computer systems in the total amount of $16,000. Her loss would be the Base Case estimate of $41,200 + $30,000 additional compensation expense + $16,000 for furniture and computers, which equaled $87,200, certainly significant in her current situation but small compared to the year 2 projections contained in Scenario 2.

In summary, Jennifer knew she should probably do more scenarios (note to students: you will have a chance to do these in the end-of-chapter problems), but she thought she had enough data to answer YES to question 2: "Is the opportunity worth it?" Now she had to figure out how to answer question 1: "Where would she get the money?"

AS5. IDENTIFYING FINANCING NEEDS AND SOURCES

The numbers in Exhibit 5.10 indicate that Jennifer will need at least $453,100 to cover her negative cumulative cash flow through Q2 as compared with her Base Case forecasted need of $421,100 (Exhibit 5.6).

She also noted that she ended Q4 with a projected cash balance of only $11,300. This seemed way too small with the huge prospects for year 2. She called a number of other suppliers and small businesses and determined she should have a cash balance of approximately $75,000 heading into year 2. Her total cash needed could be anywhere from $421,100 if the Base Case comes true to approximately $520,000 ($453,100 + $64,000) if Scenario 2 becomes reality. Where would she get that much money?

EXHIBIT 5.10	ONES Alternative Scenario 2: Forecasted Cash Flows						
Operating Cash Flow	Q1	Q2	Q3	Q4	Year 1	Year 2
Collect from customer			$525,000		$ 525,000	$ 4,290,000
Pay to supplier	$ —	$(350,000)			$(350,000)	$(2,660,000)
Pay to freight company		$ (31,500)			$ (31,500)	$ (171,600)
Pay to PM	$(20,000)	$ (20,000)	$ (20,000)	$(20,000)	$ (80,000)	$ —
Additional operating expenses	$ (7,800)	$ (7,800)	$ (7,800)	$ (7,800)	$ (31,200)	$ (31,200)
Net operating cash flow	$(27,800)	$(409,300)	$497,200	$(27,800)	$ 32,300	$ 1,427,200
One-time investments	$(16,000)		$ (5,000)		$ (21,000)	
Incremental cash flow	$(43,800)	$(409,300)	$492,200	$(27,800)	$ 11,300	$ 1,427,200
Cumulative cash flow	$(43,800)	$(453,100)	$ 39,100	$ 11,300	$ 11,300	$ 1,427,200

Like most entrepreneurs, Jennifer had invested a lot of her own money and had relatives invest a substantial amount of money to get her going. Her business was profitable and cash flow positive, and she wanted to begin to pay back her relatives. She was pretty sure she could not ask them again for funds. The events described next actually took several calls and meetings as well as serious negotiations. Presented are just summaries of the outcomes.

Initially Jennifer explored sources of funds without interest expense attached to the funds. She first called her supplier and discussed the possibility of his extending her credit in year 1 rather than waiting until year 2. He said if she had a purchase order from the retailer, he would give her 60 days of credit on $150,000 of her purchases. This $150,000 would then be due most likely in the beginning of Q3.

Next she spoke with the retailer's buyer and requested three actions: (1) a price increase to $525 per pair, (2) a purchase order for 1,000 pairs of shoes, and (3) payment in Q2 when the shoes are delivered. The buyer agreed to the higher price, much to her relief, and said the retailer would pay her $200,000 upon delivery of the shoes and the remaining $325,000 in 60 days. The retailer would also give her a purchase order containing all of these details.

Jennifer was ecstatic. She had already found $350,000 of the $520,000 she was planning to raise if she executed on this opportunity. Best of all, these were interest-free sources of capital. Her supplier was not going to charge her interest for the 60-day credit period; the retailer did not discount the price of the shoes because it was paying for the product earlier than they had initially discussed. She now had to find the remaining

$170,000. Because she needed the funds for at most three months (the end of Q3), she was optimistic about her possibilities to obtain a line of credit from a local bank. Based on the purchase order, initial talks confirmed that a local bank would fund 50% of her $325,000 receivable, holding it as security against the line of credit. The **interest rate** would be 8% annually based on the amount outstanding at the end of each day.

Reviewing her sources:

1. Supplier credit: $150,000
2. Early payment by major client: $200,000
3. Line of credit: $162,500
       Total: $512,500

She was near the $520,000 forecasted, and if she watched her cash carefully, she thought she could make it with this combination of funding sources.

AS6. INITIAL DECISION: IS IT AN IDEA OR OPPORTUNITY?

After assessing the market and fit for the business and owner, basic forecasting techniques, ratios and scenario planning were introduced to make an initial analysis of the viability of a business opportunity. Jennifer had even identified the amount of funds needed as well as likely sources for these funds. Next steps would be developing monthly projections for the first year and adding to her forecasts the additional expenses and information she had gained during her negotiations of the opportunity. Year 2 needed to be more finely forecasted to gain a clear understanding of the funds needed to undertake the explosive growth possibility in year 2 if she could persuade her new customer to sell bridesmaids' as well as brides' shoes. Based on these refined forecasts, she would then make her final decision and most likely begin seeking additional funding to support year 2. She initially assumed that she might have to take in a partner and increase equity capital in the next round of financing. For now, Jennifer felt comfortable with her analysis and decision to accept her new client and begin the next growth phase of her business. **JENNIFER WAS GOING FOR IT!**

CONCLUSIONS

Many people have good ideas, but few of these ideas are real business opportunities. In this chapter we explored the critical assessment steps to analyze an idea and determine whether the idea is truly a profitable business opportunity. We introduced the concepts of **customer value proposition (cvp), opportunity fit** for the business and the owner, **forecasts, ratio analysis (roi, break-even, and payback period)** and **scenario planning**. Finally we explored typical funding sources for entrepreneurs.

Although introduced through the entrepreneurial lens, these steps would be the same steps publicly traded companies would follow to assess opportunities. The exception may be that publicly traded companies would more quickly assess interest-bearing debt (both short and long term) as a source of funding. In this situation, Jennifer if her major customer and supplier would not have provided the funding, would have explored lines of credit and other forms of interest-bearing debt to launch this strategic initiative.

With this introduction to analysis, forecasts and the assessment of strategic initiatives, we now delve deeper into these topics in the last four chapters of this book.

KEY CONCEPTS AND TERMS

assessing, 105	fixed costs, 111	payback period, 114
break-even analysis, 113	forecasting, 105	return, 113
contribution margin, 111	interest rate, 118	variable costs, 111

QUESTIONS

Q5-1. One of the criteria for assessing whether a cool idea is a real business opportunity is the importance of solving a customer pain point. Discuss the importance of this criterion and give examples of recent products that were successful solving customers' pain and examples of products that may have failed because they did not solve a pain point.

Q5-2. When assessing an opportunity, describe the market data needed to reasonably decide to pursue the opportunity.

Q5-3. Break-even analysis calculates the sales in dollars or units required to reach zero profits. Why is this important to assess an opportunity? Is it more a measure of return or risk? Explain.

Q5-4. Explain the two major categories of investment typically necessary to pursue an opportunity.

Q5-5. Frequently when launching a new venture, the original investment needed may be less than the actual available cash needed to launch the venture. Explain.

Q5-6. Explain the logic behind the payback period calculation. Is this more a measure of risk or return?

Q5-7. Tom does a first pass on his forecasted numbers and calculates the following: Fixed costs are $200,000 per year and gross margin which is essential revenues minus variable costs equals 40%. His initial calculations show a break-even in sales dollars of $500,000. Unfortunately his first-year revenue projections are $600,000. To reduce his break-even point and reduce his risk of not making a profit, list five specific actions Tom should consider. For example, he may renegotiate with his supplier to reduce the per-unit cost of his inventory.

Q5-8. Sara has a retail clothing store. If she has a gross margin of 50%, and break-even sales of $5,000 per month, what must be her fixed expenses per month?

Q5-9. Lidija has an ROI of 40% before taxes and interest, revenues of $800,000, fixed expenses of $250,000, and variable expenses of $175,000. What must Lidija's investment in this opportunity be? Can you calculate her break-even sales in dollars of the period? If so, what is the amount?

Q5-10. Erik has an ROI of 30% before taxes and interest, revenues of $700,000, fixed expenses of $250,000, and variable expenses of $175,000. Can you calculate his break-even sales in dollars of the period? If so, what is the amount?

EXERCISES

E5-1. Natalie was the CEO of a plastic molding/extrusion company that made panels for planes and automobiles. Her new product was a plastic form that fit over electric power wires and equipment to protect birds of prey from electrocution that occurred when they landed on the towers and lines. Not only was this product beneficial to nature but reduced power outages and saved costs for public utilities.

Required:
From the following proposed cash outflows and projections, label the item as an investment, a fixed expense, or a variable expense.

a. Rent paid on additional manufacturing space. The annual amount was locked in for the term of the ten-year lease.
b. Purchase of additional plastic extrusion equipment. This equipment has an estimated life of ten years.
c. Depreciation expense on the new equipment.
d. Repairs and maintenance expense on the new equipment.
e. Installation costs to install the new equipment.
f. Plastic used in the extrusion process.
g. Labor used in the making of the insulators.
h. Shop supervisor who will be on salary.
i. Sales commissions of 5%.
j. Base sales salaries for the new salespeople.

E5-2. Debra's current operations have approximately $200,000 in fixed operating expenses. Her variety of products have gross margins of between 28% and 43%, averaging 36% and these margins approximate contribution margins as well.

Required:
Calculate Debra's current break-even revenues.

E5-3. Debra had an offer to buy additional production space. This additional space would increase her fixed expenses to $250,000 and at the same time her average margin would increase to 39%.

Required:
a. Calculate Debra's new break-even revenues.
b. Based on your calculations in Exercise 5-2 and this exercise, would you recommend Debra add the production space? What other factors should she consider?

E5-4. Tom's break-even point at his current level of operations is $3,800,000 million in revenues and his revenues recently hit $4,500,000. He has a 30% contribution margin and fixed expenses of $1,140,000. Tom is expecting slowing sales for his entire industry and his company as well. In anticipation of this trend, he wants to lower his break-even point to $3,400,000.

Required:
a. Assuming fixed costs must remain the same, how much higher must his contribution margin be to reach his desired break-even point?
b. Give examples of actions Tom could take to increase his contribution margin.

E5-5. Use the data from Exercise 5-4:

Required:
a. Assuming the contribution margin of 30% is unchangeable in the near future, how much does Tom need to reduce his fixed costs to achieve a break-even sales point of $3,400,000?
b. Give examples of actions Tom could take to decrease his fixed expenses.

E5-6. Sanju is evaluating an option to buy an asset that will lower her product production costs. The asset costs $50,000, has a 5-year life and is expected to lower her production costs from $2.50 per unit to $2.25 including depreciation factored into per-unit costs.

Required:
If the product sells for $5 per unit and her annual sales volume is 100,000 units, what is Sanju's expected payback period for this investment?

E5-7. Sanju purchased the machine considered in Exercise 5-6 and had the following expectations:

Annual Sales (100,000 units)	$500,000
Cost of Goods Sold/Unit	$ 2.25
Operating Expenses.	$150,000

Required:
Assuming the new machine is purchased, calculate the ROI using forecasted pre-tax income as the numerator.

E5-8. Ibrahim and Josephine designed a very cool umbrella they wanted to manufacture in the United States and sell through high-end retailers such as Neiman Marcus and specialty stores throughout the country. Their umbrella was incredibly waterproof to minimize things and places getting wet as the umbrellas were stored when coming in from a storm. Furthermore it was an asymmetrical design and could withstand up to 80 MPH winds. They had a purchase commitment from Neiman Marcus (NM) for 100 umbrellas on a test basis at a price to NM of $100. NM planned to retail these umbrellas for $200. If sales went well, NM was prepared to order 500 in the following quarter.

Ibrahim was trying to decide if he and Josephine should create their own manufacturing facility or simply sub out the production of their umbrellas to a third party. The manufacturing facility would be small and have the capacity to produce about 5,000 umbrellas per year. If all went as planned, sales should require about 80% of the capacity to be in use sometime in year 3.

Required:

a.   Discuss the impact of this decision on the company's break-even fixed operating costs and investments.

b.   What is the probable impact of cost per product subbed out versus manufactured in-house once production reaches the in-house production capacity?

c.   What are the major risks that you see should be considered as Ibrahim and Josephine make their decision?

E5-9.   Ibrahim and Josephine leased rather than bought space and purchased machinery to manufacture umbrellas. The investment was $75,000 for machinery that should last at least 10 years. Fixed expenses to run operations including lease expense but not depreciation expense on the machinery were projected to be $80,000 annually and the variable costs to produce the umbrellas were $30 per unit.

Required:

a.   Calculate the break-even point in units.

b.   At the last minute a salesperson was added to the team on a commission-only basis. The commission would be 10% of the retail price per unit sold by the sales person. Recalculate the break-even point with this new information.

E5-10.   At the end of year 3, Ibrahim and Josephine's company reached a steady state of sales, $400,000 on their basic umbrella. Using the information in Exercise 5-9, operating expenses would reach and remain level at $150,000 per year.

Required:

What is annual ROI using pre-tax income now that the company has reached a steady state of sales? What do you think of the business to date?

PROBLEMS

P5-1.   **Opportunity and Original Investment–Accounting Services**   Iona has her own accounting firm that employs a staff of ten doing standard bookkeeping for small companies. Each job typically includes using QuickBooks to enter monthly transactions and create financial statements. As part of this service, at the end of each quarter, Iona meets with each of her clients to perform a basic analysis of the three months looking at trends in margins and major balance sheet categories.

Reflecting on these quarterly client meetings, Iona has seen an additional service she might provide to her clients. Her clients are frequently overwhelmed with the data and instead of using the analysis to improve operations, many of them become frozen into inaction. Iona reasoned that if she simplified the data by helping each client develop a dashboard of financial metrics, she could help them connect specific management actions to dashboard metric trends thus they could better lead their businesses with data as well as with the gut-feel and hunches they were using on a day-to-day basis.

From discussions with several clients, Iona developed the following game plan for this new opportunity.

1.   As Iona was currently working 60–70 hours per week, she would have to hire an experienced accountant to oversee the staff doing the bookkeeping. This would then free her to develop the service product (e.g., create typical industry dashboard templates), develop her marketing materials and sales pitch, and begin to sell to her clients as well as all small business owners in her area. The salary and benefits for such a person would be $100,000 annually.

2.   Iona would have to provide office space for this new hire which she estimates will cost her $2,000 to renovate and furnish a portion of her leased office space.

3.   She will need a computer with printer and an additional telephone line for this person. This will require an investment of $5,000.

Required:

a.   Calculate Iona's initial investment (cash outflow) for this opportunity.

b.   What other investments need to be identified and what is the dollar impact estimated to assess this opportunity?

P5-2. **Original Investment, Break-even Analysis–Graphic Designer and Management Actions**
Zachary, a graphic designer, realized that there was a limit to his income (i.e., the number of hours he could bill in a month). In order to increase his earnings power, he decided to launch a T-shirt company, initially selling his shirts solely through the Internet. He visited the Small Business Development Center (SBDC) in his hometown and with their help launched his company. Zachary gathered the following data:

> Wholesale price of T-shirts: $7/unit
> Designs: one hour of his time: $50 per design
> T-shirt Silk Screening: $3/unit
> Packaging with company logo: $.25/unit
> Shipping: $1.25/unit
> Investment in Website redesign and ordering system: $3,000

Order fulfillment: Zachary planned to stuff the shirts and address the envelopes as he watched TV in the evening. His shipping costs would be only the $1.25 per unit estimated above. He knew this expense would grow if he was successful but as a start-up, he assumed it would take him at least a year before he had volume worries.

Monthly expenses: Zachary estimated to be $200 above the variable costs of shirt production and order fulfillment.

Zachary projected a selling price per shirt of $18.00 and the silk screener will require a run of 100 shirts for his first design.

Required:
a. How much is Zachary's investment to launch his company?
b. Would you advise Zachary to have more cash available over and above his required investment in part a? If so, why?
c. What is Zachary's expected product margin per unit?
d. Calculate Zachary's break-even sales in units per month.
e. What impact would a decrease in selling price to $16 per unit have on the break-even point? Show your calculations.
f. What actions can Zachary take to lower his break-even sales levels?

P5-3. **Break-even Analysis and ROI—Graphic Designer** Zachary decided to launch his T-shirt venture and it succeeded beyond his wildest expectations. Currently he rents 1,200 square feet of office space housing his office as well as his inventory storage and his order-fulfillment process tables. He now has his own postage meter, a dedicated computer, office furniture, and a part-time assistant responsible for fulfilling the orders and sending him a copy of orders for his record keeping. His expenses operating at his current level of business are as follows.

> Retail Price: $20/unit
> Wholesale price of T-shirts: $5/unit
> T-shirt Silk Screening: $2/unit
> Packaging with company logo: $.50/unit
> Shipping: $1.00/unit
> Payment to PayPal per customer/unit: $1
> Order fulfillment: Gillian, Zachary's assistant was paid $1,200 for 80 hours per month.

Occupancy expenses per month were:

Lease expense	$1,400
Utilities expense	50
Insurance	25
Depreciation—meter	20
Depreciation—computer	100
Depreciation—furniture	40
Total monthly	$1,635

Required:
a. What is Zachary's expected product margin per unit?
b. Calculate Zachary's break-even sales in units per month.
c. If Zachary's investment in his venture is $9,500 and Zachary sells 2,500 shirts per year, calculate Zachary's annual ROI before taxes.

P5-4. **Opportunity Assessment, ROI, Break-even and Management Actions (a continuation of Problem 5-1)** Iona, based on client interviews and requests, was considering launching a new accounting service. This service would be to help clients create a dashboard of relevant ratios to manage their business and lead growth. After a number of discussions and many hours of planning, Iona projected the following numbers for her new product launch.

Initial Investment: $5,000 equipment + $2,000 renovations + $2,500 one-time marketing expenses.

Working Capital Investment: 0 because she was a service firm. In fact, she would have to fund her new receivables but this amount would be captured in her cash flow projections.

Financial Statement Projections: Assuming she hired the senior staff accountant immediately, she would have $1,000 of ongoing incremental marketing expenses and it would take her two years for her new product line to be profitable, Iona calculated that she would need $125,000 over and above the initial investment before she achieved a positive operating cash flow (OCF). She forecasted she could pay this amount back to the bank at the end of three years. Once she achieved her steady state of product delivery, earnings before taxes (EBT) would be $35,000.

Required:
a. What would be Iona's return on investment (ROI), once she reaches steady state?
b. What type of management actions could Iona take to reduce investment and increase ROI?
c. Based on ROI would you recommend Iona launch this new service?

P5-5. **ROI and Break-even for Multiple Years Forecasted** Tom's forecasted income statement for his new product line is as follows:

Forecasted Income Statement	Year 1	Year 2	Year 3
Revenues	$150,000.00	$437,500.00	$2,250,000.00
Cost of goods sold.	97,500.00	284,375.00	1,462,500.00
Gross profit.	52,500.00	153,125.00	787,500.00
Operating expenses			
Additional compensation		75,000.00	75,000.00
Additional operating expenses . . .	20,000.00	20,000.00	20,000.00
Additional depreciation expense .	28,000.00	28,000.00	28,000.00
Operating income.	4,500.00	105,125.00	739,500.00
Tax expense (assuming 30%).	1,350.00	31,537.50	221,850.00
Net income.	$ 3,150.00	$ 73,587.50	$ 517,650.00

Additional calculations	Year 1	Year 2	Year 3
Investment	$521,000	$533,000	$605,000
Gross Margin which approximates			
Contribution Margin	35%	35%	35%
Projected Fixed Expenses	$48,000	$123,000	$123,000

Required:
a. Calculate the ROI for each year.
b. Calculate the break-even point in sales dollars for each year.
c. Based on these projections and calculations should Tom pursue this opportunity? What concerns do you have and what additional data or calculations would you recommend?

P5-6. **Opportunity Assessment Before all of the Numbers—Distillery** Hillary owned a distillery in the Southeastern region of the United States. Begun three years ago, she had developed three brand name spirits of vodka, whiskey, and gin. Sales had been brisk because of the quality of her spirits but also because of the increasing demand for craft spirits. This section of the market was expected to grow at 30% annually for the next five years and possibly beyond.

With her revenues at $1.2M, $75,000 cash in the bank, an annual profit of $130,000, and a town willing to donate her land and an old warehouse, Hillary was considering a growth opportunity to provide distilled whiskey to micro distilleries. These distilleries would then either age or further process and bottle their whiskeys to retail stores under their own labels. This market was largely untapped and industry sources estimated that this segment will grow to $30 million annually in revenues.

Hillary had been contacted by a number of these micro distilleries and developed the following estimates:

1. Sales in year 1 would be $500,000 with a 50% growth per year for the following two years.
2. Gross margin on this product should average 55% per annum.
3. Because of a significant number of micro distilleries already expressing interest in her product, Hillary thought additional marketing expenses would be minimal. Hillary estimated $10,000 per year.
4. Hillary anticipated hiring a product segment manager for this new product line. Compensation would be $70,000 per year. An assistant office manager would be hired for $40,000. These amounts include benefits.
5. Investments in equipment and trucking were substantial. She estimated two trucks at a total of $150,000 and additional distilling equipment of $175,000. The trucks had an estimated useful lives of 5 years; the equipment 10 years. Neither asset class was expected to have significant salvage value.
6. Hillary also expected to carry additional inventory of $75,000; 30% of this would be covered by credit from her grain suppliers.

Required:
a. In your opinion does this look like an opportunity worth pursuing? Please explain the basis for your opinion as well as additional data you would advise Hillary to gather before she launched this new product line.
b. How much is Hillary's initial investment to launch this business?
c. Hillary could fund this investment either by selling common stock in her company or obtaining a loan with the plant acting as security for the loan. Interest rates on these type of loans are expected to be stable at 8.5%. What would be the impact of the profit estimates for this decision?

P5-7. **Complete Opportunity Assessment Numbers—Distillery**   Using the data in Problem 5-6 and assuming: 1) 25% tax rate for this forecasting exercise; 2) that $27,500 of cash on hand was used for the equipment down payment; and 3) $350,000 of debt with an annual interest rate of 8.5% was incurred.

Required:
a. Forecast the first three years of operations. Will additional investment be needed to fund a cash burn period?
b. Calculate the return on the investment (ROI) for each of the three years.
c. Calculate the break-even sales dollar amount for each of the three years.
d. Would you advise Hillary to pursue the opportunity?

P5-8. **Opportunity Assessment**   Giovanni Mingozzi lives in London where he worked for several years in consulting before joining with several colleagues to start a gelato (type of ice cream) company—Milano Gelato. They source the gelato from a producer in Giovanni's hometown of Milan and sell it to high-end restaurants throughout the UK. The business has grown quickly, and by keeping operating costs low (e.g., running the business out of Giovanni's living room), the partners are pleased with the company's performance.

The partners are now considering selling to retail grocery stores, such as Whole Foods. Their vendor can offer products already packaged for retail sale at $2.50/unit, and Milano Gelato (MG) expects to sell them for $5/unit. MG would also need to pay an additional $.25/unit for shipping from Milan.

Although Giovanni has already established relationships with potential customers, by year 2, the company would have to hire a full-time salesperson to manage these relationships at an expected compensation of $60,000/year.

MG would need to purchase a delivery truck for $32,000 immediately and hire a driver with an expected salary of $31,000/year. The truck has a useful life of 4 years.

MG would also have to rent additional cold storage space for $17,000/year. This space would be way more than needed in year 1 but just meet the forecasted needed storage for year 3.

MG forecasts sales of 18,000 units in year 1, doubling to 36,000 units in year 2, doubling again to 72,000 units in year 3.

Required:

a. Calculate the number of units MG must sell in order to break even.

b. Complete the schedule below.

	Year 1	Year 2	Year 3
Revenue			
Cost of goods sold			
Gross profit			
Salaries expense			
Other expenses			
Operating profit			

P5-9. **Opportunity Assessment: Break-even and Return on Investment**   Juanita had built a successful restaurant over the past decade focused on Ecuadorian and Mexican food. In a very small restaurant she had successfully grown her company to just under $1M in revenues and had been consistently profitable. Perhaps most wonderfully, both her son and daughter had joined the family business, with the son running the kitchen and the daughter worrying about the books and managing the out-front staff while Juanita was the hostess most every evening.

Located in the Los Angeles, California, area, movie production studios had recently moved into the city and Juanita's daughter Victoria suggested they explore catering as a new revenue line. Juanita had catered some business lunches and found them to be profitable but she was worried the business may not be sustainable. She decided to have Victoria prove that her idea was a real business opportunity. Victoria came back with the following information.

Two movie studios had recently moved into the area and typically within all their units each needed to cater 50 lunches per week. Furthermore there was evidence that businesses linked to the studios were relocating to be near the large studio companies. Although these were small businesses, Victoria thought, based on industry trade publications that for every 10 businesses, there would be one catered lunch per week. While studying this opportunity, she also saw the possibility of catering to office buildings where a number of these smaller businesses were located. She thought she could cater at least one building per week. After her informational interviews with the studios, Victoria generated the following projections.

Revenues:
Catering jobs per week: 12
Average number of lunches per job: 30
Average revenue per lunch: $15

Immediate Cash Outflows:
Delivery vehicle with warming ovens: $40,000
Serving equipment: $2,000
Assumption: Vehicle and equipment will have 5-year service lives and no salvage value.

Expenses:
Food per lunch: $3.50
Plates and utensils per lunch: $0.50
Serving staff to be hired: 12 @ $12.00/hr. for 20 hours per week each
Additional cook: 1 @ $18.00/hr. for 20 hours per week

Required:

a. From the data given, how much will Victoria need to invest to launch this opportunity? What additional type of investments might she have to consider? Are there any additional expenses Victoria needs to consider?

b. Assuming Victoria reaches her projections quickly (i.e., the business quickly reaches a steady state of 12 catering jobs per week), how many catering jobs per week and per year will it take for Victoria to break even?

c. Once Victoria reaches steady state, what is her ROI for the catering business?

d. Would you recommend Juanita and Victoria pursue this opportunity? Support your answer with your calculations.

P5-10. **Opportunity Assessment: 3-Year Forecast, ROI, and Break-even Analysis**   Jessica was proud of what she had accomplished in her first four years of operations. The organic soaps, lotions and bath salts company she created was profitable and generated positive operating cash flow. Jessica was debt-free and had ended year 4 with over $140,000 in the bank.

Target, Inc. came to her about possibly distributing her products and she was thrilled. From the numbers they were discussing, she could increase her revenues by 50%. However, for an entrepreneur leading a small business, dealing with big box stores was tricky. She would have to carry much more inventory than she had to date, probably hire additional staff to deal with such a major client and she knew Target would want much lower margins than her existing customers. Jessica wondered if Target presented a true business opportunity. She decided that before pursuing this new opportunity, the following questions needed answers:

1. Would the new business be profitable?
2. How much money would it take to pursue? Was the current $140,000 of cash on hand sufficient? If not, how much additional funding would she need?

Assumptions:
1. Target said it would try her products in 500 stores and expected the first year's revenue to be $1,500 per store. Assuming Target expectations in year 1 were reached, Target would expand and sell Jessica's products in 1,000 stores in year 2 and 1,500 stores in year 3. Based on Target's experience with similar product classifications, sales were expected to average $1,750 per store in year 3 and $2,250 in year 4.
2. COGS for Target would average 65% of revenue, 3 percentage points less than Jessica experienced with her other customer.
3. Jessica thought she could handle the Target relationship for the first year but then she would have to hire a Target account manager. Compensation for this individual including salary and benefits was projected to be $75,000 annually from year 2 forward.
4. Other operating expenses related to the Target opportunity were estimated to be $20,000, which included travel expenses as well as administrative support.
5. Additional inventory for years 1, 2 and 3 would be $12,000, $36,000 and $180,000 based on an approximate inventory requirement by Target of 12%–13% of forecasted cost of goods sold. Jessica expected accounts payable to increase by 50% of this amount for each of the three years because she had good supplier relationships and they would give her very good terms.
6. Jessica would need to secure additional warehouse space to house this inventory increase. She thought she could buy a building adjacent to her existing building for $500,000. For depreciation purposes useful life is assumed to be 20 years with no salvage value.
7. Jessica estimated it would cost her $15,000 to create an office space with appropriate furniture and computer equipment for her new account manager. Furniture and equipment is depreciated over a useful life of 5 years and no salvage value.
8. For return on investment purposes, Jessica assumed a tax rate of 30%.

Required:
a. How much initial investment will Jessica have to make to gain Target as a customer?
b. Complete the format below capturing Jessica's projections for years 1, 2 and 3.

Jessica's Target Opportunity Forecasted Income Statement	Year 1	Year 2	Year 3
Total revenue			
Cost of goods sold.			
Gross profit.			
Operating expenses			
Additional compensation			
Additional operating expenses. . .			
Additional depreciation expense .			
Operating income.			
Tax expense (assuming 30%).			
Net income.			

c. Calculate the return on investment (ROI) for years 1, 2 and 3.
d. Ignoring tax expense, calculate the break-even sales amount for years 1, 2 and 3.
e. Because the investment will take more than Jessica has available in her cash account, how might she fund this opportunity? What impact will these have on Jessica's projected ROI? (You do not have to include calculations in this discussion.)
f. Would you advise Jessica to pursue this opportunity? Support your answers with calculations as well as other considerations you think important.

Chapter Six

Financial Statement Analysis: Basic

When you complete this chapter you should be able to:

1. Calculate and analyze ratios contained in the DuPont model.
2. Identify the connections between financial ratios and business models.
3. Calculate and analyze margins.
4. Calculate and interpret the asset turnover ratio and its components: receivables turnover, inventory turnover, and fixed asset (PP&E) turnover.
5. Analyze liquidity and cash cycle.
6. Calculate and analyze the leverage ratio and its supporting metrics: debt/equity, interest coverage, and liquidity ratios.

INTRODUCTION

With a solid grasp of how financial statements are prepared and formatted, we now turn to using them to make business decisions. Think of financial statements as the dashboard instruments in a car. The car's GPS provides information about where we have been and how we got to our current position, while the other instruments provide data on the overall condition of the vehicle. Together, they tell us where the car is headed and the likelihood of arriving there successfully. Similarly, financial statements allow us to analyze where a business has been as well as its current position. We can evaluate the overall condition of the venture and make an assessment of its likely future path.

The techniques of financial statement analysis allow us to evaluate the impact of management decisions on a company's performance. Once we know how to measure financial performance, we can better understand how it is affected by managerial decisions. Here are examples of the kinds of questions we can answer using financial statement analysis:

1. Is the business profitable? If not, why not, and what can its managers do to improve profitability?
2. Is the company using its assets efficiently?
3. Should it finance the business using equity or debt? How does this choice impact financial performance and risk?
4. What are the trends in the company's performance? How does it compare to its competitors in the industry?

In this chapter we introduce some basic tools and techniques of financial statement analysis.

COMMON-SIZE ANALYSIS

As we illustrate in Chapter 1, **common-size analysis** focuses on the income statement and balance sheet using proportions rather than dollars, euros, or other currency. On a common-size income statement, every line item is shown as a percentage of revenue; on the balance sheet, each line item is shown as a percentage of total assets. We see the real benefit of common-size analysis when we have data from comparable firms or industry data or when several years of financial statements are available. To illustrate, consider the following income statement for a small restaurant:

INCOME STATEMENT	2010	2011	2012	2013	2014
Revenue: Store.........	$275,000	$302,500	$332,750	$366,025	$402,628
Revenue: Catering	60,000	72,000	86,400	99,360	114,264
Total revenue	335,000	374,500	419,150	465,385	516,892
COGS: Food...........	(117,250)	(134,820)	(155,086)	(176,846)	(196,419)
Gross profit...........	217,750	239,680	264,065	288,539	320,473
Wage expense:					
Fixed	(50,000)	(50,000)	(60,000)	(60,000)	(60,000)
Variable...............	(50,250)	(56,175)	(62,873)	(69,808)	(77,534)
Total wages	(100,250)	(106,175)	(122,873)	(129,808)	(137,534)
General overhead.......	(50,000)	(75,000)	(85,000)	(95,000)	(110,000)
Depreciation expense....	(2,500)	(2,500)	(3,000)	(5,000)	(5,000)
Marketing	(33,500)	(37,450)	(41,915)	(46,539)	(51,689)
Operating income.......	31,500	18,555	11,277	12,192	16,250
Interest expense........	(1,016)	(1,496)	(1,626)	(1,193)	(1,193)
Income before tax	30,484	17,059	9,651	10,999	15,057
Taxes	(10,669)	(5,971)	(3,378)	(3,850)	(5,270)
Net income............	$ 19,814	$ 11,088	$ 6,273	$ 7,150	$ 9,787

It is clear the business is growing—from 2010 to 2014 total revenue increased 72%. However, net income for the same period fell by 53%, from about $21,000 to $10,000. To begin to investigate the causes of this divergence between revenue and profit, we recast the financial statements in common-size format.

Common-Size Income Statement

Consider the following common-size income statement for the small restaurant:

INCOME STATEMENT	2010	2011	2012	2013	2014
Revenue: Store............	82%	81%	79%	79%	78%
Revenue: Catering	18%	19%	21%	21%	22%
Total revenue	100%	100%	100%	100%	100%
COGS: Food..............	−35%	−36%	−37%	−38%	−38%
Gross profit..............	65%	64%	63%	62%	62%
Wage expense:	0%	0%	0%	0%	0%
Fixed..................	−15%	−13%	−14%	−13%	−12%
Variable................	−15%	−15%	−15%	−15%	−15%
Total wages	−30%	−28%	−29%	−28%	−27%
General overhead..........	−15%	−20%	−20%	−20%	−21%
Depreciation expense.......	−1%	−1%	−1%	−1%	−1%
Marketing	−10%	−10%	−10%	−10%	−10%
	0%	0%	0%	0%	0%
Operating income..........	9%	5%	3%	3%	3%
Interest expense...........	−0.3%	−0.5%	−0.5%	−0.4%	−0.4%
Income before tax	10.2%	5.7%	3.2%	3.7%	5.0%
Taxes	−3.2%	−1.6%	−0.8%	−0.8%	−1.0%
Net income...............	5.9%	3.0%	1.5%	1.5%	1.9%

How does this common-size format help us better understand the restaurant's forecasted income statement? First, on the income statement, we can quickly see all of the important margins—the gross profit margin, operating profit margin, and net profit margin. The deterioration in profitability is due to increasing cost of goods sold relative to revenue, which drove the gross margin down by 3% between 2010 and 2014 (from 65% to 62%). The common-size income statement also makes it easy to track key expense items over time. The good news is that fixed wage expense as a percentage of revenue declined over time, but this is more than offset by significant increases in general overhead and marketing expenses as a percentage of revenue. The net result of these trends is summarized by the operating profit margin, which fell from 11% in 2010 to 3.1% in 2014. It appears that management has made revenue growth a bigger priority than profitability. The key is that with common-size statements, we can see the trends clearly and quickly, which is not always the case when looking at the actual financials.

On the balance sheet, we can use the common-size percentages to see the relative importance of each asset, liability and equity account. The following information shows that total assets grew 56% from 2010 to 2014 which is less than revenue growth over the same period. However, with just the dollar figures, it is difficult to spot trends in individual line items.

BALANCE SHEET	2010	2011	2012	2013	2014
Assets					
Cash.	$15,000	$16,750	$18,725	$20,958	$23,270
A/R	4,000	5,000	6,000	7,200	8,280
Inventory.	7,000	7,800	8,988	10,339	11,790
Other assets	5,000	5,000	5,000	5,000	6,000
Total current assets	31,000	34,550	38,713	43,497	49,340
Equipment (cost)	30,000	40,000	45,000	60,000	60,000
Accumulated depreciation . . .	(2,500)	(5,000)	(8,000)	(13,000)	(18,000)
Equipment (net)	27,500	35,000	37,000	47,000	42,000
Total assets	$58,500	$69,550	$75,713	$90,497	$91,340
Liabilities					
Accounts payable.	$13,125	$14,500	$16,845	$19,386	$22,106
Wages payable.	2,670	3,100	3,185	3,686	3,894
Credit card debt	15,000	10,002	7,000	14,999	6,941
Other current liabilities	5,000	2,160	1,000	3,000	1,000
Total current liabilities.	35,795	29,762	28,030	41,071	33,941
Long-term liabilities	12,705	18,700	20,321	14,914	13,100
Owners' equity	10,000	21,088	27,362	34,512	44,299
Total	$58,500	$69,550	$75,713	$90,497	$91,340

Common-Size Balance Sheet

The common-size balance sheet shown here solves that problem. We can see that cash as a percentage of total assets has been stable. Accounts receivable increased as a percentage of assets, and while equipment (cost) rose from 51.3% in 2010 to 65.7% in 2014, there was also a large increase in accumulated depreciation. On a net basis, equipment remained stable as a proportion of assets over the period. On the liabilities and equity side of the balance sheet, we can see that equity (net worth) accounts for an increasing percentage of total assets due to the addition of positive net income to retained earnings each year.

Common-size statements are a valuable tool for financial analysis and allow us to analyze several years of data for a single firm or to compare data across firms. Common size is especially useful when comparing different companies because the percentages remove the effects of size or currency differences. However, to further understand the connections between operations and financial performance, we need to expand our tool kit, starting with one of the most common ratios, return on equity.

BALANCE SHEET	2010	2011	2012	2013	2014
Assets					
Cash....................	25.6%	24.1%	24.7%	23.2%	25.5%
A/R....................	6.8%	7.2%	7.9%	8.0%	9.1%
Inventory................	12.0%	11.2%	11.9%	11.4%	12.9%
Other assets.............	8.5%	7.2%	6.6%	5.5%	6.6%
Total current assets........	53.0%	49.7%	51.1%	48.1%	54.0%
Equipment...............	51.3%	57.5%	59.4%	66.3%	65.7%
Accumulated depreciation...	−4.3%	−7.2%	−10.6%	−14.4%	−19.7%
Total assets.............	100.0%	100.0%	100.0%	100.0%	100.0%
Liabilities					
Accounts payable..........	22.4%	20.8%	22.2%	21.4%	24.2%
Wages payable............	4.6%	4.5%	4.2%	4.1%	4.3%
Credit card debt...........	25.6%	14.4%	9.2%	16.6%	7.6%
Other current liabilities......	8.5%	3.1%	1.3%	3.3%	1.1%
Total current liabilities.......	61.2%	42.8%	37.0%	45.4%	37.2%
Long-term liabilities........	21.7%	26.9%	26.8%	16.5%	14.3%
Owners' equity...........	17.1%	30.3%	36.1%	38.1%	48.5%
Total...................	100.0%	100.0%	100.0%	100.0%	100.0%

Return on Equity and the DuPont Formula

Return on equity, or ROE, is one of the most widely used metrics for assessing financial performance. The equation is as follows:

$$ROE = \frac{Net\ Income}{Equity}$$

The numerator is the company's "bottom line" or net profit and represents what the company has earned on behalf of its owners. Think about this for a minute. To calculate net income, we start with revenue and subtract the cost of goods, all operating expenses, interest, and taxes; thus, net income is the profit after the costs of goods and services from our suppliers, employees, bankers, and government agencies have all been recognized. Whatever is left over belongs to the company's owner(s).

The denominator represents the total amount of the owners' investment or "equity" in the business. For a sole proprietorship and a partnership, the owners' investment is called owners' equity or net worth. For a corporation, the owners are shareholders and their investment includes both contributed capital and retained earnings.

ROE measures the return earned on the owners' total investment and is expressed as a percentage. For example, using the restaurant data presented earlier (a sole proprietorship), we calculate the 2014 ROE as follows:

$$ROE = \frac{Net\ Income_{2014}}{Equity_{2014}} = \frac{\$9,787}{\$44,299} = 22.1\%$$

It would appear the restaurant owners did well on their investment. However, although ROE tells us about the percentage return to the owners of a business, it does not provide insight into *how* the return was earned. For this, we turn to the **DuPont formula**, which breaks the ROE calculation into three components:

$$\text{DuPont Formula: ROE} = \frac{\text{Net Income}}{\text{Sales}} \times \frac{\text{Sales}}{\text{Total Assets}} \times \frac{\text{Total Assets}}{\text{Equity}}$$

Looking more closely at each of the components, we can see that the first is the net **profit margin**, which measures the earnings that result from each dollar of sales. The second term, Sales/Total Assets, is called asset turnover, and measures how well the business uses its assets to generate sales. The final term, Total Assets/Equity, is called financial leverage, as it provides a measure of how much debt the firm has used to acquire its assets. We can restate the DuPont formula as follows:

$$\text{ROE} = \text{Profit Margin} \times \text{Asset Turnover} \times \text{Financial Leverage}$$

In this form, we can see what "levers" drive the return owners earn from their business. Increasing any one of the three will increase the owners' return (holding all else equal). The first two terms are closely related to the firm's operations, whereas the third term, financial leverage, relates to the way the firm has been funded (i.e., the mix between debt and equity). In fact, profit margin and asset turnover can be combined to give us a measure called **return on assets**, or ROA, another often-used performance metric. The ROA equation is as follows:

$$\text{Return on Assets} = \text{ROA} = \frac{\text{Net Income}}{\text{Sales}} \times \frac{\text{Sales}}{\text{Total Assets}} = \frac{\text{Net Income}}{\text{Total Assets}}$$

ROA tells us how much return the business earns for each dollar invested in assets. Note that it differs from ROE, which only focuses on the owners' investment (equity). ROA measures the profit earned from all of the firm's assets, regardless of whether they were funded with debt or equity.

We can use the DuPont formula to compute and analyze the ROE for our restaurant example in 2014:

$$
\begin{aligned}
\text{ROE} &= \text{Profit Margin} \times \text{Asset Turnover} \times \text{Financial Leverage} \\
&= \frac{\$9,787}{\$516,892} \times \frac{\$516,892}{\$91,340} \times \frac{\$91,340}{\$44,299} \\
&= 1.89\% \times 5.66 \times 2.06 \\
&= 22.1\%
\end{aligned}
$$

By breaking ROE into the three DuPont components, we can more clearly see how the restaurant achieved a healthy ROE. The ROA, calculated as the product of the first two terms, is 10.67% (1.89% × 5.66). When this is multiplied by the financial leverage ratio of 2.06, the result is ROE of 22.1%. Financial leverage of 2.06 means that the $91,340 of total assets was funded using $44,299 of equity and $47,043 of liabilities. Although the mathematics of these calculations is straightforward, and we can agree that 22.1% is a high ROE, we have no real basis for comparison. We can apply DuPont analysis to the five-year period of financials in order to gain additional insights using trend analysis:

DuPont Analysis	2010	2011	2012	2013	2014
Profit margin.	5.91%	2.96%	1.50%	1.54%	1.89%
Asset turnover	5.73	5.38	5.54	5.14	5.66
Financial leverage.	5.85	3.30	2.77	2.62	2.06
ROE	198%	53%	23%	21%	22%
ROA	34%	16%	8%	8%	11%

Based on this analysis, the restaurant's ROE fell by 75% in 2011 and another 50% in 2012. Since asset turnover remained relatively constant during this period, the drop in ROE is due to a dramatic fall-off in net profit margin and a 50% reduction in financial leverage. The drop in profitability is problematic, but even with a net profit margin below 2.0%, the restaurant's ROE is still above 20% in 2013 and 2014. Clearly, management needs to analyze the causes for the degradation in the profit margin. However, management begins this operations analysis from a relatively strong position with respect to ROE.

DuPont analysis is a useful way to analyze a company's performance with respect to the return on the owners' investment. By decomposing ROE into three components, we gain additional insight into important levers of financial performance: profitability, asset utilization, and financial leverage. To better understand how strategic choices, operating decisions, and managerial effectiveness impact financial performance as measured by ROE, we now look at each of the three DuPont components in more detail.

Profit Margin

The focus in the DuPont formula is on net profit margin, but there are other profitability metrics that provide valuable information about the firm's pricing strategy and cost structure. The three most important are the gross margin, the operating margin, and the EBITDA (earnings before interest, taxes, depreciation, and amortization) margin. For the restaurant example, these margins have the following values:

Profitability	2010	2011	2012	2013	2014
Gross margin	65.00%	64.00%	63.00%	62.00%	62.00%
Operating (EBIT) margin	9.40%	4.95%	2.69%	2.62%	3.14%
EBITDA margin	10.15%	5.62%	3.41%	3.69%	4.11%
Profit margin	5.91%	2.96%	1.50%	1.54%	1.89%

Gross Margin

Gross margin is a metric primarily used by businesses that sell a tangible product, including manufacturers and retailers, and it is calculated as follows:

$$\text{Gross Margin} = \frac{\text{Gross Profit}}{\text{Sales}} = \frac{(\text{Sales} - \text{COGS})}{\text{Sales}}$$

Gross margin is the percentage we earn from each dollar of sales *after* subtracting the cost to manufacture or purchase the product. The cost of goods sold (COGS) for a manufacturer includes materials, labor, and overhead, and is comprised primarily of variable costs. Note that the gross margin can be improved by either raising selling prices or reducing COGS. Gross profit is a critical metric for retailers or manufacturers because this is the amount available to cover all other operating expenses, interest, and taxes. If gross profit is not carefully managed, it will be difficult for the venture to achieve profitability at the bottom line.

For our restaurant example, COGS would include the cost of the food. From the numbers given earlier, we can see that gross margin fell from 65% in 2010 to 62% in 2014. This could be due to a reduction in selling prices, possibly to spur revenue growth or in expectation of increased competition. It might also reflect higher costs for food, either due to inflation or a changing menu.

Operating Margin

The **operating margin**, one of the most widely used measures of managerial performance, is calculated as follows:

$$\text{Operating Margin} = \frac{\text{Operating Profit}}{\text{Sales}} = \frac{(\text{Sales} - \text{COGS} - \text{Operating Expenses})}{\text{Sales}}$$

Operating margin is the percentage we earn from each dollar of sales *after* subtracting all of the costs of producing, acquiring, and selling our product or service, but before interest and income taxes. By including **operating expenses**, we capture the company's fixed costs, such as rent and salaries. By looking back at the restaurant's income statements, you can see that both fixed and variable wages are part of operating expenses, along with general overhead, depreciation, and marketing costs. Over the five-year period, the restaurant's operating margin fell significantly, from 9.4% to 3.1%. As discussed earlier, this is due primarily to large increases (as a percentage of revenue) in general overhead and marketing expenses. Further analysis should be conducted to determine exactly what is causing these large increases.

The operating margin represents what is available from each dollar of sales to cover interest due to the firm's creditors and income taxes. It is a useful metric for comparing financial results across different companies because it assesses operating performance before any adjustments for debt financing (interest expense), taxes, or one-time items, none of which is directly related to the ongoing value of the firm's assets.

EBITDA Margin

The **EBITDA margin**—EBITDA is earnings before interest, taxes, depreciation, and amortization—is similar to operating profit, except that we add back depreciation and amortization. The measure provides a quick proxy for operating cash flow. Depreciation and amortization are both non-cash expenses, and adding them back to operating profit gets us closer to cash flow. The 2015 EBITDA margin is calculated as follows for our restaurant:

$$\text{EBITDA Margin}_{2014} = \frac{(\text{Operating Profit} + \text{Depreciation \& Amortization})}{\text{Sales}}$$

$$= \frac{(\$16,250 + \$5,000)}{\$516,892}$$

$$= 4.16\%$$

The three most common profit metrics are gross margin, operating margin, and net margin. Each provides insight into a company's operations and helps us assess specific aspects of performance. Although the **net margin** or net profit margin is the first lever in the DuPont formula, it is largely determined by decisions made at the gross and operating margin levels.

Asset Turnover

Most business owners, when asked whether they would like to have more assets for their business, don't hesitate before answering with an emphatic "Yes!" What they often fail to consider is that adding assets requires capital, which means those new assets need to earn a sufficient return to cover the cost of this additional capital. The real value of any business is not in the assets it owns, but in the profits and cash flows those assets generate. More specifically, value is a function of the returns to the owners after accounting for the costs of acquiring and maintaining the company's assets. It follows that a business that generates more returns from fewer assets should be more valuable. This is the idea behind **asset turnover**, the second lever of managerial performance, which measures how effectively the business utilizes its assets to generate sales and is calculated as follows:

$$\text{Asset Turnover} = \frac{\text{Sales}}{\text{Total Assets}}$$

For example, assume that two new package delivery businesses, Diligent, Inc. and Slacker Enterprises, each start operations with one identical truck costing $20,000. If at the end of the first year Diligent has generated $50,000 of revenue and Slacker only $30,000, it seems safe to conclude that Diligent has used the truck more efficiently.

Diligent's asset turnover would be 2.5 ($50,000/$20,000) and Slacker's 1.5. We need to be careful when interpreting this, however, as revenue is not profit or cash flow. To claim Diligent is doing a better job overall, we'd want to look at return on assets or the profit margins discussed earlier.

For the restaurant, 2014 asset turnover is calculated as follows:

$$\text{Asset Turnover}_{2014} = \frac{\text{Sales}_{2014}}{\text{Total Assets}_{2014}} = \frac{\$516,292}{\$91,340} = 5.66X$$

In 2014, the restaurant generated $5.66 of sales for each dollar of total assets.

Total asset turnover is a useful, but high-level measure of how well the firm is deploying its assets. Depending on the nature of the business, specific assets may be more important to generating revenue and, ultimately, profit and cash flows. For example, a steel mill's most important asset is its large investment in property, plant, and equipment. For a retailer, inventory and accounts receivable (i.e., working capital) may be the assets most responsible for generating sales. And for a technology firm, intellectual property in the form of patents or trade secrets could be most responsible for increasing sales. For the restaurant, inventory or fixed asset turnover may be key metrics because the investment in food and furniture and fixtures are two of the most important assets the business owns.

Because of this, we often measure turnover for specific types of assets, tailoring our metrics to gain additional insights into managerial performance. Although the terminology may vary, all of the following metrics are some variation of asset turnover; they measure how well the firm is managing or utilizing its assets.

Fixed Asset Turnover

Industries in which most of a firm's assets are fixed (i.e., property, plant, and equipment) are called *capital intensive*. Examples include airlines and manufacturing businesses. When evaluating performance in such industries, we often use **fixed asset turnover**, calculated as follows:

$$\text{Fixed Asset Turnover} = \frac{\text{Sales}}{\text{Net Fixed Assets}}$$

A high-fixed-assets business usually has high fixed costs. Because fixed costs are difficult to reduce in the short run, the fixed asset turnover is watched closely by lenders and investors, as a small downturn in sales can cause profitability to deteriorate quickly. For the restaurant, with $42,000 of net equipment on its 2014 balance sheet ($60,000 minus $18,000 of accumulated depreciation), fixed asset turnover is computed as follows:

$$\text{Fixed Asset Turnover}_{2014} = \frac{\text{Sales}_{2014}}{\text{Net Fixed Assets}_{2014}} = \frac{\$516,292}{\$42,000} = 12.31X$$

Inventory Turnover

For some businesses, such as a fashion retailer, the efficient acquisition and management of inventory is the most important factor in success or failure. For these types of businesses, we consider two related measures, inventory turnover and inventory days on hand. **Inventory turnover** is calculated as follows:

$$\text{Inventory Turnover} = \frac{\text{Cost of Goods Sold}}{\text{Inventory}}$$

Notice that the numerator is COGS, not sales, to remove the impact of markups. If a retailer ends the year with inventory of $35,000 and had COGS of $700,000, the inventory turnover is 20 ($700,000/$35,000). The retailer turned its inventory 20 times during the year by selling and restocking its goods. Alternatively, we can calculate **inventory days on hand** as follows:

$$\text{Inventory Days on Hand} = \frac{365 \text{ days}}{\text{Inventory Turnover}}$$

With an inventory turnover of 20, the days on hand would be 18.25 days, which means the typical item was in inventory for 18.25 days before it was sold. It should be clear that inventory turnover is at least partly a function of industry. Having 18 days of inventory might be fine for a car dealer, but problematic for a fresh fish wholesaler. For the restaurant, we can calculate the 2014 inventory turnover and days on hand as follows:

$$\text{Inventory Turnover}_{2014} = \frac{\text{Cost of Goods Sold}_{2014}}{\text{Inventory}_{2014}} = \frac{\$196,419}{\$11,790} = 16.66X$$

$$\text{Inventory Days on Hand} = \frac{365 \text{ days}}{\text{Inventory Turnover}} = \frac{365}{16.66} = 21.91 \text{ days}$$

On average, the restaurant has about 22 days or three weeks of inventory on hand. It is important to understand that this number includes items that would turn over more quickly (e.g., fish, produce, milk) as well as items that would stay in inventory longer (e.g., spices, canned goods, and frozen foods). Managers may choose to look at individual inventory items or categories to better understand how well a business is managing its inventory.

Accounts Receivable (A/R) Turnover

Many businesses grant credit to their customers and as a result carry significant accounts receivable balances on their balance sheets. The ability to manage these accounts effectively and ultimately convert this asset to cash (via collection) can be a major contributor to overall returns. The **accounts receivable (A/R) turnover** is calculated as follows:

$$\text{Accounts Receivable (A/R) Turnover} = \frac{\text{Credit Sales}}{\text{A/R}}$$

The numerator is sales, as earning revenue is the process that creates accounts receivable. Consider an advertising firm that had sales of $450,000 all on credit in the most recent year and ended the year with A/R of $125,000. The A/R turnover is 3.6. Alternatively, we can calculate **A/R days sales outstanding**, as follows:

$$\text{A/R Days Sales Outstanding} = \frac{365 \text{ days}}{\text{A/R Turnover}}$$

This metric is also called the collection period and it measures how long on average it takes the firm to collect from its customers. For our restaurant example with an A/R turnover of 3.6, the days sales outstanding is 100; that is, on average, the firm's customers take 100 days to pay for services. This may seem like a long time, but many service industries have generous credit terms. If industry convention is to grant 120-day terms, 100 days should not cause concern. However, if the firm in question gives customers 60-day terms, then a 100-day collection period may signal problems. For the restaurant, the 2014 calculation of

A/R turnover and days sales outstanding is as follows. Note that we have assumed only the catering revenue is on credit. All other sales are assumed to be cash or by credit card.[1]

$$\text{Accounts Receivable (A/R) Turnover}_{2014} = \frac{\text{Credit Sales}_{2014}}{\text{A/R}_{2014}} = \frac{\$114,264}{\$8,280} = 13.8X$$

$$\text{A/R Days Sales Outstanding} = \frac{365 \text{ days}}{\text{A/R Turnover}} = \frac{365}{13.8} = 26.45 \text{ days}$$

So the restaurant collects from its catering customers 26 days, or three to four weeks, after the event occurs and the invoice is sent. Is this good or bad? Again, it depends on the terms the restaurant extends to its customers. If the restaurant asks for payment in 15 days, then 24 days is problematic. If the terms call for payment in one month, then 24 days is healthy. The business would want to look at each account to ensure collections are being managed as efficiently as possible. The 24-day average could be due to one customer who paid immediately and another who hadn't paid even after two months. The latter is a concern even if the days sales outstanding average is reasonable.

Accounts Payable (A/P) Period

Accounts payable, that is, trade credit, is an important component of working capital for most businesses. This is financing provided to the business by suppliers willing to deliver goods or raw materials immediately, but defer payment from the business until a later date. While we consider trade credit a source of short-term financing, recall from Chapter 4 that accounts payable is classified as a component of operating cash flows, as a company's suppliers are essential to its core operations.

To assess the level of accounts payable, we use the following ratios:

$$\text{Payables Turnover} = \frac{\text{Cost of Goods Sold}}{\text{Accounts Payable}}$$

$$\text{Payables Period (Days)} = \frac{365}{\text{Payables Turnover}}$$

An important assumption is that the majority of a company's accounts payables relate to inventory purchases. Other short-term liabilities such as **wages payable**, **utilities payable**, and **rent payable** should have their own line item on the balance sheet or may be included in the accrued liabilities account. For the most part, this assumption is valid, and the calculation yields a reasonable estimate of the length of time a company waits to pay its suppliers of inventory.

For our restaurant example, the calculations for 2014 are as follows:

$$\text{Payables Turnover}_{2014} = \frac{\$196,419}{\$22,106} = 8.9X$$

$$\text{Payable Periods (Days)} = \frac{365}{8.9} = 41 \text{ days}$$

---

[1] Technically, a credit card payment creates a receivable—not from the diner, but rather from the bank that issued his or her credit card. However, these amounts are collected quickly, usually in two to three days.

At the end of 2014, our restaurant was paying its suppliers in about 41 days. Is this good or bad? The answer depends on what terms the suppliers give the restaurant. If the terms are 30 days and the restaurant is paying in 41, the suppliers may get upset and provide poorer service or lower-quality goods. Also, it is important to understand that 41 days is the average **payables period** for all of the restaurant's suppliers. For things like fresh fish or produce, which are delivered several times per week, the terms may be shorter (e.g., 10 days to pay). But items like condiments or canned goods, which are ordered less frequently, may carry more generous terms, perhaps 45 or 60 days. Businesses can conserve cash by "stretching" their payables, but this should only be a short-term strategy. Eventually, the suppliers will slow or stop shipments or may impose penalty fees until timely payment is made.

Financial Leverage and Liquidity

Financial leverage is the third lever management can use to influence ROE. Financial leverage is the relationship between debt and equity on the firm's balance sheet. Increasing leverage means increasing the proportion of debt relative to equity. Debt can be beneficial to business owners in several ways. First, in certain situations it may be more accessible than equity, making it easier for the venture to raise needed growth capital. Second, even with mandatory interest and principal payments, the cost of debt is lower than the cost of equity. Finally, due to the tax deductibility of interest payments, debt provides a tax benefit. If borrowed funds can be invested in projects whose returns exceed the after-tax cost of debt, the incremental return accrues to the firm's owners.

A simple example can illustrate these points. The firm has a project with an expected return of 15%, which requires a $20,000 investment. The expected return on the project is therefore $3,000 (15% × $20,000). Now assume the interest rate on debt is 10%, which means that if the business borrows the full $20,000, it will owe the lender interest of $2,000 (10% × $20,000). For now, ignore the effects of income taxes. The difference between the return on the project and the interest, in this case $1,000, goes to the owners. Of course, debt cuts in both directions. If the project goes badly and only returns 5% ($1,000), the owners have a problem. They still owe the bank $2,000 and will have to find the $1,000 shortfall somewhere. The results of additional leverage can be good or bad, and that uncertainty is the reason we associate leverage with risk.

Financial leverage in the DuPont formula is defined as follows:

$$\text{Financial Leverage} = \frac{\text{Total Assets}}{\text{Equity}}$$

To better understand this ratio, recall the basic accounting relationship: Assets = Liabilities + Equity. This equation recognizes that there are two ways to fund the assets of a business: with capital from creditors (liabilities) and with capital from owners (equity). If a venture is financed totally through equity, then there are no liabilities. In this case, Assets = Equity and the Financial Leverage = Total Assets/Equity = 1. There is no financial leverage because management is not using debt to finance assets; all financing is provided by the owners. However, this situation is unlikely, as liabilities are often an important source of funding, especially for new ventures.

For our restaurant example, 2014 financial leverage is computed as follows:

$$\text{Financial Leverage}_{2014} = \frac{\text{Total Assets}_{2014}}{\text{Equity}_{2014}} = \frac{\$91{,}340}{\$44{,}299} = 2.06X$$

So, $91,340 of assets was funded with $44,299 of equity, meaning the balance $(47,041) came from liabilities. This includes trade debt, that is, accounts payable, and the credit card payments.

Now let's consider the impact of this leverage on ROE. For our restaurant, return on assets (ROA) in 2014 is calculated as follows:

$$\text{Return on Assets (ROA)}_{2014} = \frac{\text{Net Income}_{2014}}{\text{Total Assets}_{2014}} = \frac{\$9,747}{\$91,340} = 10.67\%$$

If the restaurant had no debt—that is, if the financial leverage ratio was 1.0—then ROE would also be 10.67%.

$$\text{Return on Equity (ROE)}_{2014} = \text{ROA} \times \text{Financial Leverage} = 10.67\% \times 1.0 = 10.67\%$$

However, look what the actual financial leverage ratio of 2.06 does to our ROE calculation:

$$\text{Return on Equity (ROE)}_{2014} = \text{ROA} \times \text{Financial Leverage} = 10.67\% \times 2.06 = 22.09\%$$

In this example, financial leverage was used to "lever up" ROA to the benefit of the owners as measured by a large increase in ROE. Of course, with the potential rewards of financial leverage come very real risks. Liabilities require interest payments as well as the repayment of the original loan, that is, the principal. If a company cannot find projects that return more than the interest rate on the loans it incurs, then it will be paying more in interest than it is earning on the investment funded by the loan—not a good situation. A company has to earn enough income to cover its interest expense and generate sufficient cash flow to meet required periodic interest and principal payments. Failing to do so can result in insolvency, financial distress, and, ultimately, bankruptcy.

There are several other metrics closely related to financial leverage that are often used to measure the relative amounts of debt and equity on a company's balance sheet, including the two shown below. Because these are so similar to financial leverage, we omit their calculations for our restaurant.

$$\text{Debt-to-Assets Ratio} = \frac{\text{Total Liabilities}}{\text{Total Assets}}$$

$$\text{Debt-to-Equity Ratio} = \frac{\text{Total Liabilities}}{\text{Equity}}$$

In the following ratio, the emphasis is on only interest-bearing debt, which would exclude items like accounts payable or wages payable. It is helpful to know the relative magnitude of debt on which the firm must make cash payments.

$$\text{Interest-Bearing Debt-to-Assets Ratio} = \frac{\text{Interest-Bearing Liabilities}}{\text{Total Assets}}$$

We use two additional ratios used to assess a firm's ability to meet the required payments that accompany debt. This is important, because a firm without sufficient cash flow to make these payments cannot survive very long. These ratios are called **times interest earned** and **times burden covered**, and are calculated as follows:

$$\text{Times Interest Earned} = \frac{\text{Earnings Before Interest \& Taxes (EBIT)}}{\text{Interest Expense}}$$

$$\text{Times Burden Covered} = \frac{\text{Earnings Before Interest \& Taxes (EBIT)}}{\text{Interest Expense} + \dfrac{\text{Principal Repayment}}{(1 - \text{Tax Rate})}}$$

The times interest earned tells us how much EBIT or operating profit the company has relative to its interest expense.[2] Times burden covered has the same numerator, but includes both interest and principal repayment in the denominator, recognizing the reality that both are mandatory payments.[3] This formula is a bit more complicated due to the fact that principal repayments are not tax deductible. Thus the principal repayment in the denominator has to be "grossed up" to reflect the equivalent pretax amount needed to cover the actual principal repayment.

For our restaurant example, the 2014 calculations of times interest earned and times burden covered are shown below. For the latter, we make an additional two assumptions to explain the second calculation: the tax rate is 35% and the required principal repayment in 2014 is $2,000.

$$\text{Times Interest Earned}_{2014} = \frac{\text{Earnings Before Interest \& Taxes (EBIT)}_{2014}}{\text{Interest Expense}_{2014}} = \frac{\$16,250}{\$1,193} = 13.63X$$

$$\text{Times Burden Covered}_{2014} = \frac{\text{Earnings Before Interest \& Taxes (EBIT)}_{2014}}{\text{Interest Expense}_{2014} + \dfrac{\text{Principal Repayment}_{2014}}{(1 - \text{Tax Rate})}} = \frac{\$16,250}{\$1,193 + \dfrac{\$2,000}{(1 - 0.35)}} = 3.81X$$

How should we interpret these ratios? A times interest earned (TIE) of 13.63 says the restaurant's operating profit could cover its interest expense 13.63 times. Alternatively, EBIT could fall substantially before it would be below the required interest payment. This seems to imply a low level of risk to the restaurant's lenders. However, when we factor in the principal repayment, the times burden covered (TBC) is 3.81, and the lender's cushion of safety is much smaller. What are good numbers for TIE or TBC? A banker's response to that question will always be "higher," but that may not be true from the owners' perspective. If these ratios are too high, the company may be missing relatively low-risk opportunities to create value for its owners by employing leverage. To estimate the optimal level of debt for a business, we need to run numerous "what-if" scenarios and financial forecasts to see their impact on the financial statements and ratios and then make a well-informed decision.

The funding of assets is a zero-sum game—either liabilities or owners' equity must be used. Leverage (i.e., using more debt) can be beneficial to owners, because it magnifies a positive return on assets to increase ROE. We focused on the ratio of financial leverage—that is, Total Assets/Equity, because it is incorporated in the DuPont model. We also saw several similar metrics used to evaluate a firm's financial leverage.

In addition to these balance sheet ratios, there are other metrics that use income statement and balance sheet data to assess a company's ability to meet its required interest and principal payments. Times interest earned and times burden covered are both important tools for analyzing a company's debt capacity and its use of financial leverage. Clearly, this topic is a book in itself. For this introduction, knowing how to calculate and interpret these basic ratios on leverage provides a solid foundation for understanding the implications of different options for funding growth. We now turn to the related concept of liquidity.

Liquidity

Narrowly defined, **liquidity** is a measure of a company's ability to meet its near-term obligations. These typically include accounts payable, wages payable, and other current liabilities. Liquid assets are assets that can be converted to cash relatively quickly and usually include cash, short-term investments, and accounts receivable. Because liquidity is a near-term concept, the ratios we use focus on the balance sheet accounts in current

---

[2] We sometimes use earnings before interest, taxes, depreciation, and amortization (EBITDA) in the numerator as well, as this is a metric that gets us closer to operating cash flow.

[3] Some analysts include other required payments in the denominator, such as contractual lease payments, advertising commitments, and so forth.

assets and current liabilities. Recall that current assets are defined as assets that are expected to be turned into cash within one year, and current liabilities are liabilities that are anticipated to be paid within one year. The **current ratio** is as follows:

$$\text{Current Ratio} = \frac{\text{Current Assets}}{\text{Current Liabilities}}$$

The current ratio measures the amount of "excess" liquidity available to the company. If the current ratio is 1.0, there is little safety cushion, as the current assets are just enough to cover the current liabilities. So 1.0 is often thought of as the floor for the current ratio, although like all ratios, the benchmarks vary by industry. Obviously, a higher current ratio would give potential short-term lenders to the firm more comfort. Consider a new supplier from whom the business is requesting trade credit. The supplier should ask to see a recent current ratio calculation and if it is low, be cautious about extending credit.

In most industries, a company's inventory cannot be converted to cash quickly, and is, therefore, not available to pay liabilities immediately. For example, during an economic downturn, homebuilders may carry inventory of land and houses that sell slowly. For high-tech industries, inventory obsolescence may be an issue. And for a food wholesaler, a warehouse of fresh fish that cannot be sold due to a truckers' strike will never provide the business with any cash. The **acid test or quick ratio** subtracts inventory from current assets to provide a more stringent assessment of liquidity.

$$\text{Quick Ratio or Acid Test} = \frac{\text{Current Assets} - \text{Inventory}}{\text{Current Liabilities}}$$

We can now calculate our two liquidity ratios for the restaurant example:

$$\text{Current Ratio}_{2014} = \frac{\text{Current Assets}}{\text{Current Liabilities}} = \frac{\$49,339}{\$33,941} = 1.45$$

$$\text{Acid Test}_{2014} = \frac{\text{Current Assets} - \text{Inventory}}{\text{Current Liabilities}} = \frac{\$49,339 - \$11,790}{\$33,941} = 1.11$$

These results are healthy, because if the current assets—even excluding inventory—were converted into cash, the restaurant would be able to cover its current liabilities. Liquidity ratios are an important part of an overall story. They are frequently used as loan covenants by banks so that the lenders have early-warning signals with respect to the company's ability to meet its short-term financial obligations, especially the bank's interest and principal payments. For example, a bank may require that as a requirement for a loan, the company must keep its current ratio above 1.5. If the company's current ratio falls below 1.5, the loan is technically in default. The consequences, which are clearly detailed in the loan agreement, can include immediate payment of the the entire loan, forced liquidation of assets, increased interest payments, or the posting of additional collateral. None of these is good for business, and the venture should do everything possible to maintain the necessary liquidity.

Can liquidity ever be too high? The answer is yes. For example, let's assume the current ratio for a local shoe retailer is 4.0. Let's also assume that even after subtracting the substantial shoe inventory, the acid test ratio is 2.0; that is, all current assets less inventory are twice as large as current liabilities. Both these ratios indicate a liquid company with a safe current position. However, if we think about current assets, they consist of cash, which earns little or no interest; accounts receivable, which typically earn no interest; and inventory, which must be financed and carried and which is at risk of obsolescence. High levels of these current assets may indicate poor cash management, poor collection efforts, slow-paying and potentially risky customers, and slow-moving inventory—none of which is good for business. Alternatively, the current and quick ratios could be high because the company has a very low level of current liabilities. Perhaps the company is missing opportunities for additional trade credit. More trade credit would increase the current liability accounts payable, but it may be free financing, at least in the short term. In general, the company wants to minimize its investment in non-productive or "non-earning" assets and take advantage of any opportunities for interest-free financing.

Cash Flow and Liquidity

To help entrepreneurs think about liquidity from a different perspective, we expand the traditional definition to include **operating cash flow** and the **cash operating cycle**. Both of these concepts were introduced and discussed in earlier chapters, primarily Chapter 4.

Operating cash flow is an important contributor to liquidity because for many small businesses, access to cash flows from investing or financing is limited.[4] Negative operating cash flow means management must find external sources to meet the company's cash needs. If operating cash flow remains negative over a number of periods, the company will quickly burn through any cash balances, significantly reducing liquidity. When the company is unable to meet its short-term obligations (e.g., delaying payments to suppliers), it may signal the need for a major cash infusion from existing or new investors (either debt or equity).

The following data show the calculation of operating cash flow for our restaurant example over the 2010–2014 time period:

Cash Flows	2010	2011	2012	2013	2014
Operating activities:					
Net income.	$19,814	$11,088	$ 6,273	$ 7,150	$ 9,787
Add: Depreciation.	2,500	2,500	3,000	5,000	5,000
Change in working capital					
Accounts receivable.	(1,000)	(1,000)	(1,000)	(1,200)	(1,080)
Inventory.	(1,700)	(800)	(1,188)	(1,351)	(1,451)
Other current assets.	—	—	—	—	(1,000)
Accounts payable.	—	1,375	2,345	2,541	2,720
Wages payable.	430	430	85	501	208
Other current liabilities	(2,000)	(2,840)	(1,160)	2,000	(2,000)
NET: Operating cash flow.	$18,044	$10,753	$8,356	$14,640	$12,184

Operating cash flow is positive each year, which is good. The restaurant experienced a decline in 2011 and 2012 operating cash flow, due mainly to a reduction in net income, but the cash flow bounced back in 2013 and 2014. Consistent positive operating cash flow contributes to healthy liquidity, but recall from our earlier discussion that a company can also be too liquid. How the periodic operating cash flow is managed is the focus of our last liquidity factor, the cash operating cycle.

The cash operating cycle was introduced in Chapters 1 and 4 and assesses how a company manages the operating cash flows of the business. Recall how the cash operating cycle is calculated:

Cash Operating Cycle = Inventory Days on Hand + A/R Days Outstanding – A/P Days

The cash operating cycle provides an estimate of the number of days that a company must commit cash to cover its working capital needs. The measure is a function of how long its products sit in inventory, how frequently it collects from its credit customers, and how long it waits to pay its suppliers. For our restaurant in 2014, the calculation of cash operating cycle is straightforward and is a *negative* −6.1 days:

---

[4] More-established companies can increase liquidity by selling assets, but for new ventures, there are rarely assets available for sale.

$$\text{Cash Operating Cycle} = \text{Inventory Days on Hand} + \text{A/R Days Outstanding} - \text{A/P Days}$$
$$= 21.2 + 13.8 - 41.1 = -6.1 \text{ days}$$

This result is driven primarily by the 41-day payables period. The shorter the cash operating cycle, the more quickly a company converts its sales to cash and the lower its working capital needs. This will have a positive impact on liquidity, though note that carrying higher balances of accounts payable, all else equal, will be associated with lower current and quick ratios. Assessing liquidity requires considering several metrics at the same time to view the company from different angles and capture a complete picture.

In summary, the last lever in the DuPont model, financial leverage, focuses on the use of liabilities to benefit a company's owners. There are pros and cons to financial leverage, and the important issue is to understand the risks inherent in debt. We introduced several ratios used to measure leverage, along with two additional ratios, times interest earned and times burden covered. These two ratios assess the company's ability to generate profit and cash flow at a level sufficient to meet the contractual payments (interest and principal) that come with debt. Finally, the concept of liquidity was introduced and discussed, using the current and acid test ratios as well as cash flow data provided by the statement of cash flows and the operating cash cycle. In the last section of this chapter we use basic ratio analysis to examine the restaurant's operations over a five-year period, comparing results both across years and to industry data for the same period.

Using Ratios Effectively

The following figure summarizes the discussion in this chapter and shows how ROE can be broken into the three DuPont components: profitability, asset turnover, and financial leverage. It also shows how those three broad categories can be further refined to learn more about specific aspects of a venture's financial performance.

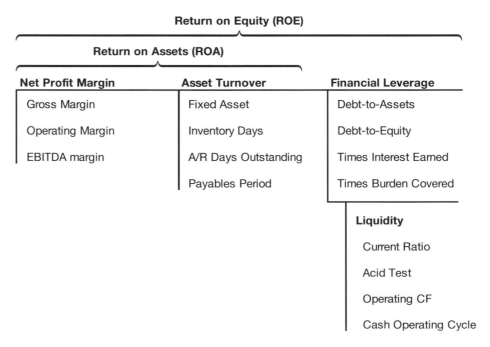

The data in the following table show our ratio calculations from throughout this chapter and extend them to the full five-year period from our restaurant example. Using this information, we can make several observations about the restaurant's forecasted financial performance:

- Profitability at all levels (gross, operating, EBITDA, and net) declines significantly before recovering slightly in 2013 and 2014.
- Total asset turnover changes little over the period, and the other turnover/control ratios are also stable over the five years.
- Leverage, as measured by the **financial leverage** and **debt-to-equity ratios**, declined over time, primarily due to increasing owners' equity.
- After 2011, times interest earned ranges from 7 to 14, which suggests that the restaurant may be able to take on more debt
- Liquidity is not very strong; the current ratio is below 1.0 in 2010 and averages just 1.2 over the five years. The quick ratio is below 1.0 in three of the five years and only 1.1 in the other two. The company's negative operating cash cycle is the result of its 40-day accounts payable outstanding.

DuPont Analysis	2010	2011	2012	2013	2014
Profit margin	5.91%	2.96%	1.50%	1.54%	1.89%
Asset turnover	5.73	5.38	5.54	5.14	5.66
Financial leverage	5.85	3.30	2.77	2.62	2.06
ROE	198%	53%	23%	21%	22%
ROA	34%	16%	8%	8%	11%

Profitability	2010	2011	2012	2013	2014
Gross margin	65.00%	64.00%	63.00%	62.00%	62.00%
Operating (EBIT) margin	9.40%	4.95%	2.69%	2.62%	3.14%
EBITDA margin	10.15%	5.62%	3.41%	3.69%	4.11%
Profit margin	5.91%	2.96%	1.50%	1.54%	1.89%

Asset turnover	2010	2011	2012	2013	2014
Fixed asset turnover	12.18	10.70	11.33	9.90	12.31
Accounts receivable turnover	83.8	74.9	69.9	64.6	62.4
Inventory turnover	16.8	17.3	17.3	17.1	16.7
Accounts payable turnover	8.9	9.3	9.2	9.1	8.9
A/R days outstanding	4	5	5	6	6
Inventory days on hand	22	21	21	21	22
A/P days outstanding	41	39	40	40	41
Operating cash cycle (days)	(15)	(13)	(13)	(13)	(13)

Financial leverage	2010	2011	2012	2013	2014
Debt-to-equity	4.9	2.3	1.8	1.6	1.1
Times interest earned	31.0	12.4	6.9	10.2	13.6

Liquidity	2010	2011	2012	2013	2014
Current ratio	0.87	1.16	1.38	1.06	1.45
Quick ratio (Acid test)	0.67	0.90	1.06	0.81	1.11
A/R days outstanding	4	5	5	6	6
Inventory days on hand	22	21	21	21	22
A/P days outstanding	41	39	40	40	41
Operating cash cycle (days)	(15)	(13)	(13)	(13)	(13)

This approach to assessing financial results—comparing a single company's performance over time—is called **time-series analysis**, and it is a good way to identify trends and changes in the company's ratios, but it is not without flaws. The primary shortcoming is that times-series analysis provides information about the relative performance of only one business over several time periods. Although this has value, it says nothing about how the business compares to competitors or other firms in the industry. Financial information for public companies is readily available, and there are also numerous sources of data for small and private businesses. In the following table, we compare several key metrics from the restaurant to industry data assembled from the Risk Management Association (RMA). Note that this comparison is focused at the beginning of the five-year period.

Ratio	Restaurant	Industry Avg.[1]
Gross margin	65.0%	58.3%
Operating margin	9.4%	2.9%
Asset turnover	5.7	5.8
Inventory turnover	16.8	48.5
Inventory days on hand	21.8	7.5
A/p turnover	8.9	71.3
Payables period (days)	40.9	5.1
Debt-to-equity	4.9	11.2
Times interest earned	31.0	2.6
Current ratio	0.9	0.9
Quick ratio	0.7	0.4

[1] Data from the Risk Management Association (RMA)

The comparison to industry data provides the following additional insights into the restaurant's financial results:

- The restaurant's gross margin is about 7 percentage points better than the industry average (65% vs. 58%), and this difference in profitability persists at the operating level.

- Total asset turnover is almost identical to the industry average, but the inventory and A/P numbers are very different; our restaurant has significantly higher levels of inventory (22 vs. 7.5 days) and takes much longer to pay its suppliers (41 vs. 5.1 days).

- The industry average for financial leverage is higher, based on the debt-to-equity ratio (11.2 vs. 4.9 X); this results in a much lower times interest earned ratio of 2.6 (vs. 31.0) due to the higher interest expense associated with more leverage.

- Finally, the current and quick ratios—which we identified as potentially problematic in our time-series analysis—appear to be well in line with industry averages; in fact, the quick ratio is higher for our restaurant.

Ratio analysis based on industry or comparable data usually provides valuable information about a company's performance and can also be used to test the validity of forecast assumptions.

CONCLUSION

There are many approaches to analyzing financial performance. In this chapter, we have focused on the DuPont model, which allows us to assess how companies employ the three "levers" of financial performance—profitability, asset utilization, and financial leverage—to affect ROE. We also introduced metrics that allow a more detailed analysis of performance and financial health, including an evaluation of liquidity and operating cash flow.

When using the DuPont model (or any tool for analyzing financial performance), we must always consider the underlying operational factors or managerial decisions that generated the financial results. As a business owner or manager, understanding how market conditions, strategic decisions, and financing choices impact your operating results, and ultimately the return earned by the company, is an essential first step in creating a successful and sustainable business model and plan for growth.

APPENDIX: RATIO SUMMARY

DuPont Model (ROE)	**Profit Margin × Asset Turnover × Leverage**
Profit Margin	$\dfrac{\text{Net Income}}{\text{Sales}}$
Asset Turnover	$\dfrac{\text{Sales}}{\text{Ending Total Assets}}$
Leverage	$\dfrac{\text{Total Assets}}{\text{Equity}}$
Profitability Ratios	
Profit Margin	$\dfrac{\text{Net Income}}{\text{Sales}}$
Gross Margin	$\dfrac{\text{Gross Profit}}{\text{Sales}}$
Operating Margin	$\dfrac{\text{Operating Profit}}{\text{Sales}}$
EBIT Margin	$\dfrac{(\text{Net Income} + \text{Taxes} + \text{Interest})}{\text{Sales}}$
EBITDA Margin	$\dfrac{(\text{EBIT} + \text{Depreciation Expense \& Amortization Expense})}{\text{Sales}}$
Asset Management Ratios	
Asset Turnover	$\dfrac{\text{Sales}}{\text{Ending Total Assets}}$
Accounts Receivable Turnover	$\dfrac{\text{Sales}}{\text{Ending Accounts Receivable}}$
A/R Days Sales Outstanding (DSO)	$\dfrac{365}{\text{Accounts Receivable Turnover}}$
Accounts Payable Turnover	$\dfrac{\text{COGS}}{\text{Ending Accounts Payable}}$
A/P Period (Days Outstanding)	$\dfrac{365}{\text{Accounts Payable Turnover}}$
Inventory Turnover	$\dfrac{\text{Cost of Goods Sold}}{\text{Ending Inventory}}$
Inventory Days on Hand (DOH)	$\dfrac{365}{\text{Inventory Turnover}}$
Fixed Asset (or PP&E) Turnover	Sales/Net PPE
Leverage (Financial Risk, Solvency)	
Leverage	$\dfrac{\text{Total Assets}}{\text{Equity}}$
Total Liabilities to Equity	$\dfrac{\text{Total Liabilities}}{\text{Equity}}$
Debt Equity	$\dfrac{\text{Interest-Bearing Debt}}{\text{Equity}}$
Times Interest Earned	$\dfrac{\text{Income Before Interest and Taxes}}{\text{Interest Expense}}$
Times Burden Covered	$\dfrac{\text{EBIT}}{\left(\text{Interest} + \dfrac{\text{Principal Repayment}}{[1 - \text{Tax Rate}]}\right)}$

continued

continued from prior page

Return Ratios	
Return on Assets	$\dfrac{\text{Net Income}}{\text{Ending Total Assets}}$
Return on Invested Capital	$\dfrac{(\text{EBIT}[1 - \text{Tax Rate}])}{(\text{Interest-Bearing Debt} + \text{Equity})}$
Return on Equity	$\dfrac{\text{Net Income}}{\text{Ending Equity}}$
Earnings per Share	$\dfrac{\text{Net Income}}{\text{Common Shares Outstanding}}$
Dividend Payout	$\dfrac{\text{Dividends}}{\text{Net Income}}$
Price/Earnings Ratio	$\dfrac{\text{Market Price}}{\text{Earnings per Share}}$
Liquidity Ratios/Cash Flow	
Current Ratio	$\dfrac{\text{Current Assets}}{\text{Current Liabilities}}$
Quick (Acid Test) Ratio	$\dfrac{(\text{Current Assets} - \text{Inventory})}{\text{Current Liabilities}}$
Working Capital	Current Assets – Current Liabilities
Accounts Receivable Turnover	$\dfrac{\text{Sales}}{\text{Ending Accounts Receivable}}$
A/R Days Sales Outstanding	$\dfrac{365}{\text{Accounts Receivable Turnover}}$
Accounts Payable Turnover	$\dfrac{\text{COGS}}{\text{Ending Accounts Payable}}$
A/P Period (Days Outstanding)	$\dfrac{365}{\text{Accounts Payable Turnover}}$
Inventory Turnover	$\dfrac{\text{Cost of Goods Sold}}{\text{Ending Inventory}}$
Inventory Days on Hand	$\dfrac{365}{\text{Inventory Turnover}}$
Operating Cash Cycle	Days A/R + Inventory Days – A/P Days

KEY CONCEPTS AND TERMS

accounts receivable (A/R) turnover, 135
acid test or quick ratio, 140
A/R days sales outstanding, 135
asset turnover, 133
cash operating cycle, 141
common-size analysis, 128
current ratio, 140
debt-to-equity ratios, 143
DuPont formula, 130
EBITDA, 133

EBITDA margin, 133
financial leverage, 143
fixed asset turnover, 134
gross margin, 132
inventory days on hand, 135
inventory turnover, 134
liquidity, 139
net margin, 133
operating cash flow, 141
operating expenses, 133
operating margin, 132

payables period, 137
profit margin, 131
rent payable, 136
return on assets, 131
return on equity, 130
times burden covered, 138
time-series analysis, 143
times interest earned, 138
utilities payable, 136
wages payable, 136

QUESTIONS

Q6-1. Define a common-size income statement and a common-size balance sheet.

Q6-2. Identify the five ratios that constitute the DuPont model.

Q6-3. Define and explain the asset turnover ratio.

Q6-4. Define and explain the leverage ratio.

Q6-5. What explains the difference between return on equity and return on assets?

Q6-6. What is the difference between gross margin, operating margin, and profit margin?

Q6-7. Show how receivables turnover (sales revenue / accounts receivable) converts to days sales outstanding.

Q6-8. Show how inventory turnover (cost of goods sold / inventory) converts to days inventory on hand.

Q6-9. Explain how we use the cash cycle in financial statement analysis.

Q6-10. Define the current ratio and the quick ratio. Why is the quick ratio also called the "acid test"?

EXERCISES

E6-1. **Financial Footprints** **Mylan, Inc.**, and **Merck & Co., Inc.**, both compete in the pharmaceutical industry. Mylan develops, manufactures, and distributes generic pharmaceuticals around the world. ("Generic" drugs are not branded and can only be produced after the patent of the original product has expired.) Merck develops, manufactures, and distributes patented, branded pharmaceuticals, such as Singulair, and branded consumer products, such as Claritin and Dr. Scholl's foot products.

Mylan, Inc.
Merck & Co., Inc.

Using the financial information below, match the company to the appropriate column, and support your conclusion with two brief financial footprint characteristics.

	Company A	Company B
Revenue	100.0%	100.0%
Cost of goods sold/Revenue	56.4%	38.5%
Gross profit percentage	43.6%	61.5%
Research and development expense/Revenue	7.4%	17.0%
Selling, general & administrative expense/Revenue	19.6%	28.0%
Operating profit/Revenue	16.6%	16.5%

E6-2. **Financial Footprints** **Darden Restaurants, Inc.**, owns and operates over 1,500 restaurants in the United States and Canada, primarily Olive Garden and LongHorn Steakhouse. All of its restaurants are full service with emphasis on fresh ingredients, regularly updated menus, and a complete bar (with an extensive wine selection). Olive Garden inner entrée prices range from $10 to $20, with the average check amount per person at $17 in the most recent year, whereas LongHorn Steakhouse prices are slightly higher generating an average check amount per person of almost $20 in the most recent year.

Darden Restaurants, Inc.
Panera Bread Company

Panera Bread Company owns 867 bakery-cafes (and franchises another 910) in the United States and Canada. The company built its brand and reputation on bread, and now serves breakfast, lunch, and dinner with a focus on comfort food (e.g., soup) and a cozy atmosphere. Panera's menu includes breakfast items in the $3 to $5 range and sandwiches in the $7 to $10 range. Customers order at a counter and serve themselves, and no alcoholic beverages are sold.

Using the ratios below, identify which company (A or B) is which (Darden Restaurants or Panera Bread). Provide at least two reasons for your choice, and be sure to specify operational characteristics, not just numbers.

	Company A	Company B
Cost of food, beverages, and paper/restaurant revenue	29.7%	30.1%
Cost of restaurant labor/restaurant revenue	29.6%	32.1%
Occupancy expenses/restaurant revenue	21.1%	17.2%
Days inventory on hand	13	38
Fixed asset turnover	3.2	1.9

E6-3. Financial Footprints Consider four companies in different spaces of the pharmaceutical industry.

Cubist
Pharmaceuticals, Inc.
CVS Caremark
Corporation

Medtronic, Inc.

Merck & Co., Inc.

1. **Cubist Pharmaceuticals, Inc.,** a biopharmaceutical company focusing on specific antibiotics used in hospitals and other acute-care institutions.
2. **CVS Caremark Corporation** combines both retail pharmacy (with close to 7,500 stores and a growing number of "Minute Clinics") with pharmacy benefit management services for corporate clients.
3. **Medtronic, Inc.,** manufactures and sells medical devices, most of which are surgically implanted, such as pacemakers and insulin pumps. The company sells to hospitals, physicians, and clinicians in approximately 140 countries.
4. **Merck & Co., Inc.,** manufactures and markets a wide range of pharmaceuticals, from prescription drugs and vaccines to branded over-the-counter items, such as Claritin and Dr. Scholl's foot care products.

The following ratios have been calculated for each of the four companies.

	Company A	Company B	Company C	Company D
$\dfrac{\text{Cost of goods sold}}{\text{Revenue}}$	81.2%	25.3%	34.4%	24.2%
$\dfrac{\text{Selling, general, and administrative}}{\text{Revenue}}$	12.5%	34.3%	27.0%	20.2%
$\dfrac{\text{Research and development}}{\text{Revenue}}$	—	9.4%	17.3%	32.7%
Operating margin	6.3%	28.8%	22.6%	26.6%
Inventory turnover	9.3	2.3	2.5	6
Inventory turnover days	38.7	157	144	60
Fixed asset turnover	14.7	6.7	2.9	5.5

Required:

Match the company to the appropriate set of ratios, and briefly explain your rationale.

E6-4. Business Models and Financial Footprints

Amazon, Inc.

1. **Amazon, Inc.** is the ubiquitous retailer of a wide array of products claiming to offer "Earth's Biggest Selection" which may well be true. Although it has many warehouses, its online business model means that it has no stores. Its retail customers pay cash (or the equivalent with credit/debit cards), but it does extend credit to its corporate customers who contract for advertising and other services.

Barnes & Noble, Inc.

2. **Barnes & Noble, Inc.** has not kept pace with Amazon, but remains one of the largest U.S. booksellers. While it does substantial business in digital books and other materials, it remains largely committed to stores, particularly on college and university campuses, which account for roughly half of its 1,361 stores in all 50 states. It extends very little credit to customers.

FedEx

3. **FedEx** provides both ground and express delivery services to a wide range of customers, including many retailers (e.g., Amazon). It extends credit to its many corporate customers and, as you would expect, it owns a large fleet of trucks and aircraft.

	Company A		Company B		Company C	
Cash	$4,917	15%	$11,448	35%	$160	4%
A/R	5,044	15%	3,364	10%	149	4%
Inventory	0	0%	6,031	19%	1,411	38%
Other current assets	1,313	4%	453	1%	327	9%
PPE and other long-term assets	22,293	66%	11,259	35%	1,685	45%
Total	$33,567	100%	$32,555	100%	$3,732	100%

Required:

Using the information on assets (millions of dollars in the first column, percentage of total assets in the second column) provided above, identify each company and provide at least one reason for your choice.

E6-5. **Business Models and Financial Footprints**   Though still working to catch up to **Google**, **Yahoo, Inc.** remains a popular search engine and generates substantial revenues through advertising and user clicks. It sells to corporate customers all over the world, and its business models require substantial computer equipment, but very few buildings, and lots of people. Yahoo uses relatively little debt to finance its business.

    Many airlines advertise on Yahoo, and one such company might be **Southwest Airlines**. Southwest is a passenger airline with most of its routes relatively short and in the U.S. It has the distinction of 40 years of profitability, which, in the airline industry, is remarkable.

    Another company that might advertise on Yahoo is **Yum! Brands**, the company that owns and operates Pizza Hut, Taco Bell, and KFC restaurants around the world. The company owns about 900 restaurants and rents another 6,700 units, and earns most revenue from units that it operates itself (rather than through franchising which it does in a limited way).

Google

Yahoo, Inc.

Southwest Airlines

Yum! Brands

	Company A	Company B	Company C
Return on equity.	6.00%	9.79%	70.90%
Return on assets	2.30%	8.40%	17.80%
Operating margin	3.6%	13.1%	16.8%
Rent expense / Revenue	5.5%	1.3%	7.4%
Days receivable outstanding	7	59	8
Days inventory on hand	0	0	29
Fixed asset turnover.	1.34	3.65	3.21

Required:

Using the ratios above, identify each company and provide at least one reason for your choice.

Use the following information for exercises 6 through 10.

Abby Waters started Waters Corporation, an office furniture business, in 2013. She designs the furniture, occasionally to custom specifications, and subcontracts all the manufacturing. Her supplier grants her credit for 30 days, and offers a discount if she pays within 15 days. She carries enough inventory so that she can usually fill her customers' orders quickly, and she sells to small and medium-sized companies to whom she offers 45 days of credit.

    Although Abby looks carefully at weekly reports regarding sales and operating costs for her company, she didn't take a step back until the end of 2015 when she considered the company's overall performance with the income statements and balance sheets below. She knew that the firm's revenues had grown by 30% in both 2014 and 2015, but she also knew that the company was experiencing a cash crunch. The 2015 balance sheet correctly shows a declining cash balance, and she was in the process of seeking additional funding.

Income Statements			
	2015	2014	2013
Revenue	$170	$130	$100
COGS	111	82	60
Gross profit.	60	48	40
SG&A	43	34	27
Operating income.	17	14	13
Interest expense.	0	0	0
Net income before taxes	17	14	13
Income tax expense.	6	5	5
Net income	$ 11	$ 9	$ 8

Balance Sheets			
	As of the end of		
	2015	**2014**	**2013**
Assets			
Cash...	$ 1	$ 3	$ 6
Accounts receivable.............................	25	16	11
Inventory......................................	26	20	15
Current assets	52	40	32
Property, plant and equipment....................	12	10	7
Total assets....................................	64	50	39
Liabilities and owners' equity			
Accounts payable...............................	10	7	5
Long-term debt	0	0	0
Capital stock	26	26	26
Retained earnings	28	17	8
Total liabilities and owners' equity	$64	$50	$39

E6-6. **Financial Ratio Calculations** Calculate ROE and its components for 2013–2015 for the Waters Corporation.

E6-7. **Financial Ratio Calculations** Calculate gross margin and operating margin for 2013–2015 for the Waters Corporation.

E6-8. **Financial Ratio Calculations** Calculate the components of asset turnover (receivables turnover, inventory turnover, and fixed asset turnover) for 2013–2015 for the Waters Corporation.

E6-9. **Financial Ratio Calculations** Calculate the cash cycle for Waters Corporation for 2013–2015.

E6-10. **Financial Ratio Analysis** Using your calculations in exercises 6 through 9 above, identify the primary causes of Abby's cash crunch. Suggest three specific changes that Abby should consider to solve her cash flow problem. Think carefully about the potential consequences of those changes for her overall.

PROBLEMS

P6-1. **Time Series Financial Statement Analysis—Kellogg** Founded in 1906, Kellogg's primary products are ready-to-eat cereals and cookies, crackers, and snacks, with brand names including Keebler and Cheez-It, and the well-known Kellogg name on Corn Flakes, Frosted Flakes, and Raisin Bran.

Required:
Use the statements below the following questions.

a. Calculate Kellogg's return on equity (ROE) in 2013.
b. Calculate the separate DuPont model components of Kellogg's ROE in 2013.
c. Calculate Kellogg's fixed asset turnover ratio in 2013.
d. Calculate Kellogg's inventory turnover ratio in 2012 and 2013. (Provide at least one possible reason for the change.)
e. Kellogg's operating margin (operating income/revenue) increased from 11.0% in 2012 to 19.2% in 2013. Using its common-sized income statement, provide two likely reasons—citing specific ratios—for this significant improvement.

KELLOGG COMPANY AND SUBSIDIARIES
Consolidated Statement of Income

(millions, except per share data)	2013	2012	2011
Net sales.	$14,792	$14,197	$13,198
Cost of goods sold.	8,689	8,763	8,046
Selling, general and administrative expense	3,266	3,872	3,725
Operating profit	2,837	1,562	1,427
Interest expense.	235	261	233
Other income (expense), net	4	24	(10)
Income before income taxes	2,606	1,325	1,184
Income taxes	792	363	320
Earnings (loss) from joint ventures	(6)	(1)	—
Net income.	$ 1,808	$ 961	$ 864

KELLOGG COMPANY AND SUBSIDIARIES
Consolidated Balance Sheet

(millions, except share data)	2013	2012
Current assets		
Cash and cash equivalents	$ 273	$ 281
Accounts receivable, net	1,424	1,454
Inventories	1,248	1,365
Other current assets.	322	280
Total current assets	3,267	3,380
Property, net.	3,856	3,782
Goodwill*	5,051	5,038
Other intangibles, net.	2,367	2,359
Other assets.	933	610
Total assets.	$15,474	$15,169
Current liabilities		
Current maturities of long-term debt	$ 289	$ 755
Notes payable	739	1,065
Accounts payable.	1,432	1,402
Other current liabilities	1,375	1,301
Total current liabilities.	3,835	4,523
Long-term debt	6,330	6,082
Deferred income taxes.	928	523
Pension liability.	277	886
Other liabilities	497	690
Commitments and contingencies		
Equity		
Common stock, $.25 par value, 1,000,000,000 shares authorized		
Issued: 419,923,540 shares in 2013 and 419,718,217 shares in 2012.	105	105
Capital in excess of par value	626	573
Retained earnings	6,749	5,615
Treasury stock, at cost		
57,121,760 shares in 2013 and 58,452,083 shares in 2012.	(2,999)	(2,943)
Accumulated other comprehensive income (loss)*	(936)	(946)
Total Kellogg Company equity	3,545	2,404
Noncontrolling interests	62	61
Total equity.	3,607	2,465
Total liabilities and equity	$15,474	$15,169

	2013	2012
Net sales.	100.0%	100.0%
Cost of goods sold.	58.7%	61.7%
Selling, general and administrative expense	22.1%	27.3%
Operating profit	19.2%	11.0%
Interest expense.	1.6%	1.8%
Other income	0.0%	0.2%
Income before income taxes	17.6%	9.3%

P6-2. **Time Series Financial Statement Analysis—General Mills** Founded in 1928, General Mills' primary products are ready-to-eat cereals and other food products (e.g., yogurt, nutrition bars, and ice cream), with brand names including Yoplait, Pillsbury, and Muir Glen, as well as its well-known Wheaties, Cheerios, and Cocoa Puffs brands.

Required:
Use the financial statements below to answer the following questions.

a. Calculate General Mills' return on equity (ROE) in the year ending May 2014.
b. Calculate the separate DuPont model components of General Mills' ROE in the year ending May 2014.
c. Calculate General Mills' fixed asset turnover ratio in May 2014.
d. Calculate General Mills' accounts payable turnover ratio in 2013 and 2014. (Provide at least one possible reason for the change.)
e. General Mills' operating margin (operating income/revenue) increased from 16.0% in May 2013 to 16.5% in May 2014. Using its common-sized income statement, provide two likely reasons—citing specific ratios—for this significant improvement.

GENERAL MILLS, INC. AND SUBSIDIARIES Consolidated Statements of Earnings			
	Fiscal Year		
(in millions, except per share data)	**2014**	**2013**	**2012**
Net sales.	$17,909.6	$17,774.1	$16,657.9
Cost of sales.	11,539.8	11,350.2	10,613.2
Selling, general, and administrative expenses.	3,408.8	3,552.3	3,380.7
Restructuring, impairment, and other exit costs	3.6	19.8	101.6
Operating profit	2,957.4	2,851.8	2,562.4
Interest, net	302.4	316.9	351.9
Earnings before income taxes and after-tax earnings from joint ventures	2,655.0	2,534.9	2,210.5
Income taxes	883.3	741.2	709.6
After-tax earnings from joint ventures	89.6	98.8	88.2
Net earnings.	$ 1,861.3	$ 1,892.5	$ 1,589.1

GENERAL MILLS, INC. AND SUBSIDIARIES Consolidated Balance Sheets		
(in millions, except par value)	May 25, 2014	May 26, 2013
ASSETS		
Current assets:		
Cash and cash equivalents	$ 867.3	$ 741.4
Receivables	1,483.6	1,446.4
Inventories	1,559.4	1,545.5
Deferred income taxes	74.1	128.0
Prepaid expenses and other current assets	409.1	437.6
Total current assets	4,393.5	4,298.9
Land, buildings, and equipment	3,941.9	3,878.1
Goodwill	8,650.5	8,622.2
Other intangible assets	5,014.3	5,015.1
Other assets	1,145.5	843.7
Total assets	$23,145.7	$22,658.0
LIABILITIES AND EQUITY		
Current liabilities:		
Accounts payable	$ 1,611.3	$ 1,423.2
Current portion of long-term debt	1,250.6	1,443.3
Notes payable	1,111.7	599.7
Other current liabilities	1,449.9	1,827.7
Total current liabilities	5,423.5	5,293.9
Long-term debt	6,423.5	5,926.1
Deferred income taxes	1,666.0	1,389.1
Other liabilities	1,643.2	1,952.9
Total liabilities	15,156.2	14,562.0
Redeemable interest	984.1	967.5
Stockholders' equity:		
Common stock, 754.6 shares issued, $0.10 par value	75.5	75.5
Additional paid-in capital	1,231.8	1,166.6
Retained earnings	11,787.2	10,702.6
Common stock in treasury, at cost, shares of 142.3 and 113.8	(5,219.4)	(3,687.2)
Accumulated other comprehensive loss	(1,340.3)	(1,585.3)
Total stockholders' equity	6,534.8	6,672.2
Noncontrolling interests	470.6	456.3
Total equity	7,005.4	7,128.5
Total liabilities and equity	$23,145.7	$22,658.0

GENERAL MILLS		
	May 2014	May 2013
Sales	100.0%	100.0%
Cost of sales	64.4%	63.9%
Selling, general and administrative expenses	19.0%	20.0%
Restructuring costs	0.0%	0.1%
Operating profit	16.5%	16.0%
Interest expense	1.7%	1.8%
Income before income taxes	14.8%	14.3%

P6-3. **Time Series Financial Statement Analysis—Whirlpool**   Whirlpool Corporation manufactures and markets major home appliances, including laundry appliances, refrigerators and
freezers, cooktops and ranges, and dishwashers. It sells globally under a variety of brand
names including Whirlpool, Maytag, KitchenAid, Consul, and Amana. The company's income

**Whirlpool
Corporation**

statements and balance sheets from the annual report for the year ending December 31, 2013, are provided below.

Required:

a. Complete the following table:

	2013	2012
Return on equity.		9.7%
Return on assets		2.8%
Leverage.		3.5
Profit margin.		2.3%
Asset turnover		1.2

b. Identify the two most important ratios that are driving the increase in ROE between 2012 and 2013.

c. Suppose that Whirlpool's management wanted to increase its asset turnover ratio. Identify two specific operational changes that management could implement that would likely cause an increase in its asset turnover ratio.

d. Below is a common-sized income statement for Whirlpool:

	2013	2012
COGS/sales	82.4%	84.1%
Gross margin/sales.	17.6%	15.9%
SG&A expense/sales	9.7%	9.7%
Amortization/sales	0.1%	0.2%
Restructuring/sales	1.0%	1.3%
Operating profit/sales.	6.7%	4.8%

Using the information above, analyze the change in Whirlpool's reported profit margin between 2012 and 2013. Identify two key factors that explain the change, and provide a likely reason for each of the factors.

e. Calculate Whirlpool's debt-equity ratio for 2013 and 2012. Provide a likely reason for the change that you observe.

f. Calculate Whirlpool's times interest earned ratio for 2013 and 2012. Provide a likely reason for the change that you observe.

WHIRLPOOL CORPORATION Consolidated Statements of Income Year Ended December 31,			
(millions of dollars, except per share data)	2013	2012	2011
Net sales.	$18,769	$18,143	$18,666
Expenses			
Cost of products sold.	15,471	15,250	16,089
Gross margin	3,298	2,893	2,577
Selling, general and administrative	1,828	1,757	1,621
Intangible amortization.	25	30	28
Restructuring costs	196	237	136
Operating profit	1,249	869	792
Other income (expense)			
Interest and sundry income (expense).	(155)	(112)	(607)
Interest expense.	(177)	(199)	(213)
Earnings (loss) before income taxes	917	558	(28)
Income tax expense (benefit).	68	133	(436)
Net earnings.	$ 849	$ 425	$ 408

WHIRLPOOL CORPORATION CONSOLIDATED BALANCE SHEETS At December 31,		
(millions of dollars, except share data)	2013	2012
Assets		
Current assets		
Cash and equivalents...	$ 1,380	$ 1,168
Accounts receivable, net of allowance of $73 and $60, respectively	2,005	2,038
Inventories	2,408	2,354
Deferred income taxes...	549	558
Prepaid and other current assets..................................	680	709
Total current assets	7,022	6,827
Property, net of accumulated depreciation of $6,278 and $6,070, respectively	3,041	3,034
Goodwill..	1,724	1,727
Other intangibles, net of accumulated amortization of $237 and $211, respectively	1,702	1,722
Deferred income taxes...	1,764	1,832
Other noncurrent assets..	291	254
Total assets..	$15,544	$15,396
Liabilities and stockholders' equity		
Current liabilities		
Accounts payable..	$ 3,865	$ 3,698
Accrued expenses	710	692
Accrued advertising and promotions................................	441	419
Employee compensation	456	520
Notes payable	10	7
Current maturities of long-term debt	607	510
Other current liabilities	705	664
Total current liabilities...	6,794	6,510
Noncurrent liabilities		
Long-term debt	1,846	1,944
Pension benefits...	930	1,636
Postretirement benefits	458	422
Other noncurrent liabilities	482	517
Total noncurrent liabilities...	3,716	4,519
Stockholders' equity		
Common stock, $1 par value, 250 million shares authorized, 109 million and 108 million shares issued and 77 million and 79 million shares outstanding, respectively	109	108
Additional paid-in capital	2,453	2,313
Retained earnings	5,784	5,147
Accumulated other comprehensive loss	(1,298)	(1,531)
Treasury stock, 32 million and 29 million shares, respectively..............	(2,124)	(1,777)
Total Whirlpool stockholders' equity	4,924	4,260
Noncontrolling interests	110	107
Total stockholders' equity	5,034	4,367
Total liabilities and stockholders' equity..............................	$15,544	$15,396

P6-4. **Time Series Financial Statement Analysis—Bed Bath & Beyond**   Bed Bath & Beyond, Inc., sells a wide assortment of home furnishings through its retail stores (including Christmas Tree Shops) and websites. Its financial statements for fiscal 2014 (ending February 28, 2015) are presented below to use in answering the following questions.

Bed Bath & Beyond, Inc.

Required:

a. Complete the following table for BBB's DuPont ratios in 2014.

	2014	2013	2012
Return on equity....................................		25.9%	25.4%
Profit margin.......................................		8.9%	9.5%
Asset turnover		1.81	1.74
Return on assets		16.1%	16.5%
Leverage..		1.6	1.5

b. Use the common-sized income statements to identify two specific expense/revenue ratios that are contributing to the decrease in profit margin. For each ratio, provide one likely operational (i.e., business) reason for the change in the ratio.

c. Calculate the current and quick ratios for BBB for 2014 and 2013. Has BBB become more or less risky in the short-term?

d. Calculate total liabilities to equity for BBB for 2014 and 2013. Provide at least two reasons for the significant increase.

BED BATH & BEYOND INC. AND SUBSIDIARIES
Consolidated Balance Sheets

(in thousands, except per share data)	February 28, 2015	March 1, 2014
Assets		
Current assets:		
Cash and cash equivalents	$ 875,574	$ 366,516
Short-term investment securities.........................	109,992	489,331
Merchandise inventories	2,731,881	2,578,956
Other current assets.....................................	366,156	354,184
Total current assets	4,083,603	3,788,987
Long-term investment securities	97,160	87,393
Property and equipment, net	1,676,700	1,579,804
Goodwill..	486,279	486,279
Other assets...	415,251	413,570
Total assets...	$6,758,993	$6,356,033
Liabilities and Shareholders' Equity		
Current liabilities:		
Accounts payable..	$1,156,368	$1,104,668
Accrued expenses and other current liabilities	403,547	385,954
Merchandise credit and gift card liabilities...................	306,160	284,216
Current income taxes payable	76,606	60,298
Total current liabilities....................................	1,942,681	1,835,136
Deferred rent and other liabilities	493,137	486,996
Income taxes payable	79,985	92,614
Long-term debt	1,500,000	—
Total liabilities..	4,015,803	2,414,746
Commitments and contingencies		
Shareholders' equity:		
Preferred stock—$0.01 par value; authorized—1,000 shares; no shares issued or outstanding........................	—	—
Common stock—$0.01 par value; authorized—900,000 shares; issued 336,667 and 334,941 shares, respectively; outstanding 174,178 and 205,405 shares, respectively	3,367	3,350
Additional paid-in capital	1,796,692	1,673,217
Retained earnings	9,553,376	8,595,902
Treasury stock, at cost...................................	(8,567,932)	(6,317,335)
Accumulated other comprehensive loss	(42,313)	(13,847)
Total shareholders' equity	2,743,190	3,941,287
Total liabilities and shareholders' equity....................	$6,758,993	$6,356,033

BED BATH & BEYOND INC. AND SUBSIDIARIES Consolidated Statements of Earnings			
	Fiscal Year Ended		
(in thousands, except per share data)	February 28, 2015	March 1, 2014	March 2, 2013
Net sales.	$11,881,176	$11,503,963	$10,914,585
Cost of sales.	7,261,397	6,938,381	6,525,830
Gross profit.	4,619,779	4,565,582	4,388,755
Selling, general and administrative expenses	3,065,486	2,950,995	2,750,537
Operating profit	1,554,293	1,614,587	1,638,218
Interest expense, net	50,458	1,140	4,159
Earnings before provision for income taxes.	1,503,835	1,613,447	1,634,059
Provision for income taxes.	546,361	591,157	596,271
Net earnings.	$ 957,474	$ 1,022,290	$ 1,037,788

Common-size Income Statement (BBB)			
	2014	2013	2013
Revenue	100.0%	100.0%	100.0%
Cost of sales.	61.1%	60.3%	59.8%
Gross profit.	38.9%	39.7%	40.2%
Selling, general and administrative expense	25.8%	25.7%	25.2%
Operating income	13.1%	14.0%	15.0%
Interest expense.	0.4%	0.0%	0.0%
Earnings before income taxes	12.7%	14.0%	15.0%
Income tax expense.	4.6%	5.1%	5.5%
Net income.	8.1%	8.9%	9.5%

P6-5.   Time Series Financial Statement Analysis—Hasbro

Hasbro, Inc.

Hasbro, Inc., manufactures, markets and distributes branded toys and games (both traditional and digital), as well as television programs based on its characters. Its best-known brands cover a wide range—from Monopoly, Life, and Jenga to Play-Doh, Playskool, and Nerf to Magic: The Gathering. Hasbro has entered partnerships with Disney and other companies that allow it to sell products based on Marvel (e.g., Spiderman) and Star Wars characters. The company sells globally, but is based in Pawtucket, Rhode Island. Although it does own two manufacturing facilities in the U.S., most of its products are manufactured by third parties in Asia.

Required:

Using the financial statements and ratio exhibits provided below, answer the following questions about Hasbro's recent financial condition and performance.

a.   Complete the following table for Hasbro's DuPont ratios in 2013.

	2013	2012	2011
Return on equity.		22.3%	27.2%
Profit margin.		8.2%	9.0%
Asset turnover		0.95	1.04
Return on assets		7.8%	9.3%
Leverage.		2.9	2.9

b.   Use the common-sized income statements to identify two specific expense/revenue ratios that are contributing to the decrease in operating margin. For each ratio, provide one likely operational (i.e., business) reason for the change in the ratio.

c.   Calculate the times interest earned for Hasbro for 2013 and 2012. Briefly comment on the likely reason for the change you observe.

d. Accounts receivable turnover decreased over the past three years. Provide one likely operational (i.e., business) reason for the decrease.

e. Complete the following table for 2011-2013.

	2013	2012	2011
Days sales outstanding		92	88
Days inventory on hand		57	55
Days payables outstanding		25	22
Cash cycle			

f. Provide one likely operational reason for changes in days inventory on hand and days payable outstanding.

HASBRO FINANCIAL STATEMENTS
Income Statements

Year ending December	2013	2012	2011
Revenue	4,082.2	4,089.0	4,285.6
Cost of goods sold.	2,059.5	2,015.8	2,211.3
Gross Profit	2,022.6	2,073.1	2,074.3
Selling general and admin. exp..	949.9	897.9	868.7
Product development.	207.6	201.2	197.6
Advertising	398.1	422.2	414.0
Operating income.	467.1	551.8	594.0
Interest expense.	105.6	91.1	89.0
Other expense	9.7	7.	18.6
Income before income taxes	351.8	453.4	486.4
Income taxes	67.9	117.4	101.0
Net income.	283.9	336.0	385.4

Balance Sheets

Year ending December	2013	2012	2011
Assets			
Cash.	682.4	849.7	641.7
Accounts receivable.	1,093.6	1,030.0	1,034.6
Inventory.	348.8	316.0	334.0
Prepaid expenses & other current assets	355.6	312.5	243.5
Total current assets	2,480.5	2,508.2	2,253.8
Gross property, plant and equipment.	736.7	711.9	671.7
Accumulated depreciation	(500.5)	(481.5)	(453.7)
Net property, plant and equipment	236.3	230.4	218.0
Long-term investments	321.9	330.7	359.8
Intangible assets	970.3	891.6	942.1
Other long-term assets	393.4	364.4	357.1
Total assets.	4,402.3	4,325.4	4,130.8

continued

Balance Sheets			
Year ending December	2013	2012	2011
Liabilities			
Accounts payable............	198.8	139.9	134.9
Accrued liabilities............	717.5	593.1	627.1
Short-term borrowings........	8.3	224.4	180.4
Current portion. of tong-term debt.........	428.4	—	—
Other current liabilities.........	10.3	3.1	—
Total current liabilities...........	1,363.3	960.4	942.3
Long-term debt.............	959.9	1,396.4	1,400.9
Other non-current liabilities.........	351.2	461.2	370.1
Total liabilities...........	2,674.5	2,818.0	2,713.3
Common stock............	104.8	104.8	104.8
Additional paid-in capital.........	779.6	655.9	630.0
Retained earnings	3,432.2	3,354.5	3,205.4
Treasury stock	(3,554.7)	(2,535.6)	(2,486.9)
Comprehensive Inc. and other...........	(34.1)	(72.3)	(35.9)
Total equity............	1,727.8	1,507.4	1,417.5
Total liabilities and equity.............	4,402.3	4,325.4	4,103.8

Common-Sized Income Statements			
Year ending December	2013	2012	2011
Revenue.........................	100.0%	100.0%	100.0%
Cost of goods sold................	50.5%	49.3%	51.6%
Gross profit.....................	49.5%	50.7%	48.4%
Selling general and admin. exp..........	23.3%	22.0%	20.3%
Product development................	5.1%	4.9%	4.6%
Advertising......................	9.8%	10.3%	9.7%
Operating income.................	11.4%	13.5%	13.9%
Interest expense..................	2.6%	2.2%	2.1%
Other expense	0.2%	0.2%	0.4%
Income before income taxes	8.6%	11.1%	11.4%
Income taxes	1.7%	2.9%	2.4%
Net income......................	7.0%	8.2%	9.0%

Year ending December	2013	2012	2011
Accounts receivable turnover..............	3.7	4.0	4.1
Inventory turnover	5.9	6.4	6.6
Accounts payable turnover	10.4	14.4	16.4

P6-6. **Cross-Sectional Financial Statement Analysis—TJX and Nordstrom** The TJX Compa-   TJX Companies, Inc.
nies, Inc., reports in its 2014 10-K that it "is the leading off-price apparel and home fashions
retailer in the United States and worldwide. Our over 3,300 stores offer a rapidly changing
assortment of quality, fashionable, brand-name and designer merchandise at prices generally
20% to 60% below department and specialty store regular prices, every day." The company's
store names include T.J. Maxx, Marshalls, and HomeGoods, operating in the U.S., Canada,
and Europe.

Nordstrom, Inc., reports in its 2014 10-K that it is "one of the leading fashion spe-   Nordstrom, Inc.
cialty retailers based in the U.S." With 290 U.S. stores located in 38 states, "as well as a
robust ecommerce business" through its websites, Nordstrom offers "an extensive selection of

high-quality brand-name and private label merchandise focused on apparel, shoes, cosmetics and accessories."

Required:

Use the financial statements for TJX and Nordstrom on the following pages to answer the following questions for the most recent year.

a. Calculate these ratios for each company: quick ratio, current ratio, accounts receivable turnover, inventory turnover, accounts payable turnover, days sales outstanding, days inventory on hand, accounts payable days, cash cycle, and fixed asset turnover ratio.

b. Based upon the results of those ratios answer the following questions:
   i. What do you think is causing the difference in the DSO between the companies?
   ii. What is your reaction to the days in inventory?
   iii. For the company that has the higher days in inventory, what actions could it implement to reduce the days and increase its inventory turns?
   iv. How would you explain the difference in fixed asset turnover?

c. Calculate the profit margin, gross margin, operating margin and selling, general, and administrative expense as a percentage of revenue for each company.

d. Based upon the results of those ratios answer the following questions:
   i. Which company has the higher gross margin percentage? What about its business model allows it to command higher margins?
   ii. What are the other key differences relating to these profitability ratios? What might be causing these differences?

e. Calculate the return on equity using the DuPont model for the two companies.

f. Based upon the results of the ratios, answer the following questions:
   i. Are the ROEs appreciably different?
   ii. Is there a significant difference in how the ROEs are achieved?
   iii. Which company is using leverage more effectively and why?
   iv. How does the DuPont model reflect differences in the business models and strategies of the two companies?

g. Calculate the debt to equity ratio and times interest earned ratios for both companies.

h. Based upon the results of the leverage ratios, answer the following questions:
   i. Which company is using more leverage?
   ii. Which company is in the better position to repay its interest?

THE TJX COMPANIES, INC. Consolidated Statements of Income			
	Fiscal Year Ended		
(amounts in thousands except per share amounts)	**January 31, 2015**	**February 1, 2014**	**February 2, 2013 (53 weeks)**
Net sales.	$29,078,407	$27,422,696	$25,878,372
Cost of sales, including buying and occupancy costs.	20,776,522	19,605,037	18,521,400
Selling, general and administrative expenses	4,695,384	4,467,089	4,250,446
Loss on early extinguishment of debt	16,830	—	—
Interest expense, net	39,787	31,081	29,175
Income before provision for income taxes.	3,549,884	3,319,489	3,077,351
Provision for income taxes.	1,334,756	1,182,093	1,170,664
Net income.	$ 2,215,128	$ 2,137,396	$ 1,906,687

THE TJX COMPANIES, INC.
Consolidated Balance Sheets

(amounts in thousands except share amounts)	Fiscal Year Ended	
	February 2, 2013	January 28, 2012
ASSETS		
Current assets:		
Cash and cash equivalents	$ 2,493,775	$ 2,149,746
Short-term investments	282,623	294,702
Accounts receivable, net	213,824	210,094
Merchandise inventories	3,217,923	2,966,490
Prepaid expenses and other current assets	356,824	345,327
Federal, state, and foreign income taxes recoverable	12,475	—
Current deferred income taxes, net	137,617	—
Total current assets	6,715,061	6,067,998
Property at cost:		
Land and buildings	888,580	722,645
Leasehold costs and improvements	2,780,932	2,720,391
Furniture, fixtures and equipment	4,671,029	4,255,210
Total property at cost	8,340,541	7,698,246
Less accumulated depreciation and amortization	4,472,176	4,103,745
Net property at cost	3,868,365	3,594,501
Non-current deferred income taxes, net	24,546	31,508
Other assets	210,539	194,328
Goodwill and tradenames, net of amortization	309,870	312,687
Total assets	$11,128,381	$10,201,022
Liabilities		
Current liabilities:		
Accounts payable	$ 2,007,511	$ 1,771,294
Accrued expenses and other current liabilities	1,796,122	1,681,834
Federal, state and foreign income taxes payable	126,001	64,715
Total current liabilities	3,929,634	3,517,843
Other long-term liabilities	888,137	732,999
Non-current deferred income taxes, net	422,516	446,071
Long-term debt	1,623,864	1,274,216
Commitments and contingencies (see note m and note o)		
Shareholders' equity		
Common stock, authorized 1,200,000,000 shares, par value $1, issued and outstanding 684,733,200 and 705,016,838, respectively	684,733	705,017
Additional paid-in capital	—	—
Accumulated other comprehensive income (loss)	(554,385)	(199,532)
Retained earnings	4,133,882	3,724,408
Total shareholders' equity	4,264,230	4,229,893
Total liabilities and shareholders' equity	$11,128,381	$10,201,022

THE TJX COMPANIES, INC. **Consolidated Statement of Cash Flows**			
		Fiscal Year Ended	
(amounts in thousands)	**January 31, 2015**	**February 1, 2014**	**February 2, 2013 (53 weeks)**
Cash flows from operating activities:			
Net income	$2,215,128	$2,137,396	$1,906,687
Adjustments to reconcile net income to net cash provided by operating activities:			
Depreciation and amortization	588,975	548,823	508,929
Loss on property disposals and impairment charges.	3,897	7,914	11,876
Deferred income tax provision	102,070	52,233	13,265
Share-based compensation	88,014	76,080	64,416
Early extinguishment of debt	16,830	—	—
Excess tax benefits from share-based compensation	(95,063)	(82,546)	(62,472)
Changes in assets and liabilities:			
(Increase) decrease in accounts receivable	(9,052)	11,979	(18,418)
(Increase) decrease in merchandise inventories.	(332,271)	35,233	27,186
(Increase) decrease in taxes recoverable	(12,475)	—	—
Decrease (increase) in prepaid expenses and other current assets.	3,719	(3,354)	(53,705)
Increase (decrease) in accounts payable	285,223	(152,271)	211,689
Increase (decrease) in accrued expenses and other liabilities	20,800	(29,590)	268,901
Increase in income taxes payable	144,977	10,994	176,076
Other.	(12,403)	(12,425)	1,290
Net cash provided by operating activities	3,008,369	2,600,466	3,055,720
Cash flows from investing activities:			
Property additions	(911,522)	(946,678)	(978,228)
Purchases of investments	(431,152)	(496,657)	(371,670)
Sales and maturities of investments.	388,037	394,914	218,828
Cash paid for acquisition of Sierra Trading Post, net of cash received	—	2,653	(190,374)
Other.	—	—	34,490
Net cash (used in) investing activities.	(954,637)	(1,045,768)	(1,286,954)
Cash flows from financing activities:			
Proceeds from issuance of long-term debt	749,475	499,555	—
Cash payments for extinguishment of debt	(416,357)	—	—
Cash payments for debt issuance expenses	(6,185)	(4,297)	(1,370)
Cash payments for rate lock agreement.	(7,937)	(3,251)	—
Cash payments on capital lease obligation	—	—	(1,456)
Cash payments for repurchase of common stock	(1,650,704)	(1,471,096)	(1,345,082)
Proceeds from issuance of common stock	143,005	146,495	133,771
Excess tax benefits from share-based compensation	95,063	82,546	62,472
Cash dividends paid.	(465,902)	(393,755)	(323,922)
Net cash (used in) financing activities	(1,559,542)	(1,143,803)	(1,475,587)
Effect of exchange rate changes on cash	(150,161)	(73,106)	11,666
Net increase in cash and cash equivalents	344,029	337,789	304,845
Cash and cash equivalents at beginning of year	2,149,746	1,811,957	1,507,112
Cash and cash equivalents at end of year	$2,493,775	$2,149,746	$1,811,957

NORDSTROM, INC. Consolidated Statements of Earnings (In millions except per share amounts)			
Fiscal year	2014	2013	2012
Net sales..	$13,110	$12,166	$11,762
Credit card revenues	396	374	372
Total revenues	13,506	12,540	12,134
Cost of sales and related buying and occupancy costs	(8,406)	(7,737)	(7,432)
Selling, general and administrative expenses	(3,777)	(3,453)	(3,357)
Earnings before interest and income taxes	1,323	1,350	1,345
Interest expense, net	(138)	(161)	(160)
Earnings before income taxes	1,185	1,189	1,185
Income tax expense..............................	(465)	(455)	(450)
Net earnings.....................................	$ 720	$ 734	$ 735

NORDSTROM, INC. Consolidated Balance Sheets		
(in millions)	January 31, 2015	February 1, 2014
Assets		
Current assets:		
Cash and cash equivalents	$ 827	$1,194
Accounts receivable, net	2,306	2,177
Merchandise inventories	1,733	1,531
Current deferred tax assets, net......................	256	239
Prepaid expenses and other	102	87
Total current assets	5,224	5,228
Land, property and equipment, net	3,340	2,949
Goodwill..	435	175
Other assets.....................................	246	222
Total assets.....................................	$9,245	$8,574
Liabilities and Shareholders' Equity		
Current liabilities:		
Accounts payable..................................	$1,328	$1,263
Accrued salaries, wages and related benefits	416	395
Other current liabilities.............................	1,048	876
Current portion of long-term debt	8	7
Total current liabilities..............................	2,800	2,541
Long-term debt, net...............................	3,123	3,106
Deferred property incentives, net.....................	510	498
Other liabilities	372	349
Commitments and contingencies		
Shareholders' equity:		
Common stock, no par value: 1,000 shares authorized; 190.1 and 191.2 shares issued and outstanding	2,338	1,827
Retained earnings	166	292
Accumulated other comprehensive loss	(64)	(39)
Total shareholders' equity	2,440	2,080
Total liabilities and shareholders' equity..................	$9,245	$8,574

P6-7. **Cross-Sectional Financial Statement Analysis—Under Armour, NIKE, lululemon** Under Armour, Inc. reports in its fiscal 2014 10-K: "Our principal business activities are the development, marketing and distribution of branded performance apparel, footwear and accessories

Under Armour, Inc.

for men, women and youth. The brand's moisture-wicking fabrications are engineered in many designs and styles for wear in nearly every climate to provide a performance alternative to traditional products. Our products are sold worldwide and are worn by athletes at all levels, from youth to professional, on playing fields around the globe, as well as by consumers with active lifestyles." It sells most of its products through wholesalers to retailers in North America, and in 2014, "sales of apparel, footwear and accessories represented 74%, 14% and 9% of net revenues, respectively. Licensing arrangements, primarily for the sale of our products, and other revenue represented the remaining 3% of net revenues." Most of its products are manufactured by unaffiliated suppliers based outside the U.S.

NIKE, Inc.

NIKE, Inc., states in its May 2014 10-K that its "principal business activity is the design, development and worldwide marketing and selling of athletic footwear, apparel, equipment, accessories and services. NIKE is the largest seller of athletic footwear and athletic apparel in the world. We sell our products to retail accounts, through NIKE-owned retail stores and internet websites (which we refer to as our "Direct to Consumer" operations) and through a mix of independent distributors and licensees, in virtually all countries around the world. Virtually all of our products are manufactured by independent contractors. Virtually all footwear and apparel products are produced outside the United States, while equipment products are produced both in the United States and abroad." In addition to Nike brands, the company owns the Converse and Hurley brands. NIKE has developed a "futures ordering program, which allows retailers to order five to six months in advance of delivery with the commitment that their orders will be delivered within a set time period at a fixed price. In fiscal 2014, 86% of our U.S. wholesale footwear shipments (excluding NIKE Golf, Hurley, and Converse) were made under the futures program."

lululemon athletica inc.

lululemon athletica Inc., reports in its 2014 10-K that it "is a designer and retailer of technical athletic apparel…. Our healthy lifestyle inspired athletic apparel is marketed under the lululemon athletica and ivivva athletica brand names. We offer a comprehensive line of apparel and accessories for women, men and female youth. Our apparel assortment includes items such as pants, shorts, tops and jackets designed for healthy lifestyle activities and athletic pursuits such as yoga, running, general fitness, and dance-inspired apparel for female youth." The company adds that its "primary target customer is a sophisticated and educated woman who understands the importance of an active, healthy lifestyle. She is increasingly tasked with the dual responsibilities of career and family and is constantly challenged to balance her work, life and health. We believe she pursues exercise to achieve physical fitness and inner peace….

As of February 1, 2015, we operated 302 corporate-owned stores located in the United States, Canada, Australia, New Zealand, the United Kingdom, and Singapore. We believe our vertical retail strategy allows us to interact more directly with, and gain feedback from, our customers, whom we call guests, while providing us with greater control of our brand."

Required:

Use the financial statements and background information for Nike, UnderArmour, and Lululemon on the following pages to answer the questions below.

a. Calculate the following liquidity ratios for each company for the past three years: quick ratio, current ratio, accounts receivable turnover, inventory turnover, accounts payable turnover, days sales outstanding, days inventory on hand, accounts payable days and cash cycle. In addition, calculate the fixed asset turnover ratio.

b. Based upon the results of those ratios answer the following questions:
   i.   What do you think is causing the difference in the DSO among the three companies?
   ii. What is your reaction to the days in inventory?
   iii. For the company that has the highest days in inventory, what actions could they implement to reduce the days and increase their inventory turns?
   iv. Do you have any other observations relating to any of these ratios?

c. Calculate the profit margin, gross margin, operating margin and selling, general and administrative expense as a percentage of sales for each company for the past three years.

d. Based upon the results of those ratios, answer the following questions:
   i.   Which company has the highest gross margin percentage? What about its business model allows it to command higher margins?
   ii. What are the other key differences relating to these profitability ratios? What may be causing these differences?

    e. Calculate the return on equity ("ROE") disaggregation (using the DuPont model) for each company for the past three years.

    f. Based upon the results of the ROE disaggregation answer the following questions:
        i. Are the ROEs appreciably different?
        ii. Is there a significant difference in how the ROEs are achieved?
        iii. Which company is using leverage the most effectively?
        iv. How does the ROE disaggregation analysis reflect differences in the business models and strategies of these three companies?

    g. Calculate the debt/equity and times interest earned ratios for the past three years.

    h. Based upon the results of these leverage ratios, answer the following questions:
        i. Which company is using the least and the most leverage?
        ii. Which company is in the best position to repay its interest?

UNDER ARMOUR, INC. AND SUBSIDIARIES Consolidated Balance Sheets (in thousands, except share data)	December 31, 2014	December 31, 2013
Assets		
Current assets		
Cash and cash equivalents.	$ 593,175	$ 347,489
Accounts receivable, net	279,835	209,952
Inventories	536,714	469,006
Prepaid expenses and other current assets.	87,177	63,987
Deferred income taxes	52,498	38,377
Total current assets.	1,549,399	1,128,811
Property and equipment, net.	305,564	223,952
Goodwill.	123,256	122,244
Intangible assets, net.	26,230	24,097
Deferred income taxes.	33,570	31,094
Other long-term assets	57,064	47,543
Total assets.	$2,095,083	$1,577,741
Liabilities and Stockholders' Equity		
Current liabilities		
Revolving credit facility.	$ —	$ 100,000
Accounts payable.	210,432	165,456
Accrued expenses	147,681	133,729
Current maturities of long-term debt	28,951	4,972
Other current liabilities	34,563	22,473
Total current liabilities	421,627	426,630
Long-term debt, net of current maturities	255,250	47,951
Other long-term liabilities.	67,906	49,806
Total liabilities	744,783	524,387
Commitments and contingencies (see Note 7)		
Stockholders' equity		
Class A Common Stock, $0.0003 1/3 par value; 400,000,000 shares authorized as of December 31, 2014 and 2013; 177,295,988 shares issued and outstanding as of December 31, 2014 and 171,628,708 shares issued and outstanding as of December 31, 2013.	59	57
Class B Convertible Common Stock, $0.0003 1/3 par value; 36,600,000 shares authorized, issued and outstanding as of December 31, 2014 and 40,000,000 shares authorized, issued and outstanding as of December 31, 2013.	12	13
Additional paid-in capital.	508,350	397,248
Retained earnings	856,687	653,842
Accumulated other comprehensive income (loss).	(14,808)	2,194
Total stockholders' equity.	1,350,300	1,053,354
Total liabilities and stockholders' equity.	$2,095,083	$1,577,741

UNDER ARMOUR, INC. AND SUBSIDIARIES Consolidated Statements of Income			
	Year Ended December 31,		
(in thousands, except per share amounts)	2014	2013	2012
Net revenues	$3,084,370	$2,332,051	$1,834,921
Cost of goods sold	1,572,164	1,195,381	955,624
Gross profit	1,512,206	1,136,670	879,297
Selling, general and administrative expenses	1,158,251	871,572	670,602
Income from operations	353,955	265,098	208,695
Interest expense, net	(5,335)	(2,933)	(5,183)
Other expense, net	(6,410)	(1,172)	(73)
Income before income taxes	342,210	260,993	203,439
Provision for income taxes	134,168	98,663	74,661
Net income	$ 208,042	$ 162,330	$ 128,778
Net income available per common share			
Basic	$0.98	$0.77	$0.62
Diluted	$0.95	$0.75	$0.61

UNDER ARMOUR, INC. AND SUBSIDIARIES			
Consolidated Statements of Cash Flows			
	Year Ended December 31,		
(in thousands)	**2014**	**2013**	**2012**
Cash flows from operating activities			
Net income.	$208,042	$162,330	$128,778
Adjustments to reconcile net income to net cash used in operating activities			
Depreciation and amortization.	72,093	50,549	43,082
Unrealized foreign currency exchange rate losses (gains).	11,739	1,905	(2,464)
Loss on disposal of property and equipment.	261	332	524
Stock-based compensation.	50,812	43,184	19,845
Deferred income taxes.	(17,584)	(18,832)	(12,973)
Changes in reserves and allowances.	31,350	13,945	13,916
Changes in operating assets and liabilities, net of effects of acquisitions:			
Accounts receivable.	(101,057)	(35,960)	(53,433)
Inventories	(84,658)	(156,900)	4,699
Prepaid expenses and other assets.	(33,345)	(19,049)	(4,060)
Accounts payable.	49,137	14,642	35,370
Accrued expenses and other liabilities.	28,856	56,481	21,966
Income taxes payable and receivable	3,387	7,443	4,511
Net cash provided by operating activities	219,033	120,070	199,761
Cash flows from investing activities			
Purchases of property and equipment.	(140,528)	(87,830)	(50,650)
Purchase of business.	(10,924)	(148,097)	—
Purchases of other assets	(860)	(475)	(1,310)
Change in loans receivable	—	(1,700)	—
Change in restricted cash	—	—	5,029
Net cash used in investing activities	(152,312)	(238,102)	(46,931)
Cash flows from financing activities.			
Proceeds from revolving credit facility	—	100,000	—
Payments on revolving credit facility	(100,000)	—	—
Proceeds from term loan	250,000	—	—
Payments on term loan	(13,750)	—	(25,000)
Proceeds from long-term debt.	—	—	50,000
Payments on long-term debt	(4,972)	(5,471)	(44,330)
Excess tax benefits from stock-based compensation arrangements	36,965	17,167	17,868
Proceeds from exercise of stock options and other stock issuances	15,776	15,099	14,776
Payments of debt financing costs	(1,713)	—	(1,017)
Net cash provided by financing activities.	182,306	126,795	12,297
Effect of exchange rate changes on cash and cash equivalents.	(3,341)	(3,115)	1,330
Net increase in cash and cash equivalents	$245,686	$ 5,648	$166,457
Cash and cash equivalents			
Beginning of period	347,489	341,841	175,384
End of period	$593,175	$347,489	$341,841

NIKE, INC.
Consolidated Balance Sheets

(in millions)	May 31,	
	2014	2013
Assets		
Current assets:		
Cash and equivalents..	$ 2,220	$ 3,337
Short-term investments (note 6)................................	2,922	2,628
Accounts receivable, net (note 1)..............................	3,434	3,117
Inventories (notes 1 and 2)....................................	3,947	3,484
Deferred income taxes (note 9)	355	308
Prepaid expenses and other current assets (notes 6 and 17)	818	756
Total current assets	13,696	13,630
Property, plant and equipment, net (note 3)......................	2,834	2,452
Identifiable intangible assets, net (note 4)	282	289
Goodwill (note 4)	131	131
Deferred income taxes and other assets (notes 6, 9, and 17)	1,651	1,043
Total assets..	$18,594	$17,545
Liabilities and shareholders' equity		
Current liabilities:		
Current portion of long-term debt (note 8)......................	$7	$57
Notes payable (note 7).......................................	167	98
Accounts payable (note 7)....................................	1,930	1,669
Accrued liabilities (notes 5, 6, and 17).........................	2,491	2,036
Income taxes payable (note 9)................................	432	84
Liabilities of discontinued operations (note 15)	—	18
Total current liabilities......................................	5,027	3,962
Long-term debt (note 8)......................................	1,199	1,210
Deferred income taxes and other liabilities (notes 6, 9, 13 and 17).......	1,544	1,292
Commitments and contingencies (note 16)		
Redeemable preferred stock (note 10).........................	—	—
Shareholders' equity:		
Common stock at stated value (note 11):		
Class a convertible — 178 and 178 shares outstanding	—	—
Class b — 692 and 716 shares outstanding	3	3
Capital in excess of stated value	5,865	5,184
Accumulated other comprehensive income (note 14)	85	274
Retained earnings	4,871	5,620
Total shareholders' equity	10,824	11,081
Total liabilities and shareholders' equity.........................	$18,594	$17,545

NIKE, INC. Consolidated Statements of Income			
	Year Ended May 31,		
(in millions, except per share data)	2014	2013	2012
Income from continuing operations:			
Revenues	$27,799	$25,313	$23,331
Cost of sales.	15,353	14,279	13,183
Gross profit.	12,446	11,034	10,148
Demand creation expense	3,031	2,745	2,607
Operating overhead expense	5,735	5,051	4,472
Total selling and administrative expense	8,766	7,796	7,079
Interest expense (income), net (Notes 6, 7, and 8).	33	(3)	4
Other expense (income), net (Note 17).	103	(15)	54
Income before income taxes	3,544	3,256	3,011
Income tax expense (Note 9)	851	805	754
Net income from continuing operations.	2,693	2,451	2,257
Net income (loss) from discontinued operations	—	21	(46)
Net income	$ 2,693	$ 2,472	$ 2,211
Earnings per share from continuing operations:			
Basic earnings per common share (Notes 1 and 12)	$3.05	$2.74	$2.45
Diluted earnings per common share (Notes 1 and 12).	$2.97	$2.68	$2.40

NIKE, INC. Consolidated Statements of Cash Flows			
	Year Ended May 31,		
(in millions)	**2014**	**2013**	**2012**
Cash provided by operations:			
Net income.	$2,693	$2,472	$2,211
Income charges (credits) not affecting cash:			
Depreciation.	518	438	373
Deferred income taxes.	(11)	20	(59)
Stock-based compensation (Note 11).	177	174	130
Amortization and other.	114	66	23
Net gain on divestitures	—	(124)	—
Changes in certain working capital components and other assets and liabilities:			
(Increase) decrease in accounts receivable	(298)	142	(323)
(Increase) in inventories	(505)	(219)	(815)
(Increase) in prepaid expenses and other current assets.	(210)	(28)	(141)
Increase in accounts payable, accrued liabilities and income taxes payable . . .	525	27	425
Cash provided by operations.	3,003	2,968	1,824
Cash (used) provided by investing activities:			
Purchases of short-term investments	(5,386)	(4,133)	(3,245)
Maturities of short-term investments.	3,932	1,663	2,663
Sales of short-term investments	1,126	1,330	1,721
Additions to property, plant and equipment.	(880)	(598)	(563)
Disposals of property, plant and equipment	3	14	2
Proceeds from divestitures.	—	786	—
Increase in other assets, net of other liabilities	(2)	(2)	(14)
Settlement of net investment hedges.	—	—	22
Cash (used) provided by investing activities	(1,207)	(940)	586
Cash used by financing activities:			
Net proceeds from long-term debt issuance	—	986	—
Long-term debt payments, including current portion	(60)	(49)	(203)
Increase (decrease) in notes payable.	75	10	(47)
Payments on capital lease obligations.	(17)	—	—
Proceeds from exercise of stock options and other stock issuances	383	313	468
Excess tax benefits from share-based payment arrangements.	132	72	115
Repurchase of common stock.	(2,628)	(1,674)	(1,814)
Dividends—common and preferred	(799)	(703)	(619)
Cash used by financing activities.	(2,914)	(1,045)	(2,100)
Effect of exchange rate changes	1	100	67
Net (decrease) increase in cash and equivalents.	(1,117)	1,083	377
Cash and equivalents, beginning of year.	3,337	2,254	1,877
Cash and equivalents, end of year.	$2,220	$3,337	$2,254

LULULEMON ATHLETICA INC. AND SUBSIDIARIES
Consolidated Balance Sheets

(amounts in thousands, except per share amounts)	February 1, 2015	February 2, 2014
Assets		
Current assets		
Cash and cash equivalents	$ 664,479	$ 698,649
Accounts receivable	13,746	11,903
Inventories	208,116	188,790
Prepaid expenses and other current assets	64,671	46,197
	951,012	945,539
Property and equipment, net	296,008	255,603
Goodwill and intangible assets, net	26,163	28,201
Deferred income taxes	16,018	18,300
Other non-current assets	7,012	4,745
	$1,296,213	$1,252,388
Liabilities and stockholders' equity		
Current liabilities		
Accounts payable	$ 9,339	$ 12,647
Accrued inventory liabilities	22,296	15,415
Accrued compensation and related expenses	29,932	19,445
Income taxes payable	20,073	769
Unredeemed gift card liability	46,252	38,343
Other accrued liabilities	31,989	29,595
	159,881	116,214
Deferred income tax liability	3,633	3,977
Other non-current liabilities	43,131	35,515
	206,645	155,706
Stockholders' equity		
Undesignated preferred stock, $0.01 Par value, 5,000 shares authorized, none issued and outstanding	—	—
Exchangeable stock, no par value, 60,000 shares authorized, issued and outstanding 9,833 and 29,955	—	—
Special voting stock, $0.000005 Par value, 60,000 shares authorized, issued and outstanding 9,833 and 29,955	—	—
Common stock, $0.005 Par value, 400,000 shares authorized, issued and outstanding 132,112 and 115,342	661	577
Additional paid-in capital	241,695	240,351
Retained earnings	1,020,619	923,822
Accumulated other comprehensive loss	(173,407)	(68,068)
	1,089,568	1,096,682
	$1,296,213	$1,252,388

LULULEMON ATHLETICA INC. Consolidated Statements of Operations and Comprehensive Income			
		Fiscal Year Ended	
(amounts in thousands, except per share amounts)	**February 1, 2015**	**February 2, 2014**	**February 3, 2013**
Net revenue	$1,797,213	$1,591,188	$1,370,358
Cost of goods sold...........................	883,033	751,112	607,532
Gross profit..................................	914,180	840,076	762,826
Selling, general and administrative expenses	538,147	448,718	386,387
Income from operations.......................	376,033	391,358	376,439
Other income (expense), net	7,102	5,768	4,957
Income before provision for income taxes..........	383,135	397,126	381,396
Provision for income taxes.....................	144,102	117,579	109,965
Net income..................................	239,033	279,547	271,431
Net income attributable to non-controlling interest ...	—	—	875
Net income attributable to lululemon athletica inc.	$ 239,033	$ 279,547	$ 270,556
Basic earnings per share	$1.66	$1.93	$1.88
Diluted earnings per share	$1.66	$1.91	$1.85

LULULEMON ATHLETICA INC.
Consolidated Statements of Cash Flows
(amounts in thousands)

	Fiscal Year Ended		
	February 1, 2015	February 2, 2014	February 3, 2013
Cash flows from operating activities			
Net income.	$239,033	$279,547	$271,431
Items not affecting cash.			
Depreciation and amortization	58,364	49,068	43,000
Stock-based compensation.	8,269	10,087	15,637
Derecognition of unredeemed gift card liability	(1,468)	(4,654)	(1,351)
Deferred income taxes.	2,087	820	(6,445)
Excess tax benefits from stock-based compensation.	(413)	(6,457)	(9,901)
Other, including net changes in other non-cash balances			
Prepaid tax installments.	(15,234)	3,067	(7,812)
Other prepaid expenses and other current assets.	(8,813)	(14,408)	(10,492)
Inventories	(26,806)	(38,507)	(51,222)
Accounts payable.	(2,198)	11,627	(13,481)
Accrued inventory liabilities	8,276	6,985	(1,785)
Other accrued liabilities	3,271	7,837	1,777
Sales tax collected	517	161	(4,232)
Income taxes payable	19,304	(35,075)	30,951
Accrued compensation and related expenses.	11,561	(6,282)	4,695
Deferred gift card revenue	11,326	9,306	13,711
Other non-cash balances.	7,373	5,217	5,632
Net cash provided by operating activities	314,449	278,339	280,113
Cash flows from investing activities			
Purchase of property and equipment.	(119,733)	(106,408)	(93,229)
Net cash used in investing activities	(119,733)	(106,408)	(93,229)
Cash flows from financing activities			
Proceeds from exercise of stock options.	2,913	8,171	11,014
Excess tax benefits from stock-based compensation.	413	6,457	9,901
Registration fees associated with shelf registration statement . . .	—	—	(393)
Purchase of non-controlling interest	—	—	(26,013)
Taxes paid related to net share settlement of equity awards.	(4,972)	(5,721)	—
Repurchase of common stock	(147,431)	—	—
Net cash (used in) provided by financing activities	(149,077)	8,907	(5,491)
Effect of exchange rate changes on cash	(79,809)	(72,368)	(651)
(Decrease) increase in cash and cash equivalents.	(34,170)	108,470	180,742
Cash and cash equivalents, beginning of period.	$698,649	$590,179	$409,437
Cash and cash equivalents, end of period.	$664,479	$698,649	$590,179

Analyzing Financial Performance: Extensions

INTRODUCTION

The DuPont model offers a simple and powerful framework for analyzing the financial performance of any company, from a small start-up to a large public firm. In the previous chapter we introduced ratio analysis focused on a small start-up company. In this chapter we focus on public corporations.

First, we will add three common ratios frequently used and referenced when analyzing large public companies to our analysis tool kit: earnings per share (EPS), price–earnings (P/E) ratio, and market-to-book ratio (often referred to as the price-to-book ratio or P/B ratio). Essentially, EPS is similar to ROE in that its focus is on the owners and how they benefited from the recent operating results of the company. The P/E and P/B ratios capture the stock market's assessment of the company by relating market value to current earnings' performance (P/E) and to the value of owners' equity on the balance sheet (P/B). Because ROE = (P/E) / (P/B) = earnings / equity, our discussion of P/E focuses on the numerator of ROE (with the E being EPS), and P/B focuses on the denominator of ROE (B for book value of equity).

Second, again within the context of a large-company focus, we will describe the organizations that develop the generally accepted accounting principles (GAAP) as well as the independent audit function and its impact on financial data. Publicly traded corporations are required to have an annual independent audit of their financial data to assure the user of this data that the financial statements have been formulated within GAAP and are a reasonable representation of the company's operating results (income statement and statement of cash flows) and current financial position (balance sheet).

Third, we will dig deeper into the financial analysis process and consider specifically the effects of unusual or non-recurring items on our analysis of ratios. These items, such as restructuring costs and losses on impairment of assets, will impact the analysis of company financial statements and require a framework to consider their effects. Ultimately, for time-series analysis and for forecasting, management and analysts typically want to understand the core operations of a business and analyze the success or failure of these operations to assess continuing operations and to predict the company's future. These predictions will then be important for estimating the value of a company.

Continuing this focus on core operations, we will return to the DuPont model and conclude this chapter by examining a variation of the DuPont model that recalibrates return on assets (ROA) to focus on the core operating activities of the business. Termed *return on invested capital* (ROIC), this ratio focuses on modifications to net income to arrive at income from core operations divided by the assets central to the business operations (i.e., operating assets). Let us begin with the three new ratios we want to add to our tool kit.

EPS, P/E RATIO, P/B RATIO: ADDITIONAL RATIOS CONNECTED TO PERFORMANCE

The DuPont model is an effective organizing tool to understand ratio analysis and help interpret the data and the related management actions that impact these ratios. We have discussed extensions of the model (e.g., the further examination of profit margin using common-size income statements, gross profit margin, operating profit margin, and EBITDA margin) and will examine the necessary adjustments to the data (data scrubbing) and possible refinements of the model (ROIC) later in this chapter. However, at the beginning as we shift our focus from new entrepreneurial ventures to publicly traded companies, we need to cover three additional ratios that are commonly discussed in business: earnings per share (EPS), price–earnings ratio (P/E ratio), and market-to-book ratio.

We will use the Tiffany Company (Tiffany's), a high-end jewelry company, to show examples of these calculations. Founded in New York City in 1837, the firm has expanded to 250 stores in over 20 countries, and has maintained its strategic focus on high-quality jewelry sold in upscale locations with an emphasis on attentive service and luxurious shopping environments.

EARNINGS PER SHARE

Following is a chart with Tiffany's EPS-Basic compared to two competitors during the same fiscal years: Coach and Signet (all numbers taken from S&P Capital IQ database). Coach, Inc. (Coach) is a marketer of fine accessories and gifts for women and men. Coach's product offerings include women's and men's bags, accessories, business cases, footwear, wearables, jewelry, sun wear, travel bags, watches, and fragrance. The company operates in two segments: direct to consumer through Coach retail stores and the Internet (coach.com), and indirect through other high-end retailers (e.g., Neiman Marcus). Accessories include women's and men's small leather goods, novelty accessories, and belts. Women's small leather goods, which coordinate with its handbags, include money pieces, wristlets, and cosmetic cases. Men's small leather goods consist primarily of wallets and card cases. Novelty accessories include time management and electronic accessories. Key rings and charms are also included in this category. The business cases assortment is primarily men's and includes computer bags, messenger-style bags, and totes. Footwear is distributed through select Coach retail stores, coach.com, and high-end U.S. department stores.

Earnings Per Share Fiscal Year End	Basic		
	2014	2013	2012
Tiffany & Company (TIF)	$ 1.42	$ 3.28	$ 3.45
Coach (COH)	$10.43	$15.44	$17.47
Signet Jewelers Ltd. (SIG)	$ 4.59	$ 4.37	$ 3.76

Note: If one-time item scrubbed
TIF 2014 income statement: EPS = $3.65

Signet Jewelers Limited (Signet) is a specialty retail jeweler with sales in the United States and United Kingdom, and also through stores in the Republic of Ireland and Channel Islands. The company is engaged in the retailing of jewelry, watches, and associated services. The business is managed as two geographical operating divisions: the U.S. division and the UK division. Signet's U.S. division operated 1,350 stores in all 50 states as of

January 28, 2012. As of January 28, 2012, 215 regional brand stores operated in 33 states. Its stores trade nationally in malls and off-mall locations as Kay Jewelers (Kay), regionally under a number of mall-based brands and in destination superstores nationwide such as Jared—The Galleria Of Jewelry (Jared). The UK division operates over 500 stores, including stores in the Republic of Ireland and in the Channel Islands.

EPS is similar to ROE in that it is a measure of return to the common shareholders of the company. The calculation is: Net Income Available to Common Shareholders/Average Number of Common Shares Outstanding. The numerator is the same as the numerator of ROE. The denominator is a measure of the owners' investment—the average number of common shares of stock outstanding. EPS is a popular number used to discuss company performance. It satisfies the quest of many to boil performance down to one number and is watched closely by analysts as well as management. As we can see by examining the EPS chart, the three companies' operational performance differed substantially. Tiffany had decreasing operations and then apparently disastrous results in fiscal 2014. However, as stated in the note to the illustrations, there occurred a one-time expense which is by definition infrequent and unlikely to happen again. If that item is removed from the income statement and EPS for 2014 recalculated, the recalculated EPS is $3.65—a much better result than reported. The other luxury brand, Coach, has done poorly as the world economies are slowly recovering. EPS has dropped significantly in all three years and compared with the other luxury brand, Tiffany, these results appear especially problematic for Coach and its executives. Signet is the true winner in this comparison as EPS has shown steady growth over the three-year period.

Although frequently used and widely followed, EPS does have two major flaws as reported in the basic calculation shown earlier. As previously highlighted in the Tiffany calculations and as will be discussed later in this chapter, net income includes many one-time or non-recurring and non-operating items. Without taking these items into account (i.e., scrubbing net income), frequently net income as reported (and therefore EPS) may not be representative of a company's operating success or failure or helpful in predicting the future results.

Second, it is not clear how well the average number of common shares outstanding is indicative of owners' investment, especially when we consider items such as stock options, debt that may be converted into common stock, and preferred stock that may be converted into common stock. Because these items have some common stockholder characteristics but are not currently common stock outstanding, the issue is this: Are they enough like common stock and therefore should be included in the denominator calculation, or should they be ignored in the EPS calculation because these funding instruments are *not* currently common stock? To deal with the issues presented by these types of hybrid securities, two EPS calculations are disclosed in public company financial statements: basic (which we present in the table above) and fully diluted. This additional disclosure does little to ameliorate the shortcomings of EPS as a measure of company performance.

In the discussion of scrubbing later in this chapter, Tiffany's, the high-end jewelry company, will be used to illustrate several complications affecting the assessment of a company's operations. But first, let's also look at Tiffany's reporting of the P/E ratio compared with those of the two comparable companies for the same time period.

PRICE–EARNINGS RATIO

The P/E ratio is simply the Market Price of a Share of Common Stock (the current price at which shares are being bought and sold)/EPS and is a measure of how the market views a company's future: The higher the P/E ratio, the brighter the future of the company as seen by the market. For Tiffany, in the chart below we observe that its P/E ratio increased gradually over the three-year period, a good result. However, if the scrubbed net income is used in the P/E calculation, the result is a not-so-bright market outlook for Tiffany as if restated EPS climb to $3.65, P/E ratio will fall to approximately 9.0. We may hypothesize all luxury brands are in disfavor with the market; we can examine the Coach trends to assess the validity of that hypothesis.

Price Earnings Ratio (P/E) Fiscal Year End	2014	2013	2012
Tiffany & Company (TIF).	23.30	20.14	18.76
Coach (COH)	10.43	15.44	17.47
Signet Jewelers Ltd. (SIG)	32.18	17.44	13.04

Note: If one-time item scrubbed
TIF 2014 income statement: EPS = $3.65
Note: all numbers taken from S&P Capital IQ database

By comparing Tiffany's P/E ratio to the P/E ratio of Coach, one can develop a sense of the relative market assessment of these two luxury brand companies. The Coach P/E has declined substantially in all three fiscal years from 17.47 to 10.43. Not all luxury brands did well in this period and apparently the poor trend in the Coach EPS is not viewed favorably by the stock market.

Signet has improved the most, especially after seeing its P/E ratio increase from 13.04 to 32.08, a tremendous surge. The stock market approves of Signet's performance and future direction and has shown it with more than doubling its P/E ratio on steadily improving operating performance. Tentatively we might conclude based on the P/E results of two very different jewelers, the market is projecting success for the jewelry industry in the slowly recovering economy.

PRICE-TO-BOOK (P/B) RATIO

The P/B ratio is Total Market Value of Common Stock/Common Owners' Equity. The P/B ratio is also known as market-to-book ratio and the Total Market Value of Common stock is sometimes referred to as Market Capitalization.

As with the P/E ratio, a higher number indicates that the stock market thinks more highly of a company's future. Let's compare Tiffany's P/B ratio to those of Coach and Signet (all numbers taken from S&P Capital IQ database):

Price to Book Ratio (P/B) Fiscal Year End	2014	2013	2012
Tiffany & Company (TIF).	4.23	2.96	3.64
Coach (COH)	4.92	7.16	8.67
Signet Jewelers Ltd. (SIG)	3.99	2.65	2.00

Note: If one-time item scrubbed
TIF 2014 income statement: EPS = $3.65

[QUERY: Pls check this insert for sense.]

Here Tiffany's ratio decreases from 2012 to 2013 and then appears to bounce back in 2014. However, we view this recovery with skepticism because of the one-time item. Coach and Signet Jewelers P/B calculations lead to similar interpretations to those based on the P/E trends. The interpretation of this trend is difficult because of the denominator, total owners' equity, used in this ratio. Total owners' equity is the contributed capital plus retained earnings over the life of the company. That is, for long-established companies, these dollar amounts are out of date and do not closely approximate the net investment made by the owners in the company. The good news is that the market values of all three companies are substantially higher than the book values of owners' equity. The bad news is that this fact is difficult to interpret.

In summary, we have added three often used calculations to our ratio analysis portfolio. One, EPS, is another measure of company performance (with flaws, as we have highlighted) and two are market gauges of the company. These latter two can be somewhat helpful, as they give the analyst and management a sense of how a company ranks in the collective mind of the stock market. We have also seen that one-time items can obscure the analysis of ratio trends.

THE FORMATION OF FINANCIAL STATEMENTS: THE UNITED STATES AS AN EXAMPLE

In the United States, public companies (i.e., those companies owned by a number of stockholders and traded through one of the public stock exchanges) are guided in their financial reporting by the generally accepted accounting principles (GAAP) issued by the Financial Accounting Standards Board (FASB); rulings and procedures issued by the U.S. government's Securities and Exchange Commission (SEC), and the U.S. taxing authority, the Internal Revenue Service; the Public Company Accounting Oversight Board (PCAOB); and the international accounting policymaker, the International Accounting Standards Board (IASB). Because there exist many industries, many companies, and many ways of doing business, estimates are a part of the measurement process (e.g., estimating the useful life of an asset to calculate depreciation) to create the financial statements, as are a variety of principles to measure an item (e.g., at least three accepted accounting methods exist to calculate the asset "inventory" to be shown on the balance sheet).

As a typical first step in assessing a company's performance, audited financial statements are gathered and analyzed. The term "audited" refers to the processes by which an independent Certified Public Accountant (CPA) reviews (audits) a company's periodically published financial statements to assess the accuracy of the data (freedom from material errors), the adherence to GAAP (both the selection of estimation procedures as well as measurement principles), and the reasonableness in total with which the financial data (statements and supporting footnotes) represent the economic realities of the company. That is, the auditors give an opinion to the question: "Do the financial statements and supporting footnotes fairly present a company's operations and financial position?" The result of this audit is an opinion that can take three basic forms: a *standard opinion* that highlights no exceptions and is often termed a "clean" opinion; a *qualified opinion*, which is a clean opinion with an exception for a specific measurement issue or possibly a change in accounting policy and therefore a consistency issue; and an *adverse opinion*, which signifies a major measurement or presentation issue that does not allow the auditor to render any opinion on the financial statements. As you might expect, an adverse opinion is a major "red flag" about a company and means all stakeholders need to be cautious when engaging in transactions with the company. Any data analysis should be viewed quite skeptically. If a company presents a qualified opinion, the reason for qualification must be examined before analytical results are interpreted and relied upon.

A clean opinion gives assurance that the statements fairly represent a company's results, although stakeholders must remember that this is an opinion and only an opinion. As we discuss in this chapter, the variability of events and how they impact a company (e.g., losses due to natural disasters and restructuring decisions) and the variety of GAAP practices that can be used to measure assets, liabilities, owners' equity, revenue, and expenses mean that even data analysis based on data supported by an unqualified opinion still poses problems for an analyst. However, the accounting profession, represented by CPAs and their audits of publicly held companies, provides an important assurance of the quality and reliability of the financial data used by all stakeholders to assess and make decisions about companies.

One Major Caution

Although the audit system just described is a valuable assurance for stakeholders using financial data, it has faced intense scrutiny and criticism, such as the following:

1. Audits are based on sampling procedures, and the sampling procedures are created based on an audit team's assessment of a company's internal controls and systems to prevent measurement errors and fraud. Any sample may not be representative of the actual population being sampled.

2. Auditors must be independent in fact and perception to render an independent opinion and have that opinion valued by users of the data. As a result, many have questioned

whether auditors can be truly independent, given that management pays them to perform the audit.

3. Many audit firms also provide a wide variety of other services to their audit clients, including consulting and tax services, for additional fees. The public has continued to scrutinize this portfolio of services: Can these audit firms be independent in judgment when audit and consulting fees are at risk? Can these audit firms really be independent in judgment when they audit systems their firms may have suggested and implemented for the client?

4. Finally there have been a number of systems failures in both companies' development of financial statements and the audit processes that have led to major fraud and stakeholder losses. The Enron and WorldCom cases as well as the major SEC decision against Fannie Mae are examples of major systems failures. These recent examples demonstrate that management and auditors may not always detect these errors and that it seems to happen more frequently than one would hope.

It is with the comfort provided by the audit function but the awareness of its weaknesses that we now continue our discussion of data analysis and comparability issues.

COMPARABILITY IN FINANCIAL STATEMENT ANALYSIS

In analyzing a company's financial performance, we often encounter unusual or non-recurring events and transactions that have a sudden and significant impact on the financial statements, especially the income statement. Some events are so visible and widely publicized that we anticipate their consequences. Hurricane Katrina in August 2005 and Hurricane Sandy in November 2012, for example, affected individuals on a massive and tragic scale, and had secondary repercussions for businesses. CSX Corporation, a major U.S. railroad, disclosed in its 2006 annual report that its costs from Katrina, before insurance, to repair 39 miles of track and major bridges and to compensate for lost revenues, amounted to $450 million.[1] And, California's record breaking ongoing drought in 2015 has such massive consequences that although California droughts are a regular occurrence, one on such a massive scale is viewed as a one-time event.

Such severe events are, fortunately, rare, but most companies experience unusual or non-recurring transactions more often. To varying degrees, typically in footnotes or in the discussion of financial results, companies provide information regarding the effects of idiosyncratic events and transactions on net income. However, determining a firm's sustainable or core earnings—a process sometimes called "normalizing earnings"—remains the responsibility of the financial statement user. This section discusses income statement formats and the nature of some common non-recurring items, and walks through an illustration of the effects of such items on earnings and ratios.

When we analyze the profitability of a company over time, our focus is on the core operations of the company. Consider, for example, Tiffany's, a company we have discussed previously. First we will examine this company's reported performance from 2008 through 2010 a turbulent period in the world economy during which time many companies reported a variety of unusual, infrequent, and extraordinary items. After we explore this time period for quality of earnings issues we will update Tiffany's operations to the fiscal year ending January 31, 2014.

Tiffany: 2008–2010: By fiscal year-end 2010, Tiffany had expanded to 233 stores in over 20 countries, but has maintained its strategic focus on high-quality jewelry sold in upscale locations with an emphasis on attentive service and luxurious surroundings. In an analysis of Tiffany's earnings from 2008 through 2010, we are concerned primarily with how well the company has controlled its costs and how effectively the company has used its prestigious brand name to command higher prices, even in the face of an economic downturn. The firm's "bottom line" net income, however, is likely to be affected in any given year by items that may distract us from this central purpose. Tiffany's income statement offers

---

[1] CSX 10-K, 2006, Note 5, p. 68. Note that CSX's insurance coverage was sufficient to cover its losses.

examples of the most common non-recurring or unusual items: discontinued operations and restructuring charges, both of which are the result of management's strategic choices.

Discontinued operations (shown at the bottom of the income statement) are the result of a company's decision to exit a portion of its business. In a separate section of the statement, companies are required to disclose the income or loss from the discontinued business and any gain or loss on the sale of the business. Consequently, the company's revenues and expenses over 2008–2010 exclude the business that was discontinued. Until late 2008, Tiffany owned and operated Iridesse, a chain of U.S. stores that specialized in pearl jewelry. In January 2009, before the end of the 2008 fiscal year, Tiffany's management decided to close all of those stores and to discontinue all Iridesse operations.[2] Consequently, it removed all of the Iridesse revenues and expenses from those income statement lines, and reported the net total, a substantial loss of $12,133,000 in the discontinued operations section. Because it took a few months into the next year to close the stores, a small effect (a loss of $853,000) was reported in fiscal 2009. The advantage of this treatment is that we can now see Tiffany's revenues and expenses across 2008, 2009, and 2010 in a way that reflects the ongoing company financial results, as it exists and will continue to operate in future years. We thus focus on net income from continuing operations in our analysis of a firm's profitability.

Restructuring charges are the result of a company's decision to significantly change the way it operates the business. These strategic choices are often in response to challenging economic circumstances, such as those raised in the most recent recession, as companies look for ways to deliver their goods and services more efficiently. Restructuring charges usually include laying off employees and closing facilities, but do not constitute discontinued operations as they do not involve exiting a separate line of business. In late 2008, for example, Tiffany's decided that it needed to decrease its staffing levels by 10%. The company offered financial incentives for employees to retire early, and laid off other employees, at a total cost to Tiffany's of $97,839 (reported in $ thousands) in higher pension charges and severance package costs.[3] Notice that Tiffany's includes these restructuring costs on its income statement as an operating expense, as these decisions are, after all, part of the process of operating a company. However, we can see clearly over the three years that this decision and its associated cost are unusual.

Operating income is a term often used, but its definition is not derived from any set of rules. Often, *operating income* is considered a synonym of *earnings before interest and taxes* (EBIT). In the case of Tiffany's in 2008, that notion of operating income would lead us to its line "Earnings from continuing operations" in the amount of $394,659. As you can see from the restructuring charge, however, this definition of operating income does not necessarily get at a notion of core, recurring profitability. As in all aspects of financial statement analysis, we need to think carefully about what we wish to measure before we begin to calculate and interpret ratios.

In addition, we need to read carefully to learn whether other unusual items may be included in the calculation of net income, but not identified separately on the income statement. Some non-recurring items are the result of changes in economic conditions rather than corporate strategic decisions. The two most common such items are *asset impairment charges* and the effects of *changes in accounting estimates*.

If economic conditions deteriorate, asset values may fall, and a company must recognize an asset impairment charge whenever it discovers that an asset's fair value has fallen permanently below its book value. The balance sheet equation effect is to reduce the value of the asset and to reduce retained earnings through the expense. In fiscal 2008, for example, Tiffany's learned that the fair value of its investment in two mining companies had significantly declined and was virtually worthless.[4] As a result, the company included a charge of more than $15 million included with the "Selling, general, and administrative expenses" (SG&A) line of its income statement. Asset impairment charges are often disclosed separately on the income statement, but Tiffany's has ag-

---

[2] Tiffany, 2008 10-K, Note C.
[3] Tiffany, 2008 10-K, Note D.
[4] Ibid, Note K.

gregated them with other administrative charges. Similarly, before closing its Iridesse stores, Tiffany's determined that some of the inventory in those stores had deteriorated in value. This particular kind of impairment is called an inventory write-down and must be aggregated with cost of goods sold. Thus, in fiscal 2008, Tiffany's recognized an extra $6.3 million charge in its cost of goods sold.[5]

TIFFANY & CO. **Consolidated Statements of Earnings**			
	Years Ended January 31,		
(in thousands, except per share amounts)	**2011**	**2010**	**2009**
Net sales.	$3,085,290	$2,709,704	$2,848,859
Cost of sales.	1,263,012	1,179,485	1,202,417
Gross profit.	1,822,278	1,530,219	1,646,442
Restructuring charges	—	—	97,839
Selling, general, and administrative expenses.	1,227,497	1,089,727	1,153,944
Earnings from continuing operations	594,781	440,492	394,659
Interest expense and financing costs.	54,335	55,041	28,977
Other income, net.	6,988	4,523	77
Earnings from continuing operations before income taxes	547,434	389,974	365,759
Provision for income taxes.	179,031	124,298	133,604
Net earnings from continuing operations.	368,403	265,676	232,155
Net loss from discontinued operations	—	(853)	(12,133)
Net earnings.	$ 368,403	$ 264,823	$ 220,022
Earnings per share: Basic			
Net earnings from continuing operations	$ 2.91	$ 2.14	$ 1.86
Net loss from discontinued operations.	—	(0.01)	(0.10)
Net earnings	$ 2.91	$ 2.13	$ 1.76
Diluted			
Net earnings from continuing operations	$ 2.87	$ 2.12	$ 1.84
Net loss from discontinued operations.	—	(0.01)	(0.10)
Net earnings	$ 2.87	$ 2.11	$ 1.74
Weighted-average number of common shares: Basic.	126,600	124,345	124,734
Diluted.	128,406	125,383	126,410

Putting all of these pieces together, we can recast Tiffany's income statement for the year ending January 31, 2009, as follows:

Net sales.	$2,848,859
Cost of sales (excluding $6,300)	1,196,117
Gross profit.	1,652,742
Selling, general, and administrative expenses (excluding $15,693).	1,138,251
Operating income, excluding unusual items	$ 514,491

These amounts reflect the results of Tiffany's core, ongoing operations in a way that will be comparable with the subsequent years.

Before we can complete our analysis of Tiffany's operating income over the period, however, we need to consider any unusual items that may have affected fiscal 2009 and 2010. In particular, during fiscal 2010, Tiffany's changed its estimate of the useful lives of some of its buildings and equipment, as the company determined that those assets had shorter lives than originally assumed.[6] Companies make countless estimates in the preparation of

---

[5] Ibid, Note C.
[6] Tiffany, 2010 10-K, Note L.

their financial statements, and the useful life of plant and equipment is but one example. When a company collects evidence that indicates that it should change an estimate, the new information is incorporated into the financial statements going forward, but no amounts from prior years are re-calculated. Thus, a change in estimate does introduce a breach in our apples-to-apples comparability across years. Because Tiffany's discloses the "extra" depreciation expense in 2010 as $17,635, which was included in SG&A, we can identify the amount of that breach, and assess the likely effect in future years of the higher depreciation expense.

One other non-recurring component that may appear on an income statement is an *extraordinary gain or loss*. Income statement items are considered "extraordinary" if they are *both* (1) unusual and (2) infrequent in occurrence.[7] In practice, the strict application of the joint requirement of "unusual and infrequent" results in very few extraordinary items. In 2006, for example, only four companies in a survey of 600 reported an extraordinary item.[8] In our everyday conversation, we would use the word "extraordinary" to describe the devastating effects of Hurricane Katrina, but companies such as CSX that recognized the costs of those effects did *not* classify those amounts as extraordinary items. Despite the terrible consequences, hurricanes in that region are not infrequent. If a company reports an extraordinary gain or loss, it is shown below the discontinued operations section, just before the presentation of bottom-line net income.

If we tried to assess Tiffany's earnings performance using only the "top-line" revenues and the "bottom-line" net income amounts, we would calculate profit margins of 7.7% in fiscal 2008, 9.8% in fiscal 2009, and 11.9% in fiscal 2010, just the kind of gradually increasing pattern that many companies like to report. If, however, we take the first step up the income statement and use "Net earnings from continuing operations" as our "bottom line," we would calculate a profit margin of 8.1% in fiscal 2008 and 9.8% in fiscal 2009, still confirming that apparent upward trend. In our next step up the income statement, we would focus on operating income ("Earnings from continuing operations"), and we might calculate reported operating margin as 13.9% in fiscal 2008, 16.3% in fiscal 2009, and 19.3% in fiscal 2010. Finally, in truly understanding Tiffany's operating performance, we should "scrub" (i.e., eliminate the effects of) the components of operating income and then common-size the components of the statement, as follows:

Tiffany's Key Data after Scrubbing (in thousands)	Year ending January 31, 2011	Year ending January 31, 2010	Year ending January 31, 2009
Net sales.	$3,085,390	$2,709,704	$2,848,859
Cost of sales.	1,263,012	1,179,485	1,196,117
Gross profit.	1,822,278	1,530,219	1,652,742
SG&A	1,209,862	1,089,727	1,138,251
Comparable operating income. . . .	$ 612,416	$ 440,492	$ 514,491

Tiffany's Margins after Scrubbing	Year ending January 31, 2011	Year ending January 31, 2010	Year ending January 31, 2009
Net sales.	100.0%	100.0%	100.0%
Cost of sales/Net sales	40.9	43.5	42.0
Gross margin	59.1	56.5	58.0
SG&A/Net sales	39.2	40.2	40.0
Comparable operating margin	19.9%	16.3%	18.0%

With cleaner data, we can now see a different pattern in Tiffany's operating margin, as it in fact decreased in fiscal 2009 and then bounced back in fiscal 2010. We can also see that most of the deterioration in fiscal 2009 is captured in the decrease in gross margin, a

---

[7] Accounting Principles Board Opinion No. 30, *Reporting the Results of Operations* (New York: AICPA, July, 1973), paragraph 20.

[8] American Institute of Certified Public Accountants, *Accounting Trends and Techniques* (New York: AICPA, 2007), Table 3-18.

significant change, which, combined with the overall 5% decrease in sales revenue, would lead us to focus on questions regarding Tiffany's pricing and product mix. Did Tiffany shift toward lower-margin and/or lower-priced products as a strategic choice in the face of the economic downturn? Did sales volume decrease as the demand for all luxury items fell? Were there additional pressures on gross margin due to cost increases? In fiscal 2010, we see Tiffany's gross margin recover, with an additional improvement (that is, decrease) in SG&A as a percent of sales, and 14% growth in sales revenue. We would focus on questions regarding product mix, but we would also consider Tiffany's efficiency improvements by examining metrics such as sales/square foot and sales/employee to assess whether the 2010 improvements in core profitability are likely to be sustainable.

Key to this kind of detailed analysis is that it improves the accuracy of our information, refines our perception of the company, and leads us to focus on the most relevant questions. As originally reported, fiscal 2008 looks like the "odd" year, the year of difficulty, with recovery occurring in the subsequent years. Certainly fiscal 2008 was the year in which Tiffany saw the need to restructure its business, but using the comparable data, we can see that in its core operations, fiscal 2009 was the difficult year, and only in time will we know for sure whether the rebound observed in fiscal 2010 will persist.

The DuPont model organizes and structures our analysis of financial ratios to better understand and forecast a company's operations, as well as to compare a specific company to its competitors or industry averages to assess performance and condition. The beginning step in most analyses is to use the financial statement data as presented in corporate quarterly and annual reports filed with the SEC.

Standard financial statements, however, often have one-time or unusual items embedded in the reporting of core operations that obscure a company's sustainable operating results. At a minimum, financial data should be examined for these items, and each item considered, to determine whether these items should be included or scrubbed out of the data before ratio analysis is completed. Three specific categories of events that may create non-recurring items or measurement changes on the income statement are: (1) strategic actions involving the sale of major business segments (discontinued operations) or organizational restructuring, (2) economic shifts resulting in asset impairments and changes in accounting estimates, and (3) natural disasters causing unusual losses. Again we emphasize that this section is a brief introduction to scrubbing of financial data before completing a time-series or comparative analysis. Many more adjustments may be necessary after an in-depth analysis of the footnotes accompanying the financial statements. These topics and techniques are typically covered in an advanced financial statement analysis course.

Tiffany's Update: Fiscal 2012–2014: Below are the comparative financial statements reported in Tiffany & Co.'s SEC 2014 10-K annual report. As we review these statements from the bottom up there is no evidence of extraordinary, unusual or infrequent items that might distort the core earnings of the company. However as we move up the income

Consolidated Statements of Earnings			
	Years Ended January 31,		
(in thousands, except per share amounts)	2014	2013	2012
Net sales.	$4,031,130	$3,794,249	$3,642,937
Cost of sales.	1,690,687	1,630,965	1,491,783
Gross profit.	2,340,443	2,163,284	2,151,154
Selling, general and administrative expenses	1,555,903	1,466,067	1,442,728
Arbitration award expense	480,211	—	—
Earnings from operations.	304,329	697,217	708,426
Interest expense and financing costs.	62,654	59,069	48,574
Other income, net.	13,191	5,428	5,099
Earnings from operations before income taxes	254,866	643,576	664,951
Provision for income taxes.	73,497	227,419	225,761
Net earnings.	$ 181,369	$ 416,157	$ 439,190

SEC Form 10-K, Tiffany & Company, Fiscal Year Ending January 31, 2014, Page K-47.

statement we see in the 2014 column an apparent one-time item termed "Arbitration award expense." Listed as $480,211 million this item significantly impacts earnings from operations and as highlighted previously in this chapter impacts the important calculations of earnings per share (EPS) and the related price earnings ratio (P/E). Clearly this expense item needs to be examined more closely for analysis purposes. We turn to the footnote in the SEC 10-K report dealing with litigation.

Litigation Footnote: Tiffany, 2013[9]

Arbitration Award. On December 21, 2013, an award was issued in favor of The Swatch Group Ltd. in an arbitration proceeding. The Arbitration was initiated in June 2011 by Swatch, who sought damages for alleged breach of agreements. In general terms, the Swatch Parties alleged that Tiffany breached the Agreements by obstructing and delaying development of [Swatch] Company's business and otherwise failing to proceed in good faith. Under the terms of the Arbitration Award, Tiffany was ordered to pay to Swatch damages of CHF 402,737,000, as well as interest from June 30, 2012 to the date of payment, two-thirds of the cost of the Arbitration and two-thirds of the Swatch Parties' legal fees, expenses and costs. These amounts were paid in full in January 2014.

As a result of the ruling, in the fourth quarter of 2013, the Company recorded a charge of $480,211,000, which includes the damages, interest, and other costs associated with the ruling and which has been classified as Arbitration award expense in the consolidated statement of earnings.

The arbitration award expense appears to be a one-time event. The result of this award against Tiffany appears to have very little future impact and is unlikely to happen in the future. To analyze continuing operations and project how Tiffany may do in the future, this one-time expense should be scrubbed out of the income calculations to better focus on normal operating results. As we did in the fiscal years 2008–2010, let us now look at the impact if we scrub out the Arbitration award expense to focus on the recurring core operations of the business. Below are the original and scrubbed statements, together with the common-sized calculations:

Tiffany's Key Data after Scrubbing		
($000s)	2014 Before Scrubbing	2014 After Scrubbing
Net sales.	$4,031,130	$4,031,130
Cost of sales.	1,690,687	1,690,687
Gross profit.	2,340,443	2,340,443
SG&A	1,555,903	1,555,903
Arbitration award expense	480,211	0
Operating income.	304,329	$784,540
Operating margin	7.5%	19.5%

The post-scrubbing operating margin calculations show a vastly different picture of Tiffany operations than those margins based on the reported numbers. A stakeholder interested in Tiffany's results, from the reported numbers and ratios based on these numbers may have been concerned about the future for Tiffany. However, with appropriate scrubbing, 2014 operations look strong and prospects for Tiffany's quite good as represented by the P/E and P/B ratios. Clearly, although not as many adjustments were required to focus the latter three years on normal, recurring operations as were required for the years 2008 through 2010, vigilance looking at the original data yielded more representative results in our assessment of Tiffany over the most recent three years.

With the Tiffany examples highlighting the importance of accessing original data (i.e., SEC 10-K data) and scrubbing to focus on analyzing normal operations, we now turn to explore specific refinements of the DuPont model to further analyze operations. Also included at the end of this chapter is an appendix containing a discussion of more Advanced DuPont model analytic techniques for a more in-depth analysis of core operations. If you remember from our discussions in Chapter 3 which focused on revenue

---

[9] Excerpts from the SEC Form 10-K, Tiffany & Company, fiscal year ended January 31, 2014, pages K69-71.

recognition and expense estimates, GAAP variability exists in part because it is difficult to reasonably capture the many economic realities that exist in the myriad of business operations. Flexibility in rules and procedures is needed to be able to capture these realities in financial statement formats. These flexibilities can be divided and introduced in two major categories: flexibility within measurement principles and flexibility within estimation procedures. Combined with the scrubbing procedures discussed in this chapter, it is difficult to draw conclusions from ratio analysis without first examining the statements for one-time adjustments and carefully reading the financial statement footnotes to understand the GAAP procedures and estimates used by the company. Typically a first cut at the analysis using the published data will be completed to gain an overview of a company's performance. In-depth analysis including data scrubbing and adjustments for GAAP variability will then be completed by the analyst as the focus of the analysis dictates (e.g., short-term loan payback risks, long-term growth possibilities, etc.). For now you need to be skeptical of data from which you are drawing your analyses but somewhat secure in the knowledge that the vast majority of companies do select GAAP principles that fairly represent the results of operations and financial position at a point in time. If you continue your exploration of financial analysis, you will learn and use increasingly sophisticated methods to get around these data issues. Let us now turn to two modifications of DuPont analysis that help the analyst focus on normal operations.

The DuPont Model: An Operating Income Focus

As stated in the introduction to the value and techniques of data scrubbing, a focus on core operating results is important. This focus enables a better assessment of management performance with respect to normal operations. Consistent with this focus on core or normal operations is the refining of the return on assets (ROA) portion of the DuPont model (profit margin × asset turnover). We will examine two of many possible refinements of the DuPont model. For a more thorough discussion of these refinements, please see the Appendix to this chapter.

Refinement 1—adjustment to identify core operations

Profit margin in the basic DuPont model is defined as Net Income/Revenues. However, as we have seen in the previous section of this chapter, many non-operating items such as restructuring costs, interest expense, legal losses, and losses due to asset impairment can be included in the calculation of net income. To truly focus on the results of operations, the numerator "Net Income" should be adjusted to better measure the results of core operations. To affect this change, we begin with "Operating Income," which is typically total revenues minus cost of goods sold and operating expenses (selling, general, and administrative). If we then reduce operating income by an estimated amount of income tax owed to the government because of these operating results, we have a clearer picture of the results of operations. This new calculation (Operating Profit – Income Taxes) is termed NOPAT, or net operating profit after taxes. If we now calculate NOPAT/Total Assets, the resultant return ratio focuses on core operations. That is, with the unusual and noncore events removed from the income statement, there exists a clearer representation of operating results that are likely to be sustained in future years.

Refinement 2—adjustment to identify operating assets

Many analysts contend that this modification of the numerator only goes halfway and that the denominator should be modified to focus on operating assets as well. Operating assets would be defined as assets critical to the core operations of a business and would include net working capital (i.e., current assets minus current liabilities); property, plant, and equipment; intangible assets; and investments in affiliates—in short, all of the resources needed to run the day-to-day operations of the company.

Net working capital is comprised of current assets such as cash balances, accounts receivables, inventories, and so forth that support the company's day-to-day operations. Cash balances are required to pay expenses and short-term debts in a timely fashion, accounts receivables support increase revenues through credit giving to customers, and inventory helps ensure against stock-outs. These assets need to be funded and are actually funded in part by current liabilities. For example, suppliers of inventories and supplies frequently give credit terms that result in the current liability accounts payable; similarly, accrued expenses such as utilities payable and wages payable help fund day-to-day operations. Because current assets and current liabilities are so intertwined they are considered together under the topic of *working capital management*; current asset levels are managed, current liabilities are used in part to fund current assets, and the amount of non-funded current assets (i.e., net working capital) is considered part of a company's operating assets. The denominator for our new ratio calculation is (Current Assets – Current Liabilities + PPE + Intangible Assets + Investments in Affiliates). Making this second refinement, ROA now becomes **return on invested capital (ROIC)** and is calculated by NOPAT/(Current Assets – Current Liabilities + PPE + Intangible Assets + Investments in Affiliates).[10] What is important to note is the assets not included in this denominator. Assets such as investments in marketable securities are not considered operating assets and are excluded from this calculation. Thus, ROIC is well suited to focusing on normal operations by refining the numerator to focus on operating profit and the denominator to focus on operating assets.

An Example: Tiffany

Below are selected balance sheet items for Tiffany taken from the SEC 10-K report, January 31, 2014. The income statement accounts are taken from the Tiffany Income Statement highlighted on page 184.

Tiffany Selected Operating Assets: 1/31/2014[11]

TIFFANY, INC. Selected Balance Sheet Accounts: Net Operationg Assets	
Current Assets	**January 31, 2014**
Accounts receivable...	$ 188,814
Inventory..	2,326,580
Deferred income taxes.......................................	101,012
Prepaid expenses...	244,947
Other current assets...	$ —
Current liabilities:	
Accounts payable and accrued liabilities...........................	$ 342,090
Income taxes payable	31,976
Merchandise and other customer credits	$ 70,309
Long-term assets	
Property, plant and equipment..................................	$ 855,094
Other assets..	$ 390,478

Return on Invested Capital is calculating the return generated by normal operations using operating assets, irrespective of how these assets are financed (either debt or owners' equity).

The denominator, Invested Capital, is calculated by taking operating current assets (typically accounts receivable, inventory, prepaid and other assets) minus operating current liabilities (all non-interest bearing current liabilities) to estimated operating net working capital employed in running day-to-day operations. This calculation is then added to long-term operating assets, property, plant, equipment, patents and other long-term miscellaneous assets. (See Appendix for a more in-depth discussion.)

---

[10] Note that many analysts use Total Assets – Current Liabilities as a quick way to calculate the denominator for ROIC.

[11] SEC Form 10-K, Tiffany & Company, Fiscal Year Ending January 31, 2014, Page K-47.

For Tiffany, fiscal year 2014, the net operating working capital investment is the sum of accounts receivable, inventory, deferred income taxes, prepaid expenses and other current assets (totaling $2,861,353) minus the sum of all current liabilities except for short-term borrowing (totaling $444,375) which equals $2,416,978 in net working capital employed in 2014. All numbers are taken from the balance sheet. If we now add long-term operating assets of property, plant and equipment and other assets totaling $1,245,573 to new operating working capital, the denominator for ROIC equals $3,662,551.

The numerator, Return, is typically operating income minus income tax expense. Remember, however, Tiffany had a one-time expense we deemed necessary to scrub out of income tax calculations. The operating income for fiscal year 2014 equals the reported amount of $304,329 plus the arbitration award expense $480,211 or $784,540. Tax expense is estimated by assuming between a 30%–35% standard tax rate. If you use 30%, then ($784,540 × (1 − tax rate) or $784,540 × (1 − 0.3) equals $549,173, the scrubbed net operating income.

Dividing the Return of $549,173 by the Investment of $3,662,551 yields an ROIC of 15%. Management generates from operations a 15% return on operating assets. This number can be then compared to the weighted cost of capital to better understand how management is doing. For example if an average dollar of capital to support operations costs management 9%, then management is making 6 cents more than capital costs. Please refer to the appendix at the end of this chapter for a broader discussion of ROIC and the DuPont model.

CONCLUSION

In this chapter we have introduced three widely used and discussed ratios: earnings per share (EPS), price/earnings (P/E) and price/book value (P/B). EPS is a ratio used to assess operational performance while the P/E and P/B ratios yield insights into the stock market assessment of the company. These ratios are typically shown by the company based on reported financial data. However, as discussed in this chapter, there are excellent reasons to modify (scrub) the financial data before ratio calculations and interpretations. Finally we discussed modifications to the useful DuPont model including, scrubbing data before calculations, using return on invested capital (ROIC) to focus on the assessment of core operations and, in the Appendix, exploring a more advanced version of the DuPont model to more thoroughly examine operating results and the impacts of capital structure on the returns to owners.

In Chapters 5, 6, and 7 we have studied financial data analysis to stimulate your knowledge, use and ability to discuss the discuss performance of any entity using the numbers. The focus on operations, liquidity/cash flow and capital structure helps organize the analysis in order to better link management actions to increase a company's success and ratio improvement.

In Chapters 8 and 9 we will use ratios to project likely operating results captured in financial statement format. Further we will then use forecasting techniques to explore alternative strategic courses of action and create a framework for data-supported decision making.

APPENDIX: ADVANCED DUPONT MODEL—FURTHER EXTENSIONS

In Chapter 6, we introduced you to the DuPont method of analyzing financial statements. This method is widely used and well respected. It is a useful way to organize the analysis of the financial statements of a business and provides valuable insight into the factors that drive the changes in ROE that we observe. To recap, the DuPont method decomposes the return on equity (ROE) into the following three components:

$$\text{DuPont Formula: ROE} = \frac{\text{Net Income}}{\text{Sales}} \times \frac{\text{Sales}}{\text{Total Assets}} \times \frac{\text{Total Assets}}{\text{Equity}}$$

The first two terms are profit margin and asset turnover. These combine to yield the return on assets (ROA), a measure of the operating performance of the company:

$$\text{Return on Assets} = \text{ROA} = \frac{\text{Net Income}}{\text{Sales}} \times \frac{\text{Sales}}{\text{Total Assets}} = \frac{\text{Net Income}}{\text{Total Assets}}$$

Following this initial breakdown, we can further analyze the operating performance of the company by looking at the gross profit and operating profit margins together with the turnover of individual assets and liabilities. This level of analysis often yields useful insights into the factors that are contributing to (or detracting from) a company's ability to increase ROA as well as areas that represent competitive advantages and potential risks.

The third term describes the financial leverage of the company by the proportion of debt versus equity in the company's capital structure. Higher levels of this ratio indicate more financial leverage and a higher level of risk as the company relies more heavily on borrowed funds with contractual payment terms. As a general proposition, we prefer our ROE to be driven to a greater extent by operating activities (ROA) than by financial leverage, and we prefer that our ROA be insulated from competition.

Advanced DuPont Analysis

Although the Traditional DuPont analysis provides useful insights, many analysts focus more on the way that we define operating activities and financial leverage. The reason is that included in the operating side of the business (that is, the activities relating to our customers) are the activities that are really creating value for a company. The non-operating activities of the company (borrowing money and investing excess cash in marketable securities) support the firm's operations, but don't create value in and of themselves. To the extent that we can better isolate the operating activities of the company, we might better understand what is really creating value for our company. That is what the Advanced DuPont method seeks to accomplish.

Another area in which the Advanced DuPont method differs from the traditional model is in the way we think about the investment in assets required to operate a particular business. Using this method, we learn that there are significant benefits to using other people's money. This is not to say that we couldn't have seen that using the Traditional DuPont method; it's just a bit easier to see it using the Advanced DuPont method.

Finally, the Advanced DuPont method causes us to think differently about financial leverage. We will see that there are significant differences between operating liabilities (such as accounts payable) and non-operating liabilities (such as borrowing money from a bank). The Traditional DuPont method doesn't make that distinction.

In this section, we discuss the Advanced DuPont method of analyzing financial statements. We will use Google, Inc., to illustrate the comparison between the two methods and, when we are done, you will get much more insight into why Google is one of the most valuable companies in the world.

Operating and Non-operating

A key aspect of any analysis is identifying the business activities that drive company success. We pursue an answer to the question: Is the company earning an acceptable rate of return on the investment that the owners have made in the business? We also want to know the extent to which the company's return on invested capital results from its operating versus its non-operating activities. The distinction between returns from operating and non-operating activities is important and plays a key role in our analysis.

Operating activities are the core activities of a company. They consist of those activities required to deliver a company's products or services to its customers. A company engages in operating activities when it conducts research and development, establishes supply chains, assembles administrative support, produces and markets its products, and follows up with after-sale customer services.

The asset side of a company's balance sheet reflects resources devoted to operating activities with accounts such as receivables, inventories, and property, plant, and equipment (PPE). Operating activities are reflected in current liabilities such as accounts payable, accrued expenses, and long-term operating liabilities such as pension and health-care obligations. The income statement reflects operating activities through accounts such as revenues, costs of goods sold, and selling, general, and administrative expenses that include wages, advertising, depreciation, occupancy, insurance, and research and development. Operating activities create the most persistent effects on the future profitability and cash flows of the company. Operations provide the primary value drivers for company stakeholders. It is for this reason that operating activities play such a prominent role in assessing profitability.

Non-operating activities relate to the investing of excess cash in marketable securities and in other non-operating investments. Non-operating activities also relate to borrowings through short- and long-term interest-bearing debt. These non-operating assets and liabilities expand and contract to buffer fluctuations in operating asset and liability levels. When operating assets grow faster than operating liabilities, companies typically increase their non-operating liabilities or seek ownership investment to fund the shortfall. Later, these liabilities decline when operating assets decline. When companies have cash in excess of what is needed for operating activities, they often invest the cash temporarily in marketable securities or in other investments to provide some return until those funds are needed for operations or to pay dividends to the owners.

The income statement reflects non-operating activities through accounts such as interest and dividend revenue, capital gains or losses relating to investments, and interest expense on borrowed funds. Non-operating expenses, net of any non-operating revenues, provide a non-operating return for a company. Although non-operating activities are important and must be managed well, they are not the main value drivers for company stakeholders.

To illustrate the distinction between operating and non-operating items, we present a condensed income statement and balance sheet for Google, Inc. (2013) in Exhibit 1 and highlight the operating items in those statements.

In the income statement, operating items are those that relate to transactions with customers. These include sales, cost of goods sold, research and development (R&D), sales and marketing, and general and administrative expenses. Many companies, like Google, group these operating items and report a subtotal for operating profit. Non-operating items relate to financial-related activities, such as borrowing money and investing excess cash in marketable securities. Generally speaking, if the item is interest expense or income or gains (losses) on sales of securities, it is non-operating.

In the balance sheet, those assets and liabilities that relate to operating items in the income statement are operating accounts in the balance sheet. In Google's case, these include accounts receivable, inventories (if Google carried inventory), fixed assets, and goodwill and other intangible assets. On the liability side, operating liabilities include accounts payable and accrued liabilities. Also, we generally include "other" assets and liabilities as operating unless the footnotes clearly indicate that they are non-operating. Generally speaking, if the debt is interest-bearing, it is non-operating, and if the asset generates interest income or dividends, it is non-operating as well.

You might wonder why we don't list cash as an operating asset. Although it is true that the cash used in the day-to-day operations of the business is an operating asset, the cash account that appears on balance sheets includes both cash and "cash equivalents" (marketable securities that will mature within three months of the balance sheet date), which are non-operating investments. Footnote disclosures reveal that most of the cash account is typically comprised of cash equivalents, and even the cash account that remains is typically invested in overnight securities. So, the only true operating component of the cash account is the cash in cash registers in stores, usually a very small proportion of the total cash balance. That's why most analysts treat the entire cash account as non-operating and understand that they are probably underestimating operating assets a little bit. Including the entire cash balance as operating, however, would significantly overstate operating assets.

EXHIBIT 1	Operating Items in Google's Income Statement and Balance Sheet (highlighted in blue)

CONSOLIDATED STATEMENTS OF INCOME	
(in millions)	2013
Revenue	$59,825
Total revenue.	59,825
Cost of goods sold	25,824
Gross profit	34,001
Selling general and admin exp.	12,002
R&D expense	7,910
Other operating expense, total.	19,912
Operating income	14,089
Interest expense.	(83)
Interest and investment income	785
Net interest expense.	702
Currency exchange gains (loss)	(379)
Other non-operating income (expense)	63
EBT excluding unusual items	14,475
Restructuring charges	(123)
Merger and related restructuring charges	—
Gain (loss) on sale of investments	201
Gain (loss) on sale of assets.	(57)
EBT including unusual items	14,496
Income tax expense.	2,282
Earnings from continuing operations	12,214
Earnings of discontinued operations	706
Net income to company	$12,920

CONSOLIDATED BALANCE SHEETS	
(in millions)	2013
Assets:	
Cash and equivalents.	$ 17,628
Short-term investments	39,819
Trading asset securities	87
Total cash and short-term investments	57,534
Accounts receivable.	8,882
Other receivables	408
Total receivables.	9,290
Inventory.	426
Other current assets.	5,636
Total current assets	72,886
Gross property, plant and equipment.	23,837
Accumulated depreciation	(7,313)
Net property, plant and equipment	16,524
Long-term investments	1,976
Goodwill.	11,492
Other intangibles	6,066
Other long-term assets	1,976
Total assets.	$110,920
Liabilities:	
Accounts payable.	2,453
Accrued expenses	6,253
Short-term borrowings.	3,374
Current port. of long-term debt	1,000
Current port. of capital leases	36
Unearned revenue, current.	1,062
Other current liabilities	1,733
Total current liabilities	15,908
Long-term debt	1,990
Capital leases.	246
Unearned revenue, non-current.	139
Other non-current liabilities	5,328
Total liabilities.	23,611
Common stock.	25,922
Retained earnings	61,262
	125
Total common equity	87,309
Total liabilities and equity	$110,920

Return on Net Operating Assets (RNOA)

In the Advanced DuPont analysis, we compute a return on net operating assets (RNOA) and decompose that return into an operating profit margin and a net operating asset turnover rate, as follows:

$$\text{RNOA} = \frac{\text{Net Operating Profit After Tax (NOPAT)}}{\text{Net Operating Assets (NOA)}} = \frac{\text{NOPAT}}{\text{Revenues}} \times \frac{\text{Revenues}}{\text{NOA}}$$

where (in millions),

$$
\begin{aligned}
\text{NOPAT} &= \text{Operating Profit} - \text{Income Tax Expense} \\
&= \$14,089 - \$2,282 \\
&= \$11,807
\end{aligned}
$$

and

$$
\begin{aligned}
\text{NOA} &= \text{Operating Assets} - \text{Operating Liabilities} \\
\text{Operating Assets} &= \$9,290 + \$426 + \$5,636 + \$16,524 + \$11,492 + \$6,066 + \$1,976 = \$51,540 \\
\text{Operating Liabilities} &= \$2,436 + \$6,253 + \$1,062 + \$1,733 + \$139 + \$5,328 = \$16,968 \\
\text{NOA} &= \$51,540 - \$16,968 = \$34,442
\end{aligned}
$$

Therefore, given Google's revenues of $59,825, RNOA is computed as follows:

$$\text{Profit Margin} = \frac{\$11,807}{\$59,825} = 19.7\%$$

$$\text{Turnover} = \frac{\$59,825}{\$34,442} = 1.74$$

$$\text{RNOA} = 19.7\% \times 1.74 = 34.3\%$$

Comparison with Traditional DuPont

The following table summarizes the computations under the two methods:

	Advanced DuPont	Traditional DuPont
Profit margin......	19.7%	21.6%
Turnover.........	1.74	0.54
Return..........	34.3%	12.0%

The Advanced DuPont gives us a much different view of Google's operating activities than the Traditional DuPont analysis. Google's operating returns are seen as much higher under the Advanced DuPont than they are under the traditional method. The reason lies primarily in the way the two models view the operating assets used in the business.

The traditional method views all of the assets of the company as operating, even those relating to investments in marketable securities. Further, it treats all liabilities the same. Consequently, under the traditional method, we view the company as using its total assets account in its operations and financing those assets, in part, with its liabilities.

The Advanced DuPont method takes a different view of the net asset investment. First, it includes as operating assets only the assets used in the core operating activities of the business. Non-operating (financial) assets are treated separately and are not included in our operating ratios.[12] And second, the Advanced DuPont method acknowledges that some of the liabilities are non-interest-bearing. Accounts payable are an example, and the Advanced DuPont method acknowledges that the company does not have the full amount invested in its total assets account because some of the capital is being supplied by outside parties at no interest.

To see the difference, consider the case of inventories. The Traditional DuPont method says that the company is using the total dollar amount of inventories in its operations. The Advanced DuPont method acknowledges that some of the inventory cost is being financed by suppliers at no cost and, as a result, the company only has an investment in the inventories that are not financed by its suppliers. This is a much different view of the operating assets of the company.

At the risk of oversimplifying, the net operating asset investment is comparable to net working capital plus net long-term assets, a much lower dollar amount than total assets. That is why the turnover rate is viewed as much higher under the Advanced DuPont method. And, because net operating profit margin doesn't differ that much between the two methods (most companies don't have much non-operating income and expense in proportion to total revenues), the return on assets differs because of the different ways that the models view the denominator, the net assets employed in the business. Google's return on net operating assets is much higher under the Advanced DuPont method because the dollar amount of the net operating assets used by Google in its business is, in fact, much lower than the total assets used to calculate ROA under the traditional method.

There is another important difference between the two methods. The Traditional DuPont method views all liabilities as the same. The Advanced DuPont method draws a distinction between interest-bearing and non-interest-bearing liabilities. Capital is supplied to the business by investors and creditors who expect a return on their investment (interest in the case of debt and dividends and capital gains in the case of shareholders). The Advanced DuPont method views these two sources as non-operating. Debt that does not carry an interest rate, however, is viewed differently. Not only are the creditors foregoing a return on their investment, but they also don't have the legal protection that is afforded to lenders. They are more a "partner" in the operating activities of the company than they are suppliers of long-term capital.

Finally, the Traditional DuPont model considers all income and expenses, whether or not related to operations. In fiscal year 2013 net income included substantial investment income, expenses related to one-time restructuring charges, losses due to currency exchanges and earnings from discontinued operations—none of which have to do with normal continuing operations.

Return on Equity (ROE)

ROE is computed the same under both the traditional and Advanced DuPont methods. Under the traditional method, ROE is computed as follows:

$$\text{ROE} = \frac{\text{Net Income}}{\text{Equity}} = \text{ROA} \times \text{Financial Leverage}$$

ROE is viewed as a function of ROA and financial leverage, and, assuming that ROA is positive, ROE increases as the company takes on more debt.

---

[12] In Google's case, the contrast in asset turnover calculations of the two models highlights that 60 percent of Google's assets are in cash and marketable securities, a portfolio of approximately $35 billion. Note that in August 2011, Google announced its purchase of Motorola for $12.5 billion, which helps to explain the company's decision to hold such a high proportion of liquid assets.

The Advanced DuPont method yields the same ROE, but its decomposition is more complicated. It views ROE as the sum of two components:

$$\text{ROE} = \frac{\text{Net Income}}{\text{Equity}} = \text{Operating Return} + \text{Non-operating Return}$$

The operating return is the same return on net operating assets (RNOA) that we computed previously. The non-operating return is computed as follows:

$$\text{Non-operating Return} = \text{Financial Leverage} \times \text{Spread}$$

where,

$$\text{Financial Leverage} = \frac{\text{Non-operating Liabilities}}{\text{Equity}}$$

and,

$$\text{Spread} = \text{RNOA} - \text{Weighted-Average Cost of Capital}$$

Financial leverage is a debt-to-equity ratio and is similar to financial leverage in the Traditional DuPont method. The spread is the difference between the return the company is able to realize on its operating assets over the cost of the funds it obtains to purchase those assets. For example, if a company borrows \$100 at 6% interest and invests that \$100 in an asset earning a yield of 10%, the spread is a positive 4% (10% − 6%). If, however, the company only earns a return of 5% on the assets, its spread is −1% (5% − 6%).

Although computation of the non-operating return is a bit complicated and is beyond the scope of this course, it is fairly easy to see the intuition underlying it. That is, if we can earn a positive spread (i.e., earn a return on the assets that is greater than the cost of the debt to buy those assets), our owners will realize a higher return on equity (ROE) if we borrow the money and purchase those assets. The excess return accrues to them. That is the same intuition we get from the Traditional DuPont model: assuming ROA is positive, we can increase ROE by taking on more debt (increasing our financial leverage). The Advanced DuPont model makes this a bit clearer: we can increase ROE by taking on more debt, but only if we can earn a return on the assets financed with the debt that is greater than the interest rate on the debt.

CONCLUSION

By reconsidering the Traditional DuPont model, we can more effectively focus on operating activities. This focus allows us to understand more completely the core, sustainable operating performance of a company, and reflects the fact that financial statement analysis is not governed by a rulebook, but by the needs and purpose of the analyst.

KEY CONCEPTS AND TERMS

return on invested capital
   (ROIC), 187

QUESTIONS

Q7-1. Define restructuring charges and give an interpretation of what these management actions may signal to the stock market and other interested parties.

Q7-2. Asset impairment is evidence of a loss due to a significant decline in the market value of long-term assets. Why is this significant information for analytic purposes? What impacts do these impairments have on current earnings? On future earnings?

Q7-3. What does the Loss on Disposal of Segment represent? Where is this amount typically located on the income statement?

Q7-4. Name two ratios used to indicate the stock market's perception of a company. Explain the underlying logic for the use of each of these ratios.

Q7-5. Define the term core or normal earnings and explain the importance of this calculation in analysis and forecasting.

Q7-6. Compare the calculations return on equity (ROE) and earnings per share (EPS). What is each ratio trying to measure? Do you see benefits of one ratio over the other?

Q7-7. Define return on investment capital (ROIC). What benefits does this ratio represent over the traditional return on assets (ROA) ratio?

Q7-8. Earnings Per Share (EPS) is frequently disclosed in two formats, Basic and Fully Dilutive. Explain the difference between the two of these calculations.

Q7-9. Goodwill impairment charges are disclosed separately from asset impairment charges. Explain what the asset goodwill represents. How is goodwill impairment different from the more general asset impairment?

Q7-10. Frequently, gains and losses due to legal settlements occur on companies' income statements. Although legal expenses seem a part of daily life for many corporations, why are these items typically scrubbed before ratios are calculated and interpreted?

EXERCISES

E7-1. Of the following, which income statement items would you typically scrub to better assess the results of core operations?

Place an X to indicate whether to:	Scrub	Do Not Scrub
Interest income.		
Restructuring charges		
Loss on sale of asset		
Income tax expense.		
Amortization expense on patents.		
Gain on disposal of segment		
Losses due to hurricane.		
Severence pay to a major executive		
Gain on early extinguishment of debt		

E7-2. Frequently entrepreneurs when launching a new venture use the cash accounting basis to record revenue and expenses and measure income. Although easy to use and understand, when performing a time series analysis of operations, cash-based accounting may make it difficult for an entrepreneur to assess operations period over period. Explain how the following expense amounts would be accounted for differently between cash-based versus accrual accounting. Calculate the dollar difference between the two methods assuming a monthly reporting period.

　　a. Frequently revenue was collected in one month for service contracts that would cover a six-month period. In June, Billie Jean and Associates collected $24,000 in service contract revenues that promised services delivered July–December.

    b.   Nathan worked on major utilities equipment inspecting and repairing equipment as required by federal and state regulations. In January he paid $18,000 for an insurance policy that would cover employee liability for the next six months.

    c.   Desi had a website developed for her company. The initial amount paid at the beginning of October when the site was functional was $12,000 and the basic structure of the website was estimated to remain as is for 36 months. Desi also signed a service contract with the website developer to update content monthly as she created it and to perform selected analytics on the users of her website. For this service she paid $750 per month and the developer gave her 30 days credit. In other words, for services performed in November, she would pay for them in December.

E7-3.   Like many entrepreneurs just launching a new venture, Robert was using cash-based accounting methods to record transactions and generate financial statements. His accounting service recently sent him his most recent quarterly results shown below.

Quick Prototyping Inc.			
	July	August	September
Sales.	$50,000	$75,000	$150,000
Salaries.	(20,000)	(33,000)	(60,000)
Software.			(7,200)
Rent	(1,500)	(1,500)	(1,500)
Insurance			(15,000)
Marketing	(3,000)		
Presentations	(4,000)	(8,000)	(15,000)
Legal fees.			(2,000)
EBT.	$21,500	$32,500	$49,300
EBT/Sales.	43.0%	43.3%	32.9%

Robert was surprised by the decline in profit margin because he felt they had a great month in September. As you review the account titles, are there accounting adjustments or items to scrub you would propose to Robert giving him a truer picture of his operations this quarter? Explain your reasoning for each of your suggestions.

E7-4.   Robert understood and made the changes by you and discussed in Exercise 7-3. He looked into those items and discovered the following information.

    1.   Software was programs purchased and would be used every month by Robert and his staff. This version should be useful for three years (36 months).

    2.   Insurance was a two-year policy and payment was required the month the insurance coverage began.

    3.   Marketing was for monthly ads in a technical journal read by potential customers. They were trying this journal for three months and then will evaluate the expense.

    4.   Legal fees were paid to file a protest over another company that used a logo and slogan very similar to Quick Prototyping Inc. The lawyer thought there would be a couple of more months of fees and the other company would then be forced to change its logo and tagline.

Required:

a.   With this additional information, reconfigure Robert's monthly income statements to better reflect normal operations during this quarter.

b.   Recalculate the EBT margin for each month. Do these calculations tell a different story?

E7-5.   Trask, Inc. reported the following EPS calculations for its most recent three years.

Trask, Inc.	Year 1	Year 2	Year 3
EPS basic.	$2.20	$2.50	$2.90
EPS fully diluted.	$2.20	$2.00	$2.30

Required:

a. Based on the EPS basic trend, do Trask's operating results seem to be improving, remaining stable, or declining? Explain.

b. In Years 2 and 3, EPS fully diluted is significantly less than EPS Basic. Give two reasons to explain this difference and explain why management is required to report both calculations.

E7-6. Tanya Enterprises had the following information for the most recent year's operations:

Fiscal Year: January–December

Net income:	$330,000
Common shares outstanding at the beginning of the year:	10,000
Common shares issued on July 1:	2,000
Common shares outstanding at the end of the year:	12,000

Required:

a. Calculate the earnings per share (EPS) for Tanya Enterprises.

b. Is this Basic EPS or Fully Dilutive EPS? Explain your answer.

E7-7. Recoil Inc., maker of devices to store corded phone chargers, iPad chargers, earbuds, and so on, reported $30,000 in its first year of operations. On its balance sheet it also listed:

Common shares outstanding: 1,000
Convertible debt:1,000 shares potentially outstanding in three years. Preferred shareholders were owed $2,000 in dividends per year.

Required:

a. Calculate the basic EPS for Recoil Inc. for the year just ended.

b. Calculate the fully dilutive EPS for Recoil. Explain the difference.

c. Discuss the benefits of preferred stock and the factors that would make it more likely or less likely for the preferred stockholders to convert their stock to common stock.

E7-8. **Pfizer Company, Inc.**, a major pharmaceutical company, for three recent years reported profit margins for Years 1, 2 and 3 of 54.6%, 49.1% and 57.9% respectively. This trend portrays an amazingly high and reasonably consistent profit margin.

Pfizer Company, Inc.

Pfizer	Year 1	Year 2	Year 3
EBT excluding unusual items.	$15,544	$16,897	$17,365
Restructuring charges	(4,740)	(3,145)	(3,802)
Merger and related restructuring charges	(81)	(781)	(613)
Impairment of goodwill.	—	—	—
Gain (loss) on sale of investments	143	141	253
Gain (loss) on sale of assets.	45	102	—
Asset writedown.	(417)	(2,002)	(834)
In process R&D expenses	(68)	—	—
Insurance settlements	—	—	—
Legal settlements.	(234)	(1,723)	(784)
Other unusual items.	482	(18)	(104)
EBT including unusual items	10,674	9,471	11,481
Income tax expense.	2,145	1,153	3,621
Earnings from continued operations	8,529	8,318	7,860
Earnings of discontinued operations	114	(30)	2,189
Extraordinary item and account. change	—	—	—
Net income to company.	$ 8,643	$ 8,288	$10,049

Required:

a. Based simply on the account titles, briefly describe each of the management actions that led to these items.

b. Based on your descriptions in *a.*, would you scrub any of these items and restate Pfizer's income for these three years? Be prepared to support your answers with a discussion of these items and how they should impact a time series analysis of Pfizer.

E7-9. Food retailing and home building supply are two industries that rely on extensive yet fast turning inventory to be successful. Below are the price-earnings ratios as of 12/31/2013 for two companies in each industry.

Food Retailing		Building Supply	
Safeway	41.9x	Home Depot	21.8x
Whole Foods Markets	26.4x	Lowe's	22.5x

Required:

a. Explain the calculation and interpretation of the price-earnings ratio.
b. What tentative conclusions can you draw between industries and between companies in each industry with just this data?

Panera Bread Company

Chipotle

McDonald's

E7-10. **Panera Bread Company**, **Chipotle** and **McDonald's** all compete for the fast-food dollar but with different strategies. Panera prides itself in health foods and fresh bakery goods; Chipotle focuses on ethnic foods sourcing many of its ingredients locally; and McDonald's while serving a variety of foods, is primarily known for its Big Mac and fries. The data table below shows the price-earnings ratio and the price-to-book ratio of the three food service companies at 12/31/2013.

December 31, 2013	Price-Earnings Ratio	Price-Book Ratio
Panera	22.0x	5.9x
Chipotle	51.8x	10.6x
McDonald's	18.2x	6.2x

Required:

a. What does the stock market think of food service companies as represented by these three well-known brands?
b. Which of the companies does the market appear to view most favorably? Use data to support your answer.

PROBLEMS

Safeway, Inc.

P7-1. **Scrubbing the Income Statement (all numbers in millions)** **Safeway, Inc.** is a national food retailer in the United States. Revenues for the most recent four years were $40,850, $41,050, $35,356 and $36,068 for years 1, 2, 3 and 4 respectively (all sales in millions).

Below are the bottom portions of Safeway's income statements for those four years. Use these data in both Exercise 7-9 and 7-10.

Safeway	Year 1	Year 2	Year 3	Year 4
EBT excluding unusual items	$1,094.6	$952.9	$475.3	$375.2
Impairment of goodwill	(1,974.2)	—	—	—
Gain (loss) on sale of investments	—	—	—	—
Gain (loss) on sale of assets	—	—	16.2	48.3
Asset writedown	(73.7)	(71.7)	(33.1)	(33.6)
Legal settlements	—	—	—	46.5
Other unusual items	—	—	—	—
EBT including unusual items	953.3	881.2	458.4	436.4
Income tax expense	144.2	290.6	91.2	141.8
Earnings from continued operations	(1,097.5)	590.6	367.2	294.6
Earnings of discontinued operations	—	—	151.0	303.5
Extraordinary item and account. change	—	—	—	—
Net income to company	$(1,097.5)	$590.6	$518.2	$598.1

Required:

a. Scrub the income statement, calculate the new "EBT including unusual items" for each year.

b. Are these modifications to the reported number significant? Explain.

P7-2. **Scrubbing the Income Statement (all numbers in millions)** Using the data from Problem 7-1 and assuming revenues for Years 1, 2, 3 and 4 are $41.0 billion, $41.0 billion, $43.6 billion, and $44.2 billion respectively:

Required:

a. Calculate the "Earnings from Continuing Operations" and "Net Income" margins for each of the four years based on reported numbers. What is your assessment of Safeway's operating performance during this time span?

b. Calculate the "Earnings from Continuing Operations" and "Net Income" margins for each of the four years based on your scrubbed numbers in Problem 7-1 part *a*.

c. Would your assessment of Safeway change because of the newly calculated earnings amounts?

If needed for purposes of this problem, use the average tax rate of 28.7%.

P7-3. **Scrubbing the Income Statement (all numbers in millions)** Merck Company, Inc. a major pharmaceutical company, for three recent years reported profit margins for Years 1, 2 and 3 of 30.3%, 2% and 13.3% respectively. This trend portrays a recovery from a disastrous Year 2. The lower portion of the earnings table below may help to tell a different story.

Merck Company, Inc.

Merck	Year 1	Year 2	Year 3
EBT excluding unusual items.	$ 8,449	$8,864	$10,547
Restructuring charges	(304)	(1,106)	(1,359)
Merger and related restructuring charges	(3,548)	(3,259)	(919)
Impairment of goodwill.	—	—	—
Gain (loss) on sale of investments	10,693	—	143
Gain (loss) on sale of assets.	—	—	127
Asset writedown.	—	(2,441)	(705)
Legal settlements.	—	(950)	—
Other unusual items	—	545	(500)
EBT including unusual items	15,290	1,653	7,334
Income tax expense.	2,268	671	942
Earnings from continued operations.	13,022	982	6,392
Earnings of discontinued operations	—	—	—
Extraordinary item and account. change.	—	—	—
Net income to company	$13,022	$ 982	$ 6,392
Minority interest in earnings	123	(121)	(120)
Net income	$12,899	$ 861	$ 6,272

Required:

a. Based simply on the account titles, briefly describe each of the management actions that led to these items.

b. Based on your descriptions, would you scrub any of these items and restate Merck's income for these three years? Be prepared to support your answers with a discussion of these items and how they should impact a time series analysis of Merck.

P7-4. **Scrubbing and Adjusting Profit Margins (all numbers in millions)** Using the data from Problem 7-3 and reported revenues of $42,600, $44,000, and $47,300 for years 1, 2, and 3 respectively.

NIKE, Inc.

Under Armour, Inc.

lululemon athletica Inc.

Required:

a. Assuming you will scrub out any of the above accounts if they are 5% of reported net income, scrub and recalculate pre-tax income for years 1, 2, and 3.

b. Assuming a tax rate of 20%, recalculate profit margin for years 1, 2 and 3. Do these recalculated numbers change your assessment of Merck?

P7-5. **Scrubbing the Income Statement—Pfizer** Pfizer Company, Inc. a major pharmaceutical company, for three recent years reported profit margins for years 1, 2, and 3 of 17.5%, 12.7%, and 16.5% respectively. This trend portrays a solid profit margin with a dip in year 2 and a bounce back in year 3.

Pfizer	Year 1	Year 2	Year 3
EBT excluding unusual items...................	$15,544	$16,897	$17,365
Restructuring charges	(4,740)	(3,145)	(3,802)
Merger and related restructuring charges	(81)	(781)	(613)
Impairment of goodwill..........................	—	—	—
Gain (loss) on sale of investments	143	141	253
Gain (loss) on sale of assets.....................	45	102	—
Asset writedown..............................	(417)	(2,002)	(834)
In process R&D expenses	(68)	—	—
Insurance settlements	—	—	—
Legal settlements..............................	(234)	(1,723)	(784)
Other unusual items	482	(18)	(104)
EBT including unusual items	10,674	9,471	11,481
Income tax expense............................	2,145	1,153	3,621
Earnings from continued operations	8,529	8,318	7,860
Earnings of discontinued operations	114	(30)	2,189
Extraordinary item and account. change............	—	—	—
Net income to company.........................	$ 8,643	$ 8,288	$10,049

Required:

a. Choose and scrub the above accounts you think do not represent the core business. You may use a materiality screen of 5% of reported net income. Recalculate pre-tax income for years 1, 2, and 3.

b. Assuming a tax rate of 20%, recalculate profit margin for years 1, 2, and 3. Do these recalculated numbers change your assessment of Pfizer?

Procter & Gamble **P7-6.** **Scrubbing the Income Statement** **Procter & Gamble** is an enormous, global manufacturer and marketer of consumer products with well-established brand names, including Tide, Crest, Gillette, Head & Shoulders, and Duracell.

Required:

Use the income statement for the past three years and answer the following questions.

a. In an analysis of P&G's profitability for the past three years, we can calculate its operating margin. What dollar amount would you use in the numerator of that ratio for each of the three years?

b. As part of the profitability analysis, we would also calculate its profit margin. What dollar amount would you use in the numerator of profit margin for each of the three years presented? Assume an income tax rate of 25% and show your calculations.

PROCTER & GAMBLE COMPANY Income Statement			
For the Fiscal Period Ending *In Millions of the reported currency, except per share items*	**2013** *USD*	**2012** *USD*	**2011** *USD*
Net sales.	84,167	83,680	81,104
Cost of products sold.	42,428	42,391	39,859
SGA expense	26,950	26,421	25,750
Goodwill and indefinite-lived intangible asset impairment charges. . . .	308	1,576	—
Operating income.	14,481	13,292	15,495
Interest expense.	667	769	831
Interest income.	87	77	62
Other non-operating income, net.	942	185	271
Earnings from continuing operations before income taxes	14,843	12,785	14,997
Income taxes on continuing operations.	3,441	3,468	3,299
Net earnings from continuing operations.	11,402	9,317	11,698
Net earnings from discontinued operations.	—	1,587	229
Net earnings.	11,402	10,904	11,927

P7-7. **Entrepreneurs and a Different Type of Scrubbing** Stavos had run his restaurant for 6 months and presented you with the monthly income statements below. Although his revenues showed reasonably consistent growth, his operating profit margin seemed to fluctuate, which he did not understand. You asked him to give you more detail about certain amounts included in the expense and he gave you the following information shown below the monthly income statements. Stavos further volunteered that he used the cash basis of accounting; that is, cash out was an expense and cash in was a sale.

Stavos Greek Cove: Casual Dining							
	January	**February**	**March**	**April**	**May**	**June**	**Total**
Sales.	$ 2,500	$3,750	$ 5,625	$8,438	$12,656	$18,984	$51,953
Food costs	875	1,313	1,800	2,700	3,797	5,695	16,180
Wait staff salaries	800	800	1,400	2,000	3,500	5,000	13,500
Occupancy costs	1,900	700	4,400	800	800	5,600	14,200
Other items							—
Total operating expenses . . .	$ 3,575	$2,813	$ 7,600	$5,500	$ 8,097	$16,295	$43,880
Operating income.	$(1,075)	$ 938	$(1,975)	$2,938	$ 4,559	$ 2,689	$ 8,073
Operating margin	−43%	25%	−35%	35%	36%	14%	16%

Occupancy costs included all expenses to operate the physical space of the restaurant, lease expense for space and equipment, insurance expense, utility expense and other miscellaneous expenses incurred to keep the doors open.

In January Stavos paid $1,200 in cash for his annual insurance premium covering the restaurant for the next twelve months. In March, he purchased and installed two television sets for $3,600. He estimated these televisions would have useful lives of 36 months with no salvage value. In June, Stavos paid $4,800 for his restaurant website which included the capability to be easily upgraded to take internet orders as well as immediately connecting to OpenTable allowing customers to make reservations.

Required:

a. Discuss items that you would allocate differently across the months that may impact Stavos's impressions of his monthly operations. Include your reasoning for proposing these alternative treatments.

b. Complete the form below after you have scrubbed the data.

c. Based on the scrubbed data, how did Stavos do? What recommendations would you make to him?

Stavos Greek Cove: Casual Dining							
	January	February	March	April	May	June	Total
Sales.							
Food costs							
Wait staff salaries							
Occupancy costs							
Other items							
Total operating expense. . .							
Operating income.							
Operating margin							

Staples, Inc.   **P7-8.**   **Staples, Inc. Price-earnings Ratio and Price-to-Book Value Ratios**

Required:

Use the income statements and selected balance sheet data provided in this problem for **Staples** to answer the following questions.

a. Calculate the price-earnings ratio and price-to-book ratio for Staples for the past three years.

b. Consider whether any amounts should be scrubbed as part of the income statement analysis. If so, what would the revised net income for each company be for those periods?

c. Based upon the scrubbing analysis performed in part *b*, recalculate the adjusted profit margin and return on equity for those periods.

d. Does the analysis performed in parts *b* and *c* change your perception of the company's future operating results?

Staples	2011	2012	2013
Stock price.	$13.89	$11.40	$15.89
Market capitalization (in millions)	16,091	11,139	9,041
Basic EPS.	$ 1.28	$1.39	$ 0.88
Price to earnings			
Price to book			

STAPLES, INC. AND SUBSIDIARIES Consolidated Statements of Income (Dollar Amounts in Thousands, Except Share Data)			
	Fiscal Year Ended		
	February 2, 2013	January 28, 2012	January 29, 2011
Sales.	$24,380,510	$24,664,752	$24,135,253
Cost of goods sold and occupancy costs	17,889,249	17,974,884	17,600,006
Gross profit.	6,491,261	6,689,868	6,535,247
Operating expenses:			
Selling, general and administrative.	4,884,284	4,991,195	4,832,444
Impairment of goodwill and long-lived assets	810,996	—	—
Amortization of intangibles.	78,900	64,902	61,689
Integration and restructuring costs.	207,016	—	57,765
Total operating expenses	5,981,196	5,056,097	4,951,898
Operating income.	510,065	1,633,771	1,583,349
Other (expense) income:			
Interest income.	5,340	7,370	7,397
Interest expense	(162,477)	(173,394)	(214,410)
Loss on early extinguishment of debt.	(56,958)	—	—
Other income (expense), net.	(30,547)	(3,103)	(9,799)
Income from continuing operations before income taxes	265,423	1,464,644	1,366,537
Income tax expense	426,270	477,247	467,577
(Loss) income from continuing operations, including the portion attributable to the noncontrolling interests.	(160,847)	987,397	898,960
Discontinued operations:			
Loss from discontinued operations, net of income taxes	(49,978)	(3,564)	(10,391)
Consolidated net (loss) income	(210,825)	983,833	888,569
(Loss) income attributed to the noncontrolling interests	(119)	(823)	6,621
(Loss) income attributed to Staples, Inc.	$ (210,706)	$ 984,656	$ 881,948
Basic Earnings Per Common Share:			
Continuing operations attributed to Staples, Inc.	$(0.24)	$1.42	$1.24
Discontinued operations attributed to Staples, Inc..	(0.07)	—	(0.01)
Net (loss) income attributed to Staples, Inc.	$(0.31)	$1.42	$1.23
Diluted Earnings per Common Share:			
Continuing operations attributed to Staples, Inc.	$(0.24)	$1.40	$1.22
Discontinued operations attributed to Staples, Inc..	(0.07)	—	(0.01)
Net (loss) income attributed to Staples, Inc.	$(0.31)	$1.40	$1.21

STAPLES, INC.			
Selected Balance Sheet Data:	February 2, 2013	January 29, 2012	January 28, 2011
Stockholders' equity	$ 6,128,000	$ 7,015,000	$ 6,944,000

P7-9. **TJX Companies, Inc. and** Abercrombie & Fitch Co. **Price-Earnings Ratio and Price-to-Book Value Ratio**

TJX Companies, Inc.

Abercrombie & Fitch Co.

Required:

Use the income statements and selected balance sheet data provided to answer parts *b*, *c* and *d*.

a. Calculate the price-earnings ratio and price-to-book ratio for both companies for the most recent year. How does the market compare these two companies?

2013	TJX	A&F
Stock price.	$ 62.73	$32.91
Market capitalization (in millions)	$32,793	$4,006
Stockholders' equity (millions)	$ 3,666	$1,818
Earnings per share (Basic)	$ 2.60	$ 2.95
Price to earnings		
Price to book		

b. For Abercrombie & Fitch Co., consider whether any amounts should be scrubbed as part of the income statement analysis. If so, what would the revised net income for each company be for those periods?

c. Based upon the scrubbing analysis performed in part b, recalculate the adjusted profit margins for all three years and the ROE for the two most recent years.

d. Does the analysis performed in parts b and c change your perception of the companies' future operating results?

ABERCROMBIE & FITCH CO. Consolidated Statements Of Operations (Thousands, except share and per share amounts)			
	2012	2011	2010
		(Restated see Note 4)	
Net sales.	$4,510,805	$4,158,058	$3,468,777
Cost of goods sold.	1,694,096	1,607,834	1,251,348
Gross profit.	2,816,709	2,550,224	2,217,429
Stores and distribution expense.	1,987,926	1,888,248	1,589,501
Marketing, general and administrative expense.	473,883	437,120	400,804
Other operating expense (income), net	(19,333)	3,472	(10,056)
Operating income.	374,233	221,384	237,180
Interest expense, net	7,288	3,577	3,362
Income from continuing operations before taxes.	366,945	217,807	233,818
Tax expense from continuing operations	129,934	74,669	78,109
Net income from continuing operations.	$ 237,011	$ 143,138	$ 155,709
Income from discontinued operations, net of tax	$ —	$ 796	$ —
Net income.	$ 237,011	$ 143,934	$ 155,709
Net income per share from continuing operations:			
Basic.	$2.89	$1.65	$1.77
Diluted.	$2.85	$1.60	$1.73
Net income per share from discontinued operations:			
Basic.	$ —	$0.01	$ —
Diluted.	$ —	$0.01	$ —
Net income per share:			
Basic.	$2.89	$1.66	$1.77
Diluted.	$2.85	$1.61	$1.73
Weighted-average shares outstanding:			
Basic.	81,940	86,848	88,061
Diluted.	83,175	89,537	89,851
Selected Balance Sheet Data—Stockholders' Equity . . .	$1,818,268	$1,931,335	NA

P7-10. **Price-Earnings Ratio and Price-to-Book Value Ratios for NIKE, Inc., Under Armour, Inc., and lululemon athletica Inc.**

NIKE, Inc.

Under Armour, Inc.

lululemon athletica Inc.

Required:

Use the financial statements, on pp. 165–173 in Chapter 6, to answer the following questions.

a. Calculate the price-earnings ratio and price-to-book ratio for all companies in the past three years. How does the market compare these three companies and how has each of these companies trended during the three-year period?

NIKE	2011	2012	2013
Stock price.	$48.19	$51.60	$78.64
Market capitalization (in millions).	39,523	49,546	55,124
Basic EPS.	$ 2.24	$ 2.48	$ 2.75
Price to earnings			
Price to book			

Note: all numbers taken from Yahoo! Finance data base.

Under Armour	2011	2012	2013
Stock price.	$35.89	$45.83	$87.30
Market capitalization (in millions).	9,237	5,084	3,715
Basic EPS.	$ 0.94	$ 1.23	$ 1.54
Price to earnings			
Price to book			

Note: all numbers taken from Yahoo! Finance data base.

lululemon athletica	2011	2012	2013
Stock price.	$46.66	$76.23	$59.03
Market capitalization (in millions).	7,625	7,061	3,662
Basic EPS.	$ 0.86	$ 1.29	$ 1.88
Price to earnings			
Price to book			

Note: all numbers taken from Yahoo! Finance data base.

b. Consider whether any amounts should be scrubbed as part of the income statement analysis. If so, what would the revised net income for each company be for those periods?

c. Based upon the scrubbing analysis performed in part *b*, recalculate the adjusted profit margin and return on equity for those periods.

d. Does the analysis performed in parts *b* and *c* change your perception of the companies' future operating results?

Chapter Eight

Forecasting Financial Performance

When you complete this chapter you should be able to:

1. Explain the process of forecasting financial statements.
2. Forecast revenues and the income statement.
3. Forecast the balance sheet.
4. Forecast the statement of cash flows.
5. Prepare multiyear forecasts of financial statements.
6. Explain the forecasting process as the manager of a business we own (inside out) and as an outside investor in a publicly-traded company using published financial statements.

INTRODUCTION

In Chapter 5, we discussed opportunity assessment and introduced you to forecasting future financial performance from the perspective of an owner of the business assessing a possible business opportunity. With inside information only an owner could know, we focused on a forecast of the income statement and estimated operating cash flow using some assumptions about working capital accounts. We also introduced the evaluative tools of break-even analysis, return on investment (ROI), and payback periods. In Chapters 6 and 7, we followed this introduction to forecasting and analysis with a more in-depth discussion of the analysis of financial statements to give users a better understanding of the drivers of financial performance. In this chapter we return to a focus on the company's future performance and illustrate techniques that will allow you to forecast all of the financial statements (income statement, balance sheet, and statement of cash flows) given a set of assumptions about the likely trends in the business that we expect to occur. These forecasted financial statements, together with our analysis framework from Chapters 6 and 7, will allow us to evaluate the expected future performance of the company. As a result of this analysis, we will be better able to evaluate the effectiveness of different strategic paths that we are contemplating or to suggest possible strategic paths that we might not have yet considered.

In this chapter, we are considering again the same questions that motivated our discussion in Chapters 5–7, but are now focusing on the future rather than the past:

1. Is my business likely to be profitable? If not, why not, and what can I do to improve profitability?
2. Will I continue to efficiently use the firm's assets?
3. Do I need external financing to support my business? If so, should I finance my business using equity or debt? What are the implications of different financing alternatives?

4. What are the trends in the performance of my business? How does my business compare to other firms in my industry? Are these trends acceptable to me? Or should I consider other strategic alternatives?

Being able to accurately forecast financial performance is critical to successfully managing the growth of any business. In this chapter we introduce some basic tools and techniques to help you in the forecasting process.

FORECASTING FINANCIAL STATEMENTS: INSIDE-OUT

In this section we discuss the forecasting process from the inside-out (i.e., from the owner's viewpoint) like we did in Chapter 5. In a later section of this chapter we will discuss the forecasting process from the outside-in, forecasting public company financial statements from publicly available data.

The forecasting process estimates future income statements, balance sheets, and statements of cash flow, in that order. The reason for this order is that each statement uses information from the preceding statement(s). We update retained earnings on the balance sheet to reflect our forecast of the company's profitability and expected dividend payments. And, the forecasted income statement and balance sheets are used in the preparation of the forecasted statement of cash flows in the same manner that we describe in Chapter 4 for the preparation of the statement of cash flows in the current year.

Overview of the Forecasting Process

Before we become immersed in the mechanics of the forecasting, let's take a moment to think about some overarching principles that guide us in the preparation of our forecasts:

1. **Should I be optimistic or conservative in my forecasts?** The short answer is neither. Accurate forecasts provide the best information for decision making. Being deliberately optimistic or conservative may cause you to make unsound decisions and to miss valuable opportunities.

2. **How much precision should I use?** It is easy to get carried away with precision in spreadsheets by taking estimates out to the *n*th decimal place. Increasing precision makes the resulting forecasts appear more "professional," but it may not make them more accurate. As you will see from our discussion, the forecasting process starts with, and is highly dependent upon, the forecasts of revenues, which are very difficult to estimate. Estimating cost of goods sold to the fifth decimal place doesn't make much sense if our revenue estimate is somewhat uncertain.

3. **Should all of my financial statements tie together?** The short answer is yes. The forecasted income statement, balance sheet, and statement of cash flows should relate in the same way that historical financial statements do as we discuss in Chapters 1 and 2. Preparing a forecasted statement of cash flows from the forecasted income statement and balance sheet, although difficult, is often a useful way to uncover errors in the forecasting process. In addition, the forecasting assumptions should be internally consistent. For example, it doesn't make much sense to forecast an increase in gross profit margins if we are forecasting a recession unless that expectation can be adequately supported.

Summary Forecasting is more art than science. It should begin with an analysis of general macroeconomic activity and a thorough understanding of the competitive forces within the broader business environment. Ideally, forecasts should be developed from the level of individual products, considering their competitive advantage, trends in manufacturing costs, logistical requirements, required marketing support, after-sale customer service, and so on. The narrower the focus, the more you will attend to the business environment in which the company operates and the more informed will be your forecasts.

HISTORICAL FINANCIAL STATEMENTS: THE STARTING POINT

In Chapter 6, we analyzed the financial performance of a small restaurant given its financial statements through the year 2014. Our initial analysis led us to conclude that the business had grown—from 2010 to 2014 total revenue increased 54%—but its net income for the same period fell by 51%, from about $19,814 to $9,787. In our initial analysis, we recast the income statement in common-size format as follows to better see trends in the relation of the income statement accounts as a percentage of sales:

Common-Size Income Statement INCOME STATEMENT	2010	2011	2012	2013	2014
Revenue: Store.	82.1%	80.8%	79.4%	78.6%	77.9%
Revenue: Catering	17.9%	19.2%	20.6%	21.4%	22.1%
Total revenue	100.0%	100.0%	100.0%	100.0%	100.0%
COGS: Food.	−35.0%	−36.0%	−37.0%	−38.0%	−38.0%
Gross profit.	65.0%	64.0%	63.0%	62.0%	62.0%
Wage expense:.	0.0%	0.0%	0.0%	0.0%	0.0%
Fixed.	−14.9%	−13.4%		−12.9%	−11.6%
Variable.	−15.0%	−15.0%	−15.0%	−15.0%	−15.0%
Total wages	−29.9%	−28.4%	−29.3%	−27.9%	−26.6%
General overhead.	−14.9%	−20.0%	−20.3%	−20.4%	−21.3%
Depreciation expense.	−0.7%	−0.7%	−0.7%	−1.1%	−1.0%
Marketing	−10.0%	−10.0%	−10.0%	−10.0%	−10.0%
Operating income.	9.4%	5.0%	2.7%	2.6%	3.1%
Interest expense.	−0.3%	−0.5%	−0.5%	−0.4%	−0.4%
Income before tax	10.2%	5.7%	3.2%	3.7%	5.0%
Taxes	−3.2%	−1.6%	−0.8%	−0.8%	−1.0%
Net income.	5.9%	3.0%	1.5%	1.5%	1.9%

This common-size analysis led us to the following observations:

1. We notice that the catering segment of our business is growing faster than the store segment.
2. Food COGS increased by 3 percentage points from 2010 to 2013, but leveled off in 2014 at 38%.
3. A portion of our wage expense is variable and remains at a constant at 15% of sales.
4. Our general overhead has increased steadily as a percentage of sales.

Given this historical analysis, our focus now is on the direction that these cost areas as a percentage of sales will take in *future* years. And, in order to answer that question, we will need to better understand the factors that are *causing* these expense areas to behave as they have in the past.

Many of the ratios we discussed in Chapter 6 involve both the income statement and the balance sheet. As we will discuss, our forecasts of the balance sheet will use our forecasted income statement, and once we have forecasted both of these statements, we will be able predict the likely level of these ratios in future years. In addition, once we have forecasted both the income statement and the balance sheet, we will be able to forecast the statement of cash flows. This last statement will provide us with important insight into the cash-generating ability of our business.

We now begin our discussion with a general overview of the forecasting process.

THE IMPACT OF THE REVENUE FORECAST ON THE INCOME STATEMENT AND THE BALANCE SHEET

The total revenue (sales) forecast is, arguably, the most difficult estimate in the forecasting process. It is also one of the most critical because analysts typically estimate other income statement and balance sheet accounts with respect to revenues. As a result, both the income statement and balance sheet grow with increases in the revenue forecast and should decline with decreases in revenue forecasts. The income statement reflects this growth concurrently. The balance sheet, however, reflects this growth differently. Some portions anticipate this growth (inventories are an example). Some reflect growth concurrently (accounts receivable). And some reflect growth with a lag (companies typically invest in new plant, property, and equipment [PPE] assets only after growth is deemed to be sustainable). And, when revenues decline, so does the income statement and balance sheet as the company shrinks in order to cope with adversity. Such actions include reduction of overhead costs and divestiture of excess assets.

Illustration 8.1 describes the impact of the revenue forecast on the income statement and the balance sheet.

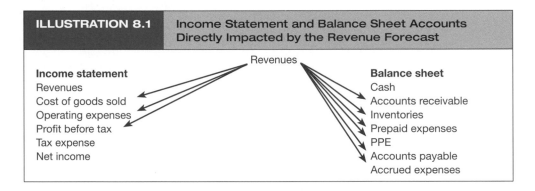

ILLUSTRATION 8.1 Income Statement and Balance Sheet Accounts Directly Impacted by the Revenue Forecast

Revenues

Income statement
Revenues
Cost of goods sold
Operating expenses
Profit before tax
Tax expense
Net income

Balance sheet
Cash
Accounts receivable
Inventories
Prepaid expenses
PPE
Accounts payable
Accrued expenses

The following accounts are impacted directly and within a relatively short period of time by the revenue forecast (we assume an increase in revenues):

- **Cost of goods sold** is impacted via the purchases account as companies increase inventories in anticipation of increased demand, with added manufacturing personnel, and with the added depreciation expense of new manufacturing PPE.

- **Operating expenses** also increase concurrently with or in anticipation of increased revenues. These expenses include increased costs for buyers, higher advertising costs, payments to sales personnel and post-sale customer support, logistics costs, salaries because of increased head count, and administrative costs.

- **Accounts receivable** increase directly with increases in revenues as more goods and services are sold on credit terms.

- **Inventories** typically increase in anticipation of higher sales volumes in order to ensure that there are sufficient stocks on hand.

- **Prepaid expenses** increase with increases in advertising and other investments in advance of sales.

- **PPE** assets are typically acquired once the revenue increase is deemed to be sustainable and the capacity constraint is reached.

- **Accounts payable** increase as inventories are purchased on credit terms.

- **Accrued expenses** also increase concurrent with increases in operating expenses.

All of these accounts increase roughly concurrently with revenue increases or with a slight lead or lag. As a result, both the income statement and the balance sheet grow or shrink together.

In the sections that follow, we discuss the forecasting process in detail, and you will notice that asset and liability accounts will be projected to grow at different rates. For example, receivables, inventories, accounts payable and accrued liabilities tend to grow roughly concurrent with the growth in sales while PPE assets tend to grow in a step fashion (as capacity is reached, we build another manufacturing plant or a new warehouse, for example). Also, companies tend to take out long-term debt and sell common stock relatively infrequently to raise large amounts of cash.

It is for these reasons that our balance sheet, which is in balance when we ended the current year, will quickly become out of balance in our first forecast year. And, since we know that assets must always equal liabilities plus equity, we need an account that we can increase or decrease to balance the balance sheet. That account is cash and we call it our "plug" account. As you will see, the amount that we estimate for our cash plug figure can be either positive or negative and the sign and magnitude of this account will tell us quite a bit about the expected performance of our company. If, for example, we see cash growing significantly we know that our business is generating a lot of excess cash. And, if we see cash becoming negative, we know that our business is losing cash (possibly because it is performing poorly or because we have invested heavily in new asset growth).

We will discuss the implications of positive and negative growth for cash later in this chapter. But, for now, just try to understand the concept of using cash as our plug figure.

ILLUSTRATION OF THE FORECASTING PROCESS

We illustrate our forecasting process by forecasting the income statement, the balance sheet, and the statement of cash flow in this order:

1. Forecast the income statement − revenues and expenses.
2. Forecast the balance sheet − assets (other than cash), liabilities, and equity. Then, plug an amount for cash to make Assets = Liabilities + Equity.
3. Forecast the statement of cash flow using the forecasted income statement and balance sheet together with the prior year's balance sheet.

To illustrate, in the following section, we begin our discussion with a forecast of the income statement, and we provide our restaurant's 2012–2014 income statements in Exhibit 8.1 as a reference point (see page 104).

EXHIBIT 8.1	Restaurant Income Statements					
Revenue Growth				**+10%**		**+10%**
	2012	**% Tot Rev**	**2013**	**% Tot Rev**	**2014**	**% Tot Rev**
Revenue: Store.........	332,750	79%	366,025	79%	402,628	78%
Revenue: Catering	86,400	21%	99,360	21%	114,264	22%
Total revenue	419,150		465,385		516,892	
COGS: Food...........	(155,086)	37%	(176,846)	38%	(196,419)	38%
Gross profit...........	264,065	63%	288,539	62%	320,473	62%
Wage expense:						
Fixed	(60,000)		(60,000)		(60,000)	
Variable	(62,873)	15%	(69,808)	15%	(77,534)	15%
Total wages	(122,873)		(129,808)		(137,534)	
General overhead.......	(85,000)		(95,000)		(110,000)	
Depreciation expense....	(3,000)		(5,000)		(5,000)	
Marketing	(41,915)	10%	(46,539)	10%	(51,689)	10%
Operating income.......	11,277		12,192		16,250	
Interest expense........	(1,626)		(1,193)		(1,193)	
Income before tax	9,651		10,999		15,057	
Taxes	(3,378)		(3,850)		(5,270)	
Net income...........	6,273		7,150		9,787	

Step 1: Forecast Revenues and Expenses

The forecast of revenues is the most difficult step in the projection process and must be done with care, as we typically forecast the remainder of the income statement and the balance sheet with an assumed relation to forecasted revenues.

We typically utilize both financial and nonfinancial sources of information in developing our forecasts. For example, we might want to consider the general level of economic activity (is the economy growing or likely to be in recession next year?) and the competitive environment (are any new restaurants planning to open or existing competition expected to close in the next year?).

For expenses, we have two possible approaches we can take:

1. **Variable expenses.** For those expenses that vary with revenues, we typically assume that the expense level will equal an assumed percentage of sales. For example, our COGS has been 38% of sales for the past two years. Unless we have reason to believe that our cost of goods sold will become more or less costly, our best guess is that COGS will remain at 38% of sales for next year.

2. **Fixed expenses.** Some of our expenses are fixed costs, meaning that they do not change with revenues over a reasonable change in sales. In our restaurant, some of our wages are fixed and some are variable. We can project the fixed portion to remain at the current level of $60,000 or, possibly, increase it by an inflation rate if we expect, for example, that our employees will be entitled to a cost-of-living increase. Another approach might be to assume a specific dollar amount say, for example, if we know one of our employees will be promoted and will receive a wage increase as a reward.

In this forecasting example, we will assume a continuation of 2014 variable cost percentages and fixed cost dollar amounts. These assumptions result in the forecast of our income statement for 2015 shown in Exhibit 8.2.

EXHIBIT 8.2	Forecasted 2015 Restaurant Income Statement			
	2014	**Forecast Assumptions**	**Est. 2015**	
Revenue: Store.........	$402,628	1.10	$442,891	(402,628 × 1.10 = 442,891)
Revenue: Catering	114,264	1.10	125,690	(114,264 × 1.10 = 125,690)
Total revenue	516,892		568,581	
COGS: Food...........	(196,419)	38.0%	(216,061)	(568,581 × 38% = 216,061)
Gross profit...........	320,473	62.0%	352,520	
Wage expense:				
Fixed...............	(60,000)	(60,000)	(60,000)	
Variable............	(77,534)	15.00%	(85,287)	(568,581 × 15% = 85,287)
Total wages	(137,534)		(145,287)	
General overhead.......	(110,000)	21.3%	(121,108)	(568,581 × 21.3% = 121,108)
Depreciation expense....	(5,000)	(5,000)	(5,000)	
Marketing	(51,689)	10%	(56,858)	(568,581 × 10% = 56,858)
Operating income.......	16,250		24,267	
Interest expense........	(1,193)	(1,193)	(1,193)	
Income before tax	15,057		23,074	
Taxes @ 35%	(5,270)	35%	(8,076)	(23,074 × 35% = 8,076)
Net income...........	$ 9,787		$ 14,998	

Explanations:

1. Revenues are expected to grow by 10%. Forecasted revenues are therefore equal to this year's revenues × (1 + growth rate %) = this year's revenues × 1.1. For 2015, est. store revenues = $402,628 × 1.1 = $442,891 and est. catering revenues

= \$114,264 × 1.1 = \$125,690, yielding total est. revenues of \$442,891 + \$125,690 = \$568,581.

2. Variable costs are projected using the forecasted total revenues of \$568,581. Forecasted COGS therefore is equal to \$568,581 × 38% = \$216,061. Variable wage expense, general overhead expense, and marketing expense are forecasted similarly.

3. Fixed costs are assumed not to change in this example. Our estimated 2015 fixed expense is therefore equal to the 2014 actual expense.

4. Tax expense is equal to estimated pretax income multiplied by our assumed tax rate of 35% (notice that tax expense is projected as a percentage of pre-tax profit, not as a percentage of revenues).

Step 2: Project Assets and Liabilities and Equity

Our next step is to forecast the balance sheet. The order of operations in the forecast of the balance sheet is described in Illustration 8.2.

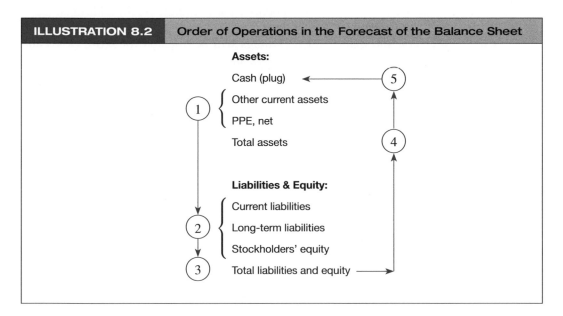

| ILLUSTRATION 8.2 | Order of Operations in the Forecast of the Balance Sheet |

Step 1.
   a. forecast current assets (other than cash), usually as a percentage of revenues
   b. forecast PPE, net with an increase for capital expenditures (CAPEX) and a decrease for depreciation expense
   c. assume no change in marketable securities

Step 2.
   d. forecast current liabilities, usually as a percentage of revenues
   e. forecast short-term and long-term debt with an increase for planned borrowing and a decrease for scheduled principal payments
   f. assume no change in common stock unless a stock sale is planned
   g. increase (decrease) retained earnings for the profit earned (loss incurred) for the period and to reduce retained earnings for any dividends paid to shareholders

Step 3. compute total liabilities and equity

Step 4. set total assets equal to total liabilities and equity

Step 5. solve (plug) for the cash balance that yields the amount for total assets in step 4.

MECHANICS OF FORECASTING ASSETS, LIABILITIES, AND EQUITY

We typically use all of the following three assumptions to forecast assets, liabilities, and equity:

1. **Forecast in relation to the change in revenues**—We use this approach to forecast most of our assets and non-interest-bearing liabilities. The underlying assumption is that, as the sales volume increases, so will receivables and inventories. Accounts payable will also grow as more inventories are purchased and accrued liabilities will increase with increases in payroll, utilities, advertising, and the like.

2. **Planned acquisitions and scheduled reductions**—We incorporate planned purchases of PPE (capital expenditures or CAPEX) and scheduled depreciation of existing and newly acquired PPE. We also assume that debt payment schedules will be paid as required.

3. **No change**—We initially assume no change in marketable securities and debt. We also assume that our paid-in capital accounts (like common stock, additional paid-in capital [APIC] and treasury stock) will remain constant unless we have reason to believe otherwise and that retained earnings will be updated for profit (loss) and dividends (we combine common stock, APIC, and retained earnings into one account called equity in this example; because we are assuming no sales or purchases of common stock, our equity account will reflect only increases from profit and decreases from dividends).

As was the case for our income statement, a useful starting point for our forecast of the balance sheet is our historical balance sheets expressed in dollars and as a percentage of revenues. These statements are presented in Exhibit 8.3.

EXHIBIT 8.3	Restaurant Balance Sheets						
	2012	**% Tot Rev (R)/ COGS (C)**	**2013**	**% Tot Rev (R)/ COGS (C)**	**2014**	**% Tot Rev (R)/ COGS (C)**	
Assets							
Cash	$18,725		$20,958		$23,269		
AR.	6,000	1.4% R	7,200	1.5% R	8,280	1.5% R	
Inventory.	8,988	5.8% C	10,339	5.8% C	11,790	6.0% C	
Other assets	5,000		5,000		6,000		
Total current assets	38,713		43,497		49,339		
Equipment	45,000		60,000		60,000		
Accumulated depreciation . . .	(8,000)		(13,000)		(18,000)		
Total assets.	$75,713		$90,497		$91,339		
Liabilities							
Accounts payable.	$16,845	10.9% C	$19,386	11.0% C	$22,106	11.3% C	
Wages payable.	3,185	0.8% R	3,686	0.8% R	3,894	0.8% R	
Credit card debt	7,000		14,999		6,941		
Other current liabilities	1,000		3,000		1,000		
Total current liabilities.	28,030		41,071		33,941		
Long-Term liabilities	20,321		14,914		13,100		
Equity	27,362		34,511		44,298		
Total	$75,713		$90,497		$91,339		

Note that, for inventories and accounts payable, we report the % COGS and not the % revenues. Since inventories are reported at cost (not at retail selling price), it is appropriate to use COGS as the measure of sales volume since COGS is also at cost and not at retail selling prices. Also, since accounts payable generally relates to inventories, we also refer to its % COGS.

In this forecasting example, we will assume a continuation of the 2014 percentages for those assets (other than cash) that are expected to vary directly with sales, and we will assume no change in other assets and liabilities. Finally, our equity will increase by our projected profit (we do not expect to pay any dividends). These assumptions result in the forecast of our income statement for 2015 shown in Exhibit 8.4.

Our forecasts use the following three approaches that we discussed earlier:

1. **Adjust in relation to the change in revenues/COGS**—We forecast accounts receivable, inventory, accounts payable, and wages payable as a percentage of estimated sales/COGS because we believe that these accounts will vary in relation to sales (COGS) volume.

2. **Scheduled reductions**—We recognize the scheduled depreciation expense of $5,000 as an increase in accumulated depreciation. We would also incorporate any scheduled debt payments (we have none in this example).

3. **No change**—We assume no change for "other assets," equipment, credit card debt, and other current liabilities unless we have reason to believe otherwise. If, for example, we had expected to acquire another piece of equipment, we would have increased our equipment account for the cost of the equipment. The depreciation of that new equipment, then, would have to be incorporated into expected depreciation expense in future years.

EXHIBIT 8.4	Forecasted 2015 Restaurant Balance Sheet			
	2014	**Forecast Assumptions Rev (R)/COGS (C)**	**Est. 2015**	
Assets				
Cash	$23,269	Plug	$ 44,241	(plug*)
AR	8,280	1.6% R	9,097	($568,581 × 1.6%)
Inventory	11,790	6.0% C	12,964	($216,061 × 6.0%)
Other assets	6,000		6,000	No change
Total current assets	49,339		72,302	
Equipment	60,000		60,000	No change
Accumulated depreciation	(18,000)	(5,000)	(23,000)	(LY balance + 2015 deprec. exp.)
Total assets	$91,339		$109,302	
Liabilities				
Accounts payable	$22,106	11.3% C	$ 24,415	($216,061 × 11.3%)
Wages payable	3,894	0.8% R	4,549	($568,581 × 0.8%)
Credit card debt	6,941		6,941	No change
Other current liabilities	1,000		1,000	No change
Total current liabilities	33,941		36,905	
Long-term liabilities	13,100		13,100	No change
Equity	44,298		59,297	($44,298 + $14,998 Profit – $0 Dividends)
Total	$91,339		$109,335	

* $44,241 = $109,302 − $9,097 − $12,964 − $6,000 − $60,000 − (−23,000)

FORECASTED STATEMENT OF CASH FLOWS

Given the projected income statement in Exhibit 8.2 and the projected comparative balance sheet in Exhibit 8.4, we can prepare the projected statement of cash flows in the same manner in which we illustrate its preparation in Chapter 4. We present our forecast of the statement of cash flows, using the indirect format, in Exhibit 8.5.

We forecast that our restaurant will generate $20,971 of cash from operating activities and we do not forecast any capital expenditures in this example. On balance, our restaurant is healthy. It is profitable, has a strong balance sheet, and is generating operating cash flow that we can use to pay down debt and/or to pay dividends.

EXHIBIT 8.5	Forecasted 2015 Income Statement, Forecasted 2016 Restaurant Balance Sheet, and Forecasted 2016 Statement of Cash Flows

Income statement	Est. 2015	Balance Sheet	2014	Est. 2015 Adjusted
Revenue: Store	$442,891	Assets		
Revenue: Catering	125,690	Cash.	$23,270	$44,241
Total Revenue.	568,581	AR.	8,280	9,097
COGS: Food.	(216,061)	Inventory.	11,790	12,964
Gross Profit	352,520	Other assets	6,000	6,000
Wage Expense:		Total Current Assets	49,340	72,302
Fixed	(60,000)	Equipment	60,000	60,000
Variable	(85,287)	Accumulated Depreciation . . .	(18,000)	(23,000)
Total wages	(145,287)	Total Assets	$91,340	$109,302
General Overhead	(121,108)	Liabilities		
Depreciation Expense	(5,000)	Accounts payable.	$22,106	$24,415
Marketing	(56,858)	Wages payable.	3,894	4,549
Operating Income.	24,267	Credit card debt	6,941	6,941
Interest Expense.	(1,193)	Other current liabilities	1,000	1,000
Income Before Tax	23,074	Total Current Liabilities	33,941	36,905
Taxes @ 35%	(8,076)	Long-term liabilities	13,100	13,100
Net Income.	$ 14,998	Equity	44,299	59,297
		Total	$91,340	$109,302

Statement of cash flows	Est. 2015	
Net income.	$14,998	from income statement
Add: depreciation.	5,000	from income statement
Less: increase in accounts receivable	(817)	$8,280 − $9,097
Less: increase in inventory.	(1,174)	$11,790 − $12,964
Add: increase in accounts payable	2,309	$24,415 − $22,106
Add: increase in wages payable.	655	$4,549 − $3,894
Net cash flow from operating activities	20,971	
Net cash flow from investing activities.	0	no CAPEX in this example
Net cash flow from financing activities.	0	no financing activities in this example
Net change in cash.	20,971	
Beginning cash.	23,270	2014 cash balance
Ending cash	$44,241	2015 cash balance (estimated)

ANALYSIS OF FORECASTED FINANCIAL STATEMENTS

Because we are comfortable with our forecasts of the financial statements, we can now perform some analysis of the statements using the techniques that we discuss in Chapter 6:

Ratio	2015	2016 est.
Profit margin	$\dfrac{\$9,787}{\$516,892} = 1.9\%$	$\dfrac{\$14,998}{\$568,581} = 2.6\%$
Asset turnover	$\dfrac{\$516,892}{\$91,339} = 5.7$	$\dfrac{\$568,581}{\$109,302} = 5.2$
ROA	$1.9\% \times 5.7 = 10.8\%$	$2.6\% \times 5.2 = 13.5\%$
Financial leverage	$\dfrac{\$91,339}{\$44,298} = 2.1$	$\dfrac{\$109,302}{\$59,297} = 1.8$
ROE	$10.8\% \times 2.1 = 22.7\%$	$13.5\% \times 1.8 = 24.3\%$

Our company is performing well and is likely to do so in the future. We forecast our ROE to increase from 22.7% to 24.3%. We expect this increase to be driven primarily by an increase in our profit margin from 1.9% to 2.6%. The increase in ROE is better than it initially appears because we also forecast our financial leverage to decline from 2.1 to 1.8. Our increase in ROE is therefore driven by an increase in ROA and not by a change in financing strategy to increase financial leverage.

POSSIBLE BALANCE SHEET ADJUSTMENTS THAT CAN BE MADE BY THE ANALYST

Notice that our forecasted cash equals $44,241 (7.8% of forecasted revenues) in the initial forecast of our balance sheet in Exhibit 8.4. This is higher than the historical cash balance equal to 4.5% of revenues. Our forecasted cash balance, higher than normal, is telling us that we are generating excess cash in the amount of $18,655 ($44,241 est. cash balance − [Est. revenues $568,581 × historical cash percent of 4.5%] = $18,655 of excess cash).

We must now decide what to do with that excess cash. There are a number of adjustments we might consider:

1. We might invest the excess cash in marketable securities to keep the excess for, say, future expansion of our restaurant.
2. We might pay off some of our interest-bearing debt.
3. We might pay a dividend (thus reducing equity).

Or, we might do any combination of the above in any dollar amount sufficient to use up the $18,655 difference. Because we have been paying off our (high-cost) credit card debt, let's assume that we use $6,941 of the excess cash to pay off the current balance of that debt and use the remainder of $11,714 to reduce our long-term debt. This results in the adjusted 2015 forecasted balance sheet shown in Exhibit 8.6.

EXHIBIT 8.6	Forecasted Adjusted 2015 Restaurant Balance Sheet				
	2015	Forecast Assumptions	Est. 2016	Adjustments	Est. 2016 Adjusted
Assets					
Cash	$23,269	Plug	$44,241	(18,655)	$25,586
AR	8,280	2%	9,097		9,097
Inventory	11,790	2%	12,964		12,964
Other assets	6,000		6,000		6,000
Total current assets	49,339		72,302		53,647
Equipment	60,000		60,000		60,000
Accumulated depreciation	(18,000)	(5,000)	(23,000)		(23,000)
Total assets	$91,339		$109,302		$90,647

Continued

Continued from previous page

EXHIBIT 8.6	Forecasted Adjusted 2015 Restaurant Balance Sheet				
	2015	Forecast Assumptions	Est. 2016	Adjustments	Est. 2016 Adjusted
Liabilities					
Accounts payable.	$22,106	4%	$ 24,415		$24,415
Wages payable.	3,894	1%	4,549		4,549
Credit card debt	6,941		6,941	(6,941)	0
Other current liabilities	1,000		1,000		1,000
Total current liabilities.	33,941		36,905		29,964
Long-term liabilities	13,100		13,100	(11,714)	1,386
Equity	44,298		59,297		59,297
Total	$91,339		$109,302		$90,647

We could, of course, have decided to invest the excess cash in marketable securities and/or pay a dividend. But, paying off our interest-bearing debt is the prudent thing to do for a young company like ours. We can, then, pay a dividend in the future once we have retired our debt.

FORECASTING FINANCIAL STATEMENTS: OUTSIDE-IN

The forecasting process that we just illustrated is inside-out; that is, we forecasted the financial results of our own business and therefore have access to all of the accounting records and other information that management rarely discloses to the outside world. Forecasting the financial results of a company using publicly available information is much harder and our estimates will be much less precise. We will cover this situational forecasting in a two-step development process.

Step 1: We will use the DuPont model and complete a "big-picture" forecast focused on profit margin and the major balance sheet categories of total assets, total liabilities, and owners' equity.

Step 2: We will complete a detailed forecast of the income statement and balance sheet as well as a forecast of the statement of cash flows.

Depending on time and purpose, each step generates useful information for evaluation and decision making. Each level of more detailed information is developed from a more thorough analysis of available data, with step 2 forecasts based on economic and industry trends, professional analysts' expectations for the company, and the "Management Discussion and Analysis" information contained in recent SEC 10-K filings. As you proceed through this two-step process, you will notice the process used to forecast the financial statements from the outside-in are exactly the same as those previously illustrated for forecasting from the inside-out—only the precision of the estimates changes. In this section, we illustrate the forecast process using a public company: Chipotle Mexican Grill (CMG).

FORECASTING CHIPOTLE MEXICAN GRILL, INC.—2014

Chipotle Mexican Grill, Inc. operates restaurants throughout the United States. As of December 31, 2014, the company operated 1,755 restaurants, serving a menu of tacos, burritos, salads, and burrito bowls, all made using fresh ingredients.

Chipotle was founded in Colorado in 1993, and McDonald's Corporation made a series of equity investments in the company beginning in February 1998, becoming the majority shareholder in 2000. Chipotle completed an initial public offering in January 2006. McDonald's sold its interest in the company during that year and currently has no ownership interest in the company.

Initial Forecasts

Exhibit 8.7 shows selected Chipotle data for the three most recent years. We will use this data to forecast the major financial statement items for 2014.

EXHIBIT 8.7	Selected Chipotle Data 2012–2014 (in millions and rounded)		
Chipotle Grill Inc.			
	2014	**2013**	**2012**
Revenues	$4,108	$3,215	$2,731
Operating income.	718	539	461
Net income.	445	327	278
Total assets.	2,546	2,009	1,669
Total liabilities	534	471	423
Stockholders' equity	$2,012	$1,538	$1,246
Profit margin.	10.8%	10.2%	10.2%
Asset turnover	1.61	1.60	1.64
ROA	17.5%	16.3%	16.7%
Financial leverage.	4.77	4.27	3.95
ROE	83.4%	69.5%	65.8%
Revenue growth	27.8%	17.7%	20.3%
Average revenue growth.	21.9%		

Using this data, we can set expectations for Chipotle's performance in 2014. It all begins with the revenue forecast and trends assessments.

Revenue in 2014 was $4.108 billion. The trend from 2012 to 2014 has clearly been upward; in fact, revenues have increased substantially each year for the last three years, averaging 22% growth per year. With such an obvious trend, any forecasts should most likely extend the trend. Without considering probable economic conditions in 2014 but based on the revenue growth rates of recent years, several estimates of revenue growth in 2015 would seem reasonable ranging from 20% to 24%. With an expected growth rate of 22%, revenues of $5.01 billion are expected (122% × $4.108 billion). We can now turn to trends in the DuPont model calculations to complete our "big-picture" forecasts for Chipotle.

Profit margin improved over years 2012–2014, again a positive trend. Let's assume slight improvement in operations in 2012 to an 11% profit margin because the trend has been increasing at a decreasing rate. This assumption yields a projected net income of $551 million (11% × $5.01 billion).

Asset turnover has ranged around 1.6 (revenues/total assets). Unlike in the cases with revenues and profit margins, no obvious trend has been exhibited. If we assume a rough median of 1.6 for asset turnover in 2015, we can estimate total assets using the formula Asset Turnover = Revenues/Total Assets → 1.6 = $5.012/Total Assets → Total Assets = $5.012/1.6 = $3.13 billion.

Financial leverage has increased over the past three years from 3.95 to 4.77. If we assume an increase to 5.0 for 2015, then estimated stockholders' equity = $3.13 billion/5 = $0.626 billion and total liabilities = $3.13 billion − $0.626 billion = $2.5 billion.

To summarize, our "big-picture" forecast for Chipotle for 2015 is:

Income Statement: Year of 2015	
Revenues	$5.01 billion ($4.108 billion × 1.22)
Net income.	$551 million ($5.01 billion × 11%)
Balance Sheet: Year End, 2015	
Total assets.	$3.13 billion ($5.01 billion/1.6)
Total liabilities	$2.50 billion ($3.13 billion − 0.626 billion)
Total owners' equity	$0.63 billion ($3.13 billion/5)

We now have set expectations for 2015 based on trends from previous years. With additional information for past years' performances we can make slightly more detailed projections of income and balance sheet statements and hone our expectations for Chipotle.

Full Information Forecasts

We now develop more detailed forecasts using much more data. Exhibit 8.8 notes selected additional information from Chipotle's 2012–2014 financial statements, including common-size income statement and balance sheet data. Exhibit 8.8 presents additional data to Exhibit 8.7 that we used in our initial forecasts.

TABLE 8.8	Selected Chipotle Data from 2012–2014		
	2014	**2013**	**2012**
Revenues	$4,108	$3,215	$2,731
Operating income	718	539	461
Net income	445	327	278
Total assets	2,546	2,009	1,669
Total liabilities	534	471	423
Stockholders' equity	$2,012	$1,538	$1,246
Profit margin	10.8%	10.2%	10.2%
Asset turnover	1.61	1.60	1.64
ROA	17.5%	16.3%	16.7%
Financial leverage	4.77	4.27	3.95
ROE	83.4%	69.5%	65.8%
Revenue growth	27.8%	17.7%	20.3%
Avg revenue growth	21.9%		
Gross profit	37.8%	37.4%	37.6%
Operating income	17.5%	16.8%	16.9%
Net income	10.8%	10.2%	10.2%
Cash and marketable securities	18.5%	18.0%	17.3%
Accounts receivable	1.2%	0.9%	1.0%
Inventory	0.4%	0.4%	0.4%
PPE, gross	41.9%	46.4%	48.0%
Accounts payable	1.7%	1.8%	2.1%
Accrued liabilities	4.3%	4.4%	4.7%

From Chipotle's Management Discussion and Analysis section of its 2014 SEC 10-K filing, we learn the company has opened about 180–190 stores per year over the past three years. Key variables in forecasting the financial statements for this company are the growth rate of new stores (and the related expenditures for PPE) and food and labor costs. Following are our forecast assumptions:

1. Revenues: $5.2 billion.

   The company provides the following schedule in its discussion of the 2014 financial statements:

	Years ended December 31,			% increase 2014 over 2013	% increase 2013 over 2012
	2014	**2013**	**2012**		
	(dollars in millions)				
Revenue	$4,108.3	$3,214.6	$2,731.2	27.8%	17.7%
Average restaurant sales	$2.472	$2.169	$2.113	14.0%	2.7%
Comparable restaurant sales increases	16.8%	5.6%	7.1%		
Number of restaurants as of the end of the period	1,783	1,595	1,410	11.8%	13.1%
Number of restaurants opened in the period, net of relocations	188	185	180		

Notice the line, "Comparable restaurant sales increase." This represents the "organic" growth of the company—that is, the increase in revenues for existing restaurants. The remainder of the revenue increase, $353.6 million for 2014 ($4,108.3 million − [$3,214.6 × 1.168]), represents the revenues generated by the 188 new stores opened during the year, or about $1.88 million per store. The distinction between organic growth and acquired or constructed growth is that the latter entails a significant investment of cash. For example, the company's statement of cash flows reveals that it spent $252.6 million on capital expenditures. Assuming that this investment related to the new stores opened during the year, each new store costs an average of $1.34 million ($252.6 million/188 stores). As we project the opening of new stores, not only will we forecast the increase in revenues, but we will also forecast the related capital expenditures.

Our forecast of revenues for 2015, then, includes the following components:

Organic growth @ 16.8% . . .	$4,798.5 million	($4,108.3 × 1.168)
New stores	$ 357.2 million	(190 stores × $1.88 million/store)
Total	$5,155.7 million	

2. Expense percentages other than depreciation: no change in 2014 % of sales.

    We forecast that each expense line will bear the same percentage to revenues in 2015 that it did in 2014.

3. Depreciation expense: $125,114,000

    Chipotle reports $110,474,000 of depreciation and amortization expense in 2014 (11.5% of the prior year PPE, net balance). We project our 2015 depreciation using the 2014 dollar amount plus the capital expenditures of 254,600 × 11.5%/2 (assuming CAPEX evenly acquired over the year). The resulting estimate of depreciation and amortization is $125,114,000.

4. Tax expense: 37.6% of pretax income, the prior-year percentage of pretax income.

5. Variable assets and liabilities: no change in the 2014 % of sales.

    As revenues grow, so do accounts receivable, inventory, other current and long-term assets, accounts payable, accrued liabilities, and other long-term liabilities. We have no reason to believe that the percentage of sales for each of these assets and liabilities will change in 2015, and therefore forecast a continuation of the 2014 percentage of sales.

6. Shareholders' equity:

    a. Paid-in capital and treasury stock: no change in paid-in capital accounts (we assume no sale or purchase of stock in 2015).

    b. Retained earnings will increase by our forecasted profit (Chipotle does not pay dividends on its common stock).

Using these assumptions, we forecast our income statement and balance sheet for 2015 as follows:

CONSOLIDATED STATEMENT OF INCOME ($000s)			
	Dec. 31, 2014		**2015 Est.**
Revenue	$4,108,269	see #1 above	$5,155,000
Restaurant operating costs (exclusive of depreciation and amortization shown separately below):			
Food, beverage, and packaging.	1,420,994	5,155,000 × 34.6%	1,783,630
Labor	904,407	5,155,000 × 22.0%	1,134,100
Other operating costs.	687,697	5,155,000 × 16.7%	860,885
General and administrative expenses	273,897	5,155,000 × 6.7%	345,385
Depreciation and amortization	110,474	110,474 + 14,640	125,114
Total operating expenses	3,397,469		4,249,114
Income from operations	710,800		905,886
Interest and other income	3,503	no change	3,503
Income before income taxes	714,303		909,389
Provision for income taxes.	(268,929)	909,389 × 37.6%	(341,930)
Net income.	$ 445,374		$ 567,459

CONSOLIDATED BALANCE SHEET ($000s)	**Dec. 31, 2014**		**2015**
Assets			
Cash and cash equivalents	$ 419,465	plug	$ 729,913
Accounts receivable.	34,839	5,155,000 × 0.8%	41,240
Inventory.	15,332	5,155,000 × 0.4%	20,620
Other current assets.	408,843	5,155,000 × 10.0%	515,500
Total current assets	878,479		1,307,273
Leasehold improvements, property and equipment, net . . .	1,106,984	+ 254,600 − 125,114	1,236,470
Other assets.	560,822	5,155,000 × 13.7%	706,235
Total assets.	$2,546,285		$3,249,978
Liabilities and shareholders' equity:			
Accounts payable.	$ 69,613	5,155,000 × 1.7%	$ 87,635
Accrued liabilities	176,097	5,155,000 × 4.3%	221,665
Total current liabilities.	245,710		309,300
Other liabilities	288,206	5,155,000 × 7.0%	360,850
Total liabilities	533,916		670,150
Shareholders' equity:			
Common stock.	354	no change	354
Additional paid-in capital	1,038,932	no change	1,038,932
Treasury stock	(748,759)	no change	(748,759)
Accumulated other comprehensive income.	(429)	no change	(429)
Retained earnings	1,722,271	+ 567,459 − 0	2,289,730
Total shareholders' equity	2,012,369		2,579,828
Total liabilities and shareholders' equity.	$2,546,285		$3,249,978

The forecast of the balance sheet involves the following steps (see Illustration 8.2):

1. Forecast individual asset and liability accounts as shown (assume no change for equity accounts other than retained earnings).
2. Compute total liabilities and equity and set total assets equal to that amount.
3. Solve (plug) for cash (i.e., the dollar amount that yields our amount for total assets).

Given our forecasted income statement and balance sheet, we can prepare our forecasted statement of cash flows for 2015, using the indirect method, as follows:

Forecasted Statement of Cash Flows		2015
Net income.	from income statement	$567,459
Add: Depreciation.	from income statement	125,114
Accounts receivable.	$ 34,839 − $ 41,240	(6,401)
Inventory.	15,332 − 20,620	(5,288)
Other current assets.	408,843 − 515,500	(106,657)
Other assets.	560,822 − 706,235	(145,413)
Accounts payable.	87,635 − 69,613	18,022
Accrued liabilities	221,665 − 176,097	45,568
Other liabilities	360,850 − 288,206	72,644
Net cash from operating activities		565,048
Capital expenditures	190 stores × $1,340/store	(254,600)
Net cash from investing activities		(254,600)
Net cash from financing activities		0
Net change in cash.		310,448
Beginning cash.		419,465
Ending cash (estimated).		$729,913

We forecast that Chipotle will generate $310 million of net cash flow in 2015 (that is, after covering all of its cash needs for additional working capital and capital expenditures). This excess cash can be invested in marketable securities to provide a store of liquidity for future expansion, or can be used to pay down debt or to pay dividends.

Forecasting the financial statements from the outside-in involves the same mechanics that we used to forecast the financial statements for our restaurant from the inside-out. The difference, of course, is in the amount of information we have available to assist us in making our forecasts. Outside investors are only privy to the information that companies disclose in their financial statements and via other public outlets (such as meetings with analysts). The outside-in forecasting process is therefore more difficult and more prone to error.

CONCLUSION

Forecasting is an integral part of strategic planning and valuation. No business can operate effectively without a sound strategic plan that is grounded in reasonable forecasts of the financial statements. For that reason, some might argue that the forecast is the most important part of the strategic planning process. The goal is not to set the bar so high that we are unlikely to reach it. That will only lead to frustration in managers and employees. Likewise, we should not set the bar so low that effort is not required to reach it. That will lead to complacency and inefficient use of resources. Our objective should be to make the forecast as accurate as we can with enough "stretch" that we must work hard in order to achieve our goals.

Forecasting begins with the all-important revenue forecast. This forecast must not be taken lightly, as the remainder of the income statement and most of the balance sheet depends on it. Revenue forecasts must not merely extrapolate historical trends. Instead, they must use all of the information that is available to us, including macroeconomic data, data on our competitive landscape, and internal data on all of the drivers of financial performance.

Given our revenue forecast, we recommend forecasting the financial statements in the following order:

1. Income statement
2. Balance sheet (because many of the balance sheet items vary in relation to revenues and because retained earnings can only be updated after we have computed net income)
3. Statement of cash flows (because it is prepared using the forecasted income statement and comparative balance sheets)

We strongly encourage you to prepare all three financial statements. Although it is not easy to get all three statements to balance, once you do, you know that all of the financial statements are prepared correctly.

It is only after we have accurately forecasted our three financial statements that we can either evaluate alternate strategic paths to determine the one that will provide the greatest increase in shareholder value or effectively value the common stock of a potential acquisition. Please take this forecasting activity seriously. If you do, you will make much better strategic and investment decisions.

KEY CONCEPTS AND TERMS

accounts payable, 208	cost of goods sold, 208	PPE, 208
accounts receivable, 208	inventories, 208	prepaid expenses, 208
accrued expenses, 208	operating expenses, 208	

QUESTIONS

Q8-1. Explain the ways in which forecasts are used by an owner of a business and the questions we want to answer through the use of forecasts.

Q8-2. Should I be optimistic or conservative in my forecasts?

Q8-3. In what ways are historical financial statements useful for the forecasting process?

Q8-4. Why is the forecast of revenues so important?

Q8-5. Explain the use of cash as a "plug" figure.

Q8-6. What is the importance of the forecast of the statement of cash flow?

Q8-7. What is the difference between variable and fixed expense and how do they change in the forecast process?

Q8-8. Describe the three ways in which assets, liabilities and equity might be expected to change in our forecast of the balance sheet.

Q8-9. Explain how the forecasting process differs between "inside out" and "outside in."

Q8-10. Why do we forecast financial statements in the order of income statement, balance sheet and statement of cash flow?

EXERCISES

E8-1. **Forecasting an Income Statement**   Violet's Catering Service reports the following income statement:

	Current Year
Sales.	$14,983
COGS.	(8,990)
Gross profit.	5,993
Operating expenses excluding depreciation	1,798
Depreciation expense.	2,053
Interest expense	375
Pre-tax profit	1,767
Tax expense @ 35%	(618)
Net income	$ 1,149

Required:

a. Using the following assumptions, forecast Violet's income statement for next year:

Sales growth rate	+15%
Gross profit.	40%
Operating expenses excluding depreciation (% sales)	12%
Depreciation expense.	$2,053
Interest expense	$375
Tax expense (% pre-tax profit).	35%

b. Assuming that Violet reports retained earnings of $3,746 in her most recent balance sheet, and that she expects to pay dividends of $311 next year, what balance will she report for retained earnings in next year's balance sheet?

E8-2. **Forecasting an Income Statement** Opie's Dog Food Company reports the following income statement:

Sales.	$30,203
COGS.	(19,028)
Gross profit.	11,175
Operating expenses excluding depreciation	3,926
Depreciation expense.	4,138
Interest expense	755
Pre-tax profit	2,356
Tax expense @ 35%.	(825)
Net income.	$ 1,531

Required:

a. Using the following assumptions, forecast Opie's income statement for next year:

Sales growth rate	+13%
Gross profit.	37%
Operating expenses excluding depreciation (% sales)	13%
Depreciation expense.	$4,138
Interest expense	$755
Tax expense (% pre-tax profit).	35%

b. Assuming that Opie reports retained earnings of $7,551 in his most recent balance sheet, and that he expects to pay dividends of $429 next year, what balance will he report for retained earnings in next year's balance sheet?

E8-3. **Forecasting an Income Statement** S&O, Inc. reports the following income statement:

Sales.	$53,510
COGS.	(31,036)
Gross profit.	22,474
Operating expenses excluding depreciation	10,702
Depreciation expense.	7,331
Interest expense.	1,338
Pre-tax profit	3,103
Tax expense @ 35%.	(1,086)
Net income.	$ 2,017

Required:

a. Using the following assumptions, forecast S&O's income statement for next year:

Sales growth rate	+22%
Gross profit.	42%
Operating expenses excluding depreciation (% sales)	20%
Depreciation expense.	$7,331
Interest expense.	$1,338
Tax expense (% pre-tax profit)	35%

b. Assuming that S&O reports retained earnings of $13,378 in its most recent balance sheet, and that the company expects to pay dividends of $740 next year, what balance will it report for retained earnings in next year's balance sheet?

E8-4. **Forecasting Balance Sheet Accounts Using Percent of Sales (COGS) and Days**   Grace's Dress Shoppe reports the following income statement and balance sheet for the current year:

Sales.	$89,183
COGS	(55,293)
Gross profit.	33,890
Operating expenses excluding depreciation	15,161
Depreciation expense.	12,218
Interest expense.	2,230
Pre-tax profit	4,281
Tax expense @ 35%	(1,498)
Net income	$ 2,783
Cash	$10,137
Accounts receivable.	4,459
Inventories	9,400
PPE, gross	122,181
Accumulated depreciation	(48,872)
Total Assets	$97,305
Accounts payable.	$ 6,635
Accrued liabilities	8,918
Total current liabilities.	15,553
Long-term debt	44,592
Common stock.	14,864
Retained earnings	22,296
Total liabilities and equity	$97,305

Required:

Using the following assumptions, forecast Grace's income statement and balance sheet for next year (use cash as your plug figure to balance the balance sheet):

Sales growth rate	+12%
Gross profit margin (% sales).	38%
Operating expenses excluding depreciation (% sales)	17%
Depreciation expense.	$12,218
Interest expense	$2,230
Tax expense (% pre-tax profit)	35%
Dividends (% forecasted net income)	20%
Accounts receivable (% sales)	5%
Inventories (% COGS)	17%
PPE, gross	No change
Accounts payable (% COGS).	12%
Accrued liabilities (% sales)	10%
Long-term debt	No change
Common stock.	No change

E8-5. **Forecasting an Income Statement and Balance Sheet** Snickers Candy Corp. reports the following income statement and balance sheet for the current year:

Sales.	$126,758
COGS.	(78,590)
Gross profit.	48,168
Operating expenses excluding depreciation	21,549
Depreciation expense.	17,366
Interest expense	3,169
Pre-tax profit	6,084
Tax expense @ 35%.	(2,129)
Net income.	$ 3,955
Cash.	$ 10,479
Accounts receivable.	6,338
Inventories	17,290
PPE, gross	173,658
Accumulated depreciation	(69,463)
Total Assets	$138,302
Accounts payable.	$ 9,431
Accrued liabilities	12,676
Total current liabilities.	22,107
Long-term debt	63,379
Common stock.	21,126
Retained earnings	31,690
Total liabilities and equity	$138,302

Required:

Using the following assumptions, forecast Snickers' income statement and balance sheet for next year (use cash as your plug figure to balance the balance sheet):

Sales growth rate	+18%
Gross profit margin (% sales).	38%
Operating expenses excluding depreciation (% sales)	17%
Depreciation expense.	$17,366
Interest expense	$3,169
Tax expense (% pre-tax profit).	35%
Dividends (% forecasted net income)	20%
Accounts receivable (% sales).	6%
Inventories (% COGS)	25%
PPE, gross	No change
Accounts payable (% COGS).	13%
Accrued liabilities (% sales)	8%
Long-term debt	No change
Common stock.	No change

E8-6. **Forecasting the Statement of Cash Flows** Using the data from E8-5 and your forecasted income statement and balance sheet, forecast the Snickers Candy Corp. statement of cash flows for next year.

E8-7. **Forecasting an Income Statement and Balance Sheet (Net loss and negative cash)** Missy's
Food Store reports the following income statement and balance sheet for the current year:

Sales.	$171,944
COGS.	(103,166)
Gross profit.	68,778
Operating expenses excluding depreciation	34,389
Depreciation expense.	23,556
Interest expense.	4,500
Pre-tax profit	6,333
Tax expense @ 35%.	(2,217)
Net income.	$ 4,116
Cash.	$ 1,735
Accounts receivable.	12,036
Inventories	36,108
PPE, gross	235,563
Accumulated depreciation	(94,225)
Total Assets	$191,217
Accounts payable.	$ 12,380
Accrued liabilities	17,194
Total current liabilities.	29,574
Long-term debt	90,000
Common stock.	28,657
Retained earnings	42,986
Total liabilities and equity	$191,217

Because competition has recently moved into the area, Missy is forecasting a 20% decline in
sales and a reduction in gross profit margin.

Required:

a. Using the following assumptions, forecast Missy's income statement and balance sheet
for next year (use cash as your plug figure to balance the balance sheet):

Sales growth rate	−20%
Gross profit margin (% sales).	30%
Operating expenses excluding depreciation (% sales)	20%
Depreciation expense.	$23,556
Interest expense	$4,500
Tax expense (% pre-tax profit).	35%
Dividends.	0
Accounts receivable (% sales).	8%
Inventories (% COGS)	40%
PPE, gross	No change
Accounts payable (% COGS).	5%
Accrued liabilities (% sales)	6%
Long-term debt	No change
Common stock.	No change

b. What does your forecasted cash balance tell you about the health of the business?

c. What actions might Missy consider to generate cash?

E8-8. **Forecasting the Statement of Cash Flows** Using the data from E8-7 and your forecasted
income statement and balance sheet, forecast Missy's statement of cash flows for next year.

E8-9. **Forecasting an income Statement and Balance Sheet with CAPEX and Borrowing**
Sparky's Golf Shop reports the following income statement and balance sheet for the current year:

Sales.	$356,730
COGS.	(239,009)
Gross profit.	117,721
Operating expenses excluding depreciation	57,077
Depreciation expense.	48,872
Interest expense.	8,918
Pre-tax profit	2,854
Tax expense @ 35%.	(999)
Net income.	$ 1,855
Cash.	$ 30,132
Accounts receivable.	17,837
Inventories	23,901
PPE, gross	488,720
Accumulated depreciation	(195,488)
Total Assets	$365,102
Accounts payable.	$ 9,560
Accrued liabilities	28,538
Total current liabilities.	38,098
Long-term debt	178,366
Common stock.	59,455
Retained earnings	89,183
Total liabilities and equity	$365,102

Sparky plans to purchase a new golf simulator machine for $50,000 and will finance the purchase, in part, by borrowing $25,000 from a local bank.

Required:
Using the following assumptions, forecast Sparky's income statement and balance sheet for next year (use cash as your plug figure to balance the balance sheet):

Sales growth rate	+25%
Gross profit margin (% sales).	33%
Operating expenses excluding depreciation (% sales)	16%
Depreciation expense.	$53,872*
Interest expense	$10,918**
Tax expense (% pre-tax profit)	35%
Dividends (% forecasted net income)	50%
Accounts receivable (% sales)	6%
Inventories (% COGS)	11%
PPE, gross	+$50,000 CAPEX
Accounts payable (% COGS).	5%
Accrued liabilities (% sales)	7%
Long-term debt	+$25,000
Common stock.	No change

* reflecting the additional depreciation on the new equipment
** reflecting the additional interest expense on the new debt

E8-10. **Forecasting the Statement of Cash Flows** Using the data from E8-9 and your forecasted income statement and balance sheet, forecast Sparky's statement of cash flows for next year.

PROBLEMS

Mylan, Inc.   **P8-1.   Forecasting an Income Statement**   Below is presented the income statement for **Mylan, Inc.** for the years ended December 31, 2014 and 2013 from their 2014 Form 10-K (Filed on 3/2/2015):

	2014	2013
Revenues:		
Total revenues	$7,720	$6,909
Cost of sales	4,192	3,869
Gross profit	3,528	3,040
Operating expenses:		
Research and development	582	508
Selling, general and administrative	1,626	1,409
Litigation settlements, net	48	(15)
Other operating (income) expense, net	(80)	3
Total operating expenses	2,175	1,905
Earnings from operations	1,353	1,136
Interest expense	333	313
Other expense (income), net	45	75
Earnings before income taxes and noncontrolling interest	975	747
Income tax provision	41	121
Net earnings	$ 933	$ 627

Required:

Part 1: Forecast the income statement for 2015 for Mylan, Inc. based upon the following assumptions (round to the nearest dollar):

Revenue growth:	11.7%
Gross profit margin:	45.7%
Research and development as a % of revenue:	7.5%
Selling, general and administrative expenses as a % of revenue:.	21.1%
Litigation settlements, net	$0
Other operating (income) expense, net	$0
Other expense (income), net	$0
Interest expense.	$333
Income tax provision as a % of pre-tax income	4.2%

Part 2: As you compare these assumptions to results for the past two years, do you have any concerns about the company's ability to meet these assumptions?

NIKE Inc.   **P8-2.   Forecasting an Income Statement and Balance Sheet**   Nike designs, develops, markets, and sells athletic footwear, apparel, equipment, and accessories for men, women, and kids worldwide. Following are the income statements and balance sheets for Nike, Inc. for 2013 and 2014:

NIKE, INC.
Consolidated Statements of Income

(In millions, except per share data)	Year Ended May 31,		
	2014	2013	2012
Income from continuing operations:			
Revenues	$27,799	$25,313	$23,331
Cost of sales	15,353	14,279	13,183
Gross profit	12,446	11,034	10,148
Demand creation expense	3,031	2,745	2,607
Operating overhead expense	5,735	5,051	4,472
Total selling and administrative expense	8,766	7,796	7,079
Interest expense (income), net (Notes 6, 7, and 8)	33	(3)	4
Other expense (income), net (Note 17)	103	(15)	54
Income before income taxes	3,544	3,256	3,011
Income tax expense (Note 9)	851	805	754
Net income from continuing operations	2,693	2,451	2,257
Net income (loss) from discontinued operations	—	21	(46)
Net income	$ 2,693	$ 2,472	$ 2,211

NIKE, INC.
Consolidated Balance Sheets

(In millions)	May 31,	
	2014	2013
Assets		
Current assets:		
Cash and equivalents	$ 2,220	$ 3,337
Short-term investments (Note 6)	2,922	2,628
Accounts receivable, net (Note 1)	3,434	3,117
Inventories (Notes 1 and 2)	3,947	3,484
Deferred income taxes (Note 9)	355	308
Prepaid expenses and other current assets (Notes 6 and 17)	818	756
Total current assets	13,696	13,630
Property, plant and equipment, net (Note 3)	2,834	2,452
Identifiable intangible assets, net (Note 4)	282	289
Goodwill (Note 4)	131	131
Deferred income taxes and other assets (Notes 6, 9, and 17)	1,651	1,043
Total assets	$18,594	$17,545
Liabilities and shareholders' equity		
Current liabilities:		
Current portion of long-term debt (Note 8)	$ 7	$ 57
Notes payable (Note 7)	167	98
Accounts payable (Note 7)	1,930	1,669
Accrued liabilities (Notes 5, 6, and 17)	2,491	2,036
Income taxes payable (Note 9)	432	84
Liabilities of discontinued operations (Note 15)	—	18
Total current liabilities	5,027	3,962
Long-term debt (Note 8)	1,199	1,210
Deferred income taxes and other liabilities (Notes 6, 9, 13 and 17)	1,544	1,292
Commitments and contingencies (Note 16)		
Redeemable preferred stock (Note 10)	—	—
Shareholders' equity:		
Common stock at stated value (Note 11):		
Class A convertible — 178 and 178 shares outstanding	—	—
Class B — 692 and 716 shares outstanding	3	3
Capital in excess of stated value	5,865	5,184
Accumulated other comprehensive income (Note 14)	85	274
Retained earnings	4,871	5,620
Total shareholders' equity	10,824	11,081
Total liabilities and shareholders' equity	$18,594	$17,545

Required:

a. Using the following assumptions, forecast Nike's income statement and balance sheet for fiscal year 2015:

Sales growth (in %)	10%
Gross profit % of sales.	45%
Operating Expenses % of sales (incl. depreciation).	32%
Interest rate (in %) – apply to prior year ending balance of Long-term debt. . . .	11%
Tax expense as a % of pre-tax profit	24%
Dividends % of net income	32%
CAPEX	$917
Depreciation expense.	$518
Accounts receivable % sales	12%
Inventories % COGS	26%
Other current assets % sales	4%
Other long-term assets	No change
Accounts payable % COGS.	13%
Accrued liabilities % sales	8%
Other current liabilities % sales	3%
Long-term debt	No change
Other long-term liabilities	No change
Common stock.	No change
AOCI.	No change

b. Using your forecasted income statement and balance sheet, together with the current year's balance sheet, prepare Nike's forecasted statement of cash flows.

c. Prepare a DuPont analysis for the current year and the forecasted year and comment on any trends you observe.

NIKE, Inc. **P8-3.** **Forecasting the Balance Sheet Using Days**

Required:

Use the following projected information for 2015 to forecast **NIKE, Inc.**'s accounts receivables, inventory and accounts payable balances as of May 2015. All amounts are in millions.

Revenue	$30,579
Cost of sales.	$16,818
Accounts receivable days	43.8
Inventory days	94.9
Accounts payable days	47.5

Staples, Inc. **P8-4.** **Forecasting Balance Sheet Amounts** Staples, Inc. reported sales of $22,492 million and cost of goods sold of $16,691 million as of January 31, 2015.

Required:

Forecast the expected balances for January 2016 for the following amounts using the assumptions included below:

Accounts or amounts:

a. Receivables
b. Merchandise inventories
c. Accounts payable
d. Total assets

Assumptions:
- Revenue will increase by 5%
- Gross margin will remain consistent with the year ended January 31, 2015.
- Expect days sales outstanding (DSO) to decrease from 31 days for 2015 to 30 for 2016.
- Expect days in inventory to decrease from 47 days for 2015 to 45 days for 2016.
- Expect days in accounts payable to increase from 41 days for 2015 to 43 days to 2016.
- Asset turnover will remain consistent at 2.18 for 2016.

P8-5. **Forecasting an Income Statement, Balance Sheet, Statement of Cash Flows, and DuPont**   TJX Companies, Inc.
analysis. TJX Companies, Inc. operates as an off-price apparel and home fashions retailer in the United States and internationally. It operates stores under the T.J. Maxx, Marshalls, HomeGoods and other well-known brand names. Following are the income statements and balance sheets for TJX for fiscal years 2014 and 2015:

THE TJX COMPANIES, INC.			
Consolidated Statements Of Income			
		Fiscal Year Ended	
(Amounts in thousands except per share amounts)	**January 31, 2015**	**February 1, 2014**	**February 2, 2013 (53 weeks)**
Net sales.	$29,078,407	$27,422,696	$25,878,372
Cost of sales, including buying and occupancy costs. . .	20,776,522	19,605,037	18,521,400
Selling, general and administrative expenses	4,695,384	4,467,089	4,250,446
Loss on early extinguishment of debt	16,830	—	—
Interest expense, net	39,787	31,081	29,175
Income before provision for income taxes.	3,549,884	3,319,489	3,077,351
Provision for income taxes.	1,334,756	1,182,093	1,170,664
Net income.	$ 2,215,128	$ 2,137,396	$ 1,906,687

THE TJX COMPANIES, INC.		
Consolidated Balance Sheets		
	Fiscal Year Ended	
(Amounts in thousands except share amounts)	**January 31, 2015**	**February 1, 2014**
Assets		
Current assets:		
Cash and cash equivalents	$ 2,493,775	$ 2,149,746
Short-term investments	282,623	294,702
Accounts receivable, net	213,824	210,094
Merchandise inventories	3,217,923	2,966,490
Prepaid expenses and other current assets.	356,824	345,327
Federal, state, and foreign income taxes recoverable	12,475	—
Current deferred income taxes, net	137,617	101,639
Total current assets	6,715,061	6,067,998
Property at cost:		
Land and buildings.	888,580	722,645
Leasehold costs and improvements	2,780,932	2,720,391
Furniture, fixtures and equipment	4,671,029	4,255,210
Total property at cost	8,340,541	7,698,246
Less accumulated depreciation and amortization	4,472,176	4,103,745
Net property at cost	3,868,365	3,594,501
Non-current deferred income taxes, net	24,546	31,508
Other assets.	210,539	194,328
Goodwill and tradenames, net of amortization	309,870	312,687
Total assets.	$11,128,381	$10,201,022

continued

THE TJX COMPANIES, INC. Consolidated Balance Sheets		
	Fiscal Year Ended	
(Amounts in thousands except share amounts)	January 31, 2015	February 1, 2014
Liabilities		
Current liabilities:		
Accounts payable.	$ 2,007,511	$ 1,771,294
Accrued expenses and other current liabilities	1,796,122	1,681,834
Federal, state and foreign income taxes payable	126,001	64,715
Total current liabilities.	3,929,634	3,517,843
Other long-term liabilities.	888,137	732,999
Non-current deferred income taxes, net	422,516	446,071
Long-term debt	1,623,864	1,274,216
Commitments and contingencies (see note m and note o)		
Shareholders' equity		
Common stock, authorized 1,200,000,000 shares, par value $1, issued and outstanding 684,733,200 and 705,016,838, respectively	684,733	705,017
Additional paid-in capital	—	—
Accumulated other comprehensive income (loss)	(554,385)	(199,532)
Retained earnings	4,133,882	3,724,408
Total shareholders' equity	4,264,230	4,229,893
Total liabilities and shareholders' equity.	$11,128,381	$10,201,022

Required:

a. Using the following assumptions, forecast TJX's income statement and balance sheet for fiscal year 2016:

Sales growth (in %)	6%
Gross profit % of sales.	29%
Operating Expenses % of sales (incl. depreciation).	16%
Interest rate (in %) – apply to prior year ending balance	4%
Tax expense as a % of pre-tax profit	38%
Dividends % of net income	21%
CAPEX	$925
Depreciation expense.	$589
Accounts receivable % sales	1%
Inventories % COGS	15%
Other current assets % sales.	2%
Other long-term assets	No change
Accounts payable % COGS.	10%
Accrued liabilities % sales	3%
Other current liabilities % sales	4%
Long-term debt	No change
Other long-term liabilities.	No change
Common stock.	No change
AOCI	No change

b. Using your forecasted income statement and balance sheet, together with the current year's balance sheet, prepare TJX's forecasted statement of cash flows.

c. Prepare a DuPont analysis for the current year and the forecasted year and comment on any trends you observe.

Macy's, Inc. **P8-6.** **Forecasting an Income Statement, Balance Sheet, Statement of Cash Flows, and Dupont Analysis** Macy's operates stores and Internet websites in the United States. Its stores and websites sell a range of merchandise, including apparel and accessories for men, women, and children; cosmetics; home furnishings; and other consumer goods. The company also operates Bloomingdale's Outlet stores that offer a range of apparel and accessories, including women's ready-to-wear, fashion accessories, jewelry, handbags, and intimate apparel, as well as men's, children's, and women's shoes. Following are the income statements and balance sheets for Macy's for fiscal years 2014 and 2015:

MACY'S, INC. Consolidated Statements of Income			
(millions, except per share data)	2014	2013	2012
Net sales.	$28,105	$27,931	$27,686
Cost of sales.	(16,863)	(16,725)	(16,538)
Gross margin	11,242	11,206	11,148
Selling, general and administrative expenses	(8,355)	(8,440)	(8,482)
Impairments, store closing and other costs.	(87)	(88)	(5)
Operating income.	2,800	2,678	2,661
Interest expense.	(395)	(390)	(425)
Premium on early retirement of debt	(17)	—	(137)
Interest income.	2	2	3
Income before income taxes	2,390	2,290	2,102
Federal, state and local income tax expense.	(864)	(804)	(767)
Net income.	$ 1,526	$ 1,486	$ 1,335

MACY'S, INC. Consolidated Balance Sheets		
(millions)	January 31, 2015	February 1, 2014
Assets		
Current assets:		
Cash and cash equivalents	$ 2,246	$ 2,273
Receivables	424	438
Merchandise inventories	5,516	5,557
Prepaid expenses and other current assets.	493	420
Total current assets	8,679	8,688
Property and equipment—net	7,800	7,930
Goodwill	3,743	3,743
Other intangible assets—net	496	527
Other assets.	743	732
Total assets.	$21,461	$21,620
Liabilities and shareholders' equity		
Current liabilities:		
Short-term debt	$ 76	$ 463
Merchandise accounts payable	1,693	1,691
Accounts payable and accrued liabilities.	3,109	2,810
Income taxes	296	362
Deferred income taxes.	362	400
Total current liabilities.	5,536	5,726
Long-term debt	7,265	6,714
Deferred income taxes.	1,081	1,273
Other liabilities	2,201	1,658
Shareholders' equity:		
Common stock (340.6 And 364.9 Shares outstanding)	4	4
Additional paid-in capital.	1,048	2,522
Accumulated equity.	7,340	6,235
Treasury stock	(1,942)	(1,847)
Accumulated other comprehensive loss	(1,072)	(665)
Total shareholders' equity	5,378	6,249
Total liabilities and shareholders' equity.	$21,461	$21,620

Required:

a. Using the following assumptions, forecast Macy's income statement and balance sheet for fiscal year 2016:

Sales growth (in %)	3%
Gross profit % of sales	40%
Operating Expenses % of sales (incl. depreciation)	30%
Interest rate (in %)—apply to prior year ending balance	7%
Tax expense as a % of pre-tax profit	36%
Dividends % of net income	28%
CAPEX	$868
Depreciation expense	$1,005
Long-term debt principal payments	$870
Accounts receivable % sales	2%
Inventories % COGS	33%
Other current assets % sales	2%
Other long-term assets	No change
Accounts payable % COGS	15%
Accrued liabilities % sales	4%
Other current liabilities % sales	7%
Other long-term liabilities	No change
Common stock	No change
Treasury stock	No change
AOCI	No change

b. Using your forecasted income statement and balance sheet, together with the current year's balance sheet, prepare Macy's forecasted statement of cash flows.

c. Prepare a Dupont analysis for the current year and the forecasted year and comment on any trends you observe.

Starbucks, Corp. **P8-7.** **Forecasting Balance Sheet Amounts** Starbucks, Corp. reported total revenues of $16,447.8 million and cost of goods sold of $6,858.8 million as of September 28, 2014.

Required:

Forecast the expected balances for September 2015 for the following amounts using the assumptions included below:

Accounts or amounts:

a. Receivables
b. Merchandise inventories
c. Accounts payable
d. Total assets

Assumptions:
- Revenue will increase by 10.6%.
- Gross margin will remain consistent with the year ended September 1, 2014.
- Expect days sales outstanding (DSO) of 14 for 2015.
- Expect days in inventory of 58 for 2015.
- Expect days in accounts payable of 28 for 2015.
- Total asset turnover will remain consistent at 1.53 for 2015.

PepsiCo, Inc. **P8-8.** **Forecasting the Income Statement and Selected Balance Sheet Information** PepsiCo, Inc. reported total revenues of $66,683 million, cost of goods sold of $30,884, and stockholders' equity of $17,578 million in 2014.

Required:

Forecast the income statement for 2015 and forecast the following amounts from the balance sheet using the assumptions and additional information included below:

a. Receivables
b. Merchandise inventories
c. Total assets
d. Accounts payable

Assumptions:

- Total revenue will grow at 3% in 2015.
- Cost of goods sold will remain at 46.3%.
- Expected days sales outstanding (DSO) will be 36 in 2015.
- Expected days in inventory will be 37 in 2015.
- Expected days in accounts payable will be 154 in 2015.
- Asset turnover will be 0.95 in 2015.

P8-9. **Forecasting an Income Statement and Balance Sheet** Southwest Airlines operates pas-   Southwest Airlines
senger airlines that provide scheduled air transportation services in the United States and
near-international markets. The company was founded in 1967 and is headquartered in Dallas,
Texas. Following are the income statements and balance sheets for Southwest Airlines for fiscal years 2013 and 2014:

SOUTHWEST AIRLINES CO. **Consolidated Statement of Income**			
	Year ended December 31,		
(in millions, except per share amounts)	**2014**	**2013**	**2012**
Operating revenues:			
Passenger..........................	$17,658	$16,721	$16,093
Freight	175	164	160
Other.............................	772	814	835
Total operating revenues	18,605	17,699	17,088
Operating expenses:			
Salaries, wages, and benefits............	5,434	5,035	4,749
Fuel and oil.........................	5,293	5,763	6,120
Maintenance materials and repairs	978	1,080	1,132
Aircraft rentals	295	361	355
Landing fees and other rentals............	1,111	1,103	1,043
Depreciation and amortization............	938	867	844
Acquisition and integration...............	126	86	183
Other operating expenses	2,205	2,126	2,039
Total operating expenses	16,380	16,421	16,465
Operating income.....................	2,225	1,278	623
Other expenses (income):			
Interest expense......................	130	131	147
Capitalized interest....................	(23)	(24)	(21)
Interest income......................	(7)	(6)	(7)
Other (gains) losses, net................	309	(32)	(181)
Total other expenses (income)	409	69	(62)
Income before income taxes	1,816	1,209	685
Provision for income taxes...............	680	455	264
Net income..........................	$ 1,136	$ 754	$ 421

SOUTHWEST AIRLINES CO. Consolidated Balance Sheet		
(in millions, except share data)	December 31, 2014	December 31, 2013
Assets		
Current assets:		
Cash and cash equivalents	$ 1,282	$ 1,355
Short-term investments	1,706	1,797
Accounts and other receivables.	365	419
Inventories of parts and supplies, at cost	342	467
Deferred income taxes.	477	168
Prepaid expenses and other current assets.	232	250
Total current assets	4,404	4,456
Property and equipment, at cost:		
Flight equipment.	18,473	16,937
Ground property and equipment	2,853	2,666
Deposits on flight equipment purchase contracts	566	764
Assets constructed for others	621	453
	22,513	20,820
Less allowance for depreciation and amortization.	8,221	7,431
	14,292	13,389
Goodwill	970	970
Other assets	534	530
	$20,200	$19,345
Liabilities and stockholders' equity		
Current liabilities:		
Accounts payable.	$ 1,203	$ 1,247
Accrued liabilities	1,565	1,229
Air traffic liability	2,897	2,571
Current maturities of long-term debt	258	629
Total current liabilities.	5,923	5,676
Long-term debt less current maturities	2,434	2,191
Deferred income taxes.	3,259	2,934
Construction obligation	554	437
Other noncurrent liabilities	1,255	771
Stockholders' equity:		
Common stock, $1.00 Par value: 2,000,000,000 shares authorized; 807,611,634 shares issued in 2014 and 2013. . .	808	808
Capital in excess of par value	1,315	1,231
Retained earnings	7,416	6,431
Accumulated other comprehensive loss	(738)	(3)
Treasury stock, at cost: 132,017,550 and 107,136,946 shares in 2014 and 2013 respectively	(2,026)	(1,131)
Total stockholders' equity	6,775	7,336
	$20,200	$19,345

Required:

a. Using the following assumptions, forecast Southwest Airlines' income statement and balance sheet for fiscal year 2015:

Sales growth (in %)	5%
Gross profit % of sales.	30%
Operating Expenses % of sales (incl. depreciation).	17%
Interest expense and other.	$(599)
Tax expense as a % of pre-tax profit	37%
Dividends % of net income	12%
CAPEX	$1,954
Depreciation expense.	$803
Long-term debt principal payments.	$561
Accounts receivable % sales	2%
Inventories % COGS	3%
Other current assets % sales.	4%
Other long-term assets	No change
Accounts payable % COGS	9%
Accrued liabilities % sales	7%
Other current liabilities % sales	18%
Other long-term liabilities	No change
Common stock and APIC.	No change
Treasury stock	No change
AOCI.	No change

b.   Using your forecasted income statement and balance sheet, together with the current
     year's balance sheet, prepare Southwest Airlines' forecasted statement of cash flows.
c.   Prepare a DuPont analysis for the current year and the forecasted year and comment on
     any trends you observe.

P8-10.   **Forecasting the Income Statement and Selected Balance Sheet Information**   Below is   **Under Armour, Inc.**
presented the balance sheets and income statement for **Under Armour, Inc.** as of December
31, 2011 and 2010 and the years ended December 31, 2011, 2010 and 2009 from their Form
10-K.

Required:
Forecast the income statement for the year ended December 2011 and forecast the following
amounts from the balance sheet using the assumptions and additional information included
below:

a.	Receivables	e.	Accounts payable
b.	Merchandise inventories	f.	Total debt
c.	Property, plant and equipment	g.	Retained earnings
d.	Total assets	h.	Stockholders' equity

Part 1. Management Assumptions:
* Under Armour management has stated they expect revenue to grow at the low end of
  their longer term growth targets of 20%–25% for 2012.
* Gross margin will decrease slightly to 48% in 2012 from 48.4% in 2011.
* SG&A expense expected to decrease from 37.4% to 37.0%
* Interest expense and other expense will remain the same percentage of sales as in 2011.
* Tax rate expected to remain at consistent rate with 2011.
* Expect days sales outstanding (DSO) to be consistent with 2011 at 33 days.
* Expect days in inventory to increase from 155 in 2011 to 165 in 2012 due to the
  forecasted milder winter.
* Expect days in accounts payable to increase from 48 days for 2011 to 50 days to 2012.
* Asset turnover will remain consistent at 1.6 for 2012.
* Fixed asset turnover rate will increase from 9.25 in 2011 to 9.6 in 2012.
* No dividends are expected to be paid and no other changes are expected to occur in
  stockholder's equity.
* Debt to equity ratio expected to be consistent with 2011 at 0.12.

Part 2. Analyst Assumptions:
- Analysts expect revenue to grow at 22.8% for 2012.
- Gross margin will increase slightly to 48.5% in 2012 from 48.4% in 2011.
- SG&A expense expected to decrease from 37.4% to 36.9%.
- Interest expense and other expense will remain the same percentage of sales as in 2011.
- Tax rate expected to remain at consistent rate with 2011.
- Expect days sales outstanding (DSO) to be consistent with 2011 at 33 days.
- Expect days in inventory to decrease from 155 in 2011 to 145 in 2012.
- Expect days in accounts payable to increase from 48 days for 2011 to 52 days to 2012.
- Asset turnover will increase from 1.6 at 2011 to 1.65 for 2012.
- Fixed asset turnover rate will increase from 9.25 in 2011 to 9.35 in 2012.
- No dividends are expected to be paid and no other changes are expected to occur in stockholder's equity.
- Debt to equity ratio expected to decrease from 0.12 in 2011 to 0.05 in 2012.

UNDER ARMOUR, INC.			
	Year Ended December 31,		
	2011	**2010**	**2009**
Net revenues	$1,472,684	$1,063,927	$856,411
Cost of goods sold.	759,848	533,420	446,286
Gross profit.	712,836	530,507	410,125
Selling, general and administrative expenses	550,069	418,152	324,852
Income from operations	162,767	112,355	85,273
Interest expense, net	($3,841)	($2,258)	($2,344)
Other expense, net.	($2,064)	($1,178)	($511)
Income before income taxes	156,862	108,919	82,418
Provision for income taxes.	59,943	40,442	35,633
Net income.	$ 96,919	$ 68,477	$ 46,785
Net income available per common share			
Basic.	$1.88	$1.35	$0.94
Diluted	$1.85	$1.34	$0.92
Weighted average common shares outstanding			
Basic.	51,570	50,798	49,848
Diluted	52,526	51,282	50,650

UNDER ARMOUR, INC.		
	December 31, 2011	December 31, 2010
Assets		
Current assets		
Cash and cash equivalents	$175,384	$203,870
Accounts receivable, net	134,043	102,034
Inventories	324,409	215,355
Prepaid expenses and other current assets.......	39,643	19,326
Deferred income taxes.......................	16,184	15,265
Total current assets	689,663	555,850
Property and equipment, net	159,135	76,127
Intangible assets, net.......................	5,535	3,914
Deferred income taxes.......................	15,885	21,275
Other long-term assets	48,992	18,212
Total assets................................	$919,210	$675,378
Liabilities and stockholders' equity		
Current liabilities		
Accounts payable...........................	$100,527	$ 84,679
Accrued expenses	69,285	55,138
Current maturities of long-term debt	6,882	6,865
Other current liabilities	6,913	2,465
Total current liabilities.......................	183,607	149,147
Long-term debt, net of current maturities	70,842	9,077
Other long-term liabilities	28,329	20,188
Total liabilities.............................	282,778	178,412
Stockholders' equity		
Class A common stock	13	13
Class B convertible common stock	4	4
Additional paid-in capital	268,223	224,887
Retained earnings	366,164	270,021
Accumulated other comprehensive income.......	2,028	2,041
Total stockholders' equity	636,432	496,966
Total liabilities and stockholders' equity..........	$919,210	$675,378

Chapter Nine

Financial Statements and Strategy Assessment

1. Describe the effects on the forecasted income statement and balance sheet of planned capital expenditures and borrowings.

2. Prepare and analyze the forecasted income statement, balance sheet, statement of cash flow, and DuPont analysis for a business scenario and make a recommendation whether to proceed.

3. Prepare and analyze a scenario analysis for a public company to test the effects on the financial statements of upper and lower bounds of revenue forecasts.

INTRODUCTION

In Chapters 6 and 7, we discussed the analysis of financial statements to give us a better understanding of where our business has been as well as its current position. In Chapter 8, we focused on our future performance and illustrated techniques that allow you to forecast future financial statements given a set of assumptions about the likely trends in our business that we expect to occur. These forecasted financial statements (income statement, balance sheet, and statement of cash flows) will allow us to evaluate the expected future performance of our company using the same ratios that we learned in Chapter 6. As a result of this analysis, we will be better able to evaluate the effectiveness of different strategic paths that we are contemplating or to suggest possible strategic paths that we might not have yet considered. In this chapter, we utilize the skills we have learned to prepare and analyze financial statements and to forecast future financial performance to examine the financial implications of strategic alternatives.

There are many benefits from the strategy assessment that we illustrate in this chapter. Such an analysis will give us a better feel for the financial statement effects of different strategies that we might be considering to allow us to make a more informed decision. Such an analysis might also help us to better anticipate problem areas that might develop, like trends that are moving in the wrong direction that might negatively impact our business if not corrected. And, finally, such an analysis might help us to anticipate future financing needs and to better communicate those needs to our providers of capital. All businesses forecast their future performance under different economic scenarios and strategic alternatives, and an understanding of this process is essential to effective management.

Before we can begin our analysis and evaluation of strategic alternatives, we need to be clear about our financial objectives; that is, we need to know the criteria that we will use to measure success. For example, are we cash constrained? If so, we might look favorably on a scenario that generates cash more quickly, even if the alternative plan under consideration might ultimately yield a higher return on invested capital. Or, are we interested in gaining market share or a significant installed base in a specific market segment?

If so, we might be willing to forego near-term returns (e.g., return on assets or return on equity) in order to strengthen our market position. Or, are we concerned about a possible violation of the terms and conditions of our loans? If so, we will need to carefully monitor the extent to which we relieve or exacerbate our loan constraints. Or, are we interested in diversifying our investment? In that case, a strategy that will allow us to take cash out of the business might be preferable. The bottom line is that we need to be mindful of our objectives before beginning our analysis and decide on the critical metrics we will use to assess alternatives and monitor strategic progress.

In the discussion that follows, we will focus on two measures of performance: return on equity (ROE) and cash flow from operating activities. Our decision rule, then, will be quite simple: the proposed course of action is desirable as long as ROE and cash flow increase, holding our financial leverage, and thus financial risk, constant. (Remember, we can always increase ROE by taking on more debt, but the increase in financial risk may not be acceptable.)

FINANCIAL STATEMENT EFFECTS OF STRATEGIC ACTIONS

In Chapter 8, we discuss forecasting of the income statement, balance sheet, and statement of cash flows assuming no change in the business operations. For those forecasts,

- There is no assumed change in operating ratios and fixed costs remain at current levels,
- There is no purchase of PPE (property, plant & equipment) assets, and
- There is no change in the level of borrowing or capital investment.

We now relax those assumptions and consider the implications on our forecasts of strategic actions that may include the purchase of PPE assets and the borrowing of money or the sale of stock to finance the purchase of those assets. Before we begin our discussion of the forecasting and analysis of proposed strategic actions, it may be helpful to first review the effects on the financial statements of purchases of PPE assets and the borrowing of money.

Purchases of PPE Assets

The purchase of PPE assets affects the financial statements in the following ways:

1. On the balance sheet, PPE assets increase by the cost of the assets purchased and cash is reduced or liabilities increased to fund the purchase,
2. In the income statement, the new PPE assets (other than land) are depreciated over their expected useful lives, and
3. Accumulated depreciation on the balance sheet becomes more negative each year as the depreciation expense in the current year is accumulated with that of all prior years, thus reducing the net book value (i.e., cost – accumulated depreciation) of the PPE assets (i.e., PPE, net).

To illustrate, let's assume that our company begins the period with $100,000 of PPE assets at cost which have been depreciated by $20,000 up to this point. These PPE assets are being depreciated over a 10-year period and the accumulated depreciation of $20,000 reflects 2 years of depreciation since their purchase. Let's also assume that we report a balance in the common stock account of $50,000, $70,000 of retained earnings, and cash of $40,000. Our balance sheet, as reflected in our BSE template, looks like this:

| | Assets | | | Equity | | | |
	Cash	PPE (cost)	Accumulated Depreciation	Common Stock	Retained Earnings	Revenue	Expenses
Beginning	40,000	100,000	(20,000)	50,000	70,000		

Now, let's assume that we purchase $30,000 of PPE assets for cash that will be depreciated over an estimated 10-year life. That purchase is recorded as follows:

| | Assets | | | Equity | | | |
	Cash	PPE (cost)	Accumulated Depreciation	Common Stock	Retained Earnings	Revenue	Expenses
Beginning	40,000	100,000	(20,000)	50,000	70,000		
Purchase of PPE for $30,000 cash	(30,000)	30,000					

Finally, at the end of the period, we recognize depreciation of *both* the existing PPE assets (in the amount of $10,000) *and* the new PPE assets (in the amount of $3,000) with the following journal entry:

| | Assets | | | Equity | | | |
	Cash	PPE (cost)	Accumulated Depreciation	Common Stock	Retained Earnings	Revenue	Expenses
Beginning	40,000	100,000	(20,000)	50,000	70,000		
Purchase of PPE for $30,000 cash	(30,000)	30,000					
Record depreciation			(13,000)		(13,000)		(13,000)

At the end of the period, then, our PPE assets will be reported as follows:

PPE, at cost	$130,000
Less: accumulated depreciation	(33,000)
PPE, net	$ 97,000

And, we will report $13,000 of depreciation expense in our income statement, reflecting the depreciation of the previously recognized PPE of $10,000 and the depreciation of the new PPE of $3,000. So, here's the first thing to remember regarding the purchase of PPE when preparing the forecasts in this chapter:

- **PPE assets increase by the cost of the assets purchased,**
- **Depreciation expense reflects the depreciation of the preexisting PPE assets and the new PPE assets purchased, and**
- **Accumulated depreciation becomes more negative each year by the depreciation expense recognized in the income statement for the current year.**

In the next year, PPE (at cost) on the balance sheet and depreciation expense in the income statement will remain at the same level as in the current year unless additional assets are purchased, and accumulated depreciation will continue to become more negative by the depreciation expense recognized in the income statement for that year.

Borrowing of Money

The borrowing of money affects the financial statements in the following ways:

1. On the balance sheet, debt (short-term or long-term) increases by the amount of money borrowed, and cash increases by the same amount
2. In the income statement, we recognize interest expense equal to the loan balance × interest rate × portion of the year for which we are accruing interest, and
3. Principal payments are reflected as a reduction in cash and a reduction in the long-term debt balance on the balance sheet (not as an expense in the income statement).

To illustrate, let's assume that our company begins the period with $100,000 of long-term debt that carries an interest rate of 5% and is being repaid at the rate of $10,000 per year. Assume also that we report $50,000 of common stock, $70,000 of retained earnings, and $220,000 of cash. Our balance sheet, as reflected in our BSE template, looks like this:

	Assets	Liabilities	Equity			
	Cash	Long-term Debt	Common Stock	Retained Earnings	Revenue	Expenses
Beginning	220,000	100,000	50,000	70,000		

Now, let's assume that, at the beginning of the year, we borrow $30,000 at a rate of 4% to be repaid over a 5-year life. That borrowing is recorded as follows:

	Assets	Liabilities	Equity			
	Cash	Long-term Debt	Common Stock	Retained Earnings	Revenue	Expenses
Beginning	220,000	100,000	50,000	70,000		
Borrow $30,000	30,000	30,000				

Finally, at the end of the year, we pay the interest on the long-term debt and make our required principal payment:

	Assets	Liabilities	Equity			
	Cash	Long-term Debt	Common Stock	Retained Earnings	Revenue	Expenses
Beginning	220,000	100,000	50,000	70,000		
Borrow $30,000	30,000	30,000				
Pay and recognize interest expense	(6,200)			(6,200)		(6,200)*
Pay principal on long-term debt	(16,000)	(16,000)**				

*Interest expense = principal × rate = $100,000 × 5% + $30,000 × 4% = $5,000 + $1,200 = $6,200
**Payments on long-term debt = $10,000 + $30,000/5 = $16,000

At the end of the year, then, our long-term debt will be reported on the balance sheet at $100,000 + $30,000 − $16,000 = $114,000.

So, here's the second thing to remember regarding the borrowing of money when preparing the forecasts in this chapter:

- **Long-term debt and cash increases by any amounts borrowed and is reduced by principal payments (note: the repayment of the debt is not an expense; only the interest on the debt is an expense).**
- **Interest expense in the income statement is equal to the interest expense on the pre-existing debt *plus* the interest expense relating to any new amounts borrowed. It is computed as principal × rate.**

Restaurant Example—Base Case Forecast

With this background, we begin our formal discussion of strategy analysis with a continuation of the restaurant example we have illustrated in the preceding chapters. For our base case, we begin with the forecast assumptions for 2015 (our first forecast year) that we used in Chapter 8 to develop the forecasts of the income statement and the balance sheet in Exhibits 8.2 and 8.3. These forecast assumptions are provided in Exhibit 9.1.

EXHIBIT 9.1	Forecast Assumptions for Base Case	
		2015
Income Statement		
Revenue growth rate: Store		10.0%
Revenue growth rate: Catering.		10.0%
COGS: Food.		38.0%
Wage Expense:		
Fixed		$60,000
Variable (% Revenues).		15.0%
General Overhead		21.3%
Depreciation expense.		$5,000
Marketing expense (% Revenues)		10%
Interest Expense.		$1,193
Taxes @ 35% of pre-tax profit		35%
Balance Sheet		
Cash.		plug
Accounts receivable (% Revenues)		1.6%
Inventory (% COGS).		6.0%
Change—Other assets.		$0
Equipment purchases (CAPEX)		$0
Accounts payable (% COGS).		11.3%
Wages payable (% Revenues)		0.8%
Change—credit card debt		$0
Change—other current liabilities		$0
Change—long-term liabilities.		$0
Equity investment.		$0

Given the forecast assumptions presented in Exhibit 9.1, our projected income statement, balance sheet, and statement of cash flow for 2015 is presented in Exhibit 9.2. We present the most recent year (2014) together with our forecasts for 2015.

EXHIBIT 9.2	Base Case Forecasts of Income Statements, Balance Sheets, and Statements of Cash Flow		
Income Statement	**2014**	**Est. 2015**	**Forecast calculations**
Revenue: Store.	$402,628	$442,891	$402,628 × 1.10
Revenue: Catering	114,264	125,690	$114,264 × 1.10
Total revenue	516,892	568,581	
COGS: Food.	(196,419)	(216,061)	$568,581 × 0.38
Gross profit.	320,473	352,520	
Wage expense:			
Fixed	(60,000)	(60,000)	No change
Variable	(77,534)	(85,287)	$568,581 × 0.15
Total wages	(137,534)	(145,287)	
General overhead.	(110,000)	(121,108)	$568,581 × 0.213
Depreciation expense.	(5,000)	(5,000)	No change
Marketing	(51,689)	(56,858)	$568,581 × 0.10
Operating income.	16,250	24,267	
Interest expense.	(1,193)	(1,193)	No change
Income before tax	15,057	23,074	
Taxes @ 35%	(5,270)	(8,076)	$23,074 × 0.35
Net income.	$ 9,787	$ 14,998	

continued

EXHIBIT 9.2 (continued)	Base Case Forecasts of Income Statements, Balance Sheets, and Statements of Cash Flow		
Balance Sheet	**2014**	**2015**	
Assets			
Cash	$ 23,269	$ 44,241	Plug*
Accounts receivable	8,280	9,097	$568,581 × 0.016
Inventory	11,790	12,964	$216,061 × 0.06
Other assets	6,000	6,000	No change
Total current assets	49,339	72,302	
Equipment	60,000	60,000	No change
Accumulated depreciation . . .	(18,000)	(23,000)	($18,000) − $5,000 (depreciation expense)
Total assets	$ 91,339	$109,302	
Liabilities			
Accounts payable	$ 22,106	$ 24,415	$216,061 × 0.113
Wages payable	3,894	4,549	$568,581 × 0.008
Credit card debt	6,941	6,941	No change
Other current liabilities	1,000	1,000	No change
Total current liabilities	33,941	36,905	
Long-term liabilities	13,100	13,100	No change
Equity	44,298	59,297	$44,298 + $14,998**
Total	$ 91,339	$109,302	
Operating cash flow	$12,184	$20,971	
DuPont			
Profit margin	1.9%	2.6%	
Asset turnover	5.7	5.2	
ROA	10.8%	13.5%	
Financial leverage	2.1	1.8	
ROE	22.7%	24.3%	

*[$109,302 − 9,097 − 12,964 − 6,000 − 60,000 − (−23,000)]

** We have assumed no capital investment or dividends in the base case.

In our base case, assuming no change in our business model and forecast assumptions, our business is projected to do quite well. Our net income is expected to increase by 53% from 2014 to 2015 and our operating cash flow will increase by over 71%. The DuPont analysis reveals that our ROE will increase from 22.7% in 2014 to 24.3% in 2015 and that the increase is driven by an increase in ROA from 10.8% to 13.5% and not by financial leverage as it is expected to decline. Overall, our business is expected to perform quite nicely, to be profitable, and generate lots of cash.

Expansion Case

Our catering business customers have continued to recommend us to others and we are beginning to develop some corporate accounts. As we survey the market, we notice that there is very little competition in our commercial market area. We think we may have an opportunity to significantly expand our catering business and that, as our reputation grows with increased visibility, we will realize an increase in our restaurant business as well. Further, we think that developing this business now will give us a significant first mover advantage over potential competition as we will be able to quickly gain significant market share and will be able to develop a solid reputation before others realize the market potential.

In order to develop this business, we will need to purchase delivery trucks and other equipment at a cost of $100,000. We are concerned about taking on too much debt and decide to borrow only half of the amount we need, financing the remaining $50,000 by contributing our own funds as an equity investment. Our bank will agree to lend us the $50,000 at 6% interest, with the principal payable over a 10-year period at $5,000 per year.

We have developed the forecast assumptions in Exhibit 9.3.

EXHIBIT 9.3	Forecast Assumptions for Expansion Case		
	2015	**2016**	**2017**
Income Statement			
Revenue growth rate: Store	17.0%	12.0%	12.0%
Revenue growth rate: Catering.	300.0%	10.0%	10.0%
COGS: Food.	38.0%	38.0%	38.0%
Wage expense:			
Fixed.	$100,000	$100,000	$100,000
Variable (% Revenues)	15.0%	15.0%	15.0%
General overhead.	18.0%	18.0%	18.0%
Depreciation expense.	$ 15,000	$ 15,000	$ 15,000
Marketing expense (% Revenues)	12%	12.0%	12.0%
Interest expense.	($ 4,193)	($ 3,893)	($ 3,593)
Taxes @ 35%	35%	35.0%	35.0%
Balance Sheet			
Cash.	plug	plug	plug
Accounts receivable (% Revenues)	2.0%	2.0%	2.0%
Inventory (% COGS).	0.8%	0.8%	0.8%
Change—other assets	$ 0	$ 0	$ 0
Equipment purchases (CAPEX)	$100,000	$ 0	$ 0
Accounts payable (% COGS).	11.3%	11.3%	11.3%
Wages payable (% Revenues)	8.0%	8.0%	8.0%
Change—credit card debt	$ 0	$ 0	$ 0
Change—other current liabilities	$ 0	$ 0	$ 0
Change—long-term liabilities.	$ 50,000	($ 5,000)	($ 5,000)
Equity investment.	$ 50,000	$ 0	$ 0

To begin, we focus on our forecast for the first year (2015) and we estimate the following for our new line of business:

1. Our catering business will triple in the first year and will grow at a 10% rate thereafter. The increased visibility from our catering business will result in an increase in our restaurant business amounting to a growth of 17% in the first year and 12% per year thereafter as the restaurant continues to benefit from the catering business.

2. Our food costs as a percentage of sales will remain constant at 38%, but we will need to hire a catering manager at an annual cost of $40,000. Our fixed wage costs will therefore rise from $60,000 to $100,000 per year. Our variable wage costs will remain at 15% of sales.

3. Our general overhead will decrease from 21.3% of sales to 18% of sales as we realize some economies of scale. To support our new business, however, we will need to increase our marketing expense from 10% of sales to 12% of sales.

4. The new equipment will be depreciated on a straight-line basis over 10 years with no salvage value, resulting in an increase in depreciation expense of $10,000 per year in addition to the $5,000 of depreciation expense we currently recognize.

5. Our interest expense will increase by $3,000 ($50,000 × 6%) in the first year and will decline by $300 ($5,000 × 6%) per year as we make our $5,000 in principal payments each year. We assume a continuation of interest expense at the same level on our existing debt.

6. We expect to carry more receivables and inventory to support the new venture. These accounts are projected at 2% of revenues (2% is approximately 7 accounts receivable days outstanding) and 8% of COGS (8% is approximately 29 inventory days on hand), respectively. We do not assume any increase in payables and accruals as we have been slow to pay our suppliers and need to reduce our indebtedness to them in order to maintain relations.

Using these forecast assumptions, we forecast our income statements, balance sheets, and statements of cash flow in Exhibit 9.4.

EXHIBIT 9.4	Forecast of Expansion Case Income Statements, Balance Sheets, and Statements of Cash Flow		
Income Statement	**2014**	**Est. 2015 Expansion**	**Expansion Forecast calculations**
Revenue: Store............	$402,628	$471,075	$402,628 × 1.17
Revenue: Catering	114,264	457,056	$114,264 × 3.00
Total revenue	516,892	928,131	
COGS: Food.............	(196,419)	(352,690)	$928,131 × 0.38
Gross profit..............	320,473	575,441	
Wage expense:			
Fixed	(60,000)	(100,000)	+$40,000/year
Variable	(77,534)	(139,220)	$928,131 × 0.15
Total wages	(137,534)	(239,220)	
General overhead.........	(110,000)	(167,064)	$928,131 × 0.18
Depreciation expense......	(5,000)	(15,000)	+$10,000
Marketing	(51,689)	(111,376)	$928,131 × 0.12
Operating income.........	16,250	42,781	
Interest expense..........	(1,193)	(4,193)	+$3,000 ($50,000 × 6%)
Income before tax	15,057	38,588	
Taxes @ 35%	(5,270)	(13,506)	$38,588 × 0.35
Net income..............	$ 9,787	$ 25,082	

Balance Sheet	**2014**	**2015**	
Assets			
Cash....................	$ 23,269	$ 57,923	Plug*
Accounts receivable........	8,280	18,563	$928,131 × 0.02
Inventory.................	11,790	28,215	$352,690 × 0.06
Other assets.............	6,000	6,000	No change
Total current assets	49,339	110,701	
Equipment	60,000	160,000	+ $100,000
Accumulated depreciation ...	(18,000)	(33,000)	($18,000) − $15,000 (depreciation expense)
Total assets...............	$ 91,339	$237,701	
Liabilities			
Accounts payable..........	$22,106	$ 39,854	$352,690 × 0.113
Wages payable............	3,894	7,425	$928,131 × 0.008
Credit card debt...........	6,941	6,941	No change
Other current liabilities	1,000	1,000	No change
Total current liabilities.......	33,941	55,220	
Long-term liabilities	13,100	63,100	+ $50,000
Equity	44,298	119,381	$44,298 + $50,000 + $25,082**
Total	$ 91,339	$237,701	

*[$237,701 − 18,563 − 28,563 − 6,000 − 160,000 − (−33,000)]
** We assume a capital investment of $50,000, but no dividends, in this expansion example.

There are a number of accounts that change as a result of our strategic decision to expand that were not affected in our "no expansion" base case:

1. Our revenue forecasts increase by the revenues attributable to the new markets we plan to develop,

2. Our fixed wage costs will increase as we hire new employees for the additional business,

3. General overhead is expected to decline as a percentage of sales as some fixed costs are spread over a larger expected revenue base,

4. **Depreciation expense will now include the depreciation of the pre-existing assets ($5,000) plus the depreciation of the new assets we expect to purchase in our expansion ($100,000/10 = $10,000),**

5. Marketing expense will increase to 12% of sales as we will need to advertise our new business in addition to the advertising related to our existing business,

6. **Interest expense will reflect both the interest on the pre-existing debt ($1,193) and the interest on the new debt ($50,000 × 6%),**

7. Accounts receivable and inventories will increase as a percentage of revenues (COGS) to reflect the receivables and inventories associated with the new venture in addition to those for our existing business,

8. **Equipment will increase by the $100,000 cost of the new equipment we will purchase in our expansion,**

9. **Accumulated depreciation will become more negative by the new depreciation expense (see #4)**

10. **Long-term debt will increase by the additional $50,000 loan we will borrow to partially finance the equipment purchase,**

11. **Equity will increase by both the additional $50,000 capital investment we will make as well as by the expected profit of $25,082.**

We have highlighted in bold the accounts relating to the purchase of PPE, the borrowing of money and the investment of additional capital into the business as these are the areas that students typically find the most difficult. Please take a moment now to make sure you understand where each of these numbers comes from.

Multi-Year Forecasts

Strategic decisions, like our expansion case above, are usually analyzed by developing forecasts over many years. We provide a 3-year forecast of our expansion plan in Exhibit 9.5 and show the calculations for the second year of the forecast (2016). The third year (2017) is computed in the same manner as the second year, and so on as far into the future as you need to forecast in order to make your strategic decision.

The first-year forecast (2016) is the same as in Exhibit 9.4. The forecast for the second year (2017) includes the following:

1. Revenue growth is based off of the year 1 (2016) forecasts. Store revenue for 2017, for example, is computed as $471,075 (2016) × 1.12 (the 12% growth rate forecasted for year 2),

2. Variable expenses are computed as a percentage of the 2017 revenues and the assumed expense percentage from Exhibit 9.1.

3. Our fixed wage expense is not projected to change from 2016 as no new employees will be added,

4. Likewise, our depreciation expense is not forecasted to change as we will not purchase new PPE assets in 2017,

5. Our interest expense will be reduced by the expected principal payment of $5,000 that will reduce long-term debt by $5,000 and will reduce interest expense by $5,000 × 6% = $300,

6. PPE assets on the balance sheet will remain at 2016 levels since no new assets will be purchased,

7. Accumulated depreciation will become more negative by the depreciation expense for 2017,

8. Long-term debt will decline by the expected principal payment of $5,000, and

EXHIBIT 9.5	Three-year Forecast of Expansion Case Income Statements, Balance Sheets, and Statements of Cash Flow				
Income Statement	**2014**	**2015**	**2016**	**2016 calculations**	**2017**
Revenue: Store..............	$402,628	$471,075	$ 527,604	$471,075 × 1.12	$ 590,916
Revenue: Catering	114,264	457,056	502,762	$457,056 × 1.10	553,038
Total revenue	516,892	928,131	1,030,366		1,143,954
COGS: Food...............	(196,419)	(352,690)	(391,539)	$1,030,366 × 0.38	(434,703)
Gross profit................	320,473	575,441	638,827		709,251
Wage expense:					
Fixed...................	(60,000)	(100,000)	(100,000)	No change	(100,000)
Variable.................	(77,534)	(139,220)	(154,555)	$1,030,366 × 0.15	(171,593)
Total wages	(137,534)	(239,220)	(254,555)		(271,593)
General overhead...........	(110,000)	(167,064)	(185,466)	$1,030,366 × 0.18	(205,912)
Depreciation expense........	(5,000)	(15,000)	(15,000)	No change	(15,000)
Marketing	(51,689)	(111,376)	(123,644)	$1,030,366 × 0.12	(137,274)
Operating income...........	16,250	42,781	60,162		79,472
Interest expense............	(1,193)	(4,193)	(3,893)	$4,193 − $5,000 × 6%	(3,593)
Income before tax	15,057	38,588	56,269		75,879
Taxes @ 35%	(5,270)	(13,506)	(19,694)	$56,629 × 0.35	(26,558)
Net income................	$ 9,787	$ 25,082	$ 36,575		$ 49,321

Balance Sheet	**2014**	**2015**	**2016**	**2016 calculations**	**2017**
Assets					
Cash.....................	$23,269	$ 57,923	$104,554	Plug*	$163,936
Accounts receivable.........	8,280	18,563	20,607	$1,030,366 × 0.02	22,879
Inventory..................	11,790	28,215	31,323	$391,539 × 0.08	34,776
Other assets...............	6,000	6,000	6,000	No change	6,000
Total current assets	49,339	110,701	162,484		227,591
Equipment	60,000	160,000	160,000	No change	160,000
Accumulated depreciation	(18,000)	(33,000)	(48,000)	($33,000) − $15,000	(63,000)
Total assets................	$91,339	$237,701	$274,484		$324,591
Liabilities					
Accounts payable...........	$22,106	$ 39,854	$ 44,244	$391,539 × 0.113	$ 49,121
Wages payable.............	3,894	7,425	8,243	$1,030,366 × 0.008	9,152
Credit card debt............	6,941	6,941	6,941	No change	6,941
Other current liabilities	1,000	1,000	1,000	No change	1,000
Total current liabilities........	33,941	55,220	60,428		66,214
Long-term liabilities	13,100	63,100	58,100	−$5,000	53,100
Equity....................	44,298	119,381	155,956	$119,380 + $36,575	205,277
Total	$91,339	$237,701	$274,484		$324,591
Cash flow from operations....	12,184	34,653	51,631		64,382
DuPont					
Profit margin...............	1.9%	2.7%	3.5%		4.3%
Asset turnover	5.7	3.9	3.8		3.5
ROA	10.8%	10.5%	13.3%		15.1%
Financial leverage...........	2.1	2.0	1.8		1.6
ROE	22.7%	21.0%	23.9%		24.2%

*[$279,545 − 20,607 − 30,911 − 6,000 − 160,000 − (−48,000)]

9. Equity will only increase by the expected profit for 2017 as we anticipate no new capital investment and no payment of dividends.

With these three-year forecasts, we can now begin to analyze whether this strategic expansion is a good idea. Following are some observations that we can glean from these expansion forecasts as compared with our initial forecasts:

- Our profitability will be significantly greater. Over the three-year forecast horizon, our net income will be $110,978 under the expansion scenario as compared with $45,595 with our existing business.

- Our asset turnover rate will decrease significantly resulting from the equipment purchase that increases assets faster than the growth in revenues.

- Our operating cash flow will grow even more dramatically, from $61,846 over the next three years without expansion to $150,666 under the expansion scenario.

- Our ROE will remain fairly constant at 21% to 24% (despite the decrease in financial leverage as our debt is retired) because our ROA will increase significantly from 10.5% to 15.1% over the three-year forecast horizon.

Given the forecasted increase in profitability, coupled with the significant increase in cash flow, expansion appears to be a viable option.

There are a few other considerations, however:

- We need to be careful not to dilute our current management talent too much as we attempt to expand. Many businesses have failed in attempting to grow as they lose focus on their core business. We need to be sure that the existing management infrastructure of the business can support the larger enterprise.

- We should complement our forecasts with additional forecasts assuming worst-case and best-case scenarios to make sure that the expansion remains viable should our forecast assumptions prove to be overly optimistic or conservative.

- We should consider whether expansion of the catering side of our business is the best course of action despite our favorable forecasts. For example, perhaps opening another restaurant might be a better strategy in the long run, as it capitalizes on our existing strength.

- We need to be certain that we can manage the debt burden. Lenders are often not very forgiving if our plans do not materialize as we expect and we run short of cash. Consequently, we might want to build in a cushion in the form of lower debt payments in the beginning of the loan to allow the business to get on a solid footing before we begin to allocate cash for debt payments.

Given the significance of these other considerations, it should be evident that financial projections are only one input into the business decision, albeit an important one.

Forecasting Using Days Rather than % Revenues (% COGS)

In the first year of our expansion scenario (see Exhibit 9.4), we forecasted accounts receivable, inventories and accounts payable using % revenues for A/R and % COGS for inventories and payables (since they are reported at cost rather than retail selling price, they should be forecasted with respect to cost of goods sold, not revenues). Business owners and managers usually find it easier to talk in terms of days, however, rather than % revenues or % COGS. It is easier for them to think in terms of "how many days will it take for me to collect my A/R" rather than "what will be my % of A/R to sales." They also prefer to think in terms of how many days it will take to sell my inventories and how many days they will take for me to pay suppliers. When preparing forecasts, then, it is quite common to use days to project these working capital accounts, and we discuss how to do that in this section.

Fortunately, there is an easy conversion from % to days: Days = 365 × % revenues (COGS).[1] So, assuming that accounts receivable will be 2% of sales is equivalent to assuming that it will take 7.3 days to collect our accounts receivable (2% × 365 = 7.3). And, when we assumed that the AR/Sales percentage would be expected to increase from

---

[1] We can illustrate this using accounts receivable. Recall that the AR turn = Sales/AR and that Days to collect = 365/AR turn. Thus, Days = 365/[sales/AR] = [365 × AR]/sales = 365 × [AR/Sales], the same AR/Sales percentage we are using in our forecasts.

1.6% in 2015 to 2.0% in 2016, we were, in effect, assuming an increase in the average collection period from 5.84 days in 2015 ($365 \times 1.6\%$) to 7.3 days in 2016.

To forecast accounts receivable using days, we use the following formula:

$$\textbf{Forecasted AR} = \frac{\textbf{Assumed days to collect} \times \textbf{Forecasted Sales}}{\textbf{365}}$$

Referring to our 2015 forecast in Exhibit 9.4 and using an assumed days to collect of 7.3,

$$\textbf{Forecasted AR} = \frac{7.3 \times \$925,131}{365} = \$18,052^{\,2}$$

We can forecast inventories and accounts payable similarly:

$$\textbf{Forecasted inventories} = \frac{\textbf{Assumed days to sell} \times \textbf{Forecasted COGS}}{\textbf{365}}$$

$$\textbf{Forecasted accounts payable} = \frac{\textbf{Assumed days to pay} \times \textbf{Forecasted COGS}}{\textbf{365}}$$

Notice that we use COGS in the numerator rather than sales in the last two formulas. Both inventories and accounts payable are reported at their purchase (wholesale) cost as opposed to accounts receivable which are reported at retail selling prices. So, we use COGS for inventories and accounts payable as our measure of volume in the numerator.

To illustrate, our assumed inventories/COGS percentage of 6% is equivalent to an assumed average days to sell of $6\% \times 365 = 21.9$. So, we forecast inventories using an assumed days to sell of 21.9 as follows:[3]

$$\textbf{Forecasted inventories} = \frac{21.9 \times \$352,690}{365} = \$21,161$$

And, our assumed accounts payable/COGS percentage of 11.3% is equivalent to an assumed average days to sell of $11.3\% \times 365 = 41.3$. So, we forecast accounts payable using an assumed days to pay of 41.3 as follows:

$$\textbf{Forecasted inventories} = \frac{41.3 \times \$352,690}{365} = \$39,907$$

These formulas for the forecasting of working capital accounts can also be useful to ask questions like, "how much cash can I generate if I can sell my inventories 5 days more quickly?" or collect my receivables 3 days more quickly or delay payment of my accounts payable by 2 days. Notice that the formula to forecast inventories multiplies days $\times$ COGS per day ($41.3 \times \frac{\$352,690}{365}$). So, how much cash can we generate by selling our inventories 5 days more quickly? $5 \times \frac{\$352,690}{365} = \$4,831$. And, the same formula can be applied to answer how much cash will I generate if I collect my receivables 3 days more quickly ($3 \times \frac{\$925,131}{365} = \$7,603$) or how much cash will I generate by delaying payment of my accounts payable by 2 days ($2 \times \frac{\$352,690}{365} = \$1,933$). Finally, to remember whether we are generating or using cash, think of the statement of cash flow . . . cash increases when we reduce assets or increase liabilities and cash decreases when assets grow and liabilities decrease.

---

[2] This is slightly less than the $18,563 forecasted amount for accounts receivable in Exhibit 9.4 and the difference is due solely to rounding of days to 1 decimal place.

[3] The forecasted amounts for inventories and payables will also differ slightly from those in Exhibit 9.4 because of rounding of the days to 1 decimal place.

CONCLUSION

In this book, we have taught you how to prepare and analyze financial statements. We have, then, used that knowledge to develop forecasts that provide useful input into investing and financial decisions as well as into the evaluation of strategic alternatives.

Financial statement forecasts are but one input into the decision-making process, and we need to be careful to use them properly. Take a step back once you complete your forecasts and make sure that the projections seem realistic. We are struck by a comment that Warren Buffett, chairman of Berkshire Hathaway and a legendary investor, made in one of the Berkshire Hathaway annual reports:

> *Be suspicious of companies that trumpet earnings projections and growth expectations. Businesses seldom operate in a tranquil, no-surprise environment, and earnings simply don't advance smoothly (except, of course, in the offering books of investment bankers).*

Be careful about blindly extrapolating growth or maintaining percentages at last year's level. That is easy to do in a spreadsheet, but may not accurately reflect how the business environment may evolve, and *forecasting* a significant level of cash does you little good when you are facing debt payments and have no cash in the bank. Use your forecasts as a decision tool, but remember, customers walking through the door to purchase the products or services offered by your business are reality, not forecasted revenues in a spreadsheet, and they should be your primary focus.

QUESTIONS

Q9-1. Explain how strategy assessment of Chapter 9 differs from the forecasting of Chapter 8.

Q9-2. Describe the benefits to be derived from strategy assessment.

Q9-3. What criteria might you use to decide whether a proposed strategy is warranted?

Q9-4. What balance sheet and income statement accounts are affected by the proposed purchase of PPE assets?

Q9-5. In what ways will depreciation expense differ from prior amounts in a forecast that contemplates the purchase of PPE assets?

Q9-6. What balance sheet and income statement accounts are affected by the proposed borrowing of money?

Q9-7. In what ways will interest expense differ from prior amounts in a forecast that contemplates the borrowing of money?

Q9-8. What factors should you consider in developing your estimate of revenue growth and forecasted gross profit margin?

Q9-9. In what ways might your operating expenses change in your forecast of an expansion scenario?

EXERCISES

E9-1. **Forecasting Retained Earnings**   Assume that your company reports a balance of retained earnings of $11,891 at the end of the year. You forecast net income of $4,947 for next year and expect to pay dividends of $989. What balance will you report for retained earnings at the end of the year?

E9-2. **Identifying Affected Accounts Resulting from Planned Capital Expenditure**   Assume that, on the first day of the next fiscal year, your company is planning a purchase of equipment for a purchase price of $50,000 that you will depreciate over its estimated useful life of 5 years (equal depreciation amounts each year and no salvage value). Using the current income statement and balance sheet for your company presented below, identify the accounts that will be directly affected by this purchase and the balance you expect to report for these accounts next year:

	Current Year
Sales.	$ 47,564
COGS	(28,538)
Gross profit.	19,026
Operating expenses excluding depreciation	3,250
Depreciation expense.	6,516
Interest expense	1,189
Pre-tax profit	8,071
Tax expense @ 35%.	(2,825)
Net income.	$ 5,246
Cash.	$ 54,502
Accounts receivable.	2,378
Inventories	4,756
PPE, gross	65,163
Accumulated depreciation	(26,065)
Total Assets	$100,734
Accounts payable.	$ 2,378
Accrued liabilities	4,756
Total current liabilities.	7,134
Long-term debt	23,782
Common stock.	57,927
Retained earnings	11,891
Total liabilities and equity	$100,734

E9-3. **Identifying Affected Accounts Resulting from Planned Capital Expenditure During the Year** Assume the same facts as in E9-2, except that the equipment will be purchased on March 31 instead of January 1. Identify the accounts that will be directly affected by this purchase and the balance you expect to report for these accounts next year.

E9-4. **Identifying Affected Accounts Resulting from Planned Borrowing** Assume that, on the first day of next year, your company is planning to borrow $40,000 that you will repay in equal annual installments over a 5-year period. The interest rate on the loan will be 5% and both the principal payment and the interest payment will be paid on the last day of the year. Using the income statement and balance sheet from E9-2, and assuming that the current long-term debt will require a principal payment of $2,378 on December 31 (your year-end) identify the accounts that will be directly affected by this borrowing and the balance you expect to report for these accounts next year.

E9-5. **Identifying Affected Accounts Resulting from Planned Borrowing During the Year** Assume the same facts as in E9-4, except that the money will be borrowed on September 30 instead of January 1. Identify the accounts that will be directly affected by this purchase and the balance you expect to report for these accounts next year.

E9-6. **Forecasting the Statement of Cash Flow—No CAPEX or Borrowing** Assume that you have forecasted the following income statement and balance sheet and desire to compute the estimated cash flows for the upcoming year. Using the following current and forecasted financial statements, prepare the forecasted statement of cash flows (note, forecasted retained earnings include dividends payments in the amount of $989):

	Current Year	Forecast
Sales.	$47,564	$54,699
COGS.	(28,538)	(32,819)
Gross profit.	19,026	21,880
Operating expenses excluding depreciation	3,250	6,564
Depreciation expense.	6,516	6,516
Interest expense.	1,189	1,189
Pre-tax profit	8,071	7,611
Tax expense @ 35%.	(2,825)	(2,664)
Net income.	$ 5,246	$ 4,947
Cash.	$ 4,502	$12,598
Accounts receivable.	2,378	2,735
Inventories	4,756	5,470
PPE, gross.	65,163	65,163
Accumulated depreciation.	(26,065)	(32,581)
Total Assets	$50,734	$53,385
Accounts payable.	$ 2,378	$ 2,735
Accrued liabilities.	4,756	5,470
Total current liabilities.	7,134	8,205
Long-term debt	23,782	21,404
Common stock.	7,927	7,927
Retained earnings	11,891	15,849
Total liabilities and equity	$50,734	$53,385

E9-7. **DuPont Analysis on Forecasted Financial Statements**   Using the current and forecasted financial statements presented in E9-5, prepare the DuPont disaggregation of ROE into profit margin, turnover, and leverage and briefly comment on any trends you observe.

E9-8. **Identifying Affected Accounts Resulting from Planned Sale of PPE**   Assume that you are forecasting the planned sale of PPE. You expect that PPE assets with a cost of $10,000 and accumulated depreciation of $7,000 will be sold for cash in the amount of $5,000. Identify the accounts that will be directly affected by this sale.

E9-9. **Forecasting an Income Statement and Balance Sheet—No CAPEX or Borrowing**   Your company reports the following income statement and balance sheet for the current year:

Sales.	$102,263
COGS.	(61,358)
Gross profit.	40,905
Operating expenses excluding depreciation	3,250
Depreciation expense.	14,010
Interest expense	2,557
Pre-tax profit	21,088
Tax expense @ 35%.	(7,381)
Net income.	$ 13,707
Cash.	$ 9,273
Accounts receivable.	5,113
Inventories	10,431
PPE, gross	140,100
Accumulated depreciation.	(56,040)
Total assets.	$108,877

continued

Accounts payable.	$ 4,909
Accrued liabilities	10,226
Total current liabilities.	15,135
Long-term debt	51,132
Common stock.	17,044
Retained earnings	25,566
Total liabilities and equity.	$108,877

Given the following forecast assumptions, prepare the projected income statement and balance sheet for the next year using the following forecast assumptions and assuming

a. the payment of dividends equal to 20% of forecasted net income,
b. no purchases of PPE assets,
c. no new borrowing, but repayment of 10% of the principal balance of the long-term debt,
d. no sales or repurchases of common stock.

Forecast assumptions:

Sales.	+20%
Gross profit percentage	35%
Operating expenses excluding depreciation	12%
Depreciation expense.	$14,010
Interest expense	$2,557
Tax expense @ 35% of pre-tax profit.	35%
Accounts receivable (% of sales).	5%
Inventories (% of COGS)	17%
Accounts payable (% of COGS).	8%
Accrued liabilities (% of sales)	10%

E9-10. **Forecasting the Statement of Cash Flows—No CAPEX or Borrowing** Using the data in E9-9 and your forecasted income E9-9 Forecasting an income statement and balance sheet – no CAPEX or borrowing.

PROBLEMS

P9-1. **Forecasting Income Statement, Balance Sheet and Statement of Cash Flows and Ratio Analysis—1 year forecast** Tabby's Toys reports the following income statement and balance sheet as of December 31, 2014:

Tabby's Toys Financial Statements for the Year Ended December 31, 2014			
Income Statement		**Balance Sheet**	
Sales.	$350,000	Cash	$ 45,780
COGS.	(234,500)	Accounts receivable.	17,500
Gross profit.	115,500	Inventories	23,450
Operating expenses excluding depreciation . . .	56,000	PPE, gross	479,500
Depreciation expense.	47,950	Accumulated depreciation . . .	(143,850)
Interest expense.	10,500	Total assets.	$422,380
Pre-tax profit	1,050		
Tax expense	(368)	Accounts payable.	$ 9,380
Net income.	$ 682	Accrued liabilities	28,000
		Total current liabilities.	37,380
		Long-term debt	210,000
		Common stock.	58,333
		Retained earnings	116,667
		Total liabilities and equity	$422,380

Tabby's Toys is currently considering expanding their square footage. This will require an investment in additional PPE of $50,000 to be made at the beginning of the year. In order to evaluate whether this is a good move, Tabby has decided to prepare a three-year forecast of its income statements, balance sheets, and statements of cash flow.

Required:

a.   Using the following forecast assumptions, prepare forecasts of Tabby's balance sheet, income statement and statement of cash flow for the next year:

Sales growth rate	+25%
Gross profit margin.	33%
Operating expense (percentage of sales). . . .	16%
Tax expense (percentage of pre-tax profit). . .	35%
Interest expense.	5% of beginning debt balance
Receivables and inventories.	6% sales and 11% COGS, respectively
Accumulated depreciation	Straight-line, 10-year, no salvage value
Accounts payable and accruals.	5% COGS and 7% sales, respectively
Long-term debt	$5,000 per year of principal payments at end of year

b.   Evaluate the desirability of this expansion prospect. Prepare a DuPont analysis (use year-end balance sheet numbers) to evaluate the effects on profitability and the company's debt level and structure. Also, give some considerations to the company's projected cash flows.

P9-2. **Forecasting Income Statement, Balance Sheet and Statement of Cash Flows and Ratio Analysis—1 year forecast**   Sparky's Landscaping Company has been operating successfully for a number of years and is contemplating the purchase of vehicles and equipment costing $500,000 as of the beginning of the year. Both the new equipment and the old PPE assets are depreciated in equal amounts over their 10-year useful life with no expected salvage value.

The company will be able to borrow $400,000 from a local bank at a 5% interest rate, the same rate as it has on its current long-term debt of $800,000. Both loans will be repaid in equal payments over a 10-year period with payments due at the end of the year.

Sparky reports the following income statement and balance sheet at the end of the most recent year:

Income Statement	
Sales.	$3,210,570
COGS.	(2,086,870)
Gross profit.	1,123,700
Operating expenses excluding depreciation . . .	449,480
Depreciation expense.	279,320
Interest expense.	44,000
Pre-tax profit	350,900
Tax expense @ 35%.	(122,815)
Net income.	$ 228,085

Balance Sheet	
Cash	$ 241,896
Accounts receivable.	160,529
Inventories	354,768
PPE, gross	2,793,196
Accumulated depreciation . . .	(1,117,278)
Total Assets	$2,433,111
Accounts payable.	$ 166,950
Accrued liabilities	128,423
Total current liabilities.	295,373
Long-term debt	800,000
Common stock.	535,095
Retained earnings	802,643
Total liabilities and equity	$2,433,111

Required:

a.   Forecast the company's income statement, balance sheet (use cash as your plug figure) and statement of cash flows for the next year using the following inputs for your forecast:

Sales.	+25% growth
Gross profit margin.	38%
Operating expenses excluding depreciation	14% sales
Tax rate.	35% of pre-tax profit
Dividends	25% net income
Accounts receivable.	8% sales
Inventories	23% COGS
Accounts payable.	10% COGS
Accrued liabilities	4% Sales
Common stock.	No change

b. Prepare a DuPont analysis on both the existing financial statement and the forecasted financial statements and comment on the forecasted financial performance compared with that of the current year.

P9-3. **Forecasting Income Statement, Balance Sheet and Statement of Cash Flows and Ratio Analysis—1 year forecast, negative cash balance**   FHS Company operates a retail store selling outdoor apparel and equipment. The store has been profitable and prospects look good. It operates in leased space in a mall. The most recent financial statements follow:

Income Statement	
Sales.	$50,000
COGS.	(32,500)
Gross profit.	17,500
Operating expenses excluding depreciation . . .	7,000
Depreciation expense.	6,850
Interest expense.	1,650
Pre-tax profit	2,000
Tax expense	(700)
Net income.	$ 1,300

Balance Sheet	
Cash	$ 6,308
Accounts receivable.	2,500
Inventory.	5,525
PPE, gross	68,500
Accumulated depreciation . . .	(27,400)
Total assets.	$55,433
Accounts payable.	$2,600
Accrued liabilities	2,000
Total current liabilities.	4,600
Long-term debt	30,000
Common stock.	8,333
Retained earnings	12,500
Total liabilities and equity	$55,433

An adjacent store is moving out of the mall and FHS Company has an opportunity to expand its square footage. This will require an investment in additional PPE of $50,000 to be purchased at the beginning of the year (all PPE assets are depreciated in equal annual amounts over a 10-year period with no expected salvage value). To partially finance the purchase, FHS has obtained a $25,000 bank loan (all loans carry an annual interest rate of 5% and will be repaid in equal annual payments over a 10-year period, with payments to be made at the end of the year).

In order to evaluate whether this is a good move, FHS has decided to prepare a one-year forecast of its income statement, balance sheet, and statement of cash flow.

Required:

a. Using the following forecast assumptions, prepare forecasts of the FHS balance sheet, income statement and statement of cash flow for the next year.

Sales.	+20% growth rate
Gross profit margin.	38%
Operating expenses excluding depreciation	14% of sales
Tax expense	35% of pre-tax profit
Net income	
Dividends	None anticipated
Cash.	Use as your plug figure
Accounts receivable.	8% of sales
Inventories	23% of COGS
Accounts payable.	10% of COGS
Accrued liabilities	4% of sales
Common stock.	No sales or purchases anticipated

b. You should discover that we have a negative forecasted cash balance in the first year. It, therefore, doesn't make sense to forecast future years until this problem is solved.
1. What target level of cash should we plan for?
2. Develop a list of options that the company might consider in order to increase its cash balance to your targeted level of cash. What are the positive and negative features of each of your options?

P9-4. **Forecasting Income Statement, Balance Sheet and Statement of Cash Flows and Ratio Analysis—3 year forecast, negative cash balance and additional capital investment** Grace's Fashion Trends sells women's clothing via the Internet. Her year-end income statement and balance sheet follow:

Income statement		Balance sheet	
Sales.	$340,000	Cash	$ 20,377
COGS.	(221,000)	Accounts receivable.	17,000
Gross profit.	119,000	Inventories	37,570
Operating expenses excluding depreciation . . .	47,600	PPE, gross	280,000
Depreciation expense.	28,000	Accumulated depreciation . . .	(112,000)
Interest expense.	3,850	Total assets.	$242,947
Pre-tax profit	39,550		
Tax expense	(13,843)	Accounts payable.	$ 17,680
Net income.	$ 25,707	Accrued liabilities	13,600
		Total current liabilities.	31,280
		Long-term debt	70,000
		Common stock.	56,667
		Retained earnings	85,000
		Total liabilities and equity	$242,947

Grace is considering a new line of shoes, which will increase her sales considerably. Moreover, the shoes have a much higher gross profit margin than her current products. In order to accommodate the additional sales volume for the new line of shoes, Grace is contemplating the purchase of an additional server and related computer and office equipment that will cost $150,000 to be purchased at the beginning of the year (all PPE assets are depreciated in equal annual amounts over a 10-year period with no expected salvage value). To partially finance the purchase, Grace's bank will lend her $75,000 (all loans carry an annual interest rate of 5% and will be repaid in equal annual payments over a 10-year period, with payments to be made at the end of the year).

In order to evaluate whether the expansion is a good idea, Grace has asked you to develop a 3-year forecast of her income statement, balance sheet and statement of cash flow. She has also asked you to prepare a DuPont analysis on the current and forecasted financial statements in order to evaluate her forecasted financial performance.

Grace feels that the additional line of shoes will increase her annual sales volume by 25% in the first year when the new products are introduced, levelling off to a 15% growth rate in the second year and a, more sustainable, 7% in the third year.

Required:

a. Prepare a forecast of Grace's income statement, balance sheet and statement of cash flow for the first year using the following inputs:

Sales growth.	+25%
Gross profit margin.	39%
Operating expenses excluding depreciation	11% of sales
Tax expense	35% of pre-tax profit
Dividends	none
Cash.	Use as your plug figure
Accounts receivable.	8% of sales
Inventories	23% of COGS
Accounts payable.	10% of COGS
Accrued liabilities	4% of sales
Common stock.	No additional investment

b. You should reveal that, while the business is forecasted to be profitable, it runs out of cash and will report a deficit cash balance of $ in the first year. Clearly, it makes no sense to continue our analysis until we solve that problem. In your discussion with Grace, she indicates that she feels strongly that this decision has real potential and is willing to invest additional capital into the business in the form of a purchase of new common stock.

   1. Compute Grace's cash/sales percentage in the current year and use that percentage to estimate the cash she will need to support her anticipated year 1 sales.
   2. Now, increase common stock by the amount needed to reach your target cash level.

c. Now that you and Grace have solved the cash issue, continue the forecast for years 2 and 3 assuming a sales growth of 15% for year 2 and 7% for year 3. All other forecast assumptions stay the same (remember, you are not purchasing additional PPE in years 2 and 3 or borrowing any new funds). You will, however, continue to depreciate the PPE assets and make the required payments on the debt.

d. Evaluate the forecasted financial statements, assuming the additional capital investment in step b and using your DuPont analysis. Does this business decision sound like a good idea?

e. You should discover that Grace's business is forecasted to perform very well. Profitability will increase significantly, but ROE will decline, primarily due to the decrease in financial leverage. You feel that financial leverage could be increased back to the level you compute for the current year without incurring undue risk. You, therefore, decide to perform one last change to your analysis to forecast the payment of $50,000 dividends in both year 2 and year 3. Now, recompute your DuPont analysis assuming the payment of dividends that will allow Grace to recoup her initial capital investment, plus take an additional $65,000 of cash out of the business. Does it appear that the business will be able to allow Grace to take some cash out of the business?

P9-5. **Forecasting Income Statement, Balance Sheet and Statement of Cash Flows and Ratio Analysis—3 year forecast, poorly performing business, negative cash balance and downsizing** Tommy Corporation sells medical equipment to doctors' offices and hospitals. It was a very profitable business, but recently has come under significant earnings pressure as a result of new competition and is reporting a net loss for the most recent year. Tommy's income statement and balance sheet for the most recent year follow:

Income statement	
Sales...............................	$623,857
COGS...............................	(436,700)
Gross profit........................	187,157
Operating expenses excluding depreciation ...	155,964
Depreciation expense................	28,000
Interest expense	10,800
Pre-tax profit	(7,607)
Tax expense........................	2,662
Net income.........................	$ (4,945)

Balance sheet	
Cash....................	$ 8,526
Accounts receivable........	31,193
Inventories	144,111
Land	120,000
Building and equipment.....	280,000
Accumulated depreciation ...	(84,000)
Total Assets	$499,830
Accounts payable..........	$ 34,936
Accrued liabilities..........	24,954
Total current liabilities.......	59,890
Long-term debt	180,000
Common stock............	103,976
Retained earnings	155,964
Total liabilities and equity	$499,830

Tommy is considering his strategic options and has asked for your help to forecast the company's financial statements.

Required:

a. Prepare a forecast of the income statement, balance sheet and statement of cash flows for the next three years using the following forecast assumptions:

Sales...............................	25% reduction in sales in year 1, followed by growth of 2% in years 2 and 3 to reflect inflation
Gross profit margin...................	A contraction to 20% to reflect increasing pricing pressure from the competition
Operating expenses excluding depreciation ...	25% of sales
Tax expense........................	35% of pre-tax profit
Dividends..........................	No dividends expected until profitability improves
Cash..............................	Use cash as your plug figure
Accounts receivable..................	5% of sales
Inventories.........................	33% of COGS
Land, Building & Equipment............	No purchases or sales
Accounts payable....................	8% of COGS
Accrued liabilities...................	4% of sales
Long-term debt	$36,000 principal payments required per year (5 year repayment)
Common stock......................	No additional investment is contemplated

b. Your forecasted balance sheet should reveal a negative cash balance in the first year of $(21,574). Tommy's company will be out of business by the end of next year unless something is done. Following discussions with Tommy, here's what the two of you have decided; you should use these new assumptions to prepare new forecasts of Tommy's financial statements for the first year only to see if we can stabilize the business:

1. You decide to eliminate a line of products that has come under particular competitive pressure. The elimination of this product line will cause sales to further decline to −31% for next year (vs. −25% originally forecast).
2. The product line you plan to eliminate, however, is unprofitable. As a result, your gross profit margin on the remaining sales will increase to 28% (from 20%).
3. You will be able to reduce office staff as a result of the smaller business, resulting in a new operating expense of 18% of sales (vs. 25% before).
4. The product line you are planning to eliminate was a higher turnover product, although less profitable. As a result, your remaining inventories, while generating more gross profit margin, will not sell as quickly and you forecast inventories at 40% of COGS (vs. 33% currently).
5. Because your business is not as strong, suppliers have begun to restrict their credit terms to you and you forecast accounts payable at 5% of COGS (vs. 8% currently).

6. All other forecast assumptions remain the same.

c. Your forecast should not yield a profitable business with a positive cash balance. It looks like you and Tommy have stabilized the business and can now look for new growth opportunities. Now, all Tommy needs to do is execute the proposed plan, no small challenge!

P9-6. **Forecasting Income Statement, Balance Sheet and Statement of Cash Flow and Ratio Analysis** J.C. Enterprises operates a manufacturing company serving the New England states. The company has been profitable and prospects look good. The most recent financial statements and current projections follow:

	CY2014	2015	2016	2017
Income statement				
Sales.	$53,400	$58,740	$64,614	$71,075
COGS.	(35,778)	(39,356)	(43,291)	(47,620)
Gross profit.	17,622	19,384	21,323	23,455
Operating expenses.	8,010	8,811	9,692	10,661
Interest expense (10%).	3,300	3,000	2,700	2,400
Pre-tax profit	6,312	7,573	8,931	10,394
Tax expense	(2,209)	(2,651)	(3,126)	(3,638)
Net income.	$ 4,103	$ 4,922	$ 5,805	$ 6,756
Balance sheet				
Cash.	$ 7,106	$ 9,551	$12,705	$16,618
Accounts receivable.	12,119	13,331	14,664	16,130
Inventories	17,822	19,604	21,564	23,720
PPE, gross	22,695	22,695	22,695	22,695
Accumulated depreciation.	(2,270)	(4,540)	(6,810)	(9,080)
Total Assets	$57,472	$60,641	$64,818	$70,083
Accounts payable.	$ 9,802	$10,782	$11,860	$13,046
Accrued liabilities.	2,670	2,937	3,231	3,554
Total current liabilities.	12,472	13,719	15,091	16,600
Long-term debt	30,000	27,000	24,000	21,000
Net worth	15,000	19,922	25,727	32,483
Total liabilities and net worth	$57,472	$60,641	$64,818	$70,083

Statement of cash flow	CY2014	2015	2016	2017
Net income.		$4,922	$ 5,805	$ 6,756
Depreciation.		2,270	2,270	2,270
Chg. A/R.		(1,212)	(1,333)	(1,466)
Chg. Inv.		(1,782)	(1,960)	(2,156)
Chg. A/P.		980	1,078	1,186
Chg. Accruals.		267	294	323
NCF—Operating activities		5,445	6,154	6,913
Chg—PPE		0	0	0
NCF—Investing		0	0	0
Chg. LTD.		(3,000)	(3,000)	(3,000)
NCF—Financing.		(3,000)	(3,000)	(3,000)
Net change in cash.		2,445	3,154	3,913
Beginning cash.		7,106	9,551	12,705
Ending cash		$9,551	$12,705	$16,618
Net profit margin.	7.7%	8.4%	9.0%	9.5%
Asset turnover	0.93	0.97	1.00	1.01
ROA	7.2%	8.1%	9.0%	9.6%
Financial leverage.	3.83	3.04	2.52	2.16
ROE	27.6%	24.6%	22.7%	20.7%

J.C. Enterprises is considering the purchase of new manufacturing equipment at a cost of $50,000 which will increase sales by 25% per year, as compared with current projected increases of 10% per year. The bank will lend the company $40,000 to be repaid over a 10-year period at the current interest rate of 10%. In order to evaluate whether this is a good move, we have decided to prepare a 3-year forecast of our income statements, balance sheets, and statements of cash flow.

Required:

a.   Using the following forecast assumptions, prepare forecasts of the J.C. Enterprises balance sheets, income statements and statements of cash flow for the next 3 years:

Sales growth rate	25%
COGS (percentage of sales).	65%
Operating expenses (percentage of sales). . .	13%
Interest expense	10% of the beginning of the year balance (assume the loan is funded at the beginning of 2014 and that the payments on debt are made on the last day of the year)
Tax expense (percentage of pre-tax profit). . .	35%
Receivables	23% of sales
Inventories	31% of sales
Accumulated depreciation	Straight-line, 10 year, no salvage value
Accounts payable.	17% of sales
Accruals	5% of sales
Long-term debt	Continue the $3,000 per year on the existing debt plus $4,000 per year on the new debt

b.   Evaluate the desirability of this expansion prospect. Prepare a DuPont analysis (use year-end balance sheet numbers) to evaluate the effects on profitability and the company's debt level and structure. Also, give some considerations to the company's projected cash flows.

Financial Statements: Introduction to the Income Statement and Balance Sheet
Body Restorations Inc. (BRI) Case Series

LEARNING OBJECTIVES

When you complete this case you should be able to:

1. Construct, understand, and discuss an income statement in good format.
2. Construct, understand, and discuss a balance sheet in good format.

INTRODUCTION

Molly was both exhilarated and exhausted. As long as she could remember, she had been into cosmetology. Perhaps it was her sensitive skin (growing up she seemed allergic to many compounds); perhaps it was the glow of the glamorous models she read about; or perhaps she saw an opportunity. After graduating from Cosmetology School while attending high school and completing her undergraduate college degree in marketing, Molly went straight into the cosmetics industry. She worked at a major high-end department store selling cosmetics, and then for L'Oreal, one of the major competitors in the industry. During this time, she had been mixing her own compounds for bath and body lotion products and selling them at craft shows, weekend farmer's markets, and holiday events. She was constantly scrambling, juggling her time between a full-time job and being an entrepreneur. She decided to quit her full-time job, became a consultant in packaging design and marketing, and with the increased flexibility in her schedule devoted more concentrated time to launch her own venture Body Restorations Inc. (BRI).

After about six months of this arrangement and while shopping in Whole Foods Market (a high-end, U.S. food retailer), Molly heard two customers discussing soap ingredients and their allergies to many of the compounds used in soaps. As they were trying to deduce the ingredients from very confusing labels, Molly offered her advice and spent about ten minutes educating these two women on products. As the women left and Molly returned to her shopping she felt a gentle tap on her shoulder. It was a buyer for the bath and body products section of the store, who had overheard the conversations and wanted to talk with Molly about her products. After their meeting, the buyer agreed to try three of Molly's products (6 variations each), in 5 stores within the region. The buyer also required Molly to obtain a $1MM product liability insurance policy and to purchase a UPC

master code.[1] As Molly left the meeting she thought "I hope we have the money to be able to deliver the products I just promised!"

In 2011 revenues had tripled to $150,000. Molly secured additional equity funding from friends plus a small loan from a regional bank and more than doubled revenues in 2012 to $345,000. The 2012 financial results are presented in Exhibit C2.1. Note for 2012, operating cash flow was ($24,000); slightly worse than the negative earnings before tax ($22,500) due to the cash tied up in accounts receivable and the growth of inventory.

The Industry

The Cosmetics and Beauty Manufacturing Industry (NAICS code 32562) is dominated by the four major players identified above. However, there were approximately 1,600 companies in 2010 when Molly agreed to sell products to Whole Foods Market and the industry was just emerging from disastrous years of the 2008 and 2009 recession. IBIS World listed this industry as a growth industry with 5% annual revenue growth expected through 2019. Although a very competitive industry, profit margins are typically high (between 10–12% Net Income/Revenues) because of the constant product innovations resulting in product differential as well as high advertising expenses to build brands and command premium prices.

The industry is considered a volatile industry with revenue swings based on consumer confidence. Swings in revenue also produce profitability swings due to the large fixed expenses, which must be paid irrespective of revenue levels. Profitability is also majorly affected by petroleum price swings because petroleum-based raw materials are major ingredients of most cosmetic products. To reduce the impact of these variables, the major companies offer lower-priced staple product lines (standard shampoos, bath soaps, fragrances, etc.) to balance the revenue swings of premium product lines.

For local companies planning to become regional and national, the industry is more volatile than for the major players and a bit more precarious because profit margins are not as high. The majority of these companies (approximately 1950 companies in 2014) follow niche strategies focusing on one portion of the market and having a focused Customer Value Proposition (CVP), a product attribute that makes their offering unique.

For BRI, the products were organic and compatible with sensitive skin. Furthermore, although Molly's products tended towards the premium range, her selling prices to retail stores were lower than those of her competitors, thus allowing the retailers to make better margins on her products. For example, one of her major competitor's bath salts sold for $8 per package and Molly knew the store paid $4. The product margin was $4/$8 or 50%. In contrast, Molly's bath salts sold for $7 per package and the store would pay in the neighborhood of $3.25. The product margin on Molly's bath salts would be $3.75/$7.00 or approximately 54%. Plus, Molly knew her products were better and had more appeal to the typical Whole Foods Market customer because they were organic.

The Problem

Developing the operations infrastructure to fulfill the Whole Foods contract would take planning, money, and people as well as bandwidth from an already stretched Molly. Molly figured she could just sleep less to provide the bandwidth but she needed money. Her family and friends had always been supportive and she was hoping they would loan funds to her or invest the money she needed to help fulfill this contract. Before she went to her family, she wanted to be able to show them what she had for resources and how she had done since she had focused more on her business. She remembered from her undergraduate program, that she should probably put together an income statement and balance sheet, but she wasn't sure the formats to use or what things went in which statement. She did however have records from her checkbook, credit cards, and the information from a

---

[1] The **Universal Product Code** (**UPC**) is a barcode symbology (i.e., a specific type of barcode) that is widely used in the United States, Canada, the United Kingdom, Australia, New Zealand and in other countries for tracking trade items in stores.

survey of her operations and inventory. Molly felt the following data was a pretty reasonable representation of her last six months of operations since she quit her full-time job and began consulting and focusing more on her company.

From Checkbook:	
Cash Paid	
Web site design	$ 5,000
Raw materials in inventory	$18,000
Labor in products in inventory	$12,000
Rent expense	$ 5,000
Packaging in inventory	$ 4,000
Purchase equipment	$ 5,000
Insurance expense	$ 500
Utilities & Telephone.	$ 800
Printed advertising materials	$ 1,000
Gas & car maintenance	$ 1,000
Sales salaries	$ 3,000
Cash Received	
Invested by owner	$ 8,000
Loan from family.	$ 3,000
Customers—craft fairs, markets, etc.	$50,000
Ending Cash	**$ 5,700**

And she knew:

Other items: No Cash Impact	
Loan for equipment	$ 5,000
Wages payable-sales salaries	$ 1,000
Accounts payable-raw materials in inventory	$ 4,000
Accounts payable-packaging in inventory	$ 2,000
Credit card debt-equipment.	$ 5,000
Depreciation equipment.	$ 2,000
Depreciation website	$ 2,500
Cost of goods sold.	$33,500

Molly knew she should be depreciating her equipment, which was essentially her manufacturing set-up but she didn't have time to worry about that. She also knew she had some of the printed materials listed above as expenses in boxes in her shop but she was not about to go out and count those materials. Finally, her inventory numbers were approximations because again, she did not have time to count the actual amount of compounds and packaging material in storage. As she grew her company, she would bake inventory counts and ordering points into a Standard Operating Procedures manual but not now.

Molly's request:

You are to take the material and create an income statement for the six-month period just ended and the balance sheet as of the last day of the period. She would then use these numbers to implement improvements to reduce expenses and forecast the likely next six months which would include her first shipments to Whole Foods.

Financial Statement Development and the Balance Sheet Equation (BSE) Format

Body Restorations Inc. (BRI) Case Series

LEARNING OBJECTIVES

When you complete this case you should be able to:

1. Reinforce the basics of constructing financial statements using the BSE format.
2. Understand standard financial statement formats.
3. Begin to understand and discuss the information contained in the income statement and balance sheet.

INTRODUCTION

Molly was both exhilarated and exhausted. As long as she could remember, she had been into cosmetology. Perhaps it was her sensitive skin (growing up she seemed allergic to many compounds); perhaps it was the glow of the glamorous models she read about; or perhaps she saw an opportunity. After graduating from Cosmetology School while attending high school and completing her undergraduate college degree in marketing, Molly went straight into the cosmetics industry. She worked at a major high-end department store selling cosmetics, and then for L'Oreal, one of the major competitors in the industry. During this time, she had been mixing her own compounds for bath and body lotion products and selling them at craft shows, weekend farmer's markets, and holiday events. She was constantly scrambling, juggling her time between a full-time job and being an entrepreneur. She decided to quit her full-time job, became a consultant in packaging design and marketing, and with the increased flexibility in her schedule devoted more concentrated time to launch her own venture Body Restorations Inc. (BRI).

After about six months of this arrangement and while shopping in Whole Foods Market (a high-end, U.S. food retailer), Molly heard two customers discussing soap ingredients and their allergies to many of the compounds used in soaps. As they were trying to deduce the ingredients from very confusing labels, Molly offered her advice and spent about ten minutes educating these two women on products. As the women left and Molly returned to her shopping she felt a gentle tap on her shoulder. It was a buyer for the bath and body products section of the store, who had overheard the conversations and wanted to talk with Molly about her products. After their meeting, the buyer agreed to try three of Molly's products (6 variations each), in 5 stores within the region. The buyer also required Molly to obtain a $1MM product liability insurance policy and to purchase a UPC

master code.[2] As Molly left the meeting she thought "I hope we have the money to be able to deliver the products I just promised!"

In 2011 revenues had tripled to $150,000. Molly secured additional equity funding from friends plus a small loan from a regional bank and more than doubled revenues in 2012 to $345,000. The 2012 financial results are presented in Exhibit C2.1. Note for 2012, operating cash flow was ($24,000); slightly worse than the negative earnings before tax ($22,500) due to the cash tied up in accounts receivable and the growth of inventory.

The Industry

The Cosmetics and Beauty Manufacturing Industry (NAICS code 32562) is dominated by four major players (L'Oreal, Procter & Gamble Co., Estee Lauder, Inc., and Unilever, USA). However, there were approximately 1,600 companies in 2010 when Molly agreed to sell products to Whole Foods Market and the industry was just emerging from the disastrous years of the 2008 and 2009 recession. IBIS World listed this industry as a growth industry with 5% annual revenue growth expected through 2019. Although a very competitive industry, net profit margins (Net Income/Revenues) are typically high (between 10–12%) because of the constant product innovations resulting in product differential as well as the increasing demand for skin products and the ability to command premium prices.

The industry is also considered a volatile industry with revenue swings based on consumer confidence. Swings in revenue also produce swings in profitability, because of the large fixed expenses that must be paid irrespective of revenue levels. Profitability is also majorly affected by petroleum price swings because petroleum-based raw materials are major ingredients of most cosmetic products. To reduce the impact of these variables, the major companies offer lower-priced staple product lines (standard shampoos, bath soaps, fragrances, etc.) to balance the revenue swings of premium product lines.

For local companies planning to become regional and national, the industry is more volatile than for the major players and a bit more precarious because profit margins are not as high. The majority of these companies (approximately 1,950 companies in 2014) follow niche strategies focusing on one portion of the market and having a focused Customer Value Proposition (CVP), a product attribute that makes their offering unique.

For BRI, the products were organic and compatible with sensitive skin. Furthermore, although Molly's products tended towards the premium range, her selling prices to retail stores were lower than those of her competitors, thus allowing the retailers to make better margins on her products. For example, one of her major competitor's bath salts sold for $8 per package and Molly knew the store paid $4. The product margin was $4/$8 or 50%. In contrast, Molly's bath salts sold for $7 per package and the store would pay in the neighborhood of $3.25. The product margin on Molly's bath salts would be $3.75/$7.00 or approximately 54%. Plus, Molly knew her products were better and had more appeal to the typical Whole Foods Market customer because they were organic.

The Future

As Molly's 2012 results indicated, she had a reasonable year for being such a young company. She was still not operating cash flow positive and she had to improve her earnings before tax (EBT) results but she was hugely positive about her future. She was positive she would expand into five more Whole Foods stores in an adjacent region and by the Q4 she thought she could launch a website that would allow online orders from individuals as well as boutique stores. She also had appointments with two other food retailers in her region. Both retailers had multiple stores in multiple regions. Molly thought 2013 could be another year of fantastic growth but she thought that might be unwise. Her current thinking was that she should slow her growth a bit and focus her efforts on better gross margins

---

[2] The **Universal Product Code** (**UPC**) is a barcode symbology (i.e., a specific type of barcode) that is widely used in the United States, Canada, the United Kingdom, Australia, New Zealand and in other countries for tracking trade items in stores.

and reducing her overhead expenses, that is her general and administrative expenses. This should allow her to generate positive earnings before tax (EBT) and hopefully a positive operating cash flow. The later result was critical because she needed to emerge from her cash burn period in order to stop seeking new investors and loans. But could the plans in her head really accomplish these two critical goals? That question had been nagging at Molly for the last three months as 2012 levels were thrilling but negative operating cash flow was a real downer.

Molly knew she did not have the ability to develop a forecasting model but she thought if she listed her expected transactions, aggregated for the year, using the Balance Sheet Equation format she learned in a well-known and intense entrepreneurship program could help her put numbers to her 2012 expectations. Over several cups of coffee one morning (you gotta' love Starbucks), Molly banged out the following forecasted transactions on her computer. While she was typing away on her keyboard, Molly also had the brilliant idea to let you do her forecasting for her!

Required:

Using the financial data given in Exhibit C2.1, the 2013 transactions below, and the BSE format (Exhibit C2.2—spreadsheet provided) enter the transactions and generate the income statement, balance sheet, and statement of cash flows for BRI.

Forecasted Transactions for 2013

1. Expected sales were $415,000, an approximate growth rate of 20%. All of these sales would be on account (accounts receivable) and all but $40,000 were expected to be collected during 2013. The average collection period was approximately 35–40 days. (Note this transaction can be done in one or two entries.)

2. Inventory of raw materials purchased will be purchased on credit in the amount of $190,000 (accounts payable). By the end of 2013 all but $30,000 is expected to be paid to BRI's suppliers. (Note this transaction can be done in one or two entries.)

3. All of beginning accounts receivable (AR) will be collected during 2013. All of beginning accounts payable (AP) will be paid within the credit terms during 2013.

4. Cost of goods sold (COGS) for 2013 should be $310,000. This amount is based on $180,000 in materials and the remaining $130,000 consisting of direct labor, packaging and manufacturing overhead to be paid in cash.

5. Selling and marketing expense (S&M) will be $72,000. As planned, this is an approximate increase of 30% over 2012. All will be paid in cash.

6. General and Administrative Expense (G&A) will be $66,000 and paid in cash. This will include the miscellaneous expense category which Molly decided to merge into G&A.

7. Depreciation expense on equipment for the year should be $2,000.

8. Financing expenses which included credit card charges and interest as well as interest on the long-term loans is expected to be $9,000 and paid in cash.

9. To continue to grow the business, Molly expects to obtain external financing. She will do this by securing a long-term loan for $20,000 and an additional $50,000 investment from an existing owner.

10. Molly will pay down $10,000 of her credit card debt (CC debt).

EXHIBIT C2.1	BRI Financial Results for 2012

Balance Sheet

Year Ending December 31	2012		
Assets			
Current assets			
Cash.	$ 15,000		
Accounts receivable.	$ 30,000		
Inventory.	$ 50,000		
Other.	$ 2,000		
Total		$ 97,000	
Long-term assets			
Equipment	$ 24,000		
Accumulated depreciation	$ (9,000)		
Total		$ 15,000	
Total assets			$112,000
Liabilities			
Accounts payable.	$ 25,000		
Payroll tax.	$ 3,000		
Credit card debt	$ 40,000		
Other.		$ 68,000	
Long-term loans		$ 30,000	
Total liabilities.			$ 98,000
Owners' equity			
Contributions		$112,000	
Retained earnings.		$ (98,000)	
Total owners' equity.			$ 14,000
Total liabilities and owners' equity			$112,000

Income Statment

Year Ending December 31	2012
Revenues	$345,000
COS	$260,000
GP	$ 85,000
Operating expenses	
S&M	$ 55,000
G&A	$ 40,000
Misc..	$ 1,500
Depreciation	$ 2,000
Total	$ 98,500
Operating income.	$ (13,500)
Financing	$ (9,000)
Earnings before tax	$ (22,500)

EXHIBIT C2.2 — BRI2013 BSE Format

BRI 2013

Transactions	Assets						Liabilities				Owner's Equity	
	Cash	Accounts Receivable	Inventory	Other	Equipment	Accumulated Depreciation	Accounts Payable	Payroll Tax Payable	Credit Card Debt	Other	Long-term Loans	Owners' Contributions	Retained Earnings
Beg Balances..........	$ 15,000	$ 30,000	$ 50,000	$ 2,000	$ 24,000	$(9,000)	$ 25,000	$ 3,000	$ 40,000		$ 30,000	$ 112,000	$ (98,000)
1) Sales.................													
2) Inventory.............													
3) Collect AR............													
4) Pay AP													
5) COGS													
6) S&M expense													
7) G&A expense													
8) Depreciation..........													
9) Financing													
10) External Financing ...													
1) Paid CC Debt.........													
End Balances..........	$ 15,000	$ 30,000	$ 50,000	$ 2,000	$ 24,000	$ (9,000)	$ 25,000	$ 3,000	$ 40,000	$ —	$ 30,000	$ 112,000	$ (98,000)

Financial Statement Development and the Balance Sheet Equation (BSE) Format
Body Restorations Inc. (BRI) Case Series

LEARNING OBJECTIVES

When you complete this case you should be able to:

1. Reinforce the basics of constructing financial statements using the BSE format.
2. Understand standard financial statement formats for the income statement, balance sheet, and statement of cash flows.
3. Begin to understand and discuss the information contained in the income statement, balance sheet, and statement of cash flows.

INTRODUCTION

Molly was both exhilarated and exhausted. As long as she could remember, she had been into cosmetology. Perhaps it was her sensitive skin (growing up she seemed allergic to many compounds); perhaps it was the glow of the glamorous models she read about; or perhaps she saw an opportunity. After graduating from Cosmetology School while attending high school and completing her undergraduate college degree in marketing, Molly went straight into the cosmetics industry. She worked at a major high-end department store selling cosmetics, and then for L'Oreal, one of the major competitors in the industry. During this time, she had been mixing her own compounds for bath and body lotion products and selling them at craft shows, weekend farmer's markets, and holiday events. She was constantly scrambling, juggling her time between a full-time job and being an entrepreneur. She decided to quit her full-time job, became a consultant in packaging design and marketing, and with the increased flexibility in her schedule devoted more concentrated time to launch her own venture Body Restorations Inc. (BRI).

After about six months of this arrangement and while shopping in Whole Foods Market (a high-end, U.S. food retailer), Molly heard two customers discussing soap ingredients and their allergies to many of the compounds used in soaps. As they were trying to deduce the ingredients from very confusing labels, Molly offered her advice and spent about ten minutes educating these two women on products. As the women left and Molly returned to her shopping she felt a gentle tap on her shoulder. It was a buyer for the bath and body products section of the store, who had overheard the conversations and wanted to talk with Molly about her products. After their meeting, the buyer agreed to try three of Molly's products (6 variations each), in 5 stores within the region. The buyer also required Molly to obtain a $1MM product liability insurance policy and to purchase a UPC

master code.[3] As Molly left the meeting she thought "I hope we have the money to be able to deliver the products I just promised!"

In 2011 revenues had tripled to $150,000. Molly secured additional equity funding from friends plus a small loan from a regional bank and more than doubled revenues in 2012 to $345,000. The 2012 financial results are presented in Exhibit C2.1. Note for 2012, operating cash flow was ($24,000); slightly worse than the negative earnings before tax ($22,500) due to the cash tied up in accounts receivable and the growth of inventory.

The Industry

The Cosmetics and Beauty Manufacturing Industry (NAICS code 32562) is dominated by the four major players identified above. However, there were approximately 1,600 companies in 2010 when Molly agreed to sell products to Whole Foods Market and the industry was just emerging from disastrous years of the 2008 and 2009 recession. IBIS World listed this industry as a growth industry with 5% annual revenue growth expected through 2019. Although a very competitive industry, profit margins are typically high (between 10–12% Net Income/Revenues) because of the constant product innovations resulting in product differential as well as high advertising expenses to build brands and command premium prices.

The industry is considered a volatile industry with revenue swings based on consumer confidence. Swings in revenue also produce profitability swings because of the large fixed expenses that must be paid irrespective of revenue levels. Profitability is also majorly affected by petroleum price swings because petroleum-based raw materials are major ingredients of most cosmetic prices. To reduce the impact of these variables, the major companies offer lower-priced staple product lines (standard shampoos, bath soaps, fragrances, etc.) to balance the revenue swings of premium product lines.

For local companies planning to become regional and national, the industry is more volatile than for the major players and a bit more precarious because profit margins are not as high. The majority of these companies (approximately 1950 companies in 2014) follow niche strategies focusing on one portion of the market and having a focused Customer Value Proposition (CVP), a product attribute that makes their offering unique.

For BRI, the products were organic and compatible with sensitive skin. Furthermore, although Molly's products tended towards the premium range, her selling prices to retail stores were lower than those of her competitors, thus allowing the retailers to make better margins on her products. For example, one of her major competitor's bath salts sold for $8 per package and Molly knew the store paid $4. The product margin was $4/$8 or 50%. In contrast, Molly's bath salts sold for $7 per package and the store would pay in the neighborhood of $3.25. The product margin on Molly's bath salts would be $3.75/$7.00 or approximately 54%. Plus, Molly knew her products were better and had more appeal to the typical Whole Foods Market customer because they were organic.

The Current Year: 2014

As Molly's 2013 results indicate (Exhibit C3.1), BRI continued to perform well for a newer company. She was still not operating cash flow positive (in fact her negative OCF was a bigger negative than in 2012) and she knew she had to improve her earnings before tax (EBT) to keep progressing towards profitability and the ability to internally finance her growth. In 2014, she was positive she would expand into five more Whole Foods stores in an adjacent region and by the Q4 she thought she could launch a website that would allow online orders from individuals as well as boutique stores and she had appointments with two other food retailers in her region. Both retailers had multiple stores in multiple regions. Molly thought 2014 could be a year of rapid growth. She had slowed growth in 2013 but now with better marketing systems in place and the purchase of new

---

[3] The **Universal Product Code (UPC)** is a barcode symbology (i.e., a specific type of barcode) that is widely used in the United States, Canada, the United Kingdom, Australia, New Zealand and in other countries for tracking trade items in stores.

production equipment, Molly thought should could achieve at least a 30% growth in sales. With continuous improvement in her product margins and her new sales processes, these actions should result in positive earnings before interest and taxes (EBIT) and hopefully a positive operating cash flow. The later result was critical because she needed to emerge from her cash burn period in order to stop seeking new investors and loans.

The transactions below are the result of Molly's planning and hard work.

Required:
Using the financial data given in Exhibit C3.1, the 2014 transactions below, and the BSE format (Exhibit C3.2 or spreadsheet provided) enter the transactions and generate the income statement, balance sheet, and statement of cash flows for BRI.

Transactions for 2014

1. Achieved sales of $590,000, an approximate growth rate of 42%. This excellent growth rate reflected the increase in number of stores and the additional SKUs ordered by Whole Foods during 2014. All of these sales were on account (accounts receivable) and all but $45,000 was collected during 2014. The average collection period was approximately 35–40 days. Note this transaction may be completed with one or two entries.

2. Inventory of raw materials were purchased for $250,000 all of which was on credit (accounts payable). By the end of 2014 all but $52,000 had been paid to BRI's suppliers. Note this transaction may be completed with one or two entries.

3. All of beginning accounts receivable (AR) was collected during 2014.

4. All of beginning accounts payable (AP) was paid within the credit terms during 2014.

5. Cost of goods sold (COGS) for 2014 amounted to $400,000. This consisted of $240,000 in materials and the remaining $160,000 which consisted of direct labor; packaging and manufacturing overhead was paid in cash.

6. Selling and marketing expense (S&M) was $82,000. As planned, this was a small increase over 2013 because Molly was determined to be more efficient and effective with her and her sales peoples' time. Her new marketing strategies worked as sales increased 40% while expenses increased less than 20%. All S&M expenses were paid in cash.

7. General and administrative expense (G&A) was $98,000 and was paid in cash.

8. Depreciation expense on equipment for the year was $5,000. The substantial increase in depreciation expense was due to the major equipment purchase in 2014.

9. Financing expenses which included credit card charges and interest as well as interest on the long-term loans was $13,000 and paid in cash.

10. To purchase the new equipment, Molly obtained a Small Business Administration backed loan for $20,000.

11. Molly paid cash for equipment costing $26,000.

EXHIBIT C3.1	BRI Financial Results for 2013

Balance Sheet, Income Statement, & Statement of Cash Flows

Balance Sheet	12/31/2013		12/31/2013
Assets		Liabilities	
Current		Current	
Cash..........................	$ 18,000	Accounts payable..............	$ 30,000
Accounts receivable..............	40,000	Payroll tax payable.............	3,000
Inventory.....................	60,000	CC Debt	30,000
Other	2,000	Other........................	—
Total current...................	$120,000	Total current..................	$ 63,000
Long-term		Long-term	
Equipment...................	24,000	Loans payable	50,000
Less: Accumulated depreciations .	(11,000)		
Net equipment	$ 13,000	Total liabilities.................	$113,000
Total assets	$133,000	Owners' equity	
		Owners' contributions.........	$162,000
		Retained ernings.............	(142,000)
		Total owners' equity...........	20,000
		Total liabilities & owners' equity...	$133,000

Income Statement		Year Ending 2013
Sales...	$ 415,000	
Cost of goods sold.....................................	$(310,000)	
Gross profit...		$ 105,000
Operating expenses		
Selling & marketing.....................................	$ (72,000)	
General & administrative	$ (66,000)	
Depreciation..	$ (2,000)	
Total operating expenses................................		$(140,000)
Operating income......................................		$ (35,000)
Financing		$ $(9,000)
Earning before tax		$ (44,000)
Tax expense..		—
Net income...		$ (44,000)

Continued

Statement of Cash Flows	Year ending 2013
Operating activities	
Customer collections	$ 405,000
Suppliers payments	$(185,000)
COGS—labor & packaging	$(130,000)
S&M	$ (72,000)
G&A	$ (66,000)
Financing	$ (9,000)
Net operating cash flow	$ (57,000)
Investing activities	—
Financing activities.	
Paid CC debt	$ (10,000)
Loan	$ 20,000
Issue common stock	$ 50,000
Total financing	$ 60,000
Change in cash.	$ 3,000
Beginning cash.	$ 15,000
Ending cash	$ 18,000

EXHIBIT C3.2 — BRI2014 BSE Format

BRI 2014

Transactions	Assets						Liabilities				Owner's Equity	
	Cash	Accounts Receivable	Inventory	Other	Equipment	Accumulated Depreciation	Accounts Payable	Payroll Tax Payable	Credit Card Desk	Long-term Loans	Owners' Contributions	Retained Earnings
Beg Balances...........	$ 18,000	$ 40,000	$ 60,000	$ 2,000	$ 24,000	$(11,000)	$ 30,000	$ 3,000	$30,000	$ 50,000	$ 162,000	$ (142,000)
1) Sales.................												
2) Inventory.............												
3) Collect AR............												
4) Pay AP												
5) COGS................												
6) S&M expense.........												
7) G&A expense												
8) Depreciation.........												
9) Financing												
10) External Financing ...												
1) Paid CC Debt........												
End Balances...........												

Financial Statement Analysis and the Board Meeting
Body Restorations Inc. (BRI) Case Series

LEARNING OBJECTIVES

When you complete this case you should be able to:

1. Understand, use, and discuss the DuPont model for ratio analysis.
2. Complete an in-depth analysis of margins.
3. Link management actions to margins and ratio improvement.
4. Complete an in-depth analysis of asset management.
5. Link management actions to ratio and asset management improvement.
6. Understand and discuss financial leverage and its impact on the return to owners.
7. Understand, calculate, and discuss liquidity ratios including net operating cash cycle.

INTRODUCTION

Molly was both exhilarated and exhausted. As long as she could remember, she had been into cosmetology. Perhaps it was her sensitive skin (growing up she seemed allergic to many compounds); perhaps it was the glow of the glamorous models she read about; or perhaps she saw an opportunity. After graduating from Cosmetology School while attending high school and completing her undergraduate college degree in marketing, Molly went straight into the cosmetics industry. She worked at a major high-end department store selling cosmetics, and then for L'Oreal, one of the major competitors in the industry. During this time, she had been mixing her own compounds for bath and body lotion products and selling them at craft shows, weekend farmer's markets, and holiday events. She was constantly scrambling, juggling her time between a full-time job and being an entrepreneur. She decided to quit her full-time job, became a consultant in packaging design and marketing, and with the increased flexibility in her schedule devoted more concentrated time to launch her own venture Body Restorations Inc. (BRI).

After about six months of this arrangement and while shopping in Whole Foods Market (a high-end, U.S. food retailer), Molly heard two customers discussing soap ingredients and their allergies to many of the compounds used in soaps. As they were trying to deduce the ingredients from very confusing labels, Molly offered her advice and spent about ten minutes educating these two women on products. As the women left and Molly returned to her shopping she felt a gentle tap on her shoulder. It was a buyer for the bath and body products section of the store, who had overheard the conversations and wanted to talk with Molly about her products. After their meeting, the buyer agreed to try three of Molly's products (6 variations each), in 5 stores within the region. The buyer also required Molly to obtain a $1MM product liability insurance policy and to purchase a UPC

master code.[4] As Molly left the meeting she thought "I hope we have the money to be able to deliver the products I just promised!"

In 2011 revenues had tripled to $150,000. Molly secured additional equity funding from friends plus a small loan from a regional bank and more than doubled revenues in 2012 to $345,000. The 2012 financial results are presented in Exhibit C2.1. Note for 2012, operating cash flow was ($24,000); slightly worse than the negative earnings before tax ($22,500) due to the cash tied up in accounts receivable and the growth of inventory.

The Industry

The Cosmetics and Beauty Manufacturing Industry (NAICS code 32562) is dominated by four major players (L'Oreal, Procter & Gamble Co., Estee Lauder, Inc., and Unilever, USA). However, there were approximately 1,600 companies in 2010 when Molly agreed to sell products to Whole Foods Market and the industry was just emerging from the disastrous years of the 2008 and 2009 recession. IBIS World listed this industry as a growth industry with 5% annual revenue growth expected through 2019. Although a very competitive industry, net profit margins (Net Income/Revenues) are typically high (between 10–12%) because of the constant product innovations resulting in product differential as well as the increasing demand for skin products and the ability to command premium prices.

The industry is also considered a volatile industry with revenue swings based on consumer confidence. Swings in revenue also produce swings in profitability, because of the large fixed expenses that must be paid irrespective of revenue levels. Profitability is also majorly affected by petroleum price swings because petroleum-based raw materials are major ingredients of most cosmetic products. To reduce the impact of these variables, the major companies offer lower-priced staple product lines (standard shampoos, bath soaps, fragrances, etc.) to balance the revenue swings of premium product lines.

For local companies planning to become regional and national, the industry is more volatile than for the major players and a bit more precarious because profit margins are not as high. The majority of these companies (approximately 1,950 companies in 2014) follow niche strategies focusing on one portion of the market and having a focused Customer Value Proposition (CVP), a product attribute that makes their offering unique.

For BRI, the products were organic and compatible with sensitive skin. Furthermore, although Molly's products tended towards the premium range, her selling prices to retail stores were lower than those of her competitors, thus allowing the retailers to make better margins on her products. For example, one of her major competitor's bath salts sold for $8 per package and Molly knew the store paid $4. The product margin was $4/$8 or 50%. In contrast, Molly's bath salts sold for $7 per package and the store would pay in the neighborhood of $3.25. The product margin on Molly's bath salts would be $3.75/$7.00 or approximately 54%. Plus, Molly knew her products were better and had more appeal to the typical Whole Foods Market customer because they were organic.

Years after Launch

In 2011 revenues had tripled to $150,000. Molly secured additional equity funding from friends and a small loan from a regional bank and more than doubled revenues in 2012 to $345,000. However, operating income continued to be negative at ($13,500), earnings before taxes (EBT) was ($22,500) and operating cash flow was also negative—($20,500).

As Molly's 2013 results indicate (Exhibit C3.1), BRI continued to perform well for a newer company. She was still not operating cash flow positive (in fact her negative OCF was a bigger negative than in 2012) and she knew she had to improve her earnings before tax (EBT) to keep progressing towards profitability and the ability to internally finance her growth. In 2014, she was positive she would expand into five more Whole Foods

---

[4] The **Universal Product Code** (**UPC**) is a barcode symbology (i.e., a specific type of barcode) that is widely used in the United States, Canada, the United Kingdom, Australia, New Zealand and in other countries for tracking trade items in stores.

stores in an adjacent region and by the Q4 she thought she could launch a website that would allow online orders from individuals as well as boutique stores and she had appointments with two other food retailers in her region. Both retailers had multiple stores in multiple regions.

The year 2014 was a good year. With better marketing systems in place and the purchase of new production equipment, operations were smoother and she thought she was poised for continuing growth. With continuous improvement in her product margins and her new sales processes, these actions helped push operating earnings and earnings before interest and taxes (EBIT) positive and she was very near to having a positive operating cash flow.

In Exhibit C4.1 are the financial statements from 2012, 2013, and 2014. She only had formal statements of cash flows for 2013 and 2014 after she finally got her accounting system in reasonable shape. Also provided in this exhibit are the common-sized income statements and balance sheets for these three years.

The Board of Advisors Meeting

At the end of every quarter, Molly held Board of Advisors meetings. For three quarters these were conference calls but at the end of the fiscal year, once her results were finalized, Molly would send her advisors a set of comparative financial statements and they would meet in person to discuss results and react to Molly's priorities for the upcoming year in detail and for the next 3–5 years from a strategic overview perspective. The meeting was typically 90 minutes and they would all adjourn for dinner, Molly's only payment to her Board of Advisors. As stated previously, Exhibit C4.1 is the financial statements Molly intended to distribute to her advisors. Exhibit C4.2 is a comparative analysis of selected ratios. Exhibit C4.3 is selected industry data for private companies in the Toilet Preparations Industry collected and published by Sage Works (NAICS 325620).

Required:

Molly would like your help to prepare for her board meeting. She has asked you to analyze the data in the exhibits and prepare questions you expect the board would ask. She emphasized the board always asked questions based on data therefore each question you formulate should state the data, percentage or ratio or trend on which the question is based. Finally, Molly remembered the board typically collected their questions around operations using the DuPont model and various margins and turnovers; liquidity and cash flows; and capital structure. She asked you to use these categories to collect your questions.

EXHIBIT C4.1	BRI Income Statements: 2012, 2013, 2014								
Income Statement	2011	2012	2013	2014	Income Statement	2011	2012	2013	2014
Sales...................	$150,000	$ 345,000	$ 415,000	$ 590,000	Sales...................		100.0%	100.0%	100.0%
Cost of goods sold.........		(260,000)	(310,000)	(400,000)	Cost of goods sold.........		(75.4%)	(74.7%)	(67.8%)
Gross profit..............		$ 85,000	$ 105,000	$ 190,000	Gross profit..............		24.6%	25.3%	32.2%
Operating expenses........					Operating expenses........				
Selling & marketing........		(55,000)	(72,000)	(82,000)	Selling & marketing........		(15.9%)	(17.3%)	(13.9%)
General & administrative		(41,500)	(66,000)	(98,000)	General & administrative		(12.0%)	(15.9%)	(16.6%)
Depreciation..............		(2,000)	(2,000)	(5,000)	Depreciation..............		(0.6%)	(0.5%)	(0.8%)
Total operating expenses....		$ (98,500)	$(140,000)	$(185,000)	Total operating expenses....		(28.6%)	(33.7%)	(31.4%)
Operating income.........		$ (13,500)	$ (35,000)	$ 5,000	Operating income.........		(3.9%)	(8.4%)	0.8%
Financing		(9,000)	(9,000)	(13,000)	Financing		(2.6%)	(2.2%)	(2.2%)
Earnings before tax		$ (22,500)	$ (44,000)	$ (8,000)	Earnings before tax		(6.5%)	(10.6%)	(1.4%)
Tax expense..............		—	—	—	Tax expense..............		0.0%	(0.0%)	0.0%
Net income..............		$ (22,500)	$ (44,000)	$ (8,000)	Net income..............		(6.5%)	(10.6%)	(1.4%)

BRI Balance Sheets: 2012, 2013, 2014									
Balance Sheet	2011	2012	2013	2014	Balance Sheet	2011	2012	2013	2014
Assets					Assets				
Current					Current				
Cash		$ 15,000	$ 18,000	$ 16,000	Cash		13.4%	13.5%	9.6%
Accounts receivable		30,000	40,000	45,000	Accounts receivable		26.8%	30.1%	26.9%
Inventory		50,000	60,000	70,000	Inventory		44.6%	45.1%	41.9%
Other		2,000	2,000	2,000	Other		1.8%	1.5%	1.2%
Total current		$ 97,000	$120,000	$133,000	Total current		86.6%	90.2%	79.6%
Long-term					Long-term				
Equipment		24,000	24,000	$ 50,000	Equipment		21.4%	18.0%	29.9%
Less: Accumulated depreciations		(9,000)	(11,000)	(16,000)	Less: Accumulated depreciations		(8.0%)	(8.3%)	(9.6%)
Net equipment		15,000	13,000	34,000	Net equipment		13.4%	9.8%	20.4%
Total assets		$ 1,120	$133,000	$167,000	Total assets		100.0%	100.0%	100.0%
Liabilities					Liabilities				
Current					Current				
Accounts payable		$ 25,000	$ 30,000	$ 52,000	Accounts payable		22.3%	22.6%	31.1%
Payroll tax payable		3,000	3,000	3,000	Payroll tax payable		2.7%	2.3%	1.8%
CC Debt		40,000	30,000	30,000	CC Debt		35.7%	22.6%	18.0%
Other		—	—	—	Other		0.0%	0.0%	0.0%
Total current		68,000	63,000	85,000	Total current		60.7%	47.4%	50.9%
Long-term					Long-term		0.0%	0.0%	0.0%
Loans payable		30,000	50,000	70,000	Loans payable		26.8%	37.6%	41.9%
Total liabilities		98,000	113,000	155,000	Total liabilities		87.5%	85.0%	92.8%
Owners' equity					Owners' equity				
Owners' contributions		112,000	162,000	162,000	Owners' contributions		100.0%	121.8%	97.0%
Retained earnings		(98,000)	(142,000)	(150,000)	Retained earnings		(87.5%)	(106.8%)	(89.8%)
Total owners' equity		14,000	20,000	12,000	Total owners' equity		12.5%	15.0%	7.2%
Total liabilities and owners' equity		$112,000	$133,000	$167,000	Total liabilities and owners' equity		100.0%	100.0%	100.0%

BRI Statement of Cash Flows: 2013, 2014		
Statement of Cash Flows	2013	2014
Operating activities		
Net income	$(44,000)	$ (8,000)
Depreciation expense	2,000	5,000
AR change	(10,000)	(5,000)
Inventory change	(10,000)	(10,000)
Other CA	—	—
AP change	5,000	22,000
Payroll tax payable change	—	—
Operating cash flows	$(57,000)	$ 4,000
Investing		
Equipment change	—	$(26,000)
Investing cash flows		$(26,000)
Financing activities		
CC Debt change	$(10,000)	$ —
Long-term debt change	20,000	20,000
Owners' contributions	50,000	—
Financing activities cash flows	60,000	20,000
Change in cash	3,000	(2,000)
Beginning cash balance	15,000	18,000
Ending cash balance	$ 18,000	$16,000

EXHIBIT C4.2	BRI Selected Ratio Analysis DuPont Model		
BRI DuPont Model with Net Income	**2012**	**2013**	**2014**
Profit margin............................	(6.5%))	(10.6%)	(1.4%)
Asset turns..............................	3.1%	3.1%	3.5%
ROA.....................................	(0.20%)	(0.33%)	(0.05%)
FinLev...................................	8.0%	6.7%	13.9%
ROE.....................................	(161%)	(220%)	(67%)
DuPont Model with EBITDA	**2012**	**2013**	**2014**
EBITDA margin...........................	(3.3%)	(8.0%)	(1.7%)
Asset turns..............................	3.1%	3.1%	3.5%
ROA.....................................	(10.3%)	(24.8%)	(6.0%)
Fin Lev..................................	8.0%	6.7%	13.9%
ROE.....................................	(82.1%)	(165.0%)	83.3%

BRI Margin Analysis			
Margin Analysis	**2012**	**2013**	**2014**
Gross margin............................	24.6%	25.3%	32.2%
Operating margin........................	(3.9%)	(8.4%)	0.8%
Profit margin............................	(6.5%)	(10.6%)	(1.4%)
EBITDA margin...........................	(3.3%)	(8.0%)	1.7%

BRI Turnover and Days Outstanding			
Turnover Analysis	**2012**	**2013**	**2014**
Accounts receivable......................	11.5	10.4	13.1
AR DO	31.7	35.2	27.8
Inventory................................	5.2	5.2	5.7
Inventory DOH	70.2	70.6	63.9
Fixed asset.............................	23.0	31.9	17.4
Accounts payable........................	10.4	10.3	7.7
APDO	35.1	35.3	47.5

BRI Liquidity and Cash Flows			
Liquidity and Cash Flow	**2012**	**2013**	**2014**
Current ratio............................	1.43	1.90	1.56
Acid test ratio...........................	0.69	0.95	0.74
Net cash cyce...........................	66.8	70.5	44.3

BRI Capital Structure			
Leverage	**2012**	**2013**	**2014**
Debt/Equity.............................	5.0	4.0	8.3
TIE	(1.50)	(3.89)	0.38

EXHIBIT C4.3	Sage Works Data for the Toiletries Production Industry

Sage Works Industry Data

Industry:	325620—Toilet Preparation Manufacturing
Sales Range:	All Sales Ranges
Data Source:	Private Companies
Location:	All Areas
Prepared On:	5/9/2014

Industry Financial Data and Ratios
Average by Year (Number of Financial Statements)

Financial Metric	Last 12 Months (6)	2013 (11)	2012 (19)	Last 5 Years (99)	All Years (160)
Current ratio	2.66	2.94	3.38	3.67	3.20
Quick ratio	1.49	2.14	1.56	2.56	2.09
Gross profit margin	46.73%	55.66%	42.31%	46.97%	48.67%
Net profit margin	5.64%	(8.57%)	5.51%	(0.75%)	(0.45%)
Inventory days	109.56	99.56	148.49	156.41	152.86
Accounts receivable days	58.20	55.11	47.48	43.50	43.66
Accounts payable days	38.24	35.74	47.52	44.88	57.95
Interest coverage ratio	18.39	18.39	15.81	15.50	13.24
Debt-to-equity ratio	0.77	0.59	1.47	1.65	2.01
Debt service coverage ratio	6.70	6.70	8.42	5.35	5.15
Return on equity	40.62%	22.89%	24.54%	23.20%	22.36%
Return on assets	27.87%	14.63%	13.17%	7.03%	5.86%
Fixed asset turnover	18.71	20.22	10.70	13.86	12.34
Profit per employee	$29,402	$29,402	$7,185	$8,492	$8,461

Growth Metric	Last 12 Months (6)	2013 (10)	2012 (18)	Last 5 Years (75)	All Years (113)
Sales growth	16.92%	10.94%	19.10%	12.53%	11.67%
Profit growth	32.82%	60.37%	25.86%	24.29%	16.74%

Industry-Specific Metrics	Last 12 Months	2013	2012	Last 5 Years	All Years
Direct labor ratio	12%	12%	11.60%	11.80%	11.30%
	(4)	(4)	(9)	(33)	(36)
Manufacturing overhead to sales	N/A	N/A	10.80%	10.40%	11.30%
			(5)	(17)	(19)
Direct materials to sales	39.20%	39.20%	43.90%	44.80%	44.30%
	(4)	(4)	(8)	(36)	(37)

EXHIBIT C4.3	Sage Works Data for the Toiletries Production Industry (Continued)

Industry Data Common Size
Average by Year (Number of Financial Statements)

Income Statement	Last 12 Months (6)	2013 (11)	2012 (19)	Last 5 Years (99)	All Years (160)
Sales (income)	100%	100%	100%	100%	100%
Cost of sales (COGS)	53.27%	44.34%	58.93%	53.03%	51.33%
Direct labor.	12%	12%	11.60%	11.80%	11.30%
Manufacturing overhead	N/A	N/A	10.80%	10.40%	11.30%
Gross profit.	46.73%	55.66%	42.31%	46.97%	48.67%
Depreciation.	0.53%	0.42%	0.99%	0.75%	1.10%
Overhead or S, G, & A expenses	24.37%	24.37%	31.13%	44.14%	45.32%
Payroll.	8.12%	8.12%	9.78%	28.46%	26.50%
Rent	4.19%	3.27%	2.92%	3.28%	2.99%
Advertising	2.10%	1.61%	4%	6.25%	6.54%
Other operating income	0%	0%	0%	0%	0%
Other operating expenses	0%	0.45%	1.11%	2.03%	1.54%
Operating profit	20.48%	35.49%	5.56%	0.04%	0.70%
Interest expense.	0.30%	0.16%	0.30%	0.91%	1.26%
Other income	0.13%	0.08%	0.04%	0.17%	0.16%
Other expenses	0%	0.07%	0.07%	0.05%	0.05%
Net profit before taxes	5.11%	(8.86%)	5.36%	(0.75%)	(0.45%)
Adjusted net profit before taxes.	5.64%	(8.57%)	5.51%	(0.75%)	(0.45%)
EBITDA.	5.94%	(8.26%)	6.68%	0.91%	1.91%
Taxes paid	0.05%	0.02%	0%	0.07%	0.06%
Net income.	5.07%	(8.88%)	5.30%	(0.81%)	(0.51%)

Balance Sheet	Last 12 Months (6)	2013 (11)	2012 (19)	Last 5 Years (99)	All Years (160)
Cash (bank funds)	9.56%	16.16%	9.21%	10.41%	8.39%
Accounts receivable.	38.70%	37.99%	26%	23.81%	23%
Inventory.	43.59%	40.82%	41.72%	39.08%	37.18%
Other current assets.	6.04%	4.35%	4.41%	3.81%	3.42%
Total current assets	86.96%	84.01%	81.69%	79.36%	76.55%
Gross fixed assets	17.54%	31.61%	32.89%	30.98%	33.67%
Accumulated depreciation	9.56%	10.56%	20.93%	17.34%	16.81%
Net fixed assets	11.51%	15.23%	15.09%	13.64%	16.86%
Other assets.	14.09%	33.69%	5.19%	7%	6.59%
Total assets	100%	100%	100%	100%	100%
Accounts payable.	13.61%	12.05%	14.02%	11.98%	15.26%
Notes payable/current portion of long-term debt	1.58%	1.05%	1.63%	1.10%	1.15%
Other current liabilities	4%	2.90%	4.62%	7.59%	9.12%
Total current liabilities	34.75%	23.68%	34.31%	35.66%	40.87%
Total long-term liabilities	3.08%	4.59%	15.02%	18.03%	18.89%
Total liabilities.	45.90%	49.27%	48.18%	53.68%	59.76%
Preferred stock.	0%	0%	0%	0%	0%
Common stock.	0.01%	0%	0.23%	0.47%	0.89%
Additional paid-in capital	0.52%	0.29%	0.69%	0.32%	0.31%
Other stock/equity	0%	0%	2.01%	1.15%	1.23%
Ending retained earnings	53.67%	29.09%	29.89%	20.72%	15.68%
Total equity.	67.79%	73.79%	53.87%	46.32%	40.24%
Total liabilities and equity.	100%	100%	100%	100%	100%

Forecasts
Body Restorations Inc. (BRI) Case Series

LEARNING OBJECTIVES

When you complete this case you should be able to:

1. Understand the key assumptions needed to build a financial projection.

2. Link forecast assumptions to an underlying strategy and business model.

3. Use the projection model to estimate funding needs and to begin understanding financing alternatives.

4. Consider the impact of uncertainty through sensitivity and scenario analysis.

INTRODUCTION

Molly was both exhilarated and exhausted. As long as she could remember, she had been into cosmetology. Perhaps it was her sensitive skin (growing up she seemed allergic to many compounds); perhaps it was the glow of the glamorous models she read about; or perhaps she saw an opportunity. After graduating from Cosmetology School while attending high school and completing her undergraduate college degree in marketing, Molly went straight into the cosmetics industry. She worked at a major high-end department store selling cosmetics, and then for L'Oreal, one of the major competitors in the industry. During this time, she had been mixing her own compounds for bath and body lotion products and selling them at craft shows, weekend farmer's markets, and holiday events. She was constantly scrambling, juggling her time between a full-time job and being an entrepreneur. She decided to quit her full-time job, became a consultant in packaging design and marketing, and with the increased flexibility in her schedule devoted more concentrated time to launch her own venture Body Restorations Inc. (BRI).

After about six months of this arrangement and while shopping in Whole Foods Market (a high-end, U.S. food retailer), Molly heard two customers discussing soap ingredients and their allergies to many of the compounds used in soaps. As they were trying to deduce the ingredients from very confusing labels, Molly offered her advice and spent about ten minutes educating these two women on products. As the women left and Molly returned to her shopping she felt a gentle tap on her shoulder. It was a buyer for the bath and body products section of the store, who had overheard the conversations and wanted to talk with Molly about her products. After their meeting, the buyer agreed to try three of Molly's products (6 variations each), in 5 stores within the region. The buyer also required Molly to obtain a $1MM product liability insurance policy and to purchase a UPC

master code.[5] As Molly left the meeting she thought "I hope we have the money to be able to deliver the products I just promised!"

In 2011 revenues had tripled to $150,000. Molly secured additional equity funding from friends plus a small loan from a regional bank and more than doubled revenues in 2012 to $345,000. The 2012 financial results are presented in Exhibit C2.1. Note for 2012, operating cash flow was ($24,000); slightly worse than the negative earnings before tax ($22,500) due to the cash tied up in accounts receivable and the growth of inventory.

The Industry

The Cosmetics and Beauty Manufacturing Industry (NAICS code 32562) is dominated by four major players (L'Oreal, Procter & Gamble Co., Estee Lauder, Inc., and Unilever, USA). However, there were approximately 1,600 companies in 2010 when Molly agreed to sell products to Whole Foods Market and the industry was just emerging from the disastrous years of the 2008 and 2009 recession. IBIS World listed this industry as a growth industry with 5% annual revenue growth expected through 2019. Although a very competitive industry, net profit margins (Net Income/Revenues) are typically high (between 10–12%) because of the constant product innovations resulting in product differential as well as the increasing demand for skin products and the ability to command premium prices.

The industry is also considered a volatile industry with revenue swings based on consumer confidence. Swings in revenue also produce swings in profitability, because of the large fixed expenses that must be paid irrespective of revenue levels. Profitability is also majorly affected by petroleum price swings because petroleum-based raw materials are major ingredients of most cosmetic products. To reduce the impact of these variables, the major companies offer lower-priced staple product lines (standard shampoos, bath soaps, fragrances, etc.) to balance the revenue swings of premium product lines.

For local companies planning to become regional and national, the industry is more volatile than for the major players and a bit more precarious because profit margins are not as high. The majority of these companies (approximately 1,950 companies in 2014) follow niche strategies focusing on one portion of the market and having a focused Customer Value Proposition (CVP), a product attribute that makes their offering unique.

For BRI, the products were organic and compatible with sensitive skin. Furthermore, although Molly's products tended towards the premium range, her selling prices to retail stores were lower than those of her competitors, thus allowing the retailers to make better margins on her products. For example, one of her major competitor's bath salts sold for $8 per package and Molly knew the store paid $4. The product margin was $4/$8 or 50%. In contrast, Molly's bath salts sold for $7 per package and the store would pay in the neighborhood of $3.25. The product margin on Molly's bath salts would be $3.75/$7.00 or approximately 54%. Plus, Molly knew her products were better and had more appeal to the typical Whole Foods Market customer because they were organic.

Years after Launch

In 2011 revenues had tripled to $150,000. Molly secured additional equity funding from friends and a small loan from a regional bank and more than doubled revenues in 2012 to $345,000. However, operating income continued to be negative at ($13,500), earnings after taxes (EBT) was ($22,500), and operating cash flow was also negative—($20,500).

Molly's 2013 results indicate she had a reasonable year for being such a young company (see Exhibit C4.1). She was still not operating cash flow positive (in fact her negative OCF was a bigger negative than in 2012) and she knew she had to improve her earnings before tax (EBT) results but she was hugely positive about her future. She was positive she would expand into five more Whole Foods stores in an adjacent region and by the Q4 she thought she could launch a website that would allow online orders from

[5] The **Universal Product Code (UPC)** is a barcode symbology (i.e., a specific type of barcode) that is widely used in the United States, Canada, the United Kingdom, Australia, New Zealand and in other countries for tracking trade items in stores.

individuals as well as boutique stores. She had appointments with two other food retailers in her region. Both retailers had multiple stores in multiple regions.

The year 2014 was another very good year. With better marketing systems in place and the purchase of new production equipment, operations were smoother and she thought she was poised for continuing growth. With continuous improvement in her product margins and her new sales processes, these actions helped push operating earnings and earnings before interest and taxes (EBIT) positive and she was very near to having a positive operating cash flow.

In Exhibit C5.1 are the financial statements from 2012, 2013, and 2014. She only had formal statements of cash flows for 2013 and 2014 once she finally got her accounting system in reasonable shape. Also included in Exhibit C5.1 are the common-sized income statements and balance sheets. Exhibit C5.2 contains the ratio analysis she presented her Board and Appendix A is the Sage Works industry data. Appendix B contains ratio definitions.

EXHIBIT C5.1 BRI Income Statements: 2012, 2013, 2014

Income Statement	2011	2012	2013	2014	Income Statement	2011	2012	2013	2014
Sales..................	$150,000	$ 345,000	$ 415,000	$ 590,000	Sales..................		100.0%	100.0%	100.0%
Cost of goods sold.........		(260,000)	(310,000)	(400,000)	Cost of goods sold.........		(75.4%)	(74.7%)	(67.8%)
Gross profit..............		$ 85,000	$ 105,000	$ 190,000	Gross profit..............		24.6%	25.3%	32.2%
Operating expenses........					Operating expenses........				
Selling & marketing........		(55,000)	(72,000)	(82,000)	Selling & marketing........		(15.9%)	(17.3%)	(13.9%)
General & administrative		(41,500)	(66,000)	(98,000)	General & administrative		(12.0%)	(15.9%)	(16.6%)
Depreciation..............		(2,000)	(2,000)	(5,000)	Depreciation..............		(0.6%)	(0.5%)	(0.8%)
Total operating expenses....		$ (98,500)	$(140,000)	$(185,000)	Total operating expenses....		(28.6%)	(33.7%)	(31.4%)
Operating income..........		$ (13,500)	$ (35,000)	$ 5,000	Operating income..........		(3.9%)	(8.4%)	0.8%
Financing		(9,000)	(9,000)	(13,000)	Financing		(2.6%)	(2.2%)	(2.2%)
Earnings before tax		$ (22,500)	$ (44,000)	$ (8,000)	Earnings before tax		(6.5%)	(10.6%)	(1.4%)
Tax expense..............		—	—	—	Tax expense..............		0.0%	(0.0%)	0.0%
Net income...............		$ (22,500)	$ (44,000)	$ (8,000)	Net income...............		(6.5%)	(10.6%)	(1.4%)

BRI Balance Sheets: 2012, 2013, 2014									
Balance Sheet	2011	2012	2013	2014	Balance Sheet	2011	2012	2013	2014
Assets					Assets				
Current					Current				
Cash.......................		$ 15,000	$ 18,000	$ 16,000	Cash.......................		13.4%	13.5%	9.6%
Accounts receivable.............		30,000	40,000	45,000	Accounts receivable.............		26.8%	30.1%	26.9%
Inventory......................		50,000	60,000	70,000	Inventory......................		44.6%	45.1%	41.9%
Other........................		2,000	2,000	2,000	Other........................		1.8%	1.5%	1.2%
Total current...................		$ 97,000	$120,000	$133,000	Total current...................		86.6%	90.2%	79.6%
Long-term					Long-term.....................				
Equipment		24,000	24,000	$ 50,000	Equipment		21.4%	18.0%	29.9%
Less: Accumulated depreciations ..		(9,000)	(11,000)	(16,000)	Less: Accumulated depreciations ..		(8.0%)	(8.3%)	(9.6%)
Net equipment		15,000	13,000	34,000	Net equipment		13.4%	9.8%	20.4%
Total assets		$ 1,120	$133,000	$167,000	Total assets		100.0%	100.0%	100.0%
Liabilities					Liabilities				
Current					Current				
Accounts payable...............		$ 25,000	$ 30,000	$ 52,000	Accounts payable...............		22.3%	22.6%	31.1%
Payroll tax payable..............		3,000	3,000	3,000	Payroll tax payable..............		2.7%	2.3%	1.8%
CC Debt		40,000	30,000	30,000	CC Debt		35.7%	22.6%	18.0%
Other........................		—	—	—	Other........................		0.0%	0.0%	0.0%
Total current...................		68,000	63,000	85,000	Total current...................		60.7%	47.4%	50.9%
Long-term					Long-term.....................		0.0%	0.0%	0.0%
Loans payable		30,000	50,000	70,000	Loans payable		26.8%	37.6%	41.9%
Total liabilities.................		98,000	113,000	155,000	Total liabilities.................		87.5%	85.0%	92.8%
Owners' equity					Owners' equity				
Owners' contributions		112,000	162,000	162,000	Owners' contributions		100.0%	121.8%	97.0%
Retained earnings		(98,000)	(142,000)	(150,000)	Retained earnings		(87.5%)	(106.8%)	(89.8%)
Total owners' equity.............		14,000	20,000	12,000	Total owners' equity.............		12.5%	15.0%	7.2%
Total liabilities and owners' equity ..		$112,000	$133,000	$167,000	Total liabilities and owners' equity ..		100.0%	100.0%	100.0%

BRI Statement of Cash Flows: 2013, 2014		
Statement of Cash Flows	2013	2014
Operating activities		
Net income	$(44,000)	$ (8,000)
Depreciation expense	2,000	5,000
AR change	(10,000)	(5,000)
Inventory change	(10,000)	(10,000)
Other CA	—	—
AP change	5,000	22,000
Payroll tax payable change	—	—
Operating cash flows	$(57,000)	$ 4,000
Investing		
Equipment change	—	$(26,000)
Investing cash flows		$(26,000)
Financing activities		
CC debt change	$(10,000)	$ —
Long-term debt change	20,000	20,000
Owners' contributions	50,000	—
Financing activities cash flows	60,000	20,000
Change in cash	3,000	(2,000)
Beginning cash balance	15,000	18,000
Ending cash balance	$ 18,000	$16,000

EXHIBIT C5.2	**BRI Selected Ratio Analysis DuPont Model**		
BRI DuPont Model with Net Income	2012	2013	2014
Profit margin	(6.5%)	(10.6%)	(1.4%)
Asset turns	3.1%	3.1%	3.5%
ROA	(0.20%)	(0.33%)	(0.05%)
FinLev	8.0%	6.7%	13.9%
ROC	(161%)	(220%)	(67%)
DuPont Model with EBITDA	2012	2013	2014
EBITDA margin	(3.3%)	(8.0%)	1.7%
Asset turns	3.1%	3.1%	3.5%
ROA	(10.3%)	(24.8%)	6.0%
Fin Lev	8.0%	6.7%	13.9%
ROE	(82.1%)	(165.0%)	83.3%

BRI Margin Analysis			
Margin Analysis	2012	2013	2014
Gross margin	24.6%	25.3%	32.2%
Operating margin	(3.9%)	(8.4%)	0.8%
Porfit margin	(6.5%)	(10.6%)	(1.4%)
EBITDA margin	(3.3%)	(8.0%)	1.7%

BRI Turnover and Days Outstanding			
Turnover Analysis	**2012**	**2013**	**2014**
Accounts receivable......................	11.5	10.4	13.1
AR DO	31.7	35.2	27.8
Inventory................................	5.2	5.2	5.7
Inventory DOH	70.2	70.6	63.9
Fixed asset..............................	23.0	31.9	17.4
Accounts payable.......................	10.4	10.3	7.7
APDO	35.1	35.3	47.5

BRI Liquidity and Cash Flows			
Liquidity and Cash Flow	**2012**	**2013**	**2014**
Current ratio............................	1.43	1.90	1.56
Acid test ratio..........................	0.69	0.95	0.74
Net cash cycle	66.8	70.5	44.3

BRI Capital Structure			
Leverage	**2012**	**2013**	**2014**
Debt/Equity.............................	5.0	4.0	8.3
TIE	(1.50	(3.89	0.38

The Board of Advisors Meeting

At the end of every quarter, Molly held Board of Advisors meetings. For three quarters these were conference calls but at the end of the fiscal year, once her results were finalized, Molly would send her advisors a set of comparative financial statements and they would meet in person to discuss results and react to Molly's priorities for the upcoming year in detail and for the next 3–5 years from a strategic overview perspective. The meeting was typically 90 minutes and they would all adjourn for dinner, Molly's only payment to her Board of Advisors.

At the beginning of 2015, Molly had her advisors meeting, which was a bit more contentious than she had expected. While they applauded Molly's revenue growth, they were concerned about her pace to achieve profitability and positive operating cash flows. She thought it might be best to reflect on the major topics of the meeting and summarize in writing the challenges (opportunities for improvement) and her responses/solutions to improve her operations and the operating income as well as operating cash flow.

Challenge 1: Product Pricing
The board had challenged her lower price points and better product quality compared to her competitors. Now that she was established in WFMI they thought WFMI should be able to price closer to her competitors and thus BRI could raise its prices to WFMI. This was critical because their next suggestion was that higher prices be included in her proposal to any new customers as well as be listed on her website for her Internet customers.

Challenge 2: Product Mix 1
Molly's gross margins were below industry averages (see Exhibit C5.3). The advisors suggested she consider better aligning her marketing efforts with her higher margin items thus increasing her overall gross margin.

Challenge 3: Product Mix 2
The board questions if Molly knew her sales of each of her specific products. They thought she should begin consolidating her product lines based on this analysis eliminating slow selling, low-margin products and consider eliminating slow selling, high-margin products if her solutions to Challenge 2: Product Mix 1 were unsuccessful. Of course she had to have some sense of which products would best sell on the Internet in order to eliminate the real dogs in her product line.

Challenge 4: Product Costs
Molly was commended for her continuous improvement of production costs/unit but the board thought she could do better. They recommended she hire a production design consultant to improve her production process and save on her direct labor costs.

Challenge 5: Marketing Strategy
With the explosion of social media and the lure of higher profit margins from Internet sales, the board thought Molly could do more to boost BRI's product recognition and Internet sales. They also thought this effort critical to extend BRI's reach and open up other regions of the country for more distribution channels.

Challenge 6: Inventory Levels
They had grilled her on her inventory levels for her finished goods. They understood she needed to deliver promptly when her major customers needed product but they encouraged her to monitor inventory days on hand more closely to reduce investment in inventories and improve her operating cash flows. They understood this challenge was closely connected to the results of her responses to the first five challenges.

Molly's Analysis and Responses

Challenge 1: Product Pricing
Molly agreed with the board that she should raise her prices. She would raise her prices enough to generate a 4 percentage point increase in gross margin during 2015. She thought WFMI would accept this level of increase and she felt very comfortable using these prices in proposals to new clients and on the Internet. This action will result in COGS/Sales to drop to 64% in 2015 and improve due to her streamlining operations to 63% in 2016, 2017, and 2018, and then to 61% in 2019. She did not think she could wring any more cost improvements from current operations but if she purchased a new building she had been looking at and hired the operations design consultant she was thinking she could drop product costs substantially.

Challenges 2&3: Product Mix 1 and 2
Molly in fact had been tracking margins by major product lines and felt she had gotten rid of the dogs and promoted the stars. She had not been reporting these efforts to the board but will now give them a schedule each meeting to show them the results of her analysis.

Challenge 4: Product Costs
As stated earlier, Molly had thought she had done a fairly good job of improving manufacturing processes and lower costs per unit. She thought she was now up against a space constraint and needed to double her production space. She was all for hiring a consultant which would cost approximately $20,000 and would happen in 2015, Q2. At the same time she would begin exploring buildings around her to better understand leasing and buying options.

Challenge 5: Marketing Strategy
Molly again agreed with her board that she had to ramp-up her Internet presence and sell more online. In an entrepreneurship program sponsored by Goldman Sachs, Molly

had learned a bit about social media but more importantly she made a close friend who was a fellow entrepreneur in the program. This entrepreneur was in the marketing/social media space and for $2,500 per quarter over the next four quarters beginning 2015, Q2 she proposed to upgrade Molly's website, expand and track her social media strategy and make it easier for customers to buy product off her website. The work would be completed by 2016, Q1 and Molly would pay quarterly beginning Q2, 2015. Once the site was renewed, she proposed to Molly a fee of $1,000 per month to refresh the site, execute on the BRI web strategy and track results of these efforts through a monthly analysis of data from Google Analytics. These payments would begin in March, 2016. Molly's friend, based on her other clients' experiences, estimated that over the months beginning in February, Q2, 2016 Molly's Internet sales would reach 20% of her current annual sales and grow similarly to the rate of growth of her store sales. Of course she would likely increase these sales exponentially if she listed her products on Amazon. com but Molly did not think this marketing channel fit her current product image or growth strategy.

Molly tempered her colleague's revenue projections to bring them more in line with her sense of the Internet market for her products. She expected $105,000 of sales in 2016 and then a 50% growth in revenues for the foreseeable future. Perhaps more importantly, Molly estimated, because she did not have to share margins with the retail stores, that her cost of goods sold as a percentage of sales would be 32% in 2016 and improve by 1% per year for the next three years. Finally, Molly expected a 10% increase per year for her Internet-focused marketing beginning at $12,500 in 2016.

Challenge 6: Inventory Levels

Molly was not sure about reducing inventory levels especially as she approached the uncharted waters (for her) of Internet sales. However, prior to this meeting she committed to reducing inventory days on hand to 50 days in 2015 and she was pretty sure that goal could be accomplished.

Additionally, Molly was nearly certain she could continue her 20% increase in same store revenues (in part from her planned price increases) in 2016 as she got the Internet sales going. In 2017, 2018, and 2019 she would increase into one other chain of food retailers in a neighboring state and planned to enter 10 more stores each year in her existing clients which would increase her revenues by an additional 20% per year 2017–2019. Molly was so excited because these estimates did not even consider being carried nationally by WFMI. She had been planting the seeds for this possibility for two years and she could not believe she would not be successful in her efforts by 2018. She thought she might eventually include this growth possibility in a best case scenario but not in her base case.

Based on these assumptions, Molly thought she could now complete her forecasts for the next five years, 2015–2019. She added the following assumptions presented below and asked you as an intern to complete these forecasts by filling in the assumptions. Once the spreadsheet provided the forecasted financial statements, she asked you to complete a DuPont model analysis, review her projected liquidity and net operating cash cycle, and succinctly summarize your thoughts on the base case results.

Additional Assumptions:

Existing Business:

1. Selling and marketing would increase 10% per year.
2. In general and administrative expenses, she would increase her salary by $30,000 in 2015, she would include the one-time fee to the operational consultant in general and administrative expenses in 2015 and these would increase 5% per year for 2016 onward.
3. Accounts receivable collection (days) would be 30, inventory days on hand would be 50, and accounts payable days would be improved to 35.

4. Other assets would stay steady at $3,000.
5. Property, plant and equipment would increase 10% per year and depreciation would approximate $7,500 per year going forward.

Opportunity (Internet):

1. Selling and marketing expense would include the website and systems development of $7,500 in 2015, the final payment of $2,500 plus $1,000 ongoing for 10 months in 2016, and $12,000 per year with 10% growth in 2017 and beyond.
2. Part-time manager of Internet sales is hired in 2016 and this increases to a full-time position in 2019. Salary for 2016–2019 is $12,500, $25,000, $35,000 and $60,000.
3. All Internet sales will be on credit cards; accounts receivable collection days will be 3. Inventory and accounts payable days will be the same as the existing business.
4. Equipment of $20,000 purchased in 2015 will begin being depreciated in 2016 at the rate of $4,000 per year.

Total Business Assumptions:

1. Tax rate will be 25%.
2. Minimum cash balance will be $15,000.
3. Interest rate on all debt will average 8%.
4. Short-term and long-term debt will be as follows:

	2014	2015	2016	2017	2018	2019
Short-term debt	$30,000	$95,408	$60,476	$ 0	$ 0	$0
Long-term debt	$70,000	$55,000	$40,000	$25,000	$10,000	$0

Required:

1. Based on the assumptions above, create a brief description of BRI's growth strategy as well as the strategy for improving existing operations.
2. Given BRI's recent financial performance, which of the above assumptions are most critical to the company's success? Which assumptions are most realistic? Which assumptions have the highest degree of uncertainty? How might BRI reduce this risk?
3. Analyze the base-case forecast (to be distributed). Will BRI need additional funding to implement the strategy? If this forecast is close to accurate, how will BRI as measured by the DuPont model perform in the future?
4. How can BRI incorporate uncertainty in its forecasts?

APPENDIX A: SAGE WORKS DATA FOR THE TOILETRIES PRODUCTION INDUSTRY:

EXHIBIT C5.3	Sage Works Data for the Toiletries Production Industry

Sage Works Industry Data

Industry:	325620—Toilet Preparation Manufacturing
Sales Range:	All Sales Ranges
Data Source:	Private Companies
Location:	All Areas
Prepared On:	5/9/2014

Industry Financial Data and Ratios
Average by Year (Number of Financial Statements)

Financial Metric	Last 12 Months (6)	2013 (11)	2012 (19)	Last 5 Years (99)	All Years (160)
Current ratio	2.66	2.94	3.38	3.67	3.20
Quick ratio	1.49	2.14	1.56	2.56	2.09
Gross profit margin	46.73%	55.66%	42.31%	46.97%	48.67%
Net profit margin	5.64%	(8.57%)	5.51%	(0.75%)	(0.45%)
Inventory days	109.56	99.56	148.49	156.41	152.86
Accounts receivable days	58.20	55.11	47.48	43.50	43.66
Accounts payable days	38.24	35.74	47.52	44.88	57.95
Interest coverage ratio	18.39	18.39	15.81	15.50	13.24
Debt-to-equity ratio	0.77	0.59	1.47	1.65	2.01
Debt service coverage ratio	6.70	6.70	8.42	5.35	5.15
Return on equity	40.62%	22.89%	24.54%	23.20%	22.36%
Return on assets	27.87%	14.63%	13.17%	7.03%	5.86%
Fixed asset turnover	18.71	20.22	10.70	13.86	12.34
Profit per employee	$29,402	$29,402	$7,185	$8,492	$8,461

Growth Metric	Last 12 Months (6)	2013 (10)	2012 (18)	Last 5 Years (75)	All Years (113)
Sales growth	16.92%	10.94%	19.10%	12.53%	11.67%
Profit growth	32.82%	60.37%	25.86%	24.29%	16.74%

Industry-Specific Metrics	Last 12 Months	2013	2012	Last 5 Years	All Years
Direct labor ratio	12%	12%	11.60%	11.80%	11.30%
	(4)	(4)	(9)	(33)	(36)
Manufacturing overhead to sales	N/A	N/A	10.80%	10.40%	11.30%
			(5)	(17)	(19)
Direct materials to sales	39.20%	39.20%	43.90%	44.80%	44.30%
	(4)	(4)	(8)	(36)	(37)

EXHIBIT C5.3	Sage Works Data for the Toiletries Production Industry (Continued)

Industrial Data Common Size
Average by Year (Number of Financial Statements)

Income Statement	Last 12 Months (6)	2013 (11)	2012 (19)	Last 5 Years (99)	All Years (160)
Sales (income)	100%	100%	100%	100%	100%
Cost of sales (COGS)	53.27%	44.34%	58.93%	53.03%	51.33%
Direct labor	12%	12%	11.60%	11.80%	11.30%
Manufacturing overhead	N/A	N/A	10.80%	10.40%	11.30%
Gross profit	46.73%	55.66%	42.31%	46.97%	48.67%
Depreciation	0.53%	0.42%	0.99%	0.75%	1.10%
Overhead or S, G, & A expenses	24.37%	24.37%	31.13%	44.14%	45.32%
Payroll	8.12%	8.12%	9.78%	28.46%	26.50%
Rent	4.19%	3.27%	2.92%	3.28%	2.99%
Advertising	2.10%	1.61%	4%	6.25%	6.54%
Other operating income	0%	0%	0%	0%	0%
Other operating expenses	0%	0.45%	1.11%	2.03%	1.54%
Operating profit	20.48%	35.49%	5.56%	0.04%	0.70%
Interest expense	0.30%	0.16%	0.30%	0.91%	1.26%
Other income	0.13%	0.08%	0.04%	0.17%	0.16%
Other expenses	0%	0.07%	0.07%	0.05%	0.05%
Net profit before taxes	5.11%	(8.86%)	5.36%	(0.75%)	(0.45%)
Adjusted net profit before taxes	5.64%	(8.57%)	5.51%	(0.75%)	(0.45%)
EBITDA	5.94%	(8.26%)	6.68%	0.91%	1.91%
Taxes paid	0.05%	0.02%	0%	0.07%	0.06%
Net income	5.07%	(8.88%)	5.30%	(0.81%)	(0.51%)

Balance Sheet	Last 12 Months (6)	2013 (11)	2012 (19)	Last 5 Years (99)	All Years (160)
Cash (bank funds)	9.56%	16.16%	9.21%	10.41%	8.39%
Accounts receivable	38.70%	37.99%	26%	23.81%	23%
Inventory	43.59%	40.82%	41.72%	39.08%	37.18%
Other current assets	6.04%	4.35%	4.41%	3.81%	3.42%
Total current assets	86.96%	84.01%	81.69%	79.36%	76.55%
Gross fixed assets	17.54%	31.61%	32.89%	30.98%	33.67%
Accumulated depreciation	9.56%	10.56%	20.93%	17.34%	16.81%
Net fixed assets	11.51%	15.23%	15.09%	13.64%	16.86%
Other assets	14.09%	33.69%	5.19%	7%	6.59%
Total assets	100%	100%	100%	100%	100%
Accounts payable	13.61%	12.05%	14.02%	11.98%	15.26%
Notes payable/current portion of long-term debt	1.58%	1.05%	1.63%	1.10%	1.15%
Other current liabilities	4%	2.90%	4.62%	7.59%	9.12%
Total current liabilities	34.75%	23.68%	34.31%	35.66%	40.87%
Total long-term liabilities	3.08%	4.59%	15.02%	18.03%	18.89%
Total liabilities	45.90%	49.27%	48.18%	53.68%	59.76%
Preferred stock	0%	0%	0%	0%	0%
Common stock	0.01%	0%	0.23%	0.47%	0.89%
Additional paid-in capital	0.52%	0.29%	0.69%	0.32%	0.31%
Other stock/equity	0%	0%	2.01%	1.15%	1.23%
Ending retained earnings	53.67%	29.09%	29.89%	20.72%	15.68%
Total equity	67.79%	73.79%	53.87%	46.32%	40.24%
Total liabilities and equity	100%	100%	100%	100%	100%

APPENDIX B: RATIO DEFINITIONS

DuPont Model = Profit Margin × Asset Turnover × Financial Leverage = Return on Owners' Equity

Profitability ratios:

Return on equity	**= Net income/Shareholders' equity**
Return on assets	= Net income/Assets
Return on invested capital	$= \dfrac{\text{Earnings before interest and taxes} \times (1 - \text{Tax rate})}{\text{Interest-bearing debt} + \text{Shareholders' equity}}$
Profit margin	**= Net income/Sales**
Earnings per share (EPS)	= Net income-pfd dividends/Common shares outstanding
Gross margin	= Gross profit/Sales
Operating margin	= Operating profit/Sales
Price to earnings	= Price per share/Earnings per share

Turnover control ratios:

Asset turnover	**= Sales/Assets**
Fixed-asset turnover	= Sales/Net property, plant, and equipment
Inventory turnover	= Cost of goods sold/Ending inventory
Inventory days on hand	= 365 days/Inventory turnover
Accounts receivable turnover	= Sales/Accounts receivable
Collection period	= Accounts receivable/Credit sales per day
	(If credit sales unavailable, use sales.)
Days' sales in cash	= Cash and securities/Sales per day
Payables period	= Accounts payable/Credit purchases per day
	(If purchases unavailable, use cost of goods sold.)

Leverage and liquidity ratios:

Assets to equity	**= Assets/Shareholders' equity**
Debt to assets	= Total liabilities/Assets
	(Interest-bearing debt is often substituted for total liabilities.)
Debt to equity	= Total liabilities/Shareholders' equity
Times interest earned	= Earnings before interest and taxes/Interest expense
Times burden covered	$= \dfrac{\text{Earnings before interest and taxes}}{\text{Interest expense} + \text{Principal payments}/(1 - \text{Tax rate})}$
Debt to assets (market value)	$= \dfrac{\text{Total liabilities}}{\text{No. equity shares} \times \text{Price/Share} + \text{Total liabilities}}$
Debt to equity (market value)	$= \dfrac{\text{Total liabilities}}{\text{No. shares} \times \text{Price per share}}$
Current ratio	= Current assets/Current liabilities
Acid test	$= \dfrac{\text{Current assets} - \text{Inventory}}{\text{Current liabilities}}$

Glossary of Terms

Accounts Payable or Trade Credit (A/P): Obligation created when inventory or supplies are purchased on credit from suppliers. A/P is found on the balance sheet as a current liability.

Accounts Payable Turnover: A short-term liquidity measure used to quantify the rate at which a company pays off its suppliers. Formula: A/P turnover = Cost of goods sold/ Accounts payable. A higher number means the company is paying its suppliers faster.

Accounts Receivable (A/R): Money owed by customers for goods or services that have been received but not yet paid for. Receivables are created when a company sells its products or services on credit. Typically expected to be collected within 12 months, A/R is shown as a current asset on the balance sheet.

Accounts Receivable (A/R) Days Sales Outstanding: is calculated as 365 Days/A/R turnover. Also see accounts receivable (A/R) turnover.

Accounts Receivable (A/R) Turnover: An accounting measure used to quantify a firm's effectiveness in extending credit and collecting from its customers. The A/R turnover ratio is an activity ratio, measuring how quickly a firm's credit customers pay. Formula: A/R turnover = Credit sales/ Accounts receivable. Note: frequently total sales is substituted for credit sales, which may not be available.

Accrual Accounting: A system where revenue is recognized when earned (products are sold or services have been performed) and expenses are recognized when incurred to generate revenues (i.e., the matching concept) during a specific period of time, regardless of when cash transactions occur.

Accrued Expense: Any expense incurred and shown on the income statement, but not paid for with cash. Usually listed as a current liability.

Accrued Liability: An expense incurred but not yet paid. Accrued liabilities can be recorded as either short- or long-term liabilities on a company's balance sheet. Similar to accrued expenses, and the terms are often used interchangeably.

Accumulated Depreciation: The aggregate depreciation of an asset up to a single point in its life. The depreciation expense of an asset during a period is added to the previous periods' accumulated depreciation to get the current accumulated depreciation. An asset's carrying value ("net" or "book" value) on the balance sheet is the difference between its purchase price and accumulated depreciation.

Acid Test Ratio or Quick Ratio: An indicator of a firm's ability to cover short-term liabilities with short-term assets without selling inventory. The acid test ratio is a far more strenuous test of liquidity than the other popular liquidity ratio, the current ratio. Formula: Acid test ratio = (Current assets –Inventory)/Current liabilities.

Asset Turnover: The amount of sales generated for every dollar of assets. It is calculated by: Asset turnover = Sales/ Total assets. Also known as the *asset turnover ratio*. This ratio is one measure of how effectively a firm uses capacity.

Assets: Owned or controlled business resources that have future, quantifiable benefits. The requirement to be reasonably quantifiable in monetary terms means a number of important assets may not be included in a company balance sheet (e.g., its people, brand name or logo, etc.).

Balance Sheet: A financial statement that summarizes a company's assets, liabilities, and owners' investment (owners' equity or net worth) at a specific point in time. These three balance sheet building blocks give investors an idea as to what the company owns and owes, as well as the amount invested by the owners. The balance sheet must follow the following formula:

Assets = Liabilities + Shareholders' equity.

This is known as the accounting or balance sheet equation.

Balance Sheet Equation Format (BSE Format): Assets = Liabilities + Shareholders' equity is used in the text to illustrate the recording of business transactions and the construction of financial statements.

Break-even Point: This is the sales in dollars or units in which sales − expenses = 0; i.e., Operating income is 0. Break-even = Periodic fixed expenses/Contribution margin = # of units needed to be sold to break even; or Break-even = Fixed expenses/(contribution margin/sales) = dollar amount of sales needed to break even.

Cash Flow: The cash that moves in and out of a business. Cash inflows usually arise from one of three activities— operating, investing or financing. Cash outflows result from expenses, investments in assets, and payments to creditors or owners.

Cash Flow from Financing Activities: A category in the cash flow statement that accounts for funding activities with the firm's capital providers. Examples include issuing dividends, borrowing or repaying loans, and the sale or repurchase of equity.

Cash Flow from Investing Activities: An item on the cash flow statement that reports the aggregate change in a company's cash position resulting from investments or the sale of fixed assets, other companies' shares, or intangible assets.

Cash Flow from Operating Activities: An accounting item indicating the cash a company gets from its ongoing, regular business activities. When entrepreneurs talk about "Happiness is a positive cash flow," they should be referring to operating cash flows.

Cash Flow Statement: A financial statement that summarizes information about the cash inflows (receipts) and cash outflows (payments) for a specific period of time. Cash flows are usually categorized as operating, investing, or financing.

Cash Operating Cycle (Cash Conversion Cycle) : = Inventory days on hand + A/R Days outstanding – A/P days. It is a measure of how many days a company is "out cash" from the time it pays for its inventory until it collects cash from its customers. Some businesses (Amazon.com, Dell, for example) have a negative cash operating cycle, which means they collect from their customers *before* they pay their supplier for the product. This is rare.

Common-Size Analysis: A financial statement that displays all items as percentages of a common base figure. Common-size statements allow for easy comparison between companies or across time periods for a given company. For the income statement the base figure is total revenue; for the balance sheet, total assets.

Common-Size Balance Sheet: In the normal balance sheet, account values are expressed in dollar terms. A common-size balance sheet lists each line item as a percentage of total assets. This type of financial statement allows for easy comparison between companies or across time periods for a given company.

Common-Size Income Statement: An income statement with each line item expressed as a percentage of total revenue (sales). A common-size income statement allows for easy comparison between companies or across time periods for a given company.

Common Stock (Common Equity or Common Shares): A security that represents ownership in a corporation. Holders of common stock exercise control by electing a board of directors and voting on corporate policy. In the event of liquidation, common shareholders have residual rights to a company's assets; that is, they are paid only after bondholders, preferred shareholders and other debtholders have been paid in full.

Comparables (Multiples or Relative) Analysis: A method that estimates value based on metrics of similar businesses. Comparables analysis uses the assumption that companies with similar risks and business models will be valued comparably by investors. Common metrics for comparison include revenue, EBITDA, and net income. Also referred to as *comparable company analysis* (CCA).

Convertible Bond: A bond that can be converted into a specified number of common shares, usually at the discretion of the bondholder.

Cost of Goods Sold (COGS) or Cost of Sales: The direct costs attributable to the production or purchase of goods sold by a company (manufacturer or retailer). For a manufacturer, COGS includes the cost of the raw materials used in creating the good along with the direct labor costs and manufacturing overhead incurred in production. It excludes indirect expenses such as distribution costs and salesforce costs. For a retailer, COGS is the wholesale price of the goods purchased for resale. A service company typically has no COGS, but instead uses "cost of services provided," which is primarily salaries.

Current Assets: Those assets that are reasonably expected to be converted into cash or used within one year over the normal course of business. Current assets include cash, accounts receivable, inventory, marketable securities, prepaid expenses, and other liquid assets that can be readily converted to cash.

Current Liabilities: A company's debts or obligations due or payable within one year. Current liabilities appear on the balance sheet and may include short-term debt, accounts payable, accrued liabilities, wages payable, taxes payable, and other short-term debts.

Current Ratio (CR): A liquidity ratio that measures a company's ability to meet short-term obligations. The formula is: Current ratio = Current assets/Current liabilities. A higher current ratio represents more liquidity.

Customer Value Proposition: A succinct summary of why a customer buys a particular product.

Debt Service Coverage (Times Burden Covered): This ratio is a measure of a company's ability to cover the principal and interest payments required by its current debt. Debt service coverage can be calculated in a number of ways: EBIT/(Interest + Principal payments) or EBITDA/(Interest + Principal payments).

Debt-to-Equity (D/E) Ratio: A measure of a company's financial leverage, that is, its use of debt to finance the business. There are many definitions of this ratio. Two common ones are Total liabilities/Stockholders' equity and Total interest-bearing debt/Stockholders' equity. The D/E ratio indicates what proportions of equity and debt are being used to finance the company's assets. A higher number means more leverage.

Depreciation: A method of allocating (expensing) the cost of a tangible fixed asset over its useful life.

Discounted Cash Flow (DCF) Analysis: A valuation method based on forecasted cash flows and their risk. DCF analysis discounts estimated future cash flows using a discount rate that reflects both the riskiness of the cash flows and the choice of debt and equity (most often the weighted-average cost of capital). The result is an estimate of the present value of the company or project that generates the cash flows.

DuPont Formula: A performance measurement that breaks return on equity (ROE) into three components: (1) profitability (net profit margin), (2) asset utilization (total asset turnover), and (3) financial leverage (Assets/Equity).

ROE = Profit margin (Profit/Sales) × Total asset turnover (Sales/Assets) × Financial leverage (Assets/Equity)

The DuPont formula tells us much more about performance than just looking at ROE in isolation.

Earnings Before Interest, Taxes, Depreciation, and Amortization (EBITDA): An indicator of a company's operating performance. EBITDA is frequently used as an approximation of operating cash flows and is popular as a comparables valuation metric.

Earnings Before Tax (EBT) or Pretax Income: An indicator of a company's operating performance calculated as:
EBT = Revenue – Expenses (excluding tax).

EBITDA Margin: A measurement of a company's operating profitability.

EBITDA Margin = EBITDA/Revenues

Because EBITDA excludes depreciation and amortization, the EBITDA margin can provide an investor with a cleaner view of a company's core profitability.

Enterprise Value (EV): A measure of a company's total market value, including debt and equity. Enterprise value is calculated as market capitalization (total stock market value) plus debt, minority interest, and preferred shares, minus "excess" cash.

Financial Leverage: (1) The use of various financial instruments (e.g., liabilities) to increase the potential return of an investment to the owners. (2) The amount of debt used to finance a firm's assets. A firm with significantly more debt than equity is considered to be highly leveraged.

Financial Statements: Records that outline the financial activities of a business, an individual, or any other entity. Financial statements for businesses usually include: income statements, balance sheet, statements of cash flows, as well as footnotes explaining the details of these statements.

Fixed Asset Turnover: The ratio of sales to fixed assets. The fixed-asset-turnover ratio measures a company's ability to generate sales from its fixed assets. A higher fixed-asset-turnover ratio shows that the company has been more effective in using the investment in fixed assets to generate revenues. The fixed-asset-turnover ratio is calculated as: Fixed Assets Turnover = Net sales/Net property, plant, and equipment.

Fixed Assets (also Property, Plant, and Equipment [PP&E]): A long-term tangible asset used in the generation of revenue. Examples include factories, vehicles, machinery, etc.

Fixed Costs: Costs that remain constant regardless of changes in the business' activity level. That is, as sales increase, the expense stays the same (e.g., fixed rent for office space).

Forecasting: A planning tool that helps management in its attempts to cope with the uncertainty of the future, relying mainly on data from the past and analysis of future trends. Forecasting starts with certain assumptions based on management's experience, knowledge, and judgment.

General and Administrative Expenses (G&A): Expenditures related to the day-to-day operations of a business. G&A expenses pertain to operating expenses rather than expenses that can be directly related to the production of any goods or services. General and administrative expenses include rent, utilities, insurance, and managerial salaries.

Gross Margin: The gross margin represents the percent of total sales revenue that the company retains after incurring the direct costs associated with producing the goods and services sold by a company. The higher the percentage, the more the company retains on each dollar of sales to service its operating costs and other obligations (e.g., interest and taxes). Gross margin (%) = (Revenue – Cost of goods sold)/Revenue.

Gross Profit: A company's revenue minus its cost of goods sold. Gross profit is the dollar-based numerator of the gross margin calculation.

Income Statement (Profit and Loss [P&L] Statement or Statement of Operations): A financial statement that measures a company's operating performance, as measured by profitability, over a specific accounting period (usually quarterly or annually). The income statement starts with revenue and then subtracts all expenses from both operating and non-operating activities. What is left is net income, or the "bottom line."

Interest Expense: The cost associated with borrowing money. Interest expense is shown on the income statement below operating profit, but before taxes. Calculated by multiplying the interest rate for a given period times the loan balance outstanding over the period.

Interest Rate: The percentage cost associated with borrowing money. Higher interest rates mean the lender feels there is more risk to the loan.

Inventory: The raw materials, work-in-process, and finished goods that are ready or will be ready for sale. Inventory represents one of the most important assets that most businesses possess, because the turnover of inventory represents one of the primary sources of revenue generation and subsequent earnings for the company's shareholders/owners. Most inventory is classified as a current asset on the balance sheet.

Inventory Days on Hand: Calculated as = 365 Days/Inventory turnover. This number is an important indicator of management's control of inventory and indicates how long an item typically stays on the shelf before it is sold.

Inventory Turnover: How many times a company's inventory is sold and replaced over a given period. It is calculated as: Inventory Turnover = Cost of goods sold/Inventory. This ratio is used to evaluate current assets or working capital management.

Liability: A debt or obligation that arises during the normal course of business operations. Liabilities are settled over time through the transfer of economic benefits, including money, goods, or services.

Line of Credit (LOC): A short-term loan provided to a company by a financial institution, usually a bank. An LOC has a maximum loan balance and often must be paid down to zero sometime during the year. The borrower can draw on the line of credit at any time, as long as it does not exceed the maximum. This arrangement is usually listed as a current liability and may be called, or required to be paid in full, by the bank at any time. LOCs are usually meant to fund cyclical cash needs (e.g., working capital).

Liquidity: A measure of a company's ability to meet its near-term obligations

Long-Term Debt: Loans, bonds, and other financial obligations payable in more than one year.

Net Income (NI) or Net Profit or the "Bottom Line": Net income is calculated by taking revenues and subtracting all expenses. It is found on a company's income statement and is an important measure of how profitable the company is over a period of time. Net income represents the owners' return after all other expenses. At the end of each period, the net income (or loss) is added to retained earnings in the owners' equity section of the balance sheet.

Net Margin (Net Profit Margin): The ratio of net profits to revenues for a company or business segment, typically expressed as a percentage that shows how much of each dollar earned by the business is left over after all expenses. Net margins are calculated as: net profit/revenue.

Operating Expenses: Expenses other than COGS incurred in the normal course of business operations.

Operating Income or Operating Profit: The profit realized after subtracting COGS and total operating expenses from revenue. Calculated as Operating income = Revenue – COGS – Operating expenses.

Operating Margin: A ratio used to assess a company's operating efficiency. Calculated as: Operating margin = Operating income/Sales.

Other Current Assets: A balance sheet item that includes the value of noncash assets (other than inventory or A/R) due within one year.

Other Current Liabilities: A balance sheet item used by companies to group together current liabilities not assigned to common liabilities such as debt obligations or accounts payable.

Owners' Equity (Shareholders' Equity or Stockholders' Equity or Net Worth): A firm's total assets minus its total liabilities. It represents the amount the owners have invested in the business either through direct investment or through the accumulation of net profits (less any dividends taken).

Payables Period (A/P Days): Measures the average time a company takes to pay its suppliers. Calculated as Payables period = 365 Days/Accounts payables turnover.

Payback Period: the amount of time to pay off the original investment in a strategic alternative. If a machine is purchased, it measures the period it will take for the benefits to pay for the cost of machine. Payback period = Original investment/periodic improvement in profitability.

Prepaid Expense: An asset (usually current) that arises when a business makes payments for goods and services to be received in the near future. Although prepaid expenses are initially recorded as assets, their value is expensed over time as the benefit is received on the income statement. An example of a prepaid expense would be paying for a full year of insurance in January.

Profit Margin: A percentage-based profitability measure calculated from the income statement. It can be computed at the gross level (Gross profit/Revenue), the operating level (Operating profit/Revenue) or the net level (Net profit/Revenue).

Property, Plant, and Equipment (PP&E): See *Fixed Assets*.

Research and Development (R&D) Expenses: Any expenses associated with the development of new or improved goods or services. This type of expense is incurred in the process of finding and creating new products or services.

Retained Earnings: Part of owners' equity on the balance sheet, the retained earnings account represents the accumulated profit (loss) of the business since its inception, minus any dividends paid out.

Return on Assets (ROA): A percentage-based indicator of how profitable a company is relative to its total assets. ROA gives an idea as to how efficient management is at using its assets to generate earnings. The formula for return on assets is: ROA = Net income/Total assets. ROA can also be calculated by multiplying the profit margin times asset turnover and is the product of the first two components of the DuPont formula.

Return on Equity (ROE): A percentage-based return metric of shareholder return. ROE measures a corporation's profitability by revealing how much profit a company generates with the money the owners have invested. ROE is calculated as: ROE = Net income/Owners' equity.

Return on Invested Capital (ROIC): NOPAT/(Current Assets – Current liabilities + PPE + Intangible assets + Investments in affiliates).

Return on Investment (ROI): A ratio used to evaluate strategic alternatives. ROI = earnings/investment. Typically investment included long-term assets + investment in net working capital + cash needed if the alternative initially generates a negative operating cash flow.

Revenue (Sales): The first line of the income statement and the result of customers purchasing the business' goods and/or services. Revenues result from selling merchandise, performing services, renting property, and lending money.

Run Rate (Burn Rate): Measures the monthly cash expenditures required to sustain ongoing operations. By taking the sum of cash and marketable securities divided by the burn rate, we can calculate the "cash-out period" or "burn-out period," that is, how many months the company can continue operating before running out of funds.

Scenario Analysis: A process of analyzing possible future events by considering alternative possible outcomes (scenarios). The analysis is designed to foster improved decision making by allowing more complete consideration of outcomes and their implications.

Selling, General, and Administrative Expense (SG&A): Reported on the income statement, it is the sum of all direct and indirect selling expenses and all general and administrative expenses.

Sensitivity Analysis: A technique used to determine how different values of an independent variable will impact a particular dependent variable under a given set of assumptions. Sensitivity analysis is a way to predict the outcome of a decision if a situation turns out to be different compared to the key prediction(s).

Short-Term Debt: A current liability on the company's balance sheet. Includes any debt incurred by the company that is due within one year (e.g., any credit card balance).

Statement of Cash Flows: See *Cash Flow Statement*.

Stockholders' Equity: See *Owners' Equity*.

Time-series Analysis: Comparing a single company's performance over time.

Times Burden Covered: See *Debt Service Coverage*.

Times Interest Earned (TIE): A metric used to measure a company's ability to meet its current interest obligations. It is calculated as EBIT/Interest Expense. It is usually quoted as a ratio and indicates how many times a company can cover its interest charges on a pretax basis.

Unearned Revenue: A liability (usually current) created when a company receives cash for a service or product that it has yet to deliver.

Valuation: The process of estimating the current worth of an asset or company. There are many techniques that can be used to determine value, for example, DCF analysis and comparables.

Variable Cost: A cost that changes in proportion to an increase in a company's activity or business. Sales commissions are an example of a variable cost. As revenue increases, so does the level of commissions.

Wages Payable: A current liability account representing wages owed to employees for work already done, but for which they have not yet been paid.

Working Capital: The difference between a company's current assets and its current liabilities. The level of working capital is often used to assess both a company's efficiency and its short-term financial health. A higher number means a company has more working capital.